THE TEACHING OF THE CATHOLIC CHURCH

 DIVISION OF THE SOCIETY OF ST. PAUL
STATEN ISLAND, N.Y. 10314

The teaching of the Catholic Church

AS CONTAINED IN
HER DOCUMENTS

ORIGINALLY PREPARED BY
JOSEF NEUNER, S.J. &
HEINRICH ROOS, S.J.

EDITED BY KARL RAHNER, S.J.

Translated by Geoffrey Stevens from the original German,
Der Glaube der Kirche
© by Verlag Friedrich Pustet, Regensburg 1965
This edition © The Mercier Press, Ltd., 1967

Nihil Obstat:
    Jeremiah J. O'Sullivan, D.D.
    Censor deputatus, November 25th 1966

Imprimatur:
    † Cornelius Ep. Corcag et Ross, December 1st 1966

Current Printing (last digit):

9 8 7 6 5

Library of Congress Catalog Number: 67-15199

Printed and bound in the U.S.A. by the Pauline Fathers and Brothers of the Society of St. Paul at Staten Island, New York as part of their communications apostolate.

CONTENTS

Translator's Foreword		7
Introduction		10
Chapter One	Revelation	17
Chapter Two	Tradition and Scripture	53
Chapter Three	God, Unity and Trinity	85
Chapter Four	Creation	103
	1 God's Creative Act	106
	2 Man	120
	3 Man's Original State	127
Chapter Five	Original Sin	131
Chapter Six	The Redeemer	143
Chapter Seven	The Mother of the Redeemer	181
Chapter Eight	The Church	197
Chapter Nine	The Sacraments	253
	1 In General	253
	2 Baptism	265
	3 Confirmation	273
	4 Eucharist	278
	5 Penance	305
	6 Indulgences	325
	7 Extreme Unction	331
	8 Order	339
	9 Matrimony	351
Chapter Ten	Grace	367

Chapter Eleven The Last Things	413
Chapter Twelve Creeds and Professions of Faith	423
Chronological List of Documents Quoted	439
Index	445
Table of Correspondence Denzinger/Neuner-Roos	455

TRANSLATOR'S FOREWORD

When the first edition of this work appeared in 1938, its compilers, Frs Josef Neuner S.J. and Heinrich Roos S.J. remarked that the originals of ecclesiastical documents concerning the Catholic faith had long been available in Denzinger's *Enchiridion,* but that these documents were not addressed solely to the learned but to all the faithful 'who have a right to know what the Church herself says about her beliefs, a right that can become a duty when the faith is threatened.' The book was thus intended to make the essential points of the essential documents available to the German-speaking faithful in their own language.

Now, by the initiative of Alba House, the same service is rendered to the English-speaking faithful.

Most of the texts quoted here are also contained in Denzinger, and, for those who wish to refer to the original language references are given to Denzinger (33rd Edition). In addition there is a table of correspondence Denzinger/Neuner-Roos which also shows the correspondence between the earlier and later editions of Denzinger.

A word now about the translation of the documents.

For the more modern documents I have thought it best to follow very closely any published English text with which the faithful are likely to be familiar already. The earlier documents have in general been translated from the Latin or Greek. In cases where a variety of texts, sometimes in both Latin and Greek, exists, I have followed the variant accepted by Neuner-Roos. In the matter of style I have tried to stick closely to the original construction possibly at the expense of beauty but not, I hope, at the expense of clarity. In the matter of vocabulary I have tried to use words which are familiar to most people and to avoid as far as possible words which have one meaning for a theologian and another for the man in the street, at least on those occasions when they could be misread by the latter.

In conclusion I should like to express my gratitude to the authors and publishers of the following books upon which I have drawn:

Denzinger's *Enchiridion Symbolorum Definitionum et Declarationum de Rebus Fidei et Morum* Ed. XXIII (Herder)
Canons & Decrees of the Council of Trent H. J. Schroeder O.P. (Herder)
The Vatican Council Dom Cuthbert Butler O.S.B. (Longmans Green)

and to the Catholic Truth Society for permission to quote the following encyclicals from their publications:

Pius XI *Casti Connubii*

Pius XII *Mystici Corporis Christi*
Divino Afflante Spiritu
Mediator Dei
Humani Generis.

In general the Douay Bible has been used since it follows more closely the Vulgate which is that almost exclusively used in the originals.

G.S.

EDITOR'S FOREWORD

Since it is not intended to add to the number of old texts in this edition, and since there have been no recent official doctrinal declarations coming within the scope of this work, this English translation makes its appearance essentially unchanged. A theologian must study the dogmatic declarations of Vatican II as a whole in the original, and the complete texts would be beyond the bounds of this book.

I am most grateful to L. Drewniak O.S.B. and F. X. Bantle for their suggestions about certain shortcomings in the translation.

Munich, April 1967   Karl Rahner, S.J.

INTRODUCTION

This collection of dogmatic documents is intended to serve the study of dogma itself rather than that of the history of dogma. The object is not to accompany the truths of Christian doctrine through the two thousand years of the Church's history and follow them through doctrinal disputes and decisions, but rather to present in the language of today those doctrinal Church documents which have been of particular significance in the Church's formulation of divine revelation.

Documents do not cover the whole of revelation. Generally speaking, the Church only set out the content of faith in writing when it was threatened. The Church exercises her magisterium in her day-to-day preaching of the Word of God far more than in documentary decrees. Thus, although the most important doctrinal documents are gathered together in this book, it does not represent the whole body of the truths of faith. It does not purport to replace dogmatic textbooks, but only to supplement them. Theological questions, some of them perhaps of the greatest importance, which have not been dealt with in ecclesiastical documents thus find no place in this book.

The compilers' greatest task has been the *choice of texts*. The first step was to gather together definitive doctrinal statements of Councils and infallible papal pronouncements. But there are also other sources which a documentation of the Church's teaching cannot ignore: often they take the form of decisions made during a period of dogmatic dispute which in the course of centuries have been accepted as the expression of the Church's teaching.

The motives governing the choice of texts also determined the *order of presentation*. A purely chronological arrangement would not have served our purpose; the texts had to be grouped into chapters according to subject. Within each chapter, however, the texts are generally arranged chronologically in order that as far as possible the originals can be seen as a whole for what they are – dogmatic documents: to divide them further, point by point, would have dismembered them, and much of the strength and beauty represented by their unity and coherence would have been lost. The consequent loss of continuity of matter is compensated to some extent by the analysis which heads each chapter, and by the subject index.

The *order of chapters* represents an organic whole: We start with theological knowledge, revelation and the sources of revelation (Chaps. 1 and 2);

the deposit of faith comprises the doctrine of the fundamental mystery of revelation, the doctrine of the triune God (Chap. 3),

and the gracious communication of this mystery to mankind (Chaps. 4–11).

In these chapters we deal first with the scene of God's revelation of himself, that is with creation (Chap. 4) which became estranged from God by original sin (Chap. 5). The communication itself took place in the incarnation of the second divine person (Chap. 6) through Mary (Chap. 7). The continuation of Christ's work of salvation is entrusted to the Church (Chap. 8) which communicates the grace of Christ to mankind in the sevenfold stream of the sacraments (Chap. 9). The sacraments assure to mankind the life of supernatural grace (Chap. 10) which is perfected after death in the beatific vision (Chap. 11). Chapter 12 brings together the most important Creeds or Symbols.

The *introductory notes* to each document are not intended to give an outline of the history of dogma. They are there only to situate the document in its historical context to the extent that this is necessary for its understanding.

It would be superfluous in this introduction to insist upon the *importance of these documents*. The Church has received from Christ the task of guarding his teaching and of promulgating it to all nations until the end of time. It is not the written word that enshrines his revelation and hands it on, but primarily the living Church; and it was for this that he promised and sent the Spirit of Truth. Her task is not to teach new truths but to maintain and hand on what was taught by Christ and his apostles. Thus the doctrinal decrees of the Church are no more than formal expressions, which have come into being in the course of the centuries, of the deposit of faith entrusted to the Church. The fact of the Church's teaching office, its attributes and its task, are best represented in the Church's own documents (see Chaps. 2 and 8).

The documents presented here do not all have the same *dogmatic value*. The most important distinction to be made is between documents which contain a definitive, infallible decision of the Church's teaching office and those which are part of her day-to-day official teaching, which do indeed demand the assent of the faithful but which do not propose what they teach with infallible authority as an article of faith. It is not possible, either, to define the dogmatic value of an ecclesiastical document by its form. *The criterion for the binding force of a doctrinal decree is always the Church's intention in so far as this is expressed in the document.* This does not mean that it is always possible to determine with absolute clarity the dogmatic value of a given document. The principle which applies here is that of the Code of Canon Law: Where the Church's intention to bind definitely is not clearly expressed there is no right to speak of an infallible decree. In the body of this book *infallible pronouncements* are indicated by their *paragraph-numbers being in heavy type.* Even when the doctrinal decrees of the popes do not purport to be infallible, they are nevertheless to be accepted as utterances of the highest ecclesiastical teaching authority and they command the interior assent of the faithful, for in them the Church is exercising the teaching authority which was given her by Christ and which obliges all who hear to accept her word. Nevertheless, this assent is not irrevocable since the decree is itself not infallible.

Of similar significance are the local Councils at which only the bishops of a certain area assembled to discuss questions of doctrine. They, too, are not infallible, and therefore not irrevocable, but they do command interior assent as above.

The significance of decrees of local Councils increases if they meet with the expressed approval of the Pope. Should the doctrinal decrees of a provincial Council be declared by the Pope to be binding on the whole of Christendom, they are equivalent to an infallible papal pronouncement. This applies especially to the decrees of the provincial Council of Carthage (cf. Nos. 206, 680–5) and Orange (cf. Nos. 218–9, 696–702).

The dogmatic significance of a document can increase on account of the respect it has enjoyed in the Church over a long period of time. Christ left the integrity of the deposit of faith as a sure legacy to his Church. If a doctrinal formula has for centuries been accepted by the whole Church as the norm of true belief, it cannot contain error. If it did, it would mean that the Church as a whole had strayed from true belief, and this is something that Christ's promise makes impossible. Thus, for example, Cyril of Alexandria's twelve propositions against Nestorius (cf. Nos. 234–45), and the *Indiculus* (list of papal decisions on the doctrine of grace) (cf. Nos. 217, 686–95), are equivalent to infallible decrees.

Canon law has its own special place. To start with, laws are not doctrinal decrees but signposts indicating for the faithful the way to their eternal goal by way of the Church. But these indications cannot be arbitrary, for the Church is bound by the norms of revelation. The Church can thus never promulgate a binding law in contradiction to the norms set by revelation. The support afforded the Church by the Holy Spirit in keeping her teaching unsullied extends also to her legislative activities. It is thus possible in connexion with laws which are binding upon the whole Church to speak of infallibility, since these laws certainly cannot be in contradiction to revealed truths.

Besides official pronouncements, there are also purely personal statements on theological questions made by popes and bishops. Such documents have dogmatic value according to the personal learning and experience of the authors, and no more. The mission to teach given by Christ attaches to the office and not to the person. And, of course, the infallibility of the Pope or of a Council has nothing to do with their personal morals.

This book, then, contains only official documents of Church doctrine. In cases where the dogmatic value of a document is still undecided on the basis given, the fact is included in the introductory notes.

EXPLANATION OF NUMBERING &C.

Each item has its own serial number in order throughout the book   237

If the item is a proposition *condemned* by the Church, this number appears in square brackets   [208]

If the item is an *infallible* pronouncement the number is in heavy type   **246**

Under the serial number in italic figures is a references to Denzinger 33rd Edition   *2779*

Where the item is omitted from Denzinger 33rd Edition but appears in pre-1963 editions the reference is in parentheses   *(1642)*

Breaks in continuity, of whatever length, are indicated by   ...

Explanatory insertions in the text are printed in italic and enclosed in parentheses

Documents are printed in roman type, introductory remarks, comments &c. in italic.

A **bold type** is used for documents emanating from General Councils & certain others of equivalent status.

CHAPTER ONE

REVELATION

As a revealed religion Christianity has its ultimate objective basis in God's speaking to mankind and mankind's acceptance of God's Word.
The truth which God reveals *is supernatural, that is to say it belongs to a domain inaccessible to our human understanding so long as that understanding is dependent upon its own powers. Even after revelation, the real mysteries of faith remain impenetrable to human understanding. In this sense God's revelation to us always remains to some extent other-worldly, a reality which is indeed given us in all its wealth but which our vision is inadequate to grasp in its entirety; 'we walk by faith, and not by sight' (2 Cor. 5:7). The relationship between faith and seeing is the relationship between the life of grace in this world and the glory of the world to come. Faith is an essential component of the life of grace, which is itself an earnest of eternal life, a sort of anticipation, but which leaves us at the mercy of many weaknesses and obscurities of our fallen human nature.*
Belief *is essentially obedient attention to the voice of God in revelation, the acceptance of a truth and a reality which is not evident to us by its own light nor by its own intelligibility but which we accept on* God's authority.
The question of how faith is acquired *is of an entirely*

different order. The ways to faith are certainly also determined by grace, but faith must have a connexion with our natural cognition; it cannot be something totally alien with no basis in human life. It must therefore be possible for man to recognize the existence of God *as creator and lord of the moral order independently of and before any revelation. Secondly, man must be able to grasp the fact that God has spoken. These two steps on the way to faith must be possible for man by use of his* natural powers of cognition *in order to be able to give reasonable assent to revelation. If man were not in a position to do this, the word of God in revelation could never demand a hearing.*

Thus it has always been one of the Church's principal cares, while setting out the supernatural character of revelation and the impossibility of the truths of faith being grasped by human understanding, to insist also on the natural capabilities of human reason and to claim for it the capability of recognizing the existence of God and the fact of revelation.

In ancient times and in the middle ages there were certainly erroneous views about our ability to know about God in this life, views which had the most important effect on the doctrine of revelation, but in those days the question was put rather differently. With the Beguards, for example, it was more a question of anticipating in this life the final state of eternal happiness. The actual problem of natural and supernatural cognition, *of the capabilities and limitations of human reason, only developed in all its breadth and depth in the nineteenth century.*

Since Kant there had been on one side the mistrust of pure reason, *believing that it was not possible by deductive thinking to arrive at any truth outside the domain of experience. So new bases were sought for the facts of religion, mainly in revelation itself. It was in fact an abandonment of the basis of all belief. Among these attempts were fideism and traditionalism, and finally also modernism, although the last-named was no longer concerned with a basis for revelation in the supernatural sense.*

On the other side there were the great rationalist *attempts to penetrate the whole domain of revealed truths by speculative methods and to arrive at a whole which could be entirely apprehended by the light of human understanding. The basic tendencies of these attempts stem from the great era of German philosophy, namely from Schelling and Hegel.*

Since in these rationalist systems revelation was removed from the realm of the supernatural and was no longer based on the authority of God's revealing himself, there could no longer be any talk of profane science being subordinate to revelation.

The Church's teaching on the subject of religious cognition embraces the following truths:

There are two kinds of religious cognition, natural and supernatural, (5, 11–14, 17, 23–5, 29, 42, 50, 54).

Man can by his natural, *deductive powers of cognition know the premisses of religion, in particular the existence of God (1, 6, 16, 31, 49, 65, 74a, 74b) even though to reach a certain judgment on the matter may be difficult for the human intellect (74a). In this world there is no direct vision of God (18–21, 62, 63). The knowledge we have of God stems from the finite things of this world (31, 49, 65) and therefore remains imperfect (analogous) (156 conclusion).*

In addition to this natural knowledge, there is a supernatural *knowledge, since God has revealed himself (9, 26, 27, 32, 42, 80, 833). God could reveal himself (50, 51), and revelation was a moral necessity for man to arrive at a true perception of natural religious truths, but, given his vocation to a supernatural goal, an absolute necessity (13, 14, 26, 33, 34, 46). Revealed truth is* entrusted to the Church *(38, 61, 64, 67, 126e, 352, 355, 357, 358, 367, 389, 390, 398h, 398i, 858) in which the spirit of truth is active (334b, 398d, 398f). The fact of revelation can be proved with certainty, particularly by miracles (2–6, 9, 10, 36, 55, 56, 66). The content of revelation is unalterable (8, 28, 48, 68, 74). Man's response to revelation is faith (9, 10, 35, 69) which is essentially different from philosophic cognition (9, 11, 29, 35, 54). It is assent by the understanding (35, 37, 54, 55, 69, 715). It is an action of grace (1, 37, 40, 57, 698–701, 715), but requires man's free assent (37, 57, 715). God's revelation obliges us to belief (38, 41, 53, 58). Belief is necessary for salvation (35, 39, 715, 718, 722). The task of reason is to lead us to revelation (5, 17, 24, 46) and to achieve a profounder grasp of the content of faith (24, 43). The limitations of reason are set by the dullness of human perception even in relation to natural religious knowledge (11, 13, 14, 33) and by our inability to penetrate fully the supernatural mysteries of faith (12, 22, 23, 25, 30, 34, 43, 59). Nevertheless, it is possible in normal scholastic terms to make valid statements (74c, 74d, 74e–g, 398h) which can, however, in the course of historical development, be completed and clarified (74h, 334b, 807a). But this is not possible in every philosophic system (74d, 74f).*

No real contradiction is possible between revealed truth and science, neither true philosophy (7, 15, 44, 61, 74d) nor natural science (205a, 205b, note to 537c) nor historical science (70, 71, 73, 308, 309); each furthers the others (7, 15, 46, 47). Science is not at liberty to set up hypotheses that conflict with revelation (22, 45, 60, 73, 120, 205a, 205b).

THE ARTICLES SUBSCRIBED BY BAUTAIN
(1840)

Professor Bautain (1796–1867) of Strasbourg is reckoned as the principal representative of fideism. *Profoundly impressed by Kant's philosophy and by his own experiences in returning to the faith, and moved also by pastoral reasons, he sought the sources of our religious and moral knowledge exclusively in divine revelation. In doing so, he denied the possibility of arriving at a certain knowledge of the existence of God and of the fact of revelation by purely natural powers. His teaching was condemned by the bishop of Strasbourg, and eventually he was required to subscribe to the articles set out by Pope Gregory XVI.*

Closely related to fideism was traditionalism *(Bonald, ob. 1840; Bonnetty, ob. 1879 (cf. Nos. 15–17); Lamennais, ob. 1854). Based on the same mistrust of human reason, it sought the sources of all religious and moral knowledge in human tradition, which ultimately goes back to the original revelation.*

Fideism and traditionalism tried to stress faith as opposed to human reason, but precisely in the interests of faith and revelation, the Church had to intervene in support of the rights of reason.

Reason and Revelation

1. *Deductive reasoning* can prove with certainty the *existence of God* and his infinite perfection. *Faith,* a gift from heaven, *only comes after revelation.* It cannot, therefore, be advanced to an atheist in proof of the existence of God.

2. The *divine character of the revelation* made to Moses can be proved with certainty from the oral and written tradition of the Synagogue and of Christianity.

1
2751

2
2752

3	3. The proof, perceptible to the senses and convincing for the eye-witnesses, constituted by the miracles of Jesus has lost none of its strength and light for later generations. We find this proof in all its certainty in the trustworthy sources of the New Testament as well as in the oral and written tradition of all Christians. This two-fold tradition is to be adduced as proof of revelation to those who either reject it, or do not yet accept it, but seek it.
2753	
4	4. One has no right to demand of an unbeliever his assent to the resurrection of our divine Saviour before having shown him sure proofs. These proofs can be deduced by process of reason from the above-mentioned traditions.
2754	
5	5. In all these questions *reason precedes faith* and must lead us to it.
2755	
6	6. Although *reason* has been weakened and darkened by original sin, it has still sufficient *strength and light* to lead us with certainty to a knowledge of the existence of God and to the revelation made to the Jews through Moses and to Christians through our adorable God-man.
2755	

PIUS IX's ENCYCLICAL *QUI PLURIBUS* (1846)

Pius IX's Encyclical comprises the result of the great controversy over fideism *and* traditionalism *(see Note to 1 above) on the one hand and* rationalism, *in the form of Hermesianism on the other. The task of human reason is to lead us to revelation, but then it must submit to the Word of God. There can be no contradiction between faith and knowledge, for both stem from God.*
The two fundamental errors of Hermes (1775–1831; from 1819 Professor of dogmatic theology at Bonn) were: (1) at the beginning of all theological knowledge there is absolute doubt; *(2) the grounds for assent to faith are no different*

from the grounds for assent to natural knowledge. In each case it is the inner necessity of the human capacity for knowledge which compels assent in order to preserve human dignity. Thereby the difference of order between natural and supernatural knowledge is removed.
The thoughts expressed in Qui pluribus *were repeated quite unequivocally in Pius IX's address* Singulari quadam.

The over-valuation of human reason   7
... *(rationalistic theologians)* continue to attempt by 2776 false and deceptive proofs to raise the power and dignity of human reason above the most holy faith in Christ, and are bold enough to maintain that this faith is contrary to reason... Faith is indeed above reason, but there can never be any real divergence or contradiction between the two, for they derive from one and the same source of immutable, eternal truth, the great and good God; each sustains the other, so that reason rightly used proves, protects and defends the truth of faith, while faith frees reason from error, gives it a marvellous light in the knowledge of things divine, confirms it and leads it to perfection...   8
Those enemies of divine revelation who place such a 2777 high value on human progress, are now attempting by covert means sacrilegiously to introduce this progress into the Catholic religion, as though religion were the work of man and not of God, or were some philosophical invention perfectible by human means...

                                                   9

The task of reason   2777
Since our holy religion was not the invention of human reason but was communicated to man by God's great mercy, it is easy for everyone to understand that religion derives all its strength from the authority of God, who has spoken, and that it can be neither deduced nor perfected by human reason. Now in order

that it shall not go astray in such an important matter, human reason must closely study divine revelation so as to attain thereby certainty that God has spoken and to render him rational worship as the Apostle so wisely teaches *(Rom. 12:1)*. For everyone must be clear about this: If God speaks, we must respond with obedient faith. Nothing is more in conformity with reason than that it should be satisfied with, and cling to, what it has recognized as being revealed by God who can neither deceive nor be deceived.

2779 How many convincing proofs we have whereby human reason must be wholly convinced that the religion of Christ is divine and that 'every basis for the articles of our faith has received its roots from above, from the Lord of Heaven' (Chrysostom). Thus there is nothing more certain than our faith, nothing firmer, nothing holier, nothing that could be more solidly based.

10 This faith... had its confirmation in the birth, life,
2779–80 death and resurrection of its divine Founder, in his wisdom, his miracles and his sayings... From these radiant and unassailable proofs human reason clearly and distinctly recognises God as the author of this faith. Further than that reason cannot go. It must of necessity put away and reject every difficulty and doubt and render God the service of the full obedience of faith, for it knows for certain that everything which faith proposes for man to believe and to do comes from God...

POPE PIUS IX's ADDRESS *SINGULARI QUADAM*
(1854)

11 *Faith and Reason*
(1642) There are educated people who recognise religion as God's greatest gift to man and who yet set such a

high value on human reason that in their folly they would place it on a level with religion. Thus according to their erroneous ideas theological disciplines are to be treated the same as philosophical ones. Yet the former are based upon the dogmas of faith, than which nothing is firmer or more unshakeable, while the latter receive their growth and light from human reason, than which nothing is less sure, differing as it does with different intellects, and subject as it is to innumerable deceptions and errors...

People who rate human reason immoderately high should be shown that this is contrary to the one, correct conception of the Apostle of the Gentiles: For if any man think himself to be something, whereas he is nothing, he deceiveth himself' *(Gal. 6:3)*. They must further be shown how presumptuous it is to wish to seek out the mysteries which God has graciously revealed to us, and to try to attain them and embrace them with man's weak and limited intellect, when they are far beyond the powers of our understanding which, in the words of the same Apostle, must be surrendered to Christ's service *(2 Cor. 10:5)*.

12
(1642)

The limitations of human reason

13
(1643)

Followers, not to say worshippers, of human reason, who acknowledge it as a sure teacher and expect to attain salvation in all things under its guidance, have obviously entirely forgotten what deep and painful wounds were inflicted on human nature by the guilt of our first father. Darkness has spread over our understanding, and our will tends to evil. Thus it is that from the earliest time the greatest thinkers, for all the great things they have written, have nevertheless marred their teaching with grave errors. Hence comes the unceasing struggle which we feel within ourselves, of which the apostle says: 'But I see another law in my members, fighting against the law of my mind' *(Rev. 7:23)*.

14 Since as a result of inherited guilt, which has come
(1644) down to all the descendants of Adam, the light of reason has now become dulled and the human race has fallen from its former state of righteousness and innocence, who can maintain that reason is adequate to grasp the truth? Surrounded by such dangers and subject to our great weaknesses, who can say that he does not for his salvation need the help of divine religion and the grace of heaven to keep him from slipping and falling?

ARTICLES SUBSCRIBED BY BONNETTY (1855)
(Cf. Note to No. 1)

15 *Faith and Reason. Reason's Capabilities*
2811 1. Even though faith be above reason, there can *never be a real conflict or contradiction* between them since both stem from the same immutable source of truth, from the great and good God, and thus each aids the other.

16 2. *Deductive thought* can prove with certainty the
2812 existence of God, the spirituality of the soul and the freedom of man. Faith comes after revelation. Consequently no appeal can be made to faith when proving the existence of God to an atheist, nor in proving the spirituality and freedom of the soul endowed with reason to an adherent of Naturalism or Fatalism.

17 *The use of reason precedes faith* and leads man to it by
2813 way of revelation and grace.

ONTOLOGIST ERRORS CONDEMNED BY POPE PIUS IX (1861)

Ontologism was an attempt to solve the problem of the natural cognition of God as follows: our knowledge must correspond to being. But in the order of being God is in the first place, therefore also in our knowledge. God must therefore be the first and most universal being encountered by our knowledge. And in fact all the things we know are known as existences, participating in the great universal and comprehensive being, the being in which all things are included. Our knowledge of the existence of God is thus not the result of deductive thought; instead, God is intuitively known as the absolute being. The highest logical abstraction of being is thus equated here with the ultimate principle of existence, with God. Such a concept bore within it the seed of pantheism and it was condemned, first by Pius IX against Gioberti (1801–52) and later once more by Leo XIII against Rosmini (1797–1855) who had revived it in a new form. Seldom has the nineteenth-century struggle over the problem of the natural knowledge of God, and ultimately of revelation, been so clearly seen as in the case of ontologism.

1. A *direct knowledge of God*, at least a provisional one, is essential to every human understanding, so that without it nothing can be known. It is the very light of understanding. [18] 2841
2. That being which we know in all things and without which we know nothing is the divine Being. [19] 2842
3. The universal, in its objective reality, is not materially different from God. [20] 2843
4. The innate knowledge of God as pure being *(ens)* surpasses and embraces all other knowledge, so that we thereby inclusively know every being under whatever guise we perceive it. [21] 2844

LETTER OF POPE PIUS IX TO THE ARCHBISHOP OF MUNICH-FREISING AGAINST THE RATIONALISM OF FROHSCHAMMER (1862)

Frohschammer (1821–1893) was from 1855 professor of philosophy at Munich. On account of his attacks on scholastic philosophy and theology, some of his writings were condemned in a letter written by Pope Pius IX in 1862 to the Archbishop of Munich-Freising. In this letter Frohschammer's principal errors are refuted. It is the temptation of every rationalistic philosophy to try to understand the universe in its unity and entirety and also to penetrate the mysteries of supernatural revelation. It tries to make a philosophy out of theology. Frohschammer, too, fell victim to this temptation. In doing so he demanded for scientific research a freedom that would accept no binding higher authority.

22 *Limitations and Tasks of Reason*
2850 ...*(Frohschammer diverges from Catholic doctrine)* in two places: First, because he *ascribes to human reason powers* which are not attributes of reason as such; secondly, because he accords reason the *freedom* to make any and every assumption and bold contention, so that the rights of the Church, her teaching office and her authority are completely undermined.

23 Above all, the author teaches that – provided that it is
2851 terminologically correctly arranged – philosophy can correctly grasp and understand not only those articles of faith which are the common object of perception to reason and faith together, but also which are only constituted by Christian religion and faith, namely man's supernatural destiny and all things connected therewith. Even the most holy mystery of the Lord's incarnation belongs (according to him) to the domain of human reason and philosophy, and human reason can, if these matters be proposed to it, attain them by means of its own principles...

It is the task of philosophy to seek earnestly after truth, and properly and zealously to cultivate human reason, which, though darkened by the guilt of the first man, is by no means extinguished; to enlighten it; to grasp the matter of its perception and many truths; to understand them and further them; and in the case of many of these truths, which are also proposed to us by faith, such as the existence, nature and attributes of God, to furnish them with proofs deriving from its own principles, and to justify and defend them. In this manner it prepares the way for these truths to be more correctly held by faith and to make even the more hidden articles of faith, which faith alone can grasp, to some extent accessible to reason... If the scholars of Germany concern themselves, with the thoroughness characteristic of this famous country, with serious and difficult scientific tasks, We welcome and approve their efforts, for whatever discoveries they make for their purposes also serve to advance holy doctrine.

But in this difficult task it cannot be allowed that all things are indiscriminately mingled, or that reason usurp those things which are reserved to faith and bring them into disorder. For there are quite certain boundaries, well known to all, which reason has never rightfully overstepped and which it cannot overstep. Clearly, among such articles of faith belongs in the first place all that has to do with man's supernatural elevation and his supernatural communion with God and what has been revealed to this purpose, for since these articles of faith are above nature they cannot be attained by natural reason and natural principles...

ERRORS CONDEMNED BY POPE PIUS IX (1864)

Errors concerning the possibility of natural knowledge of God, revelation and the obligation of obedient faith in revelation have demanded the adoption of an increasingly strict attitude by the Church. The definitive answer to all these questions was given by the first Vatican Council. However, even before this, Pius IX had formulated the most important errors in his 'Syllabus of Errors' which paved the way for the answer which was later given by the bishops of the whole world assembled for the first Vatican Council.

[26] 3. *Human reason, regardless of God*, is the sole arbiter
2903 of truth and falsehood, of good and evil, it is a law unto itself and by its natural powers is sufficient to assure the good of men and peoples.

[27] 4. *All the truths of religion derive from the natural*
2904 *powers of human reason.* Reason is thus the principal criterion by which man can and must recognize truth in any order.

[28] 5. Divine *revelation* is imperfect and thus subject to
2905 continual and *indefinite progress* corresponding to the progress of human reason.

[29] 8. Since human *reason* is on a par with religion,
2908 theological disciplines are to be treated in the same way as philosophical ones.

[30] 9. *All dogmas of the Christian religion* are, without
2909 distinction, the *object of natural science or of philosophy*; and human reason, formed by purely historical development, can of its own powers and principles arrive at a true understanding of all, even the more recondite, dogmas, provided only that such dogmas be proposed to it.

THE FIRST VATICAN GENERAL COUNCIL, THIRD SESSION (1870)

DOGMATIC CONSTITUTION ON THE CATHOLIC FAITH

From among the many drafts laid before the first Vatican General Council, only two great dogmatic constitutions were agreed. *They consisted of the first part of the draft on the* Catholic faith *(the second part dealt with various individual dogmatic questions) and the crucial part of the draft on the* Church: The primacy and the infallibility of the Roman Pope *(cf. Nos. 358–69). Thereby certainly the two most important and urgent sections of the drafts were confirmed as official doctrinal decrees.*

In the four chapters of the constitution on Catholic faith and the corresponding canons, which were adopted at the third session, the Church set out her teaching on faith in opposition to the most important nineteenth-century errors, *materialism rationalism and pantheism, but also against the dangerous currents of traditionalism and fideism (cf. Note to No. 1). The second of these four chapters contains the fundamental truths determining the relationship between* human reason *and* divine revelation: *first, the capability of human reason to know, by its own natural powers, the existence of God, Creator and Lord of the moral order; second, the fact of revelation; and third, the meaning of revelation.*

The third chapter speaks of man's response to divine revelation – faith.

The fourth chapter on faith and knowledge *draws the conclusions from the two preceding chapters.*

Chapter II. Revelation

The Natural Ability to Know God   *3004*
The same Holy Mother Church holds and teaches that God, the beginning and end of all things, may be certainly known by the natural light of human reason, by

means of created things, 'for the invisible things of him from the creation of the world are clearly seen, being understood by the things that are made' *(Rom. 1:20);*

Supernatural Revelation

32
3004 but that it pleased his wisdom and bounty to reveal himself and the eternal decrees of his will to mankind by another and a supernatural way: as the Apostle says: 'God having spoken on divers occasions, and many ways, in times past, to the fathers by the prophets; last of all, in these days, has spoken to us by his Son' *(Heb. 1:1-2).*

33
3005 It is to be ascribed to this divine revelation that such truths among things divine as of themselves are not beyond human reason can, even in the present condition of mankind, be known by everyone with facility, with firm assurance, and with no admixture of error.

34
3005 This, however, is not the reason why revelation is to be called absolutely necessary; but because God of his infinite goodness has ordained man to a supernatural end, viz. to be the sharer of divine blessings which utterly exceed the intelligence of the human mind: for 'eye hath not seen, nor ear heard, neither hath it entered into the heart of man, what things God hath prepared for them that love him' *(1 Cor. 2:9)*

(On Scripture and tradition as the vehicles of revelation see Nos. 87–9)

Chapter III. Faith

Terminology

35
3008 Since man is wholly dependent upon God, as upon his Creator and Lord, and since created reason is absolutely subject to uncreated truth, we are bound to yield to God, by faith in his revelation, the full obedience of our intellect and will. And the Catholic Church teaches that this faith, which is the beginning of man's salvation, is a super-

natural virtue whereby, inspired and assisted by the grace of God, we believe that the things which he has revealed are true; not because of the intrinsic truth of the things, viewed by the natural light of reason, but because of the authority of God himself who reveals them, and who can neither be deceived nor deceive. For faith, as the Apostle testifies, is 'the substance of things to be hoped for, the evidence of things that appear not' *(Heb. 11:1)*.

The Rational Basis of Belief
Nevertheless, in order that the obedience of our faith might be in harmony with reason, God willed that to the interior helps of the Holy Spirit there should be joined exterior proofs of his revelation, to wit, divine facts, and especially miracles and prophecies, which, as they manifestly display the omnipotence and infinite knowledge of God, are most certain proofs of his divine revelation, adapted to the intelligence of all men. Wherefore both Moses and the prophets, and most especially Christ our Lord himself, showed forth many and most evident miracles and prophecies; and of the apostles we read: 'But they going forth preached everywhere, the Lord working withal, and confirming the word with signs that followed' *(Mark 16:20)*. And again it is written: 'We have the more firm prophetical word, whereunto you do well to attend, as to a light shining in a dark place' *(2 Peter 1:19)*.

36
3009

Faith as a Work of Grace
But though the assent of faith is by no means a blind action of the mind, still no man can 'assent to the Gospel teaching', as is necessary to obtain salvation, 'without the illumination and inspiration of the Holy Spirit, who gives to all men sweetness in assenting to and believing in truth' *(Can. 7 of the II Council of Orange)*. Where-

37
3010

fore, faith itself, even when it does not work by charity, is in itself a gift of God, and the act of faith is a work appertaining to salvation, by which man yields voluntary obedience to God himself by assenting to and cooperating with his grace, which he is able to resist.

The Matter of Faith
38
3011
Further, all those things are to be believed with divine and Catholic faith which are contained in the Word of God, written or handed down, and which the Church, either by a solemn judgment, or by her ordinary and universal magisterium, proposes for belief as having been divinely revealed.

Faith Necessary to Salvation
39
3012
Since 'without faith it is impossible to please God' *(Heb. 11:6)* and to attain to the fellowship of his children, therefore without faith no one has ever attained justification, nor will anyone obtain eternal life unless he shall have persevered in faith until the end *(Mt. 10:22)*... *(The Church as protection and proof of this faith, see Nos. 355, 356)*

The Grace of Perseverence
40
3014
And the testimony *(given by the Church of the supernatural character of revelation)* is efficaciously supported by a power from on high. For our most merciful Lord gives his grace to stir up and to aid those who are astray, that they may come to a knowledge of the truth *(1 Tim. 2:4);* and to those whom he has brought out of darkness into his own admirable light *(1 Pet. 2:9)* he gives his grace to strengthen them to persevere in that light, deserting none who do not desert him. *(Cf. Council of Trent, 6th Session, 11th Chapter: No. 725).*

Therefore there is no parity between the consideration of those who haved adhered to the Catholic truth by the heavenly gift of faith, and of those who, led by human opinions, follow a false religion; for those who have received the faith under the magisterium of the Church can never have any just cause for changing or doubting that faith. Therefore, giving thanks to God the Father who has made us worthy to be partakers of the lot of the saints in light, *(Col. 1:12)* let us not neglect so great salvation, but with our eyes fixed on Jesus, the author and finisher of our faith *(Heb. 12:2)* let us hold fast the confession of our hope without wavering *(Heb. 10:23)*. [41] [3014]

Chapter IV. Faith and Reason

The twofold order of religious knowledge
The Catholic Church with one consent has also ever held and holds that there is a twofold order of knowledge, distinct both in principle and also in object: in principle, because our knowledge in the one is by natural reason, and in the other by divine faith; in object, because, besides those things which natural reason can attain, there are proposed to our belief mysteries hidden in God, which, unless divinely revealed, cannot be known. Wherefore the Apostle, who testifies that God is known by the gentiles through created things, still, when discoursing of the grace and truth which came by Jesus Christ *(John 1:17)* says: 'We speak the wisdom of God in a mystery, a wisdom which is hidden, which God ordained before the world unto our glory; which none of the princes of this world knew... but to us God hath revealed them by his Spirit. For the Spirit searcheth all things, yea, the deep things of God' *(1 Cor. 2:7–10)*. And the only-begotten Son himself gives thanks to the Father, because he has hid these things from the wise and prudent, and has [42] [3015]

revealed them to little ones *(Mt. 11:25)*.

The tasks and limitations of reason

43 Reason, indeed, enlightened by faith, when it seeks
3016 earnestly, piously, and calmly, attains by a gift from God some understanding, and that very fruitful, of mysteries; partly from the analogy of those things which it naturally knows, partly from the relations the mysteries bear to one another and to the last end of man: but reason never becomes capable of apprehending mysteries as it does those truths which constitute its proper object. For the divine mysteries by their own nature so far transcend the created intelligence that, even when delivered by revelation and received by faith, they remain covered with the veil of faith itself, and shrouded in a certain degree of darkness, so long as we are pilgrims in this mortal life, not yet with God; 'for we walk by faith and not by sight' *(2 Cor. 5:7)*.

Reason and faith cannot be contradictory

44 But although faith is above reason, there can never be any
3017 real discrepancy between faith and reason, since the same God who reveals mysteries and infuses faith has bestowed the light of reason on the human mind, and God cannot deny himself, nor can truth ever contradict truth. The false appearance of such a contradiction is mainly due, either to the dogmas of faith not having been understood and expounded according to the mind of the Church, or to the inventions of opinion having been taken for the verdicts of reason. 'We define, therefore, that every assertion contrary to a truth of enlightened faith is utterly false' *(Lateran V)*.

45 Further, the Church, which together with the apostolic
3018 office of teaching has received a charge to guard the deposit of faith, derives from God the right and duty of

proscribing false science *(1 Tim. 6:20)*, lest any should be deceived by philosophy and vain fallacy *(Col. 2:8)*. Therefore all faithful Christians are not only forbidden to defend, as legitimate conclusions of science, such opinions as are known to be contrary to the doctrines of faith, especially if they have been condemned by the Church, but are altogether bound to account them as errors which put on the fallacious appearance of truth.

Mutual aid of faith and reason
And not only can faith and reason never be opposed to one another, but they are of mutual aid one to the other; for right reason demonstrates the foundations of faith and enlightened by its light, cultivates the science of things divine; while faith frees and guards reason from errors, and furnishes it with manifold knowledge.   46 *3019*

Church and culture
So far, therefore, is the Church from opposing the cultivation of human arts and sciences, that it in many ways helps and promotes it. For the Church neither ignores nor despises the benefits to human life which result from the arts and sciences, but confesses that, as they come from God, the Lord of all science, rightly used they lead to God by the help of his grace. Nor does the Church forbid that each of these sciences in its sphere should make use of its own principles and its own method; but, while recognizing this just liberty, it stands watchfully on guard, lest sciences, setting themselves against the divine teaching, or transgressing their own limits, should invade and disturb the domain of faith.   47 *3019*

True development of faith and science
For the doctrine of faith which God has revealed has not been proposed, like a philosophical invention, to be   48 *3020*

perfected by human intelligence, but has been delivered as a divine deposit to the Spouse of Christ, to be faithfully kept and infallibly declared. Hence also the meaning of the sacred dogmas is perpetually to be retained which our Holy Mother Church has once declared; nor is that meaning ever to be departed from under the pretence or pretext of a deeper comprehension of them. 'Let, then, the intelligence, science and wisdom of each and all, of individuals and of the whole Church, in all ages and at all times, increase and flourish in abundance and vigour; but only in its own proper kind, that is to say, in one and the same doctrine, one and the same sense, one and the same judgment' *(Vincentius of Lerius)*.

CANONS ON RELIGIOUS KNOWLEDGE

Canons on chap. II: *1 – against fideism and traditionalism; 2 – against deism; 3 – against objective development of dogma; (4 – on the sources of revelation – cf. No. 91)*
Canons on chap. III: *1 & 2 – against autonomous rationalism: 3 – on the conditions for belief: against fideism and traditionalism; 4 – on the proof of revelation by miracles: against fideism: 5 – on the freedom of faith; against Hermes; 6 – against absolute doubt as the beginning of theological knowledge: against Hermes.*
Canons on chap. IV: *on the relationship of supernatural faith and natural knowledge: against rationalism.*

Canons on Chap. II – Revelation

49
3026
1. If any one shall say that the One true God, our Creator and Lord, cannot be certainly known by the natural light of human reason through created things – *anathema sit.*

50
3027
2. If any one shall say that it is impossible or inexpedient that man should be taught, by divine revelation, concerning God and the worship to be paid to him – *anathema sit.*

3. If any one shall say that man cannot be raised by divine power to a higher than natural knowledge and perfection, but can and ought, by continuous progress, to arrive at length, of himself, to the possession of all that is true and good – *anathema sit*.   51 *3028*

4. *(On Holy Scripture, Cf. No. 91)*   52 *3029*

Canons on Chap. III – Faith

1. If any one shall say that human reason is so independent that faith cannot be enjoined upon it by God – *anathema sit*.   53 *3031*

2. If any one shall say divine faith is not distinguished from natural knowledge of God and of moral truths, and therefore that it is not requisite for divine faith that revealed truth be believed because of the authority of God who reveals it – *anathema sit*.   54 *3032*

3. If any one shall say that divine revelation cannot be made credible by outward signs, and therefore that men ought to be moved to faith solely by the internal experience of each, or by private inspiration – *anathema sit*.   55 *3033*

4. If any one shall say that miracles are impossible, and that therefore all the accounts regarding them, even those contained in Holy Scripture, are to be dismissed as fabulous or mythical; or that miracles can never be known with certainty, and that the divine origin of Christianity cannot be proved by them – *anathema sit*.   56 *3034*

5. If any one shall say that the assent of Christian faith is not a free act, but is inevitably produced by the arguments of human reason; or that the grace of God is necessarily only for that living faith which works by charity – *anathema sit*.   57 *3035*

6. If any one shall say that the condition of the faithful, and of those who have not yet attained to the only true faith, is on a par, so that Catholics may have just cause for doubting, with suspended assent, the faith which they   58 *3036*

have already received under the magisterium of the Church, until they shall have obtained a scientific demonstration of the credibility and truth of their faith – *anathema sit.*

Canons on Chap. IV – Faith and Knowledge

59
3041
1. If any one shall say that in divine revelation there are no mysteries, truly and properly so-called, but that all the doctrines of faith can be understood and demonstrated from natural principles, by properly cultivated reason – *anathema sit.*

60
3042
2. If any one shall say that human sciences are to be so freely treated, that their assertions, even if opposed to revealed doctrine, may be held as true, and cannot be condemned by the Church – *anathema sit.*

61
3043
3. If any one shall assert it to be possible that sometimes, according to the progress of science, a sense is to be given to dogmas propounded by the Church different from that which the Church has understood and understands – *anathema sit.*

ARTICLES OF ROSMINI CONDEMNED BY POPE LEO XIII (1887)
(Cf. also Note to No. 18)

[62]
3201
1. In the order of created things *something divine* manifests itself directly to the human understanding, something that belongs to the divine nature.

[63]
3205
5. The being *(esse)* which man sees must necessarily have something of the necessary, eternal Being *(Ens)* of the creating, determining and perfecting cause of all contingent beings *(entes)*; and that is God.

FORM OF OATH AGAINST MODERNISM PRESCRIBED BY POPE PIUS X (1910)

Modernism *has become a generic name for the most varied attempts to reconcile Christian religion with the findings of agnostic philosophy, rationalistic science of history, and in general with all those cultural areas which in their progressive development have constantly become further estranged from religion or have set themselves in hostile opposition to it. In the* narrow sense, *modernism as it is meant here embraces those systems which in the attempt gave up the positions attacked by rationalism and sought a* new basis for religion, *no longer in the historical fact of the personality of Christ and his work, or in absolutely valid truth at all, but solely in* man's inner self. *Thus, while modernism on the one hand took up a position opposed to a-religious rationalism, it discarded on the other all the bases of Christianity as a revealed religion. After repeated individual initiatives against modernism, Pope Pius X finally formally opposed it in the decree* Lamentabili *(1907) which gives the most important errors of modernism. The Encyclical* Pascendi *(1907) gives a wide-ranging presentation of the whole system, to the extent that one can use the word system of such an incoherence as modernism, and ends with a brief summary of its errors and their refutation.*

Practically all the nineteenth century's abortive attempts to find a satisfactory solution to the problem of revelation and its proof ended up with the stamp of modernism.

In 1910 the entire body of clergy involved in pastoral or instructional work was obliged by Pius to take an oath rejecting all the essential errors of modernism concerning revelation and tradition. Precisely on account of its concise summary of modernist error it has, in addition to its disciplinary importance, considerable significance as a pronouncement of the Church's teaching office.

For the sake of coherence, the whole text is given here, though many parts of it belong more properly in chapter 2.

I firmly embrace and accept each and every thing defined by the Church's infallible magisterium and by

64

3537

it set out and declared, in particular the main articles of doctrine which are immediately opposed to the *errors of the present time.*

65 Firstly: I profess that *God*, the beginning and end of
3538 all things can be known with certainty by the natural light of reason by means of what is created, that is to say through the visible works of creation, as a cause is known by its effects, and that this can be proved.

66 Secondly: I recognize the exterior proofs of revelation,
3539 that is to say the works of God, in the first place *miracles* and prophecies, as wholly sure signs of the divine origin of the Christian religion. I hold that they are the most suitable for all men at all times, including the present.

67 Thirdly: I hold that the *Church*, the guardian and
3540 teacher of the revealed word, was immediately and directly founded by the true historical Christ himself during his life among us, and that it is built upon Peter, the Prince of the Apostles, and upon his successors.

68 Fourthly: I sincerely accept the *doctrinal teaching*
3541 which has come down from the apostles through the faithful Fathers in the same sense and meaning down to our own day. Therefore I wholly and entirely reject the false invention of the *evolution of dogmas*, whereby they pass from one meaning to a meaning other than that formerly held by the Church. Equally I condemn any error which proposes to replace the divine legacy left to the Bride of Christ and to be faithfully guarded by her by any invention of philosophical thought or by any creation of human conscience which should by human effort improve itself and perfect itself in the future in unlimited progress.

69 Fifthly: I hold it for absolutely certain and I sincerely
3542 profess that *faith* is not a blind religious feeling drawn

from the depths of the subconscious by the heart nor springing from the tendency of the morally informed will, but that it is the true consent of the understanding to truth externally comminicated *ex auditu*, by which we hold to be true on authority of the all-truthful God what has been said, and witnessed, and revealed to us by the personal God who is our Creator and Lord.

I submit myself with due respect and adhere with all my heart to all the condemnations, declarations and prescriptions contained in the encyclical *Pascendi* and in the decree *Lamentabili*, particularly in so far as they concern the so-called history of dogma. And I reject the error of those who maintain that the *belief proposed by the Church can be contrary to history* and that the articles of the Catholic faith in the sense in which they are now understood cannot be made to harmonize with the origins of the Christian religion as they really were.

I condemn and reject also the conception of those who say that a more educated Christian leads a *double existence*, the existence of a *believer* and that of a *historian*, as though it were permitted to the historian to hold something contradictory to the belief of the believer, or to advance hypotheses implying that the articles of faith are false, or doubtful, even if they are not directly denied.

Equally I reject any way of judging or interpreting Holy Scripture which takes no account of the Church's tradition, of the *analogia fidei* and the rules of the Apostolic See, and adheres to the inventions of the Rationalists and illegitimately and rashly recognizes textual criticism as the only supreme rule.

Equally do I reject the conception of those who affirm that a teacher of *theological history*, or a writer in this field, must discard all preconceived opinions about the supernatural origin of Catholic tradition or about the promise of divine help for the protection of revealed truth; that the writings of the individual Fathers should be interpreted on purely scientific principles to the exclusion of all ecclesiastical authority, and should be studied with the same freedom of judgment as that with which any profane historical monument is studied.

74
3548 Finally, I profess in general that I have nothing whatever to do with the error which causes the Modernist to believe that *sacred tradition* contains nothing divine or, what is worse, leads them to a *pantheistic* interpretation of tradition, so that there is nothing left but the naked and simple fact standing on a level with the ordinary events of history, the fact namely that men,

3549 by their own efforts and by their own care and insight continued, in the ages that followed, the School begun by Christ and his apostles. So I hold, and I shall firmly told till my dying breath, the faith of the Fathers in the certain gracious gift of the truth which has been, is and always will be in the succession of the episcopal office from the apostles so that the object of faith is not that which may seem to be better for, and better adapted to, the culture of each and every age but the absolute inalterable truth, preached from the beginning by the apostles and never to be differently believed nor differently understood.

3550 I vow that I will observe all this faithfully, wholly and absolutely and keep it unchanged, that I will never depart from it in teaching or in any way by word or in writing. And so I vow, and to this I swear, so help me God and this holy Gospel.

PIUS XII's ENCYCLICAL *HUMANI GENERIS* (1950)

On 12 August 1950 Pius XII issued his great Encyclical (almost a new 'Syllabus' of errors to be rejected) 'concerning certain false opinions which threaten to sap the foundation of Catholic teaching' as the Encyclical itself describes its theme. It opposes certain theological and philosophical tendencies which had appeared in various places, notably in France (Nouvelle Théologie) without however constituting a real system. The Encyclical is correspondingly many-sided. We reproduced the most important passages in the appropriate sections of this book (cf. 74a–f, 126 e–f, 205a + b, 398h, i, 537c [807b]. Here we give two extracts; one brings out the possibilities and limitations of knowing the Praeambula fidei, *which can be known by the light of natural reason alone without thereby denying that the knowledge when in fact complete is a supernatural act of salvation in the real order of salvation necessarily supported by grace. The second extract deals with the possibility, and more particularly the limitations of change in theology, of the conceptual formulation of divine revelation, and with the normalization of dogmatic and theological development by the Church's teaching office (more on this in nos. 398h, & i).*

Possibility and difficulty of a rational basic theology
It is the same with the Catholic faith. It is, sometimes, not without difficulty that a man makes up his mind in favour of its credentials. True, God has provided us with an amazing wealth of external evidence by which the divine origins of the Christian religion can be brought home beyond question, even to the unaided light of reason. But a man may be so blinded by prejudice, so much at the mercy of his passions and his animosity, that he can shake his head and remain unmoved; not only the evidence of external proofs, which is plain to the view, but even the heavenly inspirations which God conveys to our minds, can go for nothing.

74a
3876

[74b] A doubt is raised, whether the human reason, unaided
3890 by God's revelation and by his grace, can really prove the existence of a personal God by inference from the facts of creation. We are told that the world had no beginning; that its creation was a necessary event, owing its origin to an act of liberality which the divine Love could not refuse. So, too, God is no longer credited with an infallible foreknowledge, from all eternity, of our free human acts. All this is contrary to the declarations made by the Council of the Vatican. Are the angels (we are asked) personal beings? Is there any essential difference between matter and spirit?

[74c] *Possibility and Limitations of 'historicity' of theology*
3881 What do they make of theology? Some are for whittling away the meaning of doctrines to the utmost possible limit. Dogma must be disentangled from the forms of expression which have so long been accepted in the schools, from the philosophical notions which find favour with Catholic teachers; there must be a return, in our exposition of Catholic doctrine, to the language of Scripture and of the Fathers.

Privately they cherish the hope that dogma, when thus stripped of the elements which they regard as external to divine revelation, may be usefully compared with the theological opinions of other bodies, separated from the unity of the Church; this might lead, by degrees, to a mutual levelling-up between Catholic doctrine and the views of those who disagree with us.

[74d] There is more; when Catholic teaching has been
3882 restored to this model they see the way made clear for re-stating dogma in terms of modern philosophy, immanentism, idealism, existentialism, or what other system you will, and so meeting the needs of the day. As for the bolder spirits, they will tell you this is but

right and natural; after all, the mysteries of the faith can never be expressed in terms which exhaust the truth – only in approximate terms, perpetually needing revision, which adumbrate the truth up to a point, but suffer, inevitably, from a kind of refraction. There is no absurdity, then, they say, rather there is a strict necessity about the idea that theology should constantly be exchanging old concepts for new, as times keep on altering and it finds, in the gradual development of philosophy, new tools ready to its hand. The same divine truth, they tell us, may be expressed on the human side in two different ways, nay, in two ways which in a sense contradict one another, and yet really mean the same thing. And they go on to say that the history of dogma consists in that and nothing else; in giving some account of the various successive forms under which revealed truth has appeared, corresponding to the various theories and speculations which the centuries have brought with them.

It will be clear, from all We have been saying, that the efforts made by these thinkers not merely lead to what is called 'relativism' in doctrinal theology, but already involve it. To be sure, all are agreed that the terms representing certain ideas, however much they may have been used in the schools, and even in the authoritative teaching of the Church, are nevertheless susceptible of further perfecting and polishing; it is notorious that the Church has not always been consistent in the use of the same identical phrases. It is evident, too, that the Church cannot be tied down to any philosophy which has had a brief moment of popularity. But the framework which has been built up, over a course of centuries, by the common consent of Catholic teachers, in the effort to reach truth about such and such a doctrine, cannot be dismissed as

74e
3883

resting on a flimsy foundation of that sort. It rests on principles, on ideas, which have been inferred from a just apprehension of created things; and in the making of such inferences the star of truth, divinely revealed, has shone out to the human mind through the Church's agency, no wonder if some of these conceptions have been used, and hallowed in their use, by the General Councils, after such a fashion that they cannot, without impiety, be abandoned.

74f
3884 So numerous they are, and so important, these theological concepts which have been hammered out and polished with the utmost care, in order to express, with ever-increasing accuracy, the truths in which we believe. It is a process that has often cost centuries of labour, carried out by men of no common intellectual attainments, under the watchful eye of Authority, with light and leading, too, from the Holy Spirit. Must they now fall into disuse, be cast aside, be robbed of all their meaning? Are we to substitute for them guesswork of our own, vague and impermanent fashions of speech, borrowed from our up-to-date philosophies, which today live, and will feed the oven tomorrow? That were indeed the height of imprudence; the whole of dogma would thus become no better than a reed shaken by the wind. Treat with disrespect the terms and concepts which have been used by scholastic theologians, and the result, inevitably, is to take all the force out of what is called 'speculative' theology. It rests entirely on theological reasoning, and so, for these modern thinkers, has no real validity!

74g *Importance of scholastic philosophy*
3894 Deplorable, that a philosophy thus recognized and received by the Church should, in our day, be treated by some minds with contempt! Its style, these un-

Revelation

blushing critics inform us, is out of date, its thought-processes are too closely wedded to reason. They will have it that this philosophy of ours takes up a false position in asserting the existence of absolute truth in metaphysics; ought we not rather to say that our ideas, at least of transcendental being, can only be represented with accuracy by a series of isolated propositions, which are complementary to one another, and yet, in a sense, contradict one another? The philosophic tradition of the schools, with its clear exposition of problems and the solution it gives to them, its nice definition of concepts and all the distinction it introduces, may have been well enough as a preparation for scholastic theology, not ill suited to the medieval mind; it does not match the culture or meet the needs of our own day. An unageing philosophy? Rather, one which deals only with the immutable essence of things, whereas the mind of today is forced back on the contemplation of separate existences, of a world in continual flux. So, contemptuous of ours, they will cry up other philosophies, new or old, from the east or from the west, with the implication that any system of speculation can be harmonized with Catholic doctrines, when you have added a few corrections, filled in a few gaps. Every Catholic knows this to be a palpable illusion, at least if it be applied to immanentism and idealism, to materialism, historical or dialectical, and to existentialism, whether it denies God's existence or merely the validity of metaphysical reasoning.

PIUS XII's ENCYCLICAL
SEMPITERNUS REX (1951)

On the occasion of the fifteenth centenary of the Council of Chalcedon (451) (Cf. Nos. 247, 252) Pope Pius XII issued his Encyclical Sempiternus Rex *in which he explained the significance of this Council for the doctrine of the papal primacy and for christology. We reproduce here a short extract touching upon the question, up till then scarcely alluded to in the writings of the Church's magisterium, of the development of dogma and the history of dogmatic terminology. The conceptual expression of the truths of revelation has its history. Whereas the Encyclical* Humani generis *rightly emphasized that the historicity of the formulation of dogma did not give* carte blanche *for arbitrariness in current theology nor constitute an emancipation from the Church's magisterium (for historicity properly understood forbids any romantic revival of past times even in the history of the mind and above all in the history of dogma), the present Encyclical indicates in the fine passage we cite that there is such a thing as the history of dogma and that therefore the teaching of the Church is only properly understood if this factor is taken into account and duly studied in its interpretation.*

74h *Development of dogma from Ephesus to Chalcedon*

If one asks... how comes it that the expressions of the Council of Chalcedon show such clarity and effectiveness in the rejection of error, the reason seems to Us to be principally in the fact that they employed the really exact phrase in order to avoid any possibility of double meaning. For in the canons of Chalcedon the words 'person (πρόσωπον) and 'hypostasis' (ὑπόστασις) are used with the same meaning, while the word 'nature' (φύσις), on the contrary, has its own meaning and is never used in the sense of the other two expressions. Thus formerly the Nestorians and Eutychians believed, and certain historians of our own time maintain, that the Council of Chalcedon corrected the conclusions of the Council of Ephesus. On the contrary: the one completes the other, but in such a manner that harmonious coordination of the basic christological doctrine only comes out even more clearly in the second and third General Councils of Constantinople. Unfortunately certain old opponents of the Council of Chalcedon, the so-called monophysites, rejected such a clear, true and unimpaired article of faith because they misunderstood certain expressions of earlier authors. They did indeed reject Eutyches, who spoke in a contrary manner of the mingling of the natures of Christ, but they obstinately held fast to the well-known formula: 'There is only one nature, that which became man, in the Word of God'; a formula which St Cyril of Alexandria adopted from St Athanasius, though in the orthodox sense, since by 'nature' he meant 'person'. The Fathers of Chalcedon, however, eliminated all double meanings and unclarity in every expression, for they made use of the technical language of trinitarian theology when speaking of the incarnation of the Lord as well, and therefore equated on the one hand the terms 'nature' and 'substance' ($οὐσία$) and on the other 'person' and 'hypostasis', and made a clear distinction between the two pairs, whereas the heterodox persons mentioned above equated the nature with the person but not with the substance. Therefore in the traditional and unexceptionable terms one must say that in God there is one nature and three persons, but in Christ one person and two natures.

CHAPTER TWO

TRADITION AND SCRIPTURE

Revelation is God's Word to mankind. Faith is the acceptance of this Word by mankind. Where is man to find the Word of God?
God could have addressed the Word of his revelation to individuals independently of any human community or authority. This was the idea of the reformers. But he could also have entrusted his truth to a human community *and set up a responsible guardian for its presentation. This is what Christ did. Naturally he had also to give his Church the special* charism *to be able to preserve this truth unaltered throughout all changes of ages and cultures and throughout all changes in word and speech. Christ gave his Church this gift of grace, as a result of which she can appear before all peoples at all times in the sure knowledge that she faithfully brings them the word of Christ and his mission. 'Going therefore, teach ye all nations... and behold I am with you all days even to the consummation of the world' (Mt. 28:19-20). Christ gave his Church this gift of grace so that the coming of God's Word of revelation to the world might really be a dwelling among men. We could not in the fullest sense see Christ as the bringer of revelation if each individual human being had ultimately to receive faith and revelation directly from God and not through the Church*

founded by him in which he continues to act and teach. This is then the first source of faith: the living tradition of the Church. Every truth of revelation comes to us by way of this tradition, even Holy Scripture itself.

Of course Holy Scripture is more than this, more than just volume one of the series that makes up written tradition, to be followed by other volumes of equal standing. It is directly inspired by God and is infallible. It is therefore the direct Word of God. Nevertheless, it is not independent of tradition. Even the determination of which books were inspired by God is possible only through a living tradition, for no book directly bears the mark of its divine inspiration.

But the connexion with tradition is even closer than this: God did not want to entrust his truth solely to the dead written word. Either this written word would be given over to the free interpretation of individuals, and the interpretation thus change with the changing times and the constantly changing ideas of mankind, or it would ultimately be no more than the occasion whereby God would himself ultimately speak his revealing word to each individual according to the opportunities given by his reading or preaching. In no case could scripture be called in the fullest sense the vehicle of God's Word.

God could only entrust his truth to the sacred books in conjunction with a living tradition. The written word of Scripture *must be incorporated with the* living word of tradition, *which has the task of setting forth the full meaning of Scripture. This is how the Church has always thought of the Word of God in Scripture. It would be quite impossible to gather together Church documents on the subject of tradition alone without constantly coming upon Holy Scripture as a source of faith; but it would be equally impossible to assemble the documents relating to Scripture without constantly coming upon tradition as*

Tradition and Scripture

the yardstick of scriptural interpretation.
Besides the association of Scripture and tradition, more recent Church documents also deal with the questions raised by modern bible criticism. *These questions were answered in encyclicals by Leo XIII, Benedict XV and Pius XII, who also showed the way for modern exegesis and the proper use of Scripture in theological studies.*
The Church's teaching on tradition and Scripture can be briefly summarized as follows:
There are two sources of revelation: tradition and Scripture *(nos. 38, 78, 80, 84, 87, 90, 850);*
tradition contains divine revelation *(74, 75) and is found principally in the teaching of the Fathers of the Church and laid down in the decrees of the Councils (76, 77, 78, 90, 94, 850, 858);*
Scripture comprises the sacred books of the Old and New Testaments *(79, 81–3, 87).* They, with all their parts, are inspired by God *and have him for author (79, 81, 88, 91, 93, 98–101, 108, 109, 111, 121, 123–4, 126e)* and are therefore *(and not only in moral and religious statements – 1260)* free from error *(56, 88, 98–101, 110, 112–7, 122–6).* They are confided to the Church *(79, 81, 177, 126e)* who alone has the right to normative interpretation *(72, 86, 89, 92, 93, 104, 107, 850, 205a);*
the norm for the interpretation *of Holy Scripture* is tradition *(72, 86, 89, 92–4, 105, 118, 850, 126e). Modern ancillary sciences may serve the interpretation of Scripture (95) and should always recognize it as the Word of God (102, 103, 111, 205a, 205b). The content of Scripture can never contradict science (95, 98), not 'natural' science (96, 102, 123, 205a, 205b) nor the science of history (97, 102, 106, 119, 120, 125–6d, 126f).*

THE SECOND GENERAL COUNCIL OF CONSTANTINOPLE (553)

The ultimate foundation for Christian doctrine, which was opposed to every error in the early days of Christianity, was not the proof based on Holy Scripture alone, much less that based on theological reasoning, but the appeal to tradition. We have not inherited from this age a theoretical doctrine of tradition so much as a living awareness of the deposit of faith by means of tradition from apostolic times. We reproduce here only a few such expressions of belief.

Tradition

76 **We firmly hold and teach the faith which from the**
(212) **beginning was given to the apostles by our great God and Saviour Jesus Christ and by them proclaimed to the whole world. The holy Fathers confessed it and explained it and handed it on to the Holy Church, particularly when they came together in Council...**

THE LATERAN COUNCIL UNDER POPE MARTIN I (649)
(Cf. also Note to No. 267)

Tradition

77 17. And one who does not confess in accordance with
517 the holy Fathers by word and from the heart, really and truly, to the last word, all that has been handed down and proclaimed by the holy Fathers and by the five venerable General Councils of the Holy Catholic and Apostolic Church – *condemnatus sit.*

THE SECOND GENERAL COUNCIL OF NICAEA (787)

Tradition

Any one does not accept the whole of the Church's tradition, both written and unwritten – *anathema sit*. 78 609

THE GENERAL COUNCIL OF FLORENCE
CANON CONCERNING THE JACOBITES (1442)

This Council, concerned with the reunion of the separated East with the Church of Rome, also had to concern itself with the Canon of the sacred writings. The Jacobites included a number of apocryphal books in their Canon.

The stress on the fact that one and the same God is author of both Old and New Testaments was directed against gnostic ideas which still survived (Cf. Note to No. 164).

The solemn opening phrase preceding this extract, 'The Holy Roman Church firmly believes, confesses, and teaches...' indicates that this is a real definition. In any case, this extract was adopted, without discussion by the Council of Trent.

...One and the same God is author of the Old and the New Covenants, that is of the law, of the prophets, and of the Gospel; for, by inspiration, one and the same Holy Spirit spoke to the Saints of both Covenants. With all respect she *(the Church)* accepts their books... *(There follows the list of books comprising Holy Scripture – Cf. Nos. 82, 83)* 79 1334

THE GENERAL COUNCIL OF TRENT, FOURTH SESSION (1546)

ACCEPTANCE OF HOLY SCRIPTURE AND THE TRADITION OF THE APOSTLES

After the preparatory sessions, the Council took up ihe questions of the bases and sources of faith. The examination of these bases was most necessary, for both sources, revelation and Scripture, were attacked by the Protestants.

Erasmus *of Rotterdam had already acknowledged that several parts of Scripture were not authentic.* Luther *had distinguished three groups of books: first, those featuring God's work of salvation (John, Romans, Galatians, Ephesians, 1 Peter, and 1 John); secondly, other canonical books (Matthew, Mark, Luke, the rest of the Pauline epistles, 2 Peter and 2 and 3 John); and thirdly, non-canonical books (Hebrews, James, Jude, Apocalypse, and various books of the O.T.).*

Tradition *as a real source of faith was unanimously rejected by the Protestants. The Council tried most laboriously to achieve a more accurate definition of the term 'tradition'. External traditions, customs in the matter of fasting, penitential discipline, ritual etc. were entirely excluded, for they were of no direct significance for the life of faith. In the Decree itself they were not even mentioned. Only traditions of faith in the strictest sense are still in question, traditions which are evidence of a truth of faith as part of what the Church has held from apostolic times. This tradition can be transmitted orally or in writing in the works of the Fathers of the Church. The Council deliberately refrained from listing the individual truths of revelation at this point, but at the next session it was already appealing to tradition in the matter of the doctrine of original sin, (for example Nos. 220, 224).*

The Council sought to counter abuses in the use of Holy Scripture *in a special decree. The text was in many places corrupt, various different readings were used because there was no standard version; in particular the liturgical books had often very incomplete texts. Furthermore there was a great deal of arbitrariness in interpretation and in preaching, and not much attention was paid to obtaining ecclesiastical approval for interpretations or new editions.*

The decree recognized the Vulgate as the standard Latin version. *In this context the word 'authentic' is best rendered as 'standard' since it is not a question of the origin or author of the Sacred Books but only of the accuracy of the trans-*

lation, in the sense that the Vulgate version contains no dogmatic error and reproduces the substance of the written word of God. It is not contested that even this translation also shows considerable inadequacies in places.

Secondly, the decree provided that interpretation of Holy Scripture must be in agreement with the Church's tradition. (See also Divino afflante Spiritu' *No. 126a).*

Tradition and Scripture as Sources of Faith

The holy, ecumenical and general Council of Trent... 80
keeps this constantly in view, namely, that the purity *1501*
of the Gospel may be preserved in the Church after the errors have been removed. This *(Gospel)*, **promised of old through the prophets in the sacred Scriptures, our Lord Jesus Christ, Son of God, first promulgated from his own lips, and then commanded that it be preached to all creatures as the fount of all saving truth and rules of conduct. It also clearly perceives that these truths and rules are contained in the written books and unwritten traditions which have come down to us, having been received by the apostles from the mouth of Christ himself, or from the apostles themselves, by the dictation of the Holy Spirit, have been transmitted, as it were, from hand to hand.**

Following, then, the example of the orthodox Fathers, 81
it receives and venerates with the same piety and reverence *1501*
all the books of both Old and New Testaments – for God is the author of both – together with all traditions concerning faith and morals, for they come from the mouth of Christ or are inspired by the Holy Spirit and have been preserved in continuous succession in the Catholic Church.

It has thought it proper, moreover, to insert in this 82
decree a list of the sacred books, so that no doubt may *1501*
remain as to which books are recognized by this Council.

List of the Sacred Books

82 They are the following:
1502 Old Testament: The five books of Moses, namely Genesis, Exodus, Leviticus, Numbers, Deuteronomy; Josue, Judges, Ruth, four Books of Kings, two of Paralipomena, the First Book of Esdras, and the Second Book of Esdras called the Book of Nehemias, Tobias, Judith, Esther, Job, the Book of Psalms of David containing one hundred and fifty psalms. Proverbs, Ecclesiastes, the Song of Songs, Wisdom, Ecclesiasticus, Isaias, Jeremias with Baruch, Ezechiel, Daniel, the twelve minor prophets, i.e. Osee, Joel, Amos, Abdias, Jonas, Michaeas, Nahum, Habacuc, Sophonias, Aggaeus, Zacharias and Malachias; two Books of Machabees, the first and second.

83 New Testament: the four Gospels, according to Mat-
1503 thew, Mark, Luke and John; the Acts of the Apostles written by Luke the Evangelist; fourteen epistles of the Apostle Paul – to the Romans, two to the Corinthians, to the Galatians, Ephesians, Philippians, Colossians, two to Timothy, to Titus, Philemon, and the Hebrews; two epistles of the Apostle Peter, three of the Apostle John, one of the Apostle James, one of the Apostle Jude, and the Apocalypse of the Apostle John.

84 If any one shall not accept all these books in their en-
1504 tirety, with all their parts, as they are read in the Catholic Church and are contained in the ancient Latin Vulgate edition as sacred and canonical, and if any one shall knowingly and deliberately reject the aforesaid traditions – *anathema sit*.

The Vulgate as the standard

85 Believing it to be of no little advantage to the Church to
1506 make known which of all the Latin editions of the Sacred Books now in circulation is to be regarded as the

standard version, this Holy Council decrees and declares: this same ancient Vulgate edition which has for so many centuries been preserved by the Church is to be regarded as the standard version in public readings, disputations, sermons and expositions, and that no one shall dare or presume to reject it to any grounds.

The Church as interpreter of Holy Scripture
Further it determines, in order to restrain irresponsible minds, that no one shall presume in matters of faith or morals pertaining to the edification of Christian doctrine to rely on his own conceptions to turn Scripture to his own meaning, contrary to the meaning that Holy Mother Church has held and holds – for it belongs to her to judge the true sense and interpretation of Holy Scripture – or to interpret the Scripture in a way contrary to the unanimous consensus of the Fathers, even though such interpretations not be intended for publication...   86 *1507*

FIRST VATICAN GENERAL COUNCIL THIRD SESSION (1870)

DOGMATIC CONSTITUTION ON THE CATHOLIC FAITH

In conjunction with the teaching on revelation (cf. Nos. 31ff) the Vatican Council also had to deal with the question of the sources of revelation. In doing so, it adhered closely to the decisions of the Council of Trent in its statement of the two sources as revelation and tradition and in the rules for the interpretation of Scripture.

Chapter II. Revelation

Tradition and Scripture as Sources of Faith
...Further, this supernatural revelation, according to the universal belief of the Church, declared by the Sacred   87 *3006*

Synod of Trent, 'is contained in the *written books* and *unwritten traditions* which have come down to us, having been received by the apostles from the mouth of Christ himself, or from the apostles themselves, by the dictation of the Holy Spirit, have been transmitted, as it were, from hand to hand' *(Cf. No. 80)*. And these books of the Old and New Testament are to be received as sacred and canonical, in their integrity, with all their parts, as they are enumerated in the decree of the said Council, and are contained in the ancient Latin edition of the Vulgate.

88
3006 These the Church holds to be sacred and canonical, not because, having been carefully composed by mere human industry, they were afterwards approved by her authority, not merely because they contain revelation, with no admixture of error, but because, having been *written by the inspiration of the Holy Spirit, they have God for their author, and have been delivered as such to the Church herself.*

The Church as Interpreter of Holy Scripture

89
3007 And as the things which the Holy Synod of Trent decreed for the good of souls concerning the *interprêtation* of Divine Scripture, in order to curb rebellious spirits, have been wrongly explained by some, We, renewing the said decree, declare this to be its sense: that, in matters of faith and morals, appertaining to the building up of Christian doctrine, that is to be held as the true sense of Holy Scripture which our Holy Mother Church has held and holds, to whom it belongs to judge of the true sense and interpretation of the Holy Scripture; and therefore that it is permitted to no one to interpret the Sacred Scripture contrary to this sense, nor, likewise, contrary to the unanimous consent of the Fathers.

Chapter III. Faith

The Word of God in tradition and Scripture
...Further, all those things are to be believed with divine and Catholic faith which are contained in the word of God, written or handed down, and which the Church, either by a solemn judgment, or by her ordinary and universal magisterium, proposes for belief as having been divinely revealed... 90 3011

Canon 4 on Ch. II. If any one shall not receive as sacred and canonical the Books of Holy Scripture, entire with all their parts, as the Holy Synod of Trent has enumerated them, or shall deny that they have been divinely inspired – *anathema sit*. 91 3029

POPE LEO XIII'S ENCYCLICAL *PROVIDENTISSIMUS DEUS* ON THE STUDY OF HOLY SCRIPTURE (1893)

This encyclical represents the Church's first far-ranging treatment of the questions raised by modern Bible criticism. The Pope unhesitatingly recognizes the services by new research methods in Bible science, and wishes to use all the means of modern science towards a deeper understanding of the Sacred Books. But Holy Scripture is the Word of God, and therefore infallible. Scientific research can never leave this fact out of account. No interpretation, therefore, can neglect the criteria of faith and tradition.

The thought underlying the encyclical is the firm conviction that there can be no contradiction between the words of Holy Scripture and the findings of science, always provided that both sides honestly seek the truth and are aware of their own boundaries, for there is only one God, who created nature, who is at the helm of history, and who is the author of the Sacred Books; and he cannot be in contradiction to himself.

Faith as the norm for interpretation of the Scriptures

92 ...Accordingly, where the sense of biblical texts has been authoritatively declared, either by the sacred authors themselves under the inspiration of the Holy Spirit, as in many passages of the New Testament, or by the Church assisted by the same Holy Spirit, whether by means of a solemn judgment or by her ordinary and universal authority, it should be the special and religious care of the Catholic interpreter to explain them himself in the same way, and to prove by means of the helps which his science supplies that it is the only interpretation which can rightly be approved according to the laws of sound exegesis.

93
3283 ...In other points the analogy of the faith *(analogia fidei)* must be followed, and Catholic doctrine as it has been received from the authority of the Church must be employed as the supreme criterion. For since it is the same God who is the author both of the Sacred books and of the doctrine deposited with the Church, it is plainly impossible that a meaning should by legitimate interpretation be extracted from the former which in any way conflicts with the latter. Whence it is evident that an interpretation is to be rejected as foolish and false which either puts the sacred authors in some sort of conflict with one another, or which is opposed to the doctrine of the Church...

The importance of the Fathers of the Church in the interpretation of Scripture.
(Every Catholic interpretation of the Scriptures must draw on the wealth of Church tradition. It is not a private research project, but a deeper penetration into the meaning of Scripture on the basis of Catholic perception).

94
3284 ...Moreover the authority of the holy Fathers is very great, whom Holy Church had after the apostles to

Tradition and Scripture

plant and water and build and shepherd and rear her in her growth, so often as they all explain in one and the same manner some biblical text as belonging to doctrine of faith or morals...

(Even their personal views are worthy of appropriate respect, In second place come the views of other Catholic exegetes who work on the basis of Catholic perception.)   3285

Ancillary sciences
...But these same men... must be especially learned and practised in the true science of criticism. For unfortunately, and to the damage of religion, a system has been introduced which parades under the name of the higher criticism, according to which the origin, integrity, and authority of every kind of book is found to be decided by what they call internal arguments. It is evident, on the contrary, that in historical questions such as the origin and presentation of books, historical testimonies are of greater value than others, and should be most carefully sought out and examined; and on the other hand it is clear that these internal arguments are not usually of such weight that they can be invoked except to confirm to some extent the others...   95   3286

(To base oneself on internal criticism alone would be to abandon all sure norms and we should be at the mercy of antibiblical science which would lead to 'diversity and contradiction of opinions'.)

The Bible and the physical sciences
(Many attacks on Scripture are made in the field of the physical sciences. They are especially dangerous because of their attractive vividness).

96
3287 ...Wherefore to the teacher of Holy Scripture a knowledge of natural science will be of great assistance, enabling him more easily to discover and refute objections made against Holy Scripture in this field. No real disaccord can exist between the theologian and the scientist provided each keeps within his own limits and follows the warning of St Augustine to beware of 'affirming anything rashly, and the unknown as known'. If nevertheless there is disagreement, the same Doctor proposes a summary rule for the theologian: 'Whatever they are able to demonstrate about nature by true proofs, let us show that it is not contrary to our Scriptures. But whatever they propose in any books of theirs which is contrary to our Scriptures – that is to say, to the Catholic faith – let us also show, if we are at all able, or at all events let us believe without any doubt

3288 that it is most false.' In order to understand the justness of this rule it should be remembered, in the first place that the sacred writers, or more truly 'the Spirit of God who spoke through them, did not wish to teach men these truths (that is to say, the inward constitution of visible objects) which would not help any to salvation; and that for this reason, rather than apply themselves directly to the investigation of nature, they sometimes describe and treat the objects themselves either in language to some extent figurative, or as the common manner of speech of the period required, and indeed still requires nowadays in everyday life in regard to many things, even among the most learned men. And since in popular speech those things are first and chiefly mentioned which fall under the senses, in like manner the sacred writer, as the Angelic Doctor *(St Thomas Aquinas speaking of Moses)* warns us, 'described those things which appeared to outward sense; that is, those things which God himself, in addressing men, signified after the human fashion so as to be understood by them'...

Historical problems
These same principles it will be profitable to apply in turn to allied departments of study, especially history. For it is to be deplored that there are many who examine and make known the monuments of antiquity, the manners and institutions of peoples, and similar evidence, with great labour it is true, but too often with the purpose of discovering the stains of error in the sacred books and thereby to weaken in every way and shake their authority. And this some do with a mind utterly hostile and with a judgment not sufficiently impartial. They have as much confidence in profane literature and in the monuments of ancient history as if it were impossible that even a suspicion of error should attach to them; but upon the mere supposition of an appearance of error, and that not properly discussed, they refuse even an equal amount of belief to the books of Sacred Scripture.

97
3290

Divine origin and inerrancy of Sacred Scripture and all its components
It may indeed happen that some things have been incorrectly set down by scribes when copying the manuscripts; a supposition to be carefully weighed and not readily admitted except in regard to places where it has been properly proved... But it would be utterly impious to limit inspiration to some portions only of Sacred Scripture, or to admit that the sacred writer himself had erred. Neither is the method to be tolerated of those who extricate themselves from these difficulties by allowing without hesitation that divine inspiration extends to matters of faith and morals and nothing

98
3291

more; and this because it is their false opinion that, when the truth of propositions is in question, it is not so much what God has said that must be discovered as the reason why he said it that must be carefully weighed.

99
3292 For all the books, and the whole of them, which the Church receives as sacred and canonical, with all their parts, have been written under the dictation of the Holy Spirit, and so far is it from being possible that any error should underlie the divine inspiration that such inspiration of itself not only excludes all error, but excludes and rejects it as necessarily as it is of necessity that God, the supreme truth, be the author of absolutely no error. This is the ancient and constant faith

3293 of the Church. *(Here follows a reference to the decrees of the Councils of Florence, Trent and Vatican I)*

100
3293 Wherefore it is of no great consequence that the Holy Spirit took men for his instruments in writing, as though anything false could slip out, not indeed from the principal author but from the inspired writers. *For by his supernatural power he so excited and moved them to write, he so assisted them while they were writing, as to make them rightly conceive in their mind, and wish to write faithfully, and express fitly and with infallible truth all those things and only those things which he himself should command*; otherwise he would not himself be the author of the whole of Sacred Scripture. This the holy Fathers always regarded as an established principle. 'Therefore,' says Augustine, 'when they wrote what he showed them and said to them, it is by no means to be said that he did not write it, since his members carried out what they learned from the dictation of the Head.' And St Gregory the Great affirms: 'It is quite superfluous to enquire who wrote these things, since in any case the Holy Spirit is

Tradition and Scripture 69

faithfully believed to be the author of the book. He therefore wrote these things who dictated what was to be written; he wrote, who in this writer's, work also was the inspirer.'

101
3293
It follows then that they who think that anything false can be contained in the authentic passages of the sacred books assuredly either pervert the Catholic notion of divine inspiration or make God himself the author of error. So fully indeed were all the Fathers and Doctors persuaded that the divine writings, such as they were produced by the sacred writers, are immune from absolutely all error that for that very reason they studied no less ingeniously than conscientiously to harmonize and reconcile with one another those many passages which seemed to present some contradiction or divergence – and those passages are mostly the same as they now oppose to us in the name of the new science. They unanimously declared that those books, both as wholes and in their several parts, were all equally the effect of the divine impulse, and that God himself, who had spoken through the sacred authors, could have put down absolutely nothing that was contrary to the truth.

102
(Profane science should also concern itself with the noble task of Catholic exegesis. The guiding principle for all such work should be:) Let them hold faithfully that God, the Creator and Ruler of all things, is at the same time the author of the Scriptures; and that therefore nothing can be discovered in nature, nothing in the monuments of history, which can really be in conflict with the Scriptures. Hence, if there seem to be something of this sort, the difficulty must be carefully removed, both by having recourse to the prudent judgment of theologians and interpreters as to what is the truer and the more likely meaning of the passage

in Scripture under dispute, and again by weighing more carefully the arguments brought up on the other side. Nor must one therefore give up, if even then there remain some appearance of truth in favour of the contrary view; for since the truth cannot possibly conflict with the truth, it must be held for certain that an error has found its way, either into the interpretation of the sacred words or into the arguments of the opposing party. But if it be not clear enough that either of these things has happened, one must in the

3294 meantime delay forming an opinion. For very many objections taken from all the sciences have been urged long and vehemently against Scripture, but have now become utterly obsolete, as having nothing in them; and in the same way not a few views have been put forward upon occasion to explain certain passages of Scripture (passages not bearing directly upon the rule of faith and morals) in regard to which a more searching investigation has later led to a more correct judgment. Time indeed destroys the invention of opinion, but 'the truth abides and for ever becomes stronger' *(3 Esd. 4:38)*

Humility in the face of Scriptural problems

103 Wherefore, even as no one can flatter himself that he understands the whole of Scripture aright, wherein Augustine himself confessed that the things he did not know were more than the things he did know, so likewise, should a passage occur which is too difficult for him to explain, each one will adopt the caution and self-control of the same Doctor: 'It is better (he said) even to be perplexed by figures not understood yet profitable than, by interpreting them unprofitably, to thrust one's neck into the noose of error after having released it from the yoke of slavery...

ARTICLES OF MODERNISM CONDEMNED BY PIUS X (1907) (DECREE *LAMENTABILI*)

Modernism (cf. also Note to No. 64, and No. 72) adhered wholly to liberalist scriptural science in the matter of biblical criticism and exegesis. The articles condemned mainly concern the attitude of the Church's magisterium to the sacred books (1-4), Modernist views on divine inspiration (9-12), and finally to certain detailed questions (13-14).

1. The *ecclesiastical law* which requires that books treating of Holy Scriptures be submitted to previous censorship does not apply to workers in the fields of criticism or scientific exegesis on the Old and New Testaments. [104] *3401*

2. The Church's interpretation of the sacred books is indeed not to be scorned, but it is subject to more exact judgment and correction by exegetes. [105] *3402*

3. It follows from the ecclesiastical judgments and censures of a free and more scientific exegesis that the faith proposed by the Church is contrary to history and that Catholic dogma cannot be brought into harmony with the truer origins of the Christian religion. [106] *3403*

4. The Church's magisterium cannot, even by dogmatic definition, determine the genuine meaning of the Holy Scriptures. [107] *3404*

9. Those who believe that *God is really the author of Holy Scripture* show too much simplicity or ignorance. [108] *3409*

10. The inspiration of the books of the Old Testament consists in the fact that the Israelite authors represented religious truths from a special point of view which was hardly, if at all, known to the Gentiles. [109] *3410*

11. Divine inspiration does not extend over the whole of Scripture in such a way that each and every part of it is kept free of error. [110] *3411*

12. If he wishes to undertake useful biblical studies, [111]

3412 an exegete must in the first place abandon every preconceived notion about the divine origin of Holy Scripture and interpret it in no way differently from other, merely human, documents.

[112] 13. The Gospel parables were contrived by the Evan-
3413 gelists and by Christians of the second and third generation to explain the poor results of Jesus' preaching among the Jews.

[113] 14. In many of their accounts the Evangelists narrated
3414 not so much the truth as what they thought would, although false, be more helpful to their readers.

[114] 15. Until the Canon had been defined and constituted,
3415 the Gospels were constantly being added to and amended: there thus remains no more than a slight and uncertain trace of the Christ's teaching.

[115] 16. John's accounts are not really history but a mystical
3416 contemplation of the Gospel. The statements contained in his Gospel are theological meditations about the mystery of salvation devoid of historical truth.

[116] 17. The fourth Gospel exaggerated the miracles, not
3417 only so that they should seem to be more extraordinary but also so that they should the better show forth the work and glory of the Word Incarnate.

[117] 18. John pretends indeed to be a witness of Christ.
3418 In fact he was nothing but an outstanding witness of Christian life, or the life of Christ in the Church at the end of the first century.

[118] 19. Heterodox exegetes express the true meaning of
3419 Scripture more faithfully than Catholic exegetes.

[119] 23. There can exist, and in fact there does exist, conflict
3423 between facts related by Holy Scripture and the Church's dogma based upon them. The critic can thus reject as false things which the Church with the
[120] greatest certainty believes.
3424 24. An exegete is not to be blamed who sets up prem-

isses from which it follows that dogmas are historically false or doubtful, provided that he does not directly deny the dogmas themselves.

POPE BENEDICT XV's ENCYCLICAL
SPIRITUS PARACLITUS (1920)

In spite of Leo XIII's perfectly clearly expressed position and Pius X's condemnation of Modernism, Benedict XV had once more to intervene against false attempts to solve unsettled questions about the Scriptures. The underlying thoughts developed in this encyclical are essentially those expressed by Leo XIII, but Benedict's main task was to deal with the misinterpretation of the passage in which Leo dealt with the historical problem (cf. No. 97). The occasion for the encyclical was the fifteen-hundredth anniversary of the death of St Jerome, the greatest translator and interpreter of the sacred Scriptures.

The divine inspiration of Holy Scripture
...No page can be found in the works of this great Doctor which does not make it plain that, along with the whole Catholic Church, he firmly and constantly held: that the sacred books were written under the inspiration of the Holy Spirit; that they have God for their author and were so entrusted to the Church (cf. *Vatican I, 3rd Session, Chap. II – Nos. 87ff)*. Indeed he asserts that the books of Holy Scripture were written by the inspiration of the Holy Spirit, by his instruction, stimulus and even dictation, and were indeed written and produced by him. Wherefore he has no doubt that the individual writers placed themselves freely at the service of the divine dictation according to their several natures and gifts, for he speaks not only always of what is common to all the sacred writers – that in writing they allowed themselves to be led by the Spirit

121
3650

of God, so that God is to be regarded as the first cause of every thought and every sentence of Scripture – but he also accurately distinguishes the special characteristics of each one of them individually...

The inerrancy of Holy Scripture

122 *(Leo XIII declared that Holy Scripture was inerrable cf. No.98ff)* ... The words of Our Predecessor leave no room for doubt and allow no escape. In spite of this, Venerable Brethren, there have been, not only among those outside the Church but also among her own sons, even to Our great sorrow among priests and teachers of the sacred science, people who, pridefully relying on their own judgment, have openly rejected or secretly opposed the Church's magisterium on this point.

3652 Certainly We approve the decision of those who wish to free themselves and others from the difficulties of Holy Scripture and therefore make use of all means of study and criticism and seek new ways and means. But they sadly miss their goal if they leave the prescriptions of Our Predecessor out of account and overstep the sure boundaries and limits set by the Fathers.

Divine inspiration extends to both religious and profane matters

123 These prescriptions and boundaries have certainly been
3652 overstepped by the opinion of recent exegetes who distinguish between a primary or religious and a secondary or profane element in Scripture; that Divine inspiration applies to every sentence, to every word even, of Holy Scripture, but its effect, in particular absolute truth and freedom from error, is restricted to the primary or religious element. They believe that only what concerns religion was intended and taught by God. Everything else belongs to profane disciplines and

is in the service of revealed truth, as it were an outer garment of divine truth, and was permitted by him and remains subject to the shortcomings of the writer. It is therefore not to be wondered at that there are many things in Scripture concerning the physical sciences, history, and the like, which cannot be reconciled with modern scientific progress. There are some who maintain that this notion is not contrary to the prescriptions of Our Predecessor who said, indeed, that the sacred writers wrote about the external appearances of natural things, which might be deceptive.

But it is apparent from the Pope's very words how rash and wrong such contentions are. Admittedly Leo XIII very wisely followed Augustine's and Thomas's example in teaching that the outward appearance of things must be taken into account. But the outward appearance of things casts no stain of falsity on Holy Scripture. For it is the teaching of sound philosophy that the meaning of those things that can be directly known, the knowing of which is proper to it, is not deceptive. In addition, Our Predecessor rejected any distinction between primary and secondary elements as they are called, removed all ambiguity, and clearly showed that the opinion of those who believe that in matters concerning the truth of statements one does not need to ask what God said so much as why he said it, is very far from the truth. He likewise taught the divine inspiration for all parts of Scripture without selection or distinction, and that no error could occur in the inspired text. It is wrong either to limit divine inspiration to certain parts of Holy Scripture or to admit that the sacred writer has erred. 124 3652

The historical truth of Scripture
They also depart no less from the teaching of the 125

3653 Church, as confirmed by Jerome and the other Fathers, who hold the view that the historical parts of Holy Scripture are not based on the absolute truth of facts but upon what are called relative truths and on the views of ordinary people. They are even bold enough to infer as much from the words of Pope Leo, for he said that the principles of natural science could be transferred to historical disciplines. Thus they maintain that, as the sacred writers wrote about natural things according to their outward appearance, so, too, they described events without any knowledge as they appeared to be in the eyes of the ordinary people or from the false testimony of others, in doing which they neither gave the source of their information nor made the accounts of others their own.

126 Why should We continually have to refute this false, entirely misleading assumption, unjust as it is to Our Predecessor? Where is the similarity between history and the things of nature? Physics has to do with what is apparent to the senses and must therefore agree with appearances, but the principal law of history is that the accounts of facts must agree with the facts as they actually occurred. If one once adopts this attitude, how can that truth of Holy Scripture stand, free of all error, the truth which, as Our Predecessor made so clear throughout his encyclical, must be believed? Although he says that the same principles can usefully be applied to history and to related scientific fields, he did not set this up as a general rule but only urged their use for the refutation of the illusions of our opponents and for the defence of the historical truth of Holy Scripture by meeting the attacks with their own weapons...
(2187)

POPE PIUS XII's ENCYCLICAL
DIVINO AFFLANTE SPIRITU (1943)

On the fiftieth anniversary of Leo XIII's encyclical Providentissimus Deus *(cf. Nos. 92ff) Pope Pius XII published this encyclical 'on biblical studies and opportune means of promoting them'. In it the Pope enlarges significantly on Leo's 'great charter of scriptural studies'.*

The use of the original text and its relation to the Vulgate
The study of ancient languages and recourse to the original texts had already been strongly recommended by the Fathers of the Church, and especially by St Augustine, to any Catholic exegete who would approach the understanding and explanation of the Sacred Scriptures... For it is the duty of the interpreter with the greatest care and veneration to seize eagerly upon every smallest detail of what has flowed from the pen of the sacred writer under God's inspiration, in order to reach a deeper and fuller understanding of his meaning. Let him therefore use every diligence to acquire a more and more thorough knowledge of biblical and other oriental languages, and assist his work of interpretation with all the aids that any branch of philosophy may supply... By these means *(those used by Jerome and the exegetes of the sixteenth and seventeenth centuries)* then, the interpreter must explain the original text, for this, being the actual work of the sacred writer himself, has greater authority and weight than any translation however excellent, be it ancient or modern. And the accomplishment of this task will be easier and more effective if to a knowledge of languages is added a sound skill in the art of criticism applied to the said text... And it is not to be supposed that this critical use of the original texts is in any way contrary to the wise prescriptions of the Council of Trent con- 126a

3825 cerning the Latin Vulgate *(cf. No. 85)*... As for the decree of the Council of Trent requiring the Vulgate to be regarded as the standard Latin version, this, as everybody knows, concerns only the Latin Church and her public use of the Scriptures, and obviously in no way derogates from the authority and value of the original texts... It's *(the Vulgate's)* authenticity is therefore more properly called *juridical* than *critical*. Consequently the said authority of the Vulgate in matters of doctrine in no ways forbids – indeed today it almost requires – this same doctrine to be proved and corroborated also by means of the original texts; nor does it forbid the aid of these texts to be generally invoked for the better manifestation and explanation of the true meaning of Holy Writ. Nor, finally, does this same decree of the Council of Trent prohibit translations into the vernacular, made even from the original texts themselves, to be provided for the use and benefit of the faithful and for the easier understanding of the Word of God, as We know to have been done in many places laudably and with the approval of the authority of the Church.

Literal and 'spiritual' meaning

126b *3826* Well equipped, then, with a knowledge of ancient languages and with the aids afforded by the art of criticism, the Catholic exegete must approach the most important of the tasks imposed upon him: that of discovering and expounding the genuine sense of the sacred books. In doing so interpreters should bear in mind that their chief aim must be to discern and determine what is known as the literal sense of the words of the Bible... But commentators must have as their chief object to show what is the theological doctrine touching faith and morals of each book and text, so that their commentary may not only assist teachers of theology in expounding and corroborating the dogmas of faith, but also be useful to priests in their work of explaining Christian doctrine to the people, and help all the faithful to lead a holy and Christian life.

By giving an interpretation such as We have described, that is, a primarily theological one, they will effectively silence those who assert that in biblical commentaries they find hardly anything to raise their minds to God, nourish their souls, and foster their interior life, and therefore maintain that recourse should be had to a spiritual and socalled mystical interpretation... *3827*

It is true that not every spiritual sense is excluded from Sacred Scripture; what was said and done in the Old Testament was wisely so ordained and disposed by God that the past would spiritually foreshadow what was to happen in the new covenant of grace. It is therefore the duty of the exegete to discover and expound not only the 'literal' meaning of the words which the sacred writer intended and expressed, but also their spiritual significance, on condition of its being established that such meaning has been given to them by God. For God alone was able to know this spiritual significance, and he alone could reveal it to us. And in fact this sense is declared and taught to us by the divine Saviour himself in the Holy Gospels; the apostles, following the example of the Master, exhibit it both in speech and in writing; and it is shown in the perpetual and traditional teaching of the Church, as well as in the most ancient liturgical usage, wherever it is proper to apply the well-known adage: the norm of prayer is the norm of belief. This spiritual sense, therefore, intended and ordained by God himself, must be shown forth and explained by Catholic commentators with the diligence which the dignity of the word of God demands; but they must be *3828* scrupulously careful not to propound other metaphorical meanings as though they were the genuine sense of Holy Scripture... since the faithful... want to know what it is that God himself means to say to us in the Sacred Scriptures, rather than what some eloquent speaker or writer is expounding with a dexterous use of the words of the Bible...

Importance of determining the literary genre *of individual books in order to arrive at the literal meaning*

126c
3830
But frequently the literal sense is not so obvious in the words and writings of ancient oriental authors as it is with the writers of today. For what they intended to signify by their words is determined not only by the laws of grammar or philology, nor merely by the context; it is absolutely necessary for the interpreter to go back in spirit to those remote centuries of the East, and to make proper use of the aids afforded by history, archaeology, ethnology, and other sciences, in order to discover what literary forms the writers of that early age intended to use, and did in fact employ. For to express what they had in mind the ancients of the East did not always use the same forms and expressions as we use today; they used those that were current among people of their own time and place; and what these were the exegete cannot determine *a priori*, but only from a careful study of ancient oriental literature. This study has been pursued during the past few decades with greater care and industry than formerly, and has made us better acquainted with the literary forms used in those ancient times, whether in poetical descriptions, or in the formulation of rules and laws of conduct, or in the narration of historical facts and events. It has now also clearly demonstrated the unique pre-eminence among all the ancient nations of the East which the

people of Israel enjoyed in historical writing both in regard to the antiquity of the events recorded and in regard to the accuracy with which they are related... At the same time, no one who has a just conception of biblical inspiration will be surprised to find that the sacred writers, like the other ancients, employ certain arts of exposition and narrative, certain idioms especially characteristic of the semitic languages (known as 'approximations') and certain hyperbolical and even paradoxical expressions designed for the sake of emphasis. The Sacred Books need not exclude any of the forms of expression that were commonly used in human speech by the ancient people, especially of the East, to convey their meaning, so long as they are in no way incompatible with God's sanctity and truth... In many cases in which the sacred authors are accused of some historical inaccuracy or the inexact recording of some events, it is found to be a question of nothing more than those customary and characteristic forms of expression or styles of narrative which were current in human intercourse among the ancients, and which were in fact quite legitimately and commonly employed. A just impartiality therefore demands that when these are found in the word of God, which is expressed in human language for men's sake, they should be no more stigmatized as error than when similar expressions are employed in daily use. Thus a knowledge and careful appreciation of ancient modes of expression and literary forms and styles will provide a solution to many of the objections made against the truth and historical accuracy of Holy Writ...

LETTER FROM THE SECRETARY OF THE PONTIFICAL COMMISSION ON BIBLICAL STUDIES TO CARDINAL SUHARD, ARCHBISHOP OF PARIS (16 January 1948)

This letter is not actually a decree of the Commission (cf. Note to 198) but represents an important application of the principles given in No. 126e and an interpretation of earlier decisions of the Commission (cf. No. 198)

126d
3863 As regards the composition of the Pentateuch, the Commission already recognized in the decree of 27 June 1906 that one could maintain that in the composition of his work Moses may have used written documents or oral traditions and admit post-Mosaic modifications and additions. There is nobody nowadays who doubts the existence of such sources or does not admit the gradual accretions to the Mosaic laws due to the social and religious conditions of later times, a process that is also shown in the historical accounts... We therefore invite Catholic scholars to study these problems without prejudice in the light of sound criticism and the findings of other sciences interested in the matter. Such studies will undoubtedly establish the great part played by Moses as a writer and as a law-giver.

3864 The question of the literary forms of the first eleven chapters of Genesis is much more complicated and obscure. These literary forms do not correspond to any of our classic categories and cannot be judged in the light of Graeco-Latin or modern literary *genres*. Their historicity can be neither affirmed or denied *en bloc* without unjustifiably applying to them the rules of a literary *genre* in which they cannot be classified... To declare *a priori* that the accounts in them do not contain history in the modern sense of the word would easily lead to the misunderstanding that they contain no history in any sense of the word, while relating in a simple and colourful language suitable to the mentality of a not very developed mankind the basic truths underlying the economy of salvation, and at the same time the popular description of the origins of the human race and the chosen people.

PIUS XII's ENCYCLICAL *HUMANI GENERIS* (1950)
(Cf. also Note to 74a)

Rules for the interpretation of inerrable Scripture
There are those who boldly pervert the sense of the definition laid down by the Vatican Council as to its divine authorship; they bring up again the old argument, so often censured, which contends that the inerrancy of Scripture only extends to what it tells us about God, about morals, and about religion. They even use misguided language about the human meaning of the sacred books, under which a divine meaning is concealed, and only this divine meaning, they claim, is infallible. In their interpretation of Scripture they will not take into account the harmony of revealed truths with one another, nor pay attention to the tradition of the Church. They will make of Holy Scripture, as scholars interpret it each after his own fashion, a balance by which they can assay the teaching of the Fathers and of the Church, when they ought to be interpreting Holy Scripture according to the mind of the Church, since the Church, by our Lord Christ's own appointment, is authorized to guard and to interpret the whole deposit of divine revelation. 126e 3887

Comment on 126d
It was clearly laid down in that letter that the first eleven chapters of Genesis, although it is not right to 126f 3898

judge them by modern standards of historical composition, such as would be applied to the great classical authors, or to the learned of our own day, do nevertheless come under the heading of history; in what exact sense, it is for the further labours of the exegete to determine. These chapters have a *naif*, symbolical way of talking, well suited to the understanding of a primitive people. But they do disclose to us certain important truths, upon which the attainment of our eternal salvation depends, and they do also give a popularly-written description of how the human race, and the chosen people in particular, came to be. It may be true that these old writers of sacred history drew some of their material from the stories current among the people of their day. So much may be granted; but it must be remembered on the other side that they did so under the impulse of divine inspiration, which preserved them from all error in selecting and assessing the material they used.

3899 These excerpts from current stories, which are found in the sacred books, must not be put on a level with mere myths, or with legend in general. Myths arise from the untrammelled exercise of the imagination; whereas in our sacred books, even in the Old Testament, a love of truth and a cult of simplicity shine out, in such a way as to put these writers on a demonstrably different level from their profane contemporaries.

CHAPTER THREE

GOD, UNITY AND TRINITY

The reality of God's life in three persons is the mystery *of mysteries of our faith. Our life as Christians begins with our being baptized into this life and attains its eternal perfection in participation in the Beatific Vision. It is the mystery of the distinction in God which are the reality of the inherently undifferentiated* unity *of the divine Nature. This divine Nature is three persons*, Father Son and Holy Spirit. *The entire divine Nature with all its characteristics is their undivided possession. The sole bases of their distinction are the mutual relationships between them in which they possess this nature on the basis of their origin: the Father, himself without origin, is the origin of the Son and the Holy Spirit; the Son, on the basis of his having been begotten from all eternity by the Father, origin of the Holy Spirit; the Holy Spirit on the basis of his proceeding from the Father and the Son as from an origin. These distinctions of persons are real, not merely notional, distinctions. But at the same time the Persons and the Nature are* one *and the same reality. And that is why the Persons themselves while maintaining their distinction, most fully permeate each other, so that 'we worship one God in Trinity and Trinity in Unity' (Athanasian Creed).*
The decrees of the Church's magisterium guard the

articles of faith included in these statements against attacks on two fronts. The first attacks the truth of the relationships of the divine Nature and the divine Persons by emphasizing the unity of Nature *and thus obscuring the* distinction of Persons *(Sabellianism), or exaggerates the distinction of Persons at the expense of the unity of Nature (Tritheism). The second attacks the Catholic understanding of the relationships between the Persons by proposing false doctrines either about the Son's being begotten by the Father (Arianism) or the Holy Spirit's proceeding from the Father and the Son (Macedonianism, Photianism).*

The Church unfolds the basic fact of revelation, the mystery of the one triune God, in the following articles: There is one *personal* God *(140, 155, 190, 193, 194, 828, 829, 831, 838) transcending the world (178, 189, 190, 195, 196), containing in himself all* perfection *(155, 163, 190), and* omniscient *(74b, 190, 192).*

In God there are three Persons, *Father Son and Holy Spirit (127, 141, 143, 144, 155, 157, 254, 267, 828, 829, 831–3, 836, 838) who possess* one *divine* Nature *(127, 140, 144, 148, 149, 151–3, 155, 156, 160, 254, 267, 836, 838, 840). In each of these Persons there is the* whole undivided Godhead *(131, 132, 143, 155, 156, 267, 838). In the Father (145), in the Son (128, 134, 135, 146, 829–32, 836, 837, 839), and in the Holy Spirit (129, 136–8, 142, 147, 831, 835, 836, 840).*

There is a real distinction *between the three Persons (127, 130, 150, 151, 154, 156, 159, 836, 838). The reason for this distinction is the mutual* relationships *of the Persons on account of their origins (148, 149, 150, 156, 160).*

The Father has the divine Nature of himself (145,155, 158, 162), the Son is eternally begotten of the Father

God, Unity and Trinity

(133, 146, 155, 156, 158, 159, 162, 829, 831, 832, 836, 839), the Holy Spirit proceeds from the Father and the Son (147, 155, 158, 159, 162, 831, 833, 836, 840).

The Father, Son and Holy Spirit mutually interpenetrate each in perfect fusion (153, 161) and possess one and the same outward action in the world (139, 153, 162, 267, 287).

On the relationship between the Trinity and mankind in grace see the analysis on p. 368 f.

LETTER OF POPE DIONYSIUS TO BISHOP DIONYSIUS OF ALEXANDRIA (ca. 260)

Dionysius, Bishop of Alexandria about the middle of the third century, was principally concerned with combating the false teaching of Sabellianism (Modalism), which on account of its insistence on the unity of God reduced the trinity of Persons to a threefold mode or manifestation of the one God. In his conflict with this false doctrine Dionysius put too much emphasis on the real distinction of divine Persons so that his opponents accused him of tritheism. The question was put to Pope Dionysius in Rome and was thus the occasion for the first important decision of the Church's magisterium on the mystery of the Most Blessed Trinity. In opposition to Sabellius it laid down the real distinction of the three divine Persons, but also rejected with equal decisiveness any form of tritheism. It also defined with absolute clarity the true divinity of Christ.

Unity and Trinity in God

127 It is reasonable to speak next against those who in the matter of the *(divine)* monarchy, which is a most solemn teaching of the Church of God, divide it into three powers, three separate natures *(hypostases)* and three Godheads, and in so dividing destroy it. For I have heard that among you there are preachers and teachers of the divine word who maintain this opinion, and who are, so to speak, diametrically opposed to the opinion of Sabellius. For he *(Sabellius)* blasphemes by saying that the Son is the Father and vice-versa, while they in a certain sense preach three Gods in that they divide the sacred unity into three different natures each entirely separate from the others. For it is necessary that the divine Word be united to the God of all things

and that the Holy Spirit remains and dwells in God, and that the divine Trinity should come together and be gathered into One, as into a point, in the almighty God of all things. For the false doctrine of Marcion, which cuts and divides the monarchy into three principles (ἀρχὰς), is a diabolical teaching and not that of the true disciples of Christ nor of those who accept the teaching of the Saviour. For they know well that the Trinity is proclaimed in Holy Scripture and that three gods are taught neither in the Old nor in the New Testament... *(There follows an exposition of the doctrine that the Son of God was not created but begotten by the Father from all eternity.)*

Therefore, neither is the wonderful and divine unity to be separated into three godheads nor is the dignity and supreme greatness of the Lord to be diminished by the word 'creating' (ποίησις); but one must believe in God, the Father almighty, in Christ Jesus his Son, and in the Holy Spirit; and that the Word (λόγος) is united with the God of all things. For he says: 'I and the Father are one' *(John 10:30)* and 'I am in the Father, and the Father in me' *(John 14:11)*. In this way the *divine Trinity* and the *holy doctrine of monarchy* (unity) will be preserved...

THE COUNCIL OF ROME UNDER POPE DAMASUS I (382)

Arius had denied the divinity of Christ. After the General Council of Nicaea (Nos. 829ff) the true doctrine gradually prevailed in a severe struggle. But shortly afterwards a new heresy arose, denying the divinity of the Holy Spirit. The most important decrees, concerning the doctrine of the divinity of the Holy Spirit are the 'Tome' of Pope Damasus and the Creed of the General Council of Constantinople (No. 831).

129 1. We anathametize those who do not wholly freely
153   proclaim that he *(the holy Spirit)* is of one power and
      substance with the Father and the Son.
130 2. We likewise anathematize those who follow the error
154   of Sabellius in saying that the Father and the Son are
      one and the same.
131 3. We anathematize Arius and Eunomius who with
155   equal impiety but in different words assert that the Son
      and the Holy Spirit were created.
132 10. Any one who does not say that the Father is always,
162   and the Son always, and the Holy Spirit always, is
      heretical.
133 11. Any one who does not say that the Son is born of
163   the Father, that is, of his divine substance, is heretical.
134 12. Any one who does not say that the Son of God is
164   true God, as the Father is true God, that he can do
      all things, and knows all things, and is equal to the
      Father, is heretical.
135 13. Any one who says that *(the Son)* while incarnate
165   upon earth was not in heaven with the Father, is
      heretical.
136 16. Any one who does not say that the Holy Spirit,
168   like the Son, is really and truly from the Father, of the
      divine substance, and true God, is heretical.
137 17. Any one who does not say that the Holy Spirit can
169   do all things, and knows all things, and is everywhere
      present, is heretical.
138 18. Any one who says that the Holy Spirit is a creature,
170   or created through the Son, is heretical.
139 19. Any one who does not say that the Father made all
171   things, that is things visible and invisible, through the
      Son and his Holy Spirit, is heretical.
140 20. Any one who does not say that there is only one
172   godhead, one might, one majesty, one power, one glory,
      one lordship, one kingdom, one will and one truth of

the Father and of the Son and of the Holy Spirit, is heretical.

21. Any one who does not say there are three true Persons, the Father, the Son, and the Holy Spirit, equal, eternally living, containing all things visible and invisible, able to do all things, judging all things, animating all things, creating all things and maintaining all things, is heretical.

22. Any one who does not say that the Holy Spirit is to be adored, as the Father and Son *(are adored)* is heretical.

24. Any one who in saying God the Father, God the Son, and God the Holy Spirit, divides them and means gods, and who does not, on account of the one godhead and might which we believe and know to belong to the Father and the Son and the Holy Spirit, say God; who excludes the Son or the Holy Spirit and believes only God the Father may be called God, and who thus believes in one God, is heretical in all things and indeed a Jew; for the name of gods was given by God to the angels and all the Saints, but for the Father and the Son and the Holy Spirit, on account of one and the same godhead, we are shown and taught the name not of 'gods' but 'God', for we were baptized solely in the Father, Son and Holy Spirit, and not in the name of archangels or angels, as heretics or Jews or pagans in their madness do.

This, then, is the salvation of Christians, that believing in the Trinity, that is in the Father, Son and Holy Spirit, and baptized in them, we believe without doubt that theirs is the only one true godhead and might, majesty and substance.

CREED OF THE (ELEVENTH) COUNCIL OF TOLEDO (675)

This small local Council, attended by only seventeen bishops has now probably no significance today except for the wonderful confession of faith which was recited at its opening. In it were gathered together some of the profoundest thinking and clearest formulation of the two principal mysteries of Christianity, the Trinity and the Incarnation. The sources were earlier dogmatic decrees, especially those of the sixth Toledo Council, various Creeds, in particular the 'Athanasian' (No. 836f), and the works of the great Doctors of the Church, mainly Augustine and Fulgentius. On account of the great regard subsequently paid to this Creed it can be numbered among the most important doctrinal declarations of the Church.

144 / 525 We confess and believe that the holy and ineffable Trinity, Father, Son and Holy Spirit, one God, is by nature of one substance, one nature, one majesty and power.

Three persons

145 / 525 And we profess that the Father is not born, nor created, but unborn. For he himself, from whom the Son had his birth and the Holy Spirit his procession, has his origin from no one. He is therefore the source and origin of the whole godhead. He himself is therefore the father of his essence, who ineffably begot the Son out of his ineffable substance. God *(begot)* God, and light *(begot)* light. From him, therefore, is 'all paternity in heaven and earth' *(Eph. 3:15).*

146 / 526 We confess also the *Son*, born of the substance of the Father, without beginning, before time, for at no time did the Father exist without the Son, nor the Son without the Father. The Son therefore is God from the Father, and the Father is God, but not from the Son. He is

indeed the Father of the Son, but not God from the Son, but the latter is the Son of the Father and God from the Father. But in all things the Son is equal to God the Father, for his being born had no beginning and no end. And we believe that he is of the same substance with the Father, wherefore he is called ὁμοούσιος with the Father, that is, of the same substance as the Father, for ὅμος in Greek means 'one' and ὄυσια means 'substance' and being joined they mean 'of one substance'. It is to be believed that the Son was not generated or born from nothing or from some other substance but from the womb of the Father, that is, from his substance. The Father is therefore eternal, and the Son also eternal. If he was always Father, he always had a Son, whose Father he was, and therefore we confess that the Son was born of the Father without beginning. Yet we do not, because he was born of the Father call this Son a part of a divided nature, but we assert that the perfect Father begot the perfect Son without diminution or division, for it pertains to the godhead alone not to have a dissimilar *(inaequalem)* Son. And this Son of God is Son by nature, not by adoption, of whom it must be believed that God the Father begot him neither by act of will nor of necessity for in God there is no necessity nor does will come before knowledge.

We also believe that the *Holy Spirit,* who is the third Person of the Trinity, is one and the same God with God the Father and the Son, of one substance and one nature, not, however, born or created but proceeding, and that he is the Spirit of them both. In our belief, therefore, this Holy Spirit is neither unbegotten nor begotten, for if we were to say unbegotten we should assume two Fathers, or if begotten we should be shown to teach two Sons. And he is called the Spirit not of the Father alone, nor of the Son alone, but of both Father and Son. For he does not

147
527

proceed from the Father to the Son, nor from the Son to the sanctification of creation, but he is shown to have proceeded at the same time from both, for he is to be acknowledged as the love or the sanctity of both. Hence we believe that the Holy Spirit is sent by both, as the Son is sent by the Father. But he is not less than the Father and the Son, as the Son acknowledges that on account of taking a body he is less than the Father and the Holy Spirit.

148
528 This is the account of the holy *Trinity*, which one must call, and believe to be, not threefold but Trinity. Nor can it properly be said that in the one God there is Trinity, but that the one God is Trinity. In the names of the Persons, which express a relationship, the Father is related to the Son, and the Son to the Father, and the Holy Spirit to both. But while we speak of three related persons, we believe in *one* nature or substance.

One Substance

149
528 Although we profess three Persons we do not profess three substances, but *one substance* and three persons. In so far as the Father is Father, it is not to himself but to the Son; and in so far as the Son is Son, it is not to himself but to the Father; and likewise the Holy Spirit is related not to himself but to the Father and the Son, inasmuch as he is called the Spirit of the Father and the Son. So when we say 'God', this does not express a relationship to another, as of the Father to the Son or the Son to the Father or of the Holy Spirit to the Father and Son; 'God' is used himself alone.

529 For if we are asked about the individual Person, we must answer that he is God. Therefore one may say God the Father, God the Son, and God the Holy Spirit, separately; but they are not three gods, he is one God. Likewise, the Father, the Son and the Holy Spirit, each

individually is to be called almighty; but there are not three almighties, but one almighty, as we profess one light and one beginning. It must also be confessed and believed that each single Person is wholly God in himself and that all three Persons together are one God. They have one, or undivided, equal godhead, majesty or power, which is not diminished in the individuals nor augmented in the three. For it is not less when one individual Person is called God, and not greater when all three Persons together are called God.

This Holy Trinity therefore is not a stranger to number, but is not conceived in number. For in the relationship of Persons number is discernible, but the substance of the Godhead comprises nothing that can be numbered. Solely in the fact that they are related to one another is there any indication of number, but they know no number in their relationship with themselves. Thus this Holy Trinity properly has one name so that it cannot be used of the Three Persons in the plural. Wherefore, we believe, it is said in the Sacred Scriptures: 'Great is our Lord, and great his power: and of his wisdom there is no number' (Ps. 146:5).   150   530

Unity is not identity

Although we have said that these three Persons are one God, we cannot on that account say that the Father is the same as the Son, or the Son the same as the Father, or the Holy Spirit is the Father or the Son.   151   530

For the Father is not the same as the Son, nor the Son the same as the Father, nor the Spirit the same as the Father or the Son, although the Father is the same thing as the Son, and the Son is the same thing as the Father, and the Holy Spirit is the same thing as the Father and the Son, that is, by their nature one God. For when we say that the Father is not the same as the Son, we refer to the distinction of Persons. But when we say that the Father is the same *(thing)* as the Son, and the Son as the Father, and the Holy Spirit as the Father and the Son, this clearly refers to the nature or substance whereby he is God, since in substance they are one: we distinguish the Persons, but we do not divide the Godhead.

152 We therefore recognize the Trinity in the distinction of
531 Persons, but profess its unity as to nature or substance. These Three, therefore are One – in nature, that is, not in person.

The distinction of Persons does not mean they are separable

153 Nevertheless these Three Persons are not to be con-
531 sidered as separable, since it is our belief that none existed or acted before or after another or without another, for they are inseparable in what they are and in what they do.

For we believe that there was no interval of time between the Father begetting, the Son begotten and the Holy Spirit proceeding, in which the begetter preceded the begotten or was without the begotten, or which the Holy Spirit in proceeding appeared later than the Father and the Son. Wherefore we profess and believe that this Holy Trinity is inseparable and distinct. We speak according to the teaching of our forefathers, therefore, of three Persons so that they may be known, not so that they may be separated. For if we pay attention to what Holy Scripture says about wisdom: 'She is the brightness of eternal light' *(Wis. 7:26)*, we see that, as the brightness belongs inseparably to the light, the Son cannot be separated from the Father. If we do not confuse these three Persons who have one inseparable nature, we do not thereby say that they are separable.

532 The Holy Trinity, indeed, has deigned to show this

clearly to us, for precisely in the names which, by its wish, are used to identify the Persons it made provision that one *(Person)* could not be understood without the other, for one cannot conceive of a Father without a Son, nor is a Son found without a Father. Indeed, the very relationship of the personal names forbids them to be separated, for if they are names separately they are by implication together. No one can hear one of those names without being obliged to understand the other.

Altough, then, these Three are One and this One is 154 Three, each of the Persons retains his own characteristics *(proprietas)*: the Father is eternal, not begotten; the Son is eternal, begotten, the Holy Spirit, proceeding not begotten, from eternity...

THE FOURTH LATERAN GENERAL COUNCIL (1215)

More than four hundred bishops answered Pope Innocent III's call to the twelfth General Council, held at the Lateran in Rome. A solemn Creed was prepared, directed against the many heretical teachings, especially that of the Albigenses, and contained also the basic truths about the mystery of the Most Holy Trinity. Extracts from this Creed are at Nos. 155, 171, 339, 813. The whole Creed (Chap. I: On the Catholic Faith) at Nos. 837b–d.

In addition, the Council acted against Joachim de Fiore (1130–1191) who in his teaching about the Blessed Trinity had spoken against Peter the Lombard. The Council approved the teaching of Peter, which subsequently became the basis of scholastic theology.

Chapter I. On the Catholic Faith

We firmly believe and simply confess that there is only 155
one true God, eternal, immense, unchangeable, in- 800

comprehensible, omnipotent and ineffable, the Father, the Son and the Holy Spirit: three Persons, but one essence, substance or wholly simple nature: the Father from no one, the Son from the Father alone, and the Holy Spirit equally from both: and from the beginning, always, and without end: the Father begetting, the Son being born, and the Holy Spirit proceeding: of the same substance, equal, equally omnipotent and equally eternal: one origin of all things...

Chapter II. On the Errors of Abbot Joachim

156
804 We, therefore, with the approval of the Sacred Council believe and confess with Peter the Lombard that there is one highest, incomprehensible and ineffable thing which is truly Father, Son and Holy Spirit, at the same time three Persons and each one singly a Person; and therefore in God there is only Trinity, not quaternity. For each of the three Persons is that thing, that is, that divine substance, essence or nature, which alone is the beginning of all things, apart from which there is no other. And that thing is not generating, nor generated, nor proceeding, but it is the Father who generates, the Son who is generated, and the Holy Spirit who proceeds; so that there may be distinction of persons but unity in nature.

805 Although the Father is different, the Son is different, and the Holy Spirit is different, there is no different thing, for what the Father is the Son and the Holy Spirit are wholly also; so in the orthodox Catholic faith we believe them to be of one substance. For the Father, generating the Son from eternity, gave him his substance, as he himself testifies: 'That which my Father hath given me, is greater than all' *(John 10:29)*. It cannot be said that he gave him a part of his substance and retained a part for himself, since the substance of the Father is indivisible, being entirely simple. Nor can it be said that in generating him the Father transferred his substance to the Son, as though he gave it to the Son and did not retain it himself, for if so he would have ceased to be substance. It is therefore clear that the Son, on being born received the substance of the Father without any diminution, and the Father and Son thus have the same substance. Thus the Father and the Son and the Holy Spirit, who proceeds from both, are the same thing.

But when the Truth prays to the Father for his disciples, 'that they may be one, as we also are one' *(John 17:23)* the word 'one' as applied to the disciples is to be taken in the sense of a union of charity in grace, but in the case of the divine persons in the sense of unity of identity of nature. So the Truth said on another occasion, 'Be you therefore perfect, as also your heavenly Father is perfect' *(Mt. 5:48)* as though he would say more clearly, 'Be ye perfect in the perfection of grace as your heavenly Father is perfect in the perfection of nature', in other words each in his own way. For between Creator and creature no similarity can be expressed without including a greater dissimilarity... *806*

THE GENERAL COUNCIL OF FLORENCE

DECREE FOR THE JACOBITES (1442)

The Council of Florence was meant to serve the reunion of the separated East with Rome. The decree upon which the unity of faith was to be based had in the first place to set out clearly the doctrine about God. Individual Eastern Churches still showed tendencies to an anthropomorphic notion of God. The procession of the Holy Spirit from the Father and the Son was also expressly taught. The denial of his procession from the Son as well had been the reason for the breaking away of the Eastern Church.

The Jacobites, the faithful of the Church of Syria, had been separated from Rome since the condemnation of monophysitism at Chalcedon (451) (cf. No. 252). At the Council of Florence they were reunited to the Mother Church.

157 Based on the voice of our Lord and Saviour, the Most
1330 Holy Roman Church believes, professes and teaches one true God, omnipotent, unchangeable, and eternal, Father, Son and Holy Spirit, one in essence, threefold in persons.

158 The Father not begotten, the Son begotten of the Father,
1330 the Holy Spirit proceeding from the Father and the Son.

159 The Father is not the Son or the Holy Spirit; the Son
1330 is not the Father or the Holy Spirit; the Holy Spirit is not the Father or the Son. But the Father is only the Father, the Son only the Son, and the Holy Spirit only the Holy Spirit. The Father alone begot the Son out of his substance; the Son alone was begotten by the Father alone; the Holy Spirit alone proceeds from both Father and Son.

160 These three Persons are one God, and not three gods.
1330 For the three have one substance, one essence, one nature, one godhead, one immensity, one eternity, and all things are one *(in them)* except where there is the opposition *(confrontation)* of relationship.

161 'On account of this unity the Father is wholly in the Son,
1331 and wholly in the Holy Spirit; the Son wholly in the Father and wholly in the Holy Spirit; the Holy Spirit wholly in the Father and wholly in the Son. None precedes the other in eternity, none exceeds in greatness, nor excels in power. For it is from eternity and without beginning that the Son took his origin from the Father, and from eternity and without beginning that the Holy Spirit proceeds from the Father and the Son' *(Fulgentius)*

162 What the Father is or has, he has not from another but
1331 from himself; he is the origin without origin. What the

Son is or has, he has from the Father; he is origin from origin. What the Holy Spirit is or has, he has at the same time from the Father and the Son. But the Father and Son are not two origins, but one origin. As the Father and the Son and the Holy Ghost are not three origins of creation but one origin...

CHAPTER FOUR

CREATION
GOD'S CREATIVE ACT – MAN
– MAN'S ORIGINAL STATE

The triune God has shared the wealth of his truth and grace with mankind. Catholic dogma teaches about the fact of God's communication to the world, its extent and its scope.
The first question in this dogma of revelation concerns itself with the world in which God revealed himself. In it, it is not first and foremost a matter of the fact of the laws of persistence and development given to the world but of the world in its relationship with God. This is the doctrine of Creation.
It is made up of three principal parts: the doctrines of God's creative act, of man, and of man's elevation to the supernatural.
God's creative act. *Two basic thoughts are found in all the Church's documents on the doctrine of creation. The first is:* All that is was made by God. *Any doctrine of a Principle alien or inimical to God, confronting the Creator-God, is thereby rejected. Matter, and in particular the human body, also comes from God, and is therefore good. This is the ultimate basis for the Church's rejection of any form of rigourism or unbalanced spiritualism. The second deals with* the freedom of God's creative act. *Philosophical thought, starting from the data provided by the world, necessarily tries to discover*

the laws and essential consistencies of the world. All attempts to submit God, the founder of the world, to these binding consistencies have been condemned by the Church. God transcends the world; it is his free work, which he creates without thereby in any way altering himself. He himself is the beginning and the end, the foundation and the final goal, of everything that has come into existence.

Man. *The Church's decrees concerning man do not, of course, constitute a complete doctrine of man. Yet they do contain all the essentials for an overall conception of man and the life of the human soul. Principal among them are the truths of the* Spirituality, Freedom, Uniqueness (Individuality), and immortality *of the human soul, of the* direct creation *of the soul by God, and of the* relationship *between the human* soul and body.

Man's supernatural elevation. *The doctrine of man's original state only receives its full importance in conjunction with the doctrine of grace. Here, therefore, we shall only indicate two fundamental ideas which are of vital importance in the whole question of man's relationship to the supernatural. The first is the fact that in his original state man had gifts which he lost as a result of original sin. Second is the* gratuitous *nature of these gifts, which lie beyond the claims of human nature. They were freely bestowed by God. In part they were preternatural, that is to say they did not belong to the nature of man, but could belong to the nature of a created being of a higher order, such as freedom from pain, death and concupiscence; in part they were supernatural in the fullest sense, that is, they were beyond the claims of any created nature. In this truly supernatural order belongs sanctifying grace, participation in the life of God.*

The Church's teaching on creation contains the following principal truths:

Creation

God created *the whole world, visible and invisible, out of nothing (165, 166, 170, 171, 189, 190, 191, 193, 197, 198, 828, 829, 831, 838).* Not from eternity *but from the beginning of time (74b, 171, 172, 173, 174, 183, 191)* in *order to share his goodness (180, 184, 185, 191), for his own glory (186, 188, 197) and for the sanctification of man (180, 186, 187). The* angels *were created (74b, 165, 171, 191), and* Man *(167–9, 171, 191, 198) and the* material *world (171, 191). All that is created is good (165, 167, 169, 171, 177, 186). God guides the world by his* Providence *(170, 192, 201). Matter and spirit are essentially different (74b, 74g, 194).*

Man's soul *is also created by God (164, 176) at conception (199, 200). It is not begotten by the parents (204), it is one (202, 203), free (201, 708, 710, 742, 743, 784–6, 792, 796, 797), immortal (205), the form of the human body (203, 205). Every man has his own spiritual soul (205).*

The first man was provided with sanctifying grace (198, 211–3, 217, 221, 222), was not subject to death (198, 206, 215, 221) and free of concupiscence (198, 214, 225). These gifts were not owed to human nature (207–10, 212–6, 807b).

1 GOD'S CREATIVE ACT

THE PROVINCIAL COUNCIL OF CONSTANTINOPLE (543) CANONS CONDEMNING THE ORIGENISTS

Under the Patriarch Menas, the Council established a series of canons against the Origenists which were confirmed by the signature of Pope Vigilius. The doctrine condemned in these canons is not that of Origen so much as that of the Origenists. Influenced by Platonic philosophy, this system sought to explain the whole origin of the world by laws of inner necessity. In such a system there could be no question of creation's being a free act of God. It should be noted that from the very beginning the Church had always emphasized the freedom of God as the ultimate origin of the world, as opposed to any systematic explanation involving only ineluctable laws.

163 If any one says or holds that God's power is finite, or
410 that he has created all that he could create – *anathema sit*.

THE COUNCIL OF BRAGA (PORTUGAL) (561) CANONS CONDEMNING THE PRISCILLIANISTS

Priscillian (ob. 385) was the founder of a Manichean gnostic sect in Spain. According to his teaching the devil is the Evil Principle and the creator of matter; the soul is of divine nature and its being tied to the body is the punishment of exile for previously committed sins. This doctrine was taken over from the Origenists.
In these canons it should be noted that the Church intervened from the beginning against the decrying of matter, and

especially against denigration of the human body. Everything that is, is good, including the material world, for it was all made by God.

5. If any one believe that human souls or angels consist of the substance of God, as Manichees and Priscillianists say – *anathema sit*.   164 / 455

7. If any one say that the devil was not originally created by God as a good angel and that his nature is not the work of God, but that he emerged from darkness and had no creator but is himself the principle and subtance of evil, as Manichees and Priscillianists say – *anathema sit*.   165 / 457

8. If any one believe that the devil made certain creatures in the world, and makes thunder and lightning and tempests and droughts by his own authority, as Priscillian said – *anathema sit*.   166 / 458

See also Can. 9 (No. 201)

11. If any one condemn human marriage, and abhors the begetting of children, as Manichees and Priscillianists say – *anathema sit*.   167 / 461

12. If any one say that the construction of the human body is the work of the devil, or that conceptions take place in the wombs of mothers by the activities of evil spirits, and therefore does not believe in the resurrection of the body, as Manichees and Priscillianists say – *anathema sit*.   168 / 462

13. If any one say the creation of all flesh is not the work of God, but of wicked angels, as Manichees and Priscillianists say – *anathema sit*.   169 / 463

PROFESSION OF FATH PRESCRIBED BY POPE INNOCENT III FOR THE WALDENSES (1208)

The Albigenses were the successors of the ancient Manichees and were therefore dualists. From 1180 they were known in central France under this name. Their main doctrines were: Matter is evil and was created by the devil out of nothing; Jesus Christ therefore had no real body, but only the appearance of a body; the sacraments together with any worship of God connected with perceptible signs is objectionable. The highest moral principle is abstention from matter.
In part the great movements of the time towards poverty followed the same line, in particular the Waldenses, or Waldensians (named after their founder, Peter Waldo of Lyons – ob. ca. 1217) and, in Italy the Lombards. They were bluntly opposed to the outward display of power and the increasing secularization of the Church in the time of Innocent III. Francis and Dominic fought for the same evangelical ideal, but strictly within the Church, in contrast with the Waldensians who fell into heresy (cf. Notes to Nos. 203 and 405).

170
421 Father, Son, and Holy Spirit, one God... is creator, maker, governor and disposer of all things corporeal and spiritual, visible and invisible. We believe that the Old and the New Testaments have one and the same author, God... who in enduring Trinity created all things from nothing...

THE FOURTH LATERAN GENERAL COUNCIL (1215)

Chapter I. The Catholic Faith

The Fourth Lateran Council represents the Church's final and ultimate position in relation to the Albigensian and Waldensian heresies. The teaching of this Council about creation was largely adopted by the First Vatican Council... The Omission in the following passage will be found in No. 155 above.

We firmly believe and simply confess that there is only one true God, eternal, immense, unchangeable, incomprehensible, omnipotent and ineffable, the Father, the Son and the Holy Spirit... one origin of all things: Creator of all things, visible and invisible, spiritual and corporeal; who by his own omnipotent power from the beginning of time created in the same way both orders of creation, spiritual and corporeal, that is the angelic order and the earthly; and then the order of humanity, as it were common to both, being composed of spirit and body. For the devil and other wicked spirits were made by God good by nature, but they of themselves became bad. Man indeed sinned at the suggestion of the devil... 171 *800*

ARTICLES OF ECKHART CONDEMNED BY POPE JOHN XXII (1329)

It was only towards the end of his life that Eckhart was attacked for his teaching. After his death in 1327 twenty-eight articles from his works and sermons were condemned. It has never been definitely decided whether he really meant these heretical statements in the sense in which they were condemned by the Church. They are reproduced here because their condemnation brings out so clearly God's freedom in his work of creation.

1. Asked why God did not create the world earlier, he replied that God could not have created the world earlier because nothing can act until it is; therefore, as soon as God was, he made the world. [172] *951*
2. Equally it can be conceded that the world is from eternity. [173] *952*

[174] 3. Equally, once and at the same time, when God was,
953 when he begot his co-eternal Son, in all things equal God, he also created the world.

[175] 26. All creatures are a pure nothing: I do not say they
976 are a bit or that they are something, but that they are a pure nothing.

In addition, objection was taken to the following:

[176] There is something in the soul which is un created and
977 uncreatable; if the whole soul were such, it would be uncreated and uncreatable. And this is the understanding *(intellectus).*

THE GENERAL COUNCIL OF FLORENCE

DECREE FOR THE JACOBITES (1442)

The decree of reunion of the separated East with Rome (cf. also Note to No. 157) contained among other things the condemnation of old heresies, including Manicheeism. This was a system whose line of thought continually found new adherents. The decree thus becomes part of the documentation of the Church's teaching on creation.

177 *(The Most Holy Roman Church)* **most firmly believes,**
1333 **professes and preaches that the one true God, Father, Son and Holy Spirit is the Creator of all things visible and invisible. Who, when he so wished, out of his bounty created all creatures, spiritual as well as corporeal. They are good, since they were created by the highest God, but mutable, because they were created out of nothing.**

1334 **She** *(the Church)* **affirms that evil has no nature, for all nature, as nature, is good.**

She also professes one and the same God to be the author of the Old and New Testaments, that is the Law and the Prophets and the Gospels, for the Saints of both Testaments spoke under the inspiration of the same Holy Spirit; and she receives and venerates their books...

Furthermore, she anathematizes the unreason of the Manichees who supposed two first principles, one for visible things and one for invisible things, and said that the God of the Old Testament was different from the God of the New Testament... 1336

THE PROVINCIAL COUNCIL OF COLOGNE (1860)
SECTION 3 – CREATION

As well as disciplinary decrees, the Cologne Synod of 1860 issued comprehensive doctrinal articles concerning the most important items of dogma. The following extracts are the clearest and most concise statement of the whole doctrine of creation. The occasion for them was given by the heretical views of Hermes and Günther. As documents of a local Council they are not infallible, but they are nevertheless the teaching of an official ecclesiastical authority.

Chapter XI. Against Pantheism

...Pastors should explain to their faithful how godless, indeed how utterly nonsensical it is to say: God, of whom we are taught by Scripture, creeds and reason that he is infinite, immense, and immutable is the world which is constantly subject to change. They should also show how how blasphemous it is and how contrary to God's holiness and justice to maintain that God himself is in man the performer of all wicked deeds. It should also not be difficult to show men who consider things calmly how this error is already rejected by the testimony of their own consciences, and how dangerous for human society is an error which does not hesitate to transfer man's wickedness to God and to qualify disturbances of good order as so many developments of the godhead. This would mean that, whatever blasphemy he might commit, man was not to be blamed. 178

Finally, any one who knows that God exists of himself and is infinite, and therefore infinitely far removed from all other mutable things, will easily see that God cannot have the same nature as the things of this world...

Chapter XII. God's Freedom in Creation

179 'God... when he so wished, out of his bounty, created all creatures, spiritual as well as corporeal' *(Council of Florence: cf. No. 177)*, for he had no need for the world, not in order to obtain from it something of perfection – for he is all perfection and sufficient unto himself – and not in order to effect his inner life by the act of creation – for this life is fulfilled by his knowing and loving his own infinite Being.
If one will speak of a necessary activity, this occurs in the inner action of the divine Persons and requires no perfecting by an external creation, for it is already perfect.

180 One can also not say that God necessarily created the world so that he should be known to those things which are distinct from him, made or to be made by him, in the same way as he knows himself. For the knowledge and consciousness of God require no completion by the acknowledgment of anything existing apart from him. He can in no way be perfected by things outside himself. The knowledge of the possibility of the world, which he could of course not lack, he had from his perfect insight into his own being which contains the original design of all things and into his creative power. It is as a result of his goodness that when God creates he necessarily communicates good things and necessarily wishes to do good to what he has created. But his goodness does not so impel him that

he must of necessity create. For, as it is for men, God alone, or his essence, is the highest good for himself as well, which he must necessarily always will and love. But he can love his own infinite being or the goodness in himself without creating anything. Though God necessarily wills his own goodness, he does not necessarily will the things that his goodness wills; for his goodness can exist without other things.

It is also clear that in the same entirely simple act whereby God necessarily wills and loves himself and his goodness he also freely wills all other things; for this act is eternal and is therefore adequate without increase for everything else: it is rich enough for everything. 181

As it was for God to create the world or not, so it was for him to create this world or another. In fact the same proofs of God's freedom in the creation of the world, prove also that he was free to create this or another world. 182

The earnest consideration of this complete freedom in the creation of the world will lead Christians to the greatest thankfulness to God's goodness for making us out of nothing though compelled thereto by no necessity.

The world did not exist from eternity, but was created by God in time. The act by which he willed the existence of the world was always present in God, for in him there is no time sequence and no waiting, but it was first effective in time, or to express it better, at the beginning of time. 183

Chapter XIII. The Goal of the Created World

If one asks the reason which moved God to create, that is, the purpose of the Creator, the answer runs: 184

Nothing outside himself could have moved him. Since he is sufficient unto himself, he cannot aspire to anything for himself.

185 But since God has in fact created, and since he necessarily creates what he does out of love for his own interior goodness, we rightly say: God was moved by his goodness to a free creation. In this sense St Augustine also says, 'Because he is good, we are good.'

186 But if one no longer asks about the reason which moved God to create, that is, about the Creator's purpose, but about the purpose which God the Creator aspired to for his work – the purpose of the work, that is – then we must say that he aspired to, and still always aspires to, what is so bound up with his action that it cannot be separated from it. And that is as follows: First: When God creates he must necessarily communicate *some good* to the creatures, for the 'being' which they have acquired is a good. It is in this sense that St Augustine says, 'Inasmuch as we are, we are good'. The second thing that could not be lacking in God's work was the *revelation of divine perfection*, particularly of power, wisdom and goodness. This revelation is called God's external honour, for God is praised thereby. But that God really intended the recognition and love of his perfection, or in other words his external honour, is beyond all doubt. This is shown by a consideration of created things which of their nature necessarily reveal God's perfections, and of man who is equipped with understanding so that he can know and love God in his works: because he is holy, he must necessarily wish to be known from his works. Thus we understand the many sayings of Holy Scripture urging us to praise God by considering the greatness of created things.

187 Very closely bound up with the glorification of God

is the *happiness of man*, for by glorifying God men increase their merit and their happiness. Conversely, the greater goods God gives to man, the greater are the proofs of his goodness, and his honour is increased accordingly. So each reinforces the other. But if one asks about the order of priority of the two purposes, the answer must be: the ultimate purpose of the work is the glorification of God. The happiness of creatures and of men in particular, must be subordinated to it, for the glorification of God is of a higher order than man's happiness, since it concerns God. It is therefore fitting that man's happiness should be subordinate to and should serve the glorification of God.

But it must not be concluded therefrom that God's goodness to man is thereby diminished: the goods which God gives us are not diminished by being directed to God's honour. On the contrary, the more zealously we seek God's honour in them, the more are we ourselves enriched; for God does not seek honour in this world as though thereby he acquired something he does not already possess; no, he demands only the preservation of right order. 188

ERRORS CONDEMNED BY POPE PIUS IX (1864)
(cf. Note to No. 26)

Against Pantheism and Deism
1. There is no supreme, all-wise, all-provident divine Being distinct from the totality of things, and God is the same as the nature of things and therefore subject to changes. God is truly in man and in the world and everything is God and has the very same substance of God. God is one and the same thing as the world and therefore spirit and matter, necessity and liberty, truth [189] 2901

and falsehood, good and evil, just and unjust.

2902   2. All action by God on men and on the world is to be denied.

FIRST VATICAN GENERAL COUNCIL, THIRD SESSION (1870)

The First Vatican Council was the Church's great expression of her position in relation to the errors of the nineteenth century. In opposition to materialism (the doctrine that only matter exists) and pantheism (equating the world and God) in all its forms it was first of all necessary to set forth the fundamental truth about God, the Creator of heaven and earth, and then the true doctrine of the meaning of creation. This is what is dealt with in the first chapter and the corresponding canons. This chapter corresponds very closely to the decree of the Fourth Lateran Council (cf. No. 171).

Chapter I. God, the Creator of All Things

God

190
3001   The Holy Catholic Apostolic Roman Church, believes and confesses that there is one true and living God, Creator and Lord of heaven and earth, almighty, eternal, immense, incomprehensible, infinite in intellect, in will, and in all perfection; who, as being one, sole, absolutely simple and immutable spiritual substance, is to be declared as really and essentially distinct from the world, of supreme beatitude in and from himself, and ineffably exalted above all things which exist, or are conceivable, except himself.

Creation

191
3002   This one and only true God, of his own goodness and almighty power, not for the increase or acquirement of his own happiness, but to manifest his perfection by the

blessing which he bestows on creatures, and with absolute freedom of counsel, created out of nothing, from the very first beginning of time, both the spiritual and the corporeal creature, to wit, the angelical and the mundane, and afterwards the human creature, as partaking, in a sense, of both, consisting of spirit and of body.

Providence

God protects and governs by his Providence all things which he has made, 'reaching from end to end mightily, and ordering all things sweetly' *(Wis. 8:1)*. For 'all things are bare and open to his eyes' *(Heb. 4:13)* even those which are yet to be by the free action of creatures.

192
3003

CANONS

God, Creator of all things

1. If any one shall deny One true God, Creator and Lord of things visible and invisible – *anathema sit*.

193
3021

2. If any one shall not be ashamed to affirm that, except matter, nothing exists – *anathema sit*.

194
3022

3. If any one shall say that the substance and essence of God and of all things is one and the same – *anathema sit*.

195
3023

4. If any one shall say that finite things, both corporeal and spiritual, or at least spiritual, have emanated from the divine substance or that the divine essence by the manifestation and evolution of itself becomes all things; or, lastly that God is universal or indefinite being, which by determining itself constitutes the universality of things, distinct according to genera, species and individuals – *anathema sit*.

196
3024

5. If any one does not confess that the world, and all things which are contained in it, both spiritual and material, have been, in their whole substance, produced by God out of nothing; or shall say that God created,

197
3025

not by his will, free from all necessity, but by a necessity equal to the necessity whereby he loves himself; or shall deny that the world was made for the glory of God – *anathema sit.*

DECREE OF THE BIBLICAL COMMISSION
(30 JUNE 1909)

Some exegetes tried to get round the difficulties which modern science found in the account of creation by means of a purely allegorical interpretation of the first chapters of Genesis. The decision of the Biblical Commission quoted here concerns this attempt. From this decision it results that the facts gathered in these chapters are historical happenings but that many other details, for example the six-days duration, are literary clothing.
The Bible Commission was set up by an instrument of Leo XIII dated 30 October 1902 to further biblical studies and decide upon unsettled questions. By order of Pius X, dated 18 November 1907, its decisions have the same weight as those of Roman Congregations. The decision below is thus not infallible but must be regarded as the standard Church doctrine (cf. Nos. 126d and 126f)

198
3514

The historical character of the first chapters of Genesis
Q. 3. Whether in particular the historical meaning of words may be called in doubt when it is a question of the facts narrated in these chapters which touch upon the foundations of the Christian religion, such as, for example, the creation of all things by God at the beginning of time, the particular creation of man, the formation of the first woman from the first man, the unity of the human race, the original happiness of our first parents in a state of justice, integrity and immortality, the commandment given by God to man to test his obedience, the transgression of the divine commandment at the instigation of the devil in the

form of a serpent, the ejection of our first parents from their primal state of innocence, and finally the promise of the Redeemer to come.
Answer: No.

2 MAN

THE PROVINCIAL COUNCIL OF CONSTANTINOPLE (543) CANONS CONDEMNING THE ORIGENISTS
(Cf. Note to No. 163)

199 *Against the doctrine of the transmigration of souls*
403 If any one says or holds that human souls have had a previous existence, that is that they were previously minds and holy powers and have had their fill of the Beatific Vision and have turned to evil and thus grown cold to the love of God and are thus called $\psi\upsilon\kappa\grave{\alpha}s$ (meaning cold) and in punishment have been banished into bodies – *anathema sit.*

THE COUNCIL OF BRAGA (561) CANONS CONDEMNING THE PRISCILLIANISTS
(Cf. Note to No. 164)

200 *Against transmigration of souls and fatalism*
456 6. If any one say that human souls sinned in a previous heavenly existence and were on that account banished into human bodies on earth, as Priscillian said – *anathema sit.*
201 9. If any one believe that human souls are bound to a
459 blind fate as pagans and Priscillian said – *anathema sit.*

THE FOURTH GENERAL COUNCIL OF CONSTANTINOPLE (869–70) CANONS CONDEMMING PHOTIUS

The eighth General Council met in Constantinople in the

stormy years of the separation of the East from the Roman Church, at a time when Photius was Patriarch of Constantinople. The Council's decisions against Photius were a last great victory for the papacy in the East (cf. No. 336). Various errors which had been taught by Photius, including that of two souls, were condemned by the Council. It is not possible to say with certainty from those writings of his which are still available whether Photius intended them in the sense in which they are here condemned.
The Council's intention is to exclude a dual principle in the life of the soul: in man there is not a special principle for the sensual and for the spiritual life but one single bearer of all human functions of living. The meaning of the Canon is therefore the unity of man and of the life of his soul.

The uniqueness of the soul

10. Both the Old and the New Testament teach, and all the enlightened Fathers and Doctors of the Church profess the same opinion, that man has one rational and intellectual soul. Nevertheless... certain people have impudently taught that he has two souls and attempt to justify this heresy with unreasonable arguments... 202 657

This Holy General Council therefore anathematizes... the inventors of such an impiety. 658

THE GENERAL COUNCIL OF VIENNE (1311–2) AGAINST THE ERRORS OF PETER JOHN OLIEU

Olieu (1248–98) was one of the leading figures of the 'Spirituals' in the great struggle over poverty in the Franciscan Order. They favoured the evangelical ideal of poverty in all its strictness as opposed to the opposite tendency among the Conventuals. In his lifetime he was called before the General Chapter of his Order in Paris. After his death, his teaching was once more indicted by the Conventuals in order to hit at the Spirituals by condemnation of the leader of their party.

The question came before the Council of Vienne, where among other things his doctrine of the relation of body and soul was dealt with. The decision reproduced is the infallible teaching of a General Council.
The meaning of the decision. *The problem lies in the fact that the soul, as a spiritual entity, is by nature independent of matter. How can it then in man be associated with the body and become one being? Olieu's answer to this was that the soul, as a spiritual entity, was associated with the body not directly but by means of a principle of sensible organic life quite distinct from itself. The Council's teaching: the Soul, of itself, directly and not through any principle separate from itself, is, in its inner disposition to be associated with the body, the form of the body. Thus the Church's doctrine is laid down, that the soul itself is the vehicle of the life of the body. The importance of this decision lies in its adherence to the unity and integrity of man. The splitting of the life of the human soul into spiritual life and sensible life was precisely what had such destructive effect in the Albigensian and Waldensian heresies which conceived of spirit and matter, good and evil, as equal foundations of the world. It destroys any sound conception of man.*

203 *The Soul as Form of the Body*
902 **Further, with the approval of the said Holy Council, we reject as erroneous and contrary to the truth of the Catholic faith any doctrine or position which rashly asserts, or calls into doubt, that the substance of the rational or intellectual soul is not truly and of itself the form of the human body. So that the truth of the pure faith shall be known to all, and that the entry of all errors that might slip in shall be barred, We define that from now on whoever shall presume to assert, defend, or obstinately hold that the rational or intellectual soul is not in itself and essentially the form of the human body, is to be censured as a heretic.**

ERRORS OF THE ARMENIANS CONDEMNED BY POPE BENEDICT XII (1341)

We are not concerned here with whether the Armenians did in fact teach traducianism but with the Church's rejection of it. Condemned as early as 498 by Pope Anastasius II in a letter to the Bishops of Gaul (DZ 360f), traducianism maintained that the human soul was generated like the body by the parents. This heresy did not spring from a recognition that some intellectual characteristics are inherited, but from a desire to explain original sin, it being apparently easier to understand its being inherited if the soul is generated by the parents.

5. A teacher among the Armenians... taught that the human soul of the son is generated by the soul of his father, as the body is generated by the body, and that angels also come one from another, for since the human rational soul and the angel, intellectual by nature, are beings like spiritual lights, they generate other spiritual lights from themselves.

[204]
1007

THE FIFTH LATERAN GENERAL COUNCIL EIGHTH SESSION (1513)

Pietro Pomponazzi (1464–1525) taught the Aristotelian doctrine of the soul in Padua, not in the sense in which it had continued to flourish in scholastic tradition, but as it had been introduced into Spain under Arab influence. He followed the interpretation of Averroes: On account of its capability of grasping universals, the spirit of man could not be a single individual entity; since, however, the principle of organic and sensible life in its activity in individual men was essentially bound up with matter, because it was individual, its existence ceased on death. (This teaching had already been condemned indirectly by the Council of Vienne, since a soul which is not itself individual cannot be the form of the individual bodily life of the individual man *(cf. No. 203)*. The Lateran Council condemned this teaching and proclaimed the individuality and immortality of the individual human soul as infallible dogma.

205 *Individuality and immortality of the human soul*
1440 Since the sower of cockle, ancient enemy of the human race... has dared to oversow and to cause to grow in the field of the Lord certain most pernicious errors always rejected by the faithful, in particular concerning the nature of the rational soul, viz. that it is mortal, or that one and the same soul is found in all men, and since some people, rash in their philosophical thinking, assert this to be, at least philosophically speaking, true; We, therefore, desirous of applying the appropriate remedy to such a mischief, and with the approval of this sacred Council, condemn and reject all those who assert that the intellectual soul is mortal or one soul common to all men, or who call in doubt that it *(the soul)* is not only truly and of itself and essentially the form of the human body, as is stated in the canon of Clement V, Our Predecessor of blessed memory, issued by the Council of Vienne, but is also immortal and can be multiplied in accordance with the multitude of bodies into which it is infused, has been and will be so multiplied...

PIUS XII's ENCYCLICAL *HUMANI GENERIS* (1950)
(cf. Note to 74a; 126e)

After Pope Pius XII in an address on 30th November 1941 had declared that the question of the association of man with the animal kingdom so far as his body was concerned was an open question, he again declared freedom for discussion for this matter, in certain conditions, in his encyclical Humani Generis. *At the same time, however, it was made clear that the doctrine of polygenism (i.e. denial that all men since*

Adam *stem from one set of parents) is not compatible with dogma, in particular not with the dogma of original sin.*

Origin of man and revelation

Thus, the teaching of the Church leaves the doctrine of evolution an open question, as long as it confines its speculations to the development, from other living matter already in existence, of the human body. (That souls are immediately created by God is a view which the Catholic faith imposes on us.) In the present state of scientific and theological opinion, this question may be legitimately canvassed by research, and by discussion between those who are expert in both subjects. At the same time, the reasons for and against either view must be weighed and adjudged with all seriousness, fairness, and restraint; and there must be a readiness on all sides to accept the arbitrament of the Church, as being entrusted by Christ with the task of interpreting the Scriptures aright, and the duty of safeguarding the doctrines of the faith. There are some who take rash advantage of this liberty of debate, by treating the subject as if the whole matter were closed – as if the discoveries hitherto made, and the arguments based on them, were sufficiently certain to prove, beyond doubt, the development of the human body from other living matter already in existence. They forget, too, that there are certain references to the subject in the sources of divine revelation, which call for the greatest caution and prudence in discussing it.

205a
3896

Common origin of all men (monogenism)

There are other conjectures, about polygenism (as it is called), which leave the faithful no such freedom of debate. Christians cannot lend their support to a theory which involves the existence, after Adam's time,

205b
3987

of some earthly race of men, truly so called, who were not descended ultimately from him, or else supposes that Adam was the name given to some group of our primordial ancestors. It does not appear how such views can be reconciled with the doctrine of original sin, as this is guaranteed to us by Scripture and tradition, and proposed to us by the Church. Original sin is the result of a sin committed, in actual historical fact, by an individual man named Adam, and it is a quality native to all of us, only because it has been handed down by descent from him.

3 MAN'S ORGINAL STATE

PROVINCIAL COUNCIL OF CARTHAGE (418)

Against Pelagius (cf. p. 134) the Council laid down that Adam was originally blessed with the gift of immortality. The canons of the Council were approved by Pope Zosimus. See also No. 221, Canon 1, Council of Trent, 5th Session.

1. Whoever shall say that Adam the first man was made mortal so that he would die in the body whether he sinned or did not sin, that is that he would quit the body not as punishment for sin but by necessity of nature[1]. – *anathema sit.*

206
222

ERRORS OF MICHAEL DU BAY CONDEMNED BY POPE PIUS V (1567)

In conjunction with his teaching on grace (cf. Nos. 771–89) du Bay denied that the gifts with which the first man was honoured and which he lost by original sin were preternatural or supernatural. Thus in his view their loss was not just the cessation of a gratuitous privilege but also a substantial injury to human nature as such.

21. The elevation and exaltation of human nature to participation in the divine nature was due to the integrity of its primal condition and is therefore to be called natural, not supernatural.

[207]
1921

1. In the language of the first centuries of Christianity the word 'nature' did not mean the purely natural powers of man independently of his supernatural or preternatural gifts, but his original state before the first sin, which included natural capabilities, supernatural elevation and preternatural gifts.

[208] 28. The integrity of the first creation was not an un-
1926   entitled exaltation of human nature, but was its natural condition.
[209] 55. God could not from the beginning have created
1955   man as he is now born.
[210] 78. The immortality of the first man was not a gift of
1978   grace but his natural condition.

THE PROVINCIAL COUNCIL OF COLOGNE (1860)

Chapter XV. Man's Original Condition
(Cf. Note to No. 177)

211 With the Council of Trent we teach that the first man was endowed with sanctity and justice. This condition of original justice was supernatural and in no way an entitlement of human nature; God could therefore have created man without endowing him with supernatural gifts.

212 Supernatural are those gifts whereby nature is raised to a higher order, that is to say whereby it reaches a perfection which is beyond its own powers and beyond anything which it can demand.

That this view of gifts beyond nature is no mere scholastic invention we know from the Holy See's condemnation of the teaching of du Bay *(cf. 207–10 above)*

213 Thus the sanctifying grace is supernatural whereby man was raised so far above his condition that he became by adoption the son of God and is thus capable of attaining the bliss which consists in the direct vision of God and is beyond all the natural powers of man.

214 Also supernatural and gratuitous was the complete subordination of concupiscence to understanding, that is the great gift of integrity whereby God so ordered

the motions and desires of man's soul that they always obeyed the commands of reason. Since, namely, man consists of a rational soul and a body, it can in itself happen that he allows himself to be impelled to seek the good of the body more than that of the soul and that concupiscence would be rebellious were it not kept in check.

It cannot be said that God's wisdom and goodness necessarily had to endow man with the perfect balance of higher and lower powers that existed in Adam... It therefore follows naturally that the immortality of the body and its freedom from suffering were supernatural gifts. The nature of the body, subject as it is to death and decay, has no claim to these gifts and they are also not due to man by any right. 215

We therefore declare: Any one who teaches that the wisdom and goodness of God require him to give man sanctifying grace, freedom from concupiscence, or immortality of the body, *errs* from the Catholic truth. Equally, anyone who maintains that freedom from concupiscence necessarily belong to the idea or nature of man, and finally anyone who says that the gifts accorded to Adam are only to be designated as supernatural because God the Creator gave them to him and not man himself *(is in error).* 216

5 *Teaching of the Catholic Church*

CHAPTER FIVE

ORIGINAL SIN

The world in which God was to reveal himself is God's work in so far as it is good, orderly and raised to its supernatural end. But it is also the work of man, for Adam, the first man, by his sin in Paradise lost the supernatural gifts, grace, and the preternatural gifts, freedom from concupiscence, suffering and death. The original sin of the first man became the inherited sin of all men. Because of it man needs redemption, for he is guilty before God and needs a redeemer to make the atonement man owes to God.
The Church has always had to stress two fundamental truths in her doctrine of original sin. First, the fact *of* original sin, *the loss of supernatural life and man's consequent total inability to attain by his own powers the supernatural goal assigned him by God. Original sin therefore represents a loss which man can never make good by his own efforts. The fact of original sin had to be set out in opposition to Pelagius whose moral preaching demanded only the human act of will and thus denied the necessity of man's whole activity being raised to the domain of the supernatural.*
The second basic truth is the goodness of human nature (as such) *in spite of original sin. Man has indeed, by the loss of his supernatural elevation, been robbed of his*

orientation to direct personal community of life with the triune God, and on account of the loss of his preternatural gifts also achieves the perfecting of his natural gifts only with much greater difficulty than in Paradise. But the inner goodness of his pure nature as such remains. Original sin does not consist in a weakening or corruption, of human nature as such, but is primarily 'sin' – that is, participation by every man in the state of guilt before God into which Adam entered by the first sin. Thus, fallen human nature is, at least within certain limits, in the position to be good and to act accordingly; in particular it is capable of receiving by God's grace the lost supernatural gifts. This proper conception of original sin is an essential prerequisite to the proper doctrine of justification, whereas conversely the original sin doctrine of Luther and the Reformers actually only represents a part of the Protestant doctrine of justification.

The following points thus arise in the Church's teaching on original sin:
Adam sinned and thereby forfeited the supernatural and preternatural gifts (198, 217, 218, 221).
Adam's sin affects all his descendants (205b, 217, 219, 222) and every individual human being (223, 224, 712). Original sin is inherited by descent from Adam by generation (223, 224, 712, 205b). Original sin is wilful on account of Adam's free choice (227–9).
Original sin is distinguished from personal *sin by the absence of personal consent (434). Its punishment therefore is not Hell, but loss of the Beatific Vision. (434, 812, 843).*
Original sin means loss of grace *(217, 221, 222, 710) and results in death (221, 222) and concupiscence (225), which is not itself a sin (225), and in weakening the understanding and the will (13, 14, 700, 701, 710) but not in*

the destruction of free will *(708, 710, 742, 743, 784–6, 792, 796, 797).*
Original sin is wiped out in baptism by the reparation made by Christ (217, 223, 224, 225, 434, 435, 439, 558, 704–712, 718, 831).

THE PROVINCIAL COUNCIL OF CARTHAGE (418)

The first Church decrees on the subject of original sin were made as the result of Pelagianism. In conjunction with his teaching about grace (cf. Nos. 680–5) Pelagius also denied original sin. To start with, Pelagius himself confined himself to preaching a morality based on great emphasis on the will. His disciple Caelestius, however, at first in Rome, where they both lived until the Visigoth invasion of 410, and later in Africa, built up a theological system which was the source of the disputed articles about original sin and grace. In 416 he was charged and condemned by a Synod in Carthage for the following heresies: Adam was created mortal; he would have died whether he had sinned or not; Adam's sin harmed himself alone, and not the human race; children at birth are in the same state as Adam before the fall; Adam's death and sin are not the reason why the whole of mankind must die, nor will the whole of mankind rise again on account of Christ's resurrection; the Law leads to the Kingdom of Heaven equally with the Gospel; even before the Lord's coming there were men without sin.

These articles were the starting point for all subsequent decisions and condemnations, first of all in Carthage where more than two hundred bishops were assembled, whose findings were later confirmed by Pope Zosimus, and later in the list of papal decisions relating to the doctrine of grace, and at the Council of Orange (Details in Note to No. 680). The text of Canon 2 of Carthage's condemnation was adopted as Canon 4 by the fifth session of the Council of Trent (No. 224).

LIST OF PAPAL DECISIONS CONCERNING THE DOCTRINE OF GRACE (INDICULUS)
(Cf. also Note to No. 686)

1. In Adam's fall into sin all men lost their original capability and innocence and no one can by his own free will rise up out of the depths of this fall if he is not sustained by the grace of the merciful God, in accordance with the pronouncement of Pope Innocent of blessed memory in his letter to the Council of Carthage: 'He *(Adam)* made use of his free will when he thoughtlessly used his goods, fell into the abyss of sin, sank and found nothing whereby he might again rise up. Betrayed for all time by his freedom, he would have remained under the burden of this fall had not the advent of Christ later raised him up by grace, who washed away all previous guilt by the cleansing of the regeneration of baptism. 217 *239*

THE SECOND COUNCIL OF ORANGE (529)
(Cf. Note to No. 696)

1. If any one say that through the offence of Adam's sin the entire man, i.e. body and soul, was changed for the worse *(cf. Trent, 5th Session: No. 221)* but believes that only the body was subject to corruption while the freedom of the soul remained unharmed, he is deceived by the error of Pelagius and contradicts Scripture which says: 'The soul that sinneth, the same shall die' *(Ez. 18:20)*, 'Know you not, that to whom you yield yourselves servants to obey, his servants you are whom you obey?' *(Rom. 6:16)*, and, 'By whom a man is overcome, of the same also he is the slave' *(2 Peter 2:19)*. 218 *371*

2. If anyone maintain that the fall was harmful to Adam alone and not to his descendants or that only 219 *372*

bodily death, which is a punishment of sin but not sin itself, which is the death of the soul, has passed to the whole of the human race by one man, he ascribes an injustice to God, contradicting the Apostle who says: 'Wherefore as by one man sin entered into this world, and by sin death; so also death passed upon all men, in whom all have sinned' *(Rom. 5:12)*[1].

THE GENERAL COUNCIL OF TRENT
FIFTH SESSION (1546)

The next occasion for dealing with the question of original sin, by the Council of Trent, was Luther's erroneous conception that original sin consisted in evil concupiscence which is permanent in man and is not washed away by baptism: man remains a sinner, but the sin is no longer laid to his charge. However, in its exposition the Council was not content just to reject Luther's teaching but expounded the whole doctrine of original sin in the context of the other truths of faith. The Pelagian errors are once more attacked and rejected, as also those of the Manichees and Priscillianists who denied original sin in the case of the children of a Christian marriage. The doctrine is set out in detail in five canons and deals with the following points:

Adam's sin and its effects on Adam;

the transmission of Adam's sin to his descendants (the express mention of the classical text of Rom. 5:12 was aimed at Erasmus who denied that it dealt with original sin);

the wiping out of original sin solely by the Passion of Christ and the application of his merits in baptism.

The necessity of baptizing children. Canon 2 of the Council of

1. The Council quotes the Vulgate *'in quo omnes peccaverunt'* to which the Douai version most closely corresponds. The original Greek text has 'because all men have sinned'. Knox makes 'All alike were guilty...' into the beginning of a new, parenthetical, sentence embracing v. 13 and most of v. 14. Either of these readings serves in the context to emphasize the guilt of all men.

Carthage (418) against Pelagius served with minor alterations as the basis for this.
Up to this point the canons are directed against Pelagianism and related errors.
Then comes the nature of original sin. Here the ideas of Luther and the Reformers are condemned and two truths are defined: 1 – original sin is entirely washed away by baptism; 2 – the concupiscence remaining after baptism is not a sin.
The rider – Mary, the one exception. Canon 2, on the universality of original sin led to a discussion on the one exception in favour of Mary. This canon does not, of course, amount to a proclamation of the doctrine of the Immaculate Conception but means only that in insisting on the universality of original sin the Council did not wish to deny it.

DECREE ON ORIGINAL SIN

In order that our Catholic faith without which 'it is impossible to please God' *(Heb. 11:6)* **may be free of errors and be maintained pure and unstained, in order that Christian people may not be 'carried about with every wind of doctrine'** *(Eph. 4:14)* **– for the ancient serpent, the eternal enemy of mankind, has conjured up, among the very many evils which press upon the Church of God in these times of ours, new as well as old dissensions concerning original sin and its remedy – this Most Holy Ecumenical and General Council of Trent, duly assembled in the Holy Spirit, to revoke errors and strengthen the wavering... by the testimony of Holy Scripture, the holy Fathers and most reverend Councils, and in accordance with the judgment and consensus of the Church herself, on the matter of original sin ordains, confesses and declares:**   220   1510

1. If anyone do not confess that Adam, the first man, by his transgression of God's commandment in Paradise immediately lost the sanctity and justice in which he had   221   1511 been constituted, and by the offence of this sin drew upon himself the wrath and indignation of God and the death with which God had threatened him, and with death captivity in the power of him who had the empire of death, that is to say the devil *(Heb. 2:14)*, and that the whole Adam by the offence of this sin was changed in body and soul for the worse, *anathema sit*.

222
1512
2. If anyone assert that Adam's sin harmed himself alone and not his *posterity*, and that the holiness and justice received from God which he lost, was lost for himself alone and not for us too; or that stained by the sin of disobedience, he passed on to all mankind death and bodily punishment but not sin as well, which is the death of the soul, *anathema sit*. For he contradicts the Apostle who says: 'Wherefore as by one man sin entered into this world, and by sin death; so also death passed upon all men, in whom all have sinned'[1]

223
1513
3. If anyone asert that this sin of Adam's, which was one in origin and is passed on by propagation not by imitation, and is in each and proper to each, can be taken away by the powers of human nature or by any remedy other than by the merits of the *one mediator* our Lord Jesus Christ who reconciled us to God by his blood, 'made unto us...justice and sanctification and redemption' *(1 Cor. 1:30)*; or deny that this merit of Christ Jesus is applied, to adults and to children, in the sacrament of baptism duly administered in the Church's form – *anathema sit*. 'For there is no other name under heaven given to men, whereby we must be saved' *(Acts 4:12)*. Hence the words: 'Behold the Lamb of God, behold him who taketh away the sins of the world' *(cf. John 1:29)* and: 'As many of you as have been baptized in Christ, have put on Christ' *(Gal. 3:27)*.

1. Cf. footnote to No. 219.

4. If anyone deny that children newly come from their mother's womb should be baptized, even if they come of baptized parents; or says that they are baptized for the remission of sins but bear nothing of the original sin from Adam which must be expiated in the bathing of regeneration to lead to eternal life, whence it follows that in their case the form of baptism 'for the remission of sins' is not understood in the true sense but in a false sense – *anathema sit*. For what the Apostle said: 'Wherefore as by one man sin entered into the world, and by sin death; so also death passed upon all men, in whom all have sinned' *(Rom. 5:12)* is not be to understood otherwise than the way in which the Catholic Church, which is spread over the whole world, has always understood it. By this rule of faith, according to apostolic tradition, even children who in themselves can have committed no sin are therefore truly baptized for the remission of sins so that by regeneration there may be cleansed in them what they contracted by generation[1]. For 'unless a man be born again of water and the Holy Ghost, he cannot enter into the kingdom of God' *(John 3:5)*. **224** *1514*

5. If any one deny that the *guilt of original sin is remitted* by the grace of our Lord Jesus Christ conferred in baptism or assert that everything that has the true and proper nature of sin is not taken away but is erased or not reckoned – *anathema sit*. For God hates nothing in those who are reborn, since 'there is nothing worthy of damnation in those who are buried together with Christ by baptism into death' *(cf. Rom 6:4)* 'who walk not according to the flesh' *(Rom. 8:1)*, who, putting off the old man and putting on the new who is created according to God *(cf. Eph. 4:22ff; Col. 3:9f)*, innocent, unstained, **225** *1515*

---

1. Up to this point this canon is taken from Canon 2 of Carthage.

pure and guiltless, have become the beloved sons of God, 'heirs indeed of God, and joint-heirs with Christ' *(Rom. 8:17)* so that henceforth nothing holds them back from entry into heaven. The Holy Council, however, knows and confesses that there remains in those who have been baptized concupiscence or the inclination to sin. But since this is left for us to wrestle with, it cannot harm those who do not consent to it but manfully resist it by the grace of Jesus Christ. Rather, he who strives lawfully will be crowned *(cf. 2 Tim. 2:5)*. **Of this concupiscence which the Apostle occasionally calls 'sin'** *(cf. Rom. 6:12ff; 7:7; 7:14–20)*, **this Holy Council declares that the Catholic Church has never understood its being called sin in the sense of real and actual sin in those who have been regenerated, but only as coming from sin and inclining towards sin. If anyone think to the contrary –** *anathema sit.*

226 **But this same Holy Council declares it is not its in-**
1516 **tention to include in this decree, in so far as it concerns original sin, the Blessed and Immaculate Virgin Mary, Mother of God, but that the Constitutions of Pope Sixtus IV of blessed memory are to be observed under the penalties contained in those Constitutions, which it renews.**

ERRORS OF DU BAY CONDEMNED BY PIUS V (1567)

Cf. Nos. 771-89 and Note to No. 771. Du Bay regarded original sin as inherent disorder of the human will. Luther spoke about the decay of human nature as a whole, but du Bay conceived original sin not so much as a state of man's fallen nature as the habitual perversion of the human will in fallen man. This sinful direction of the will, with which every man is born, is only removed by consious conversion to God in pure love. In the Catholic conception the wilful element, which must exist in original sin if it is really to be sin, does not lie in the individual man but in the free action of Adam.

46. The wilful element is not a part of the nature and definition of sin, and it is not a question of definition, but of its cause and origin, whether every sin must be wilful. [227] *1946*

47. Therefore, original sin truly has the nature of sin without relation or respect to the will from which it had its cause. [228] *1947*

48. Original sin is wilful on account of the habitual will of the child and it habitually dominates the child because the child makes no contrary decision of will. [229] *1948*

49. From this habitually dominant will it results that a child dying without the sacrament of regeneration, when it reaches the use of reason, hates and blasphemes God and resists his law. [230] *1959*

CHAPTER SIX

THE REDEEMER

One Member of the Most Holy Trinity, *the only-begotten Son of the Father, in the course of time assumed* human nature *from the Virgin Mary by the power of the Holy Spirit. Thus he was able by his obedience, obedience unto the death of the Cross, to make satisfaction for our sins, and by his merits to embody us in the Holy Spirit in his divine-human life for the glory of the Father so that the Father might be all in all.*
The significance for our salvation of the mystery of the God-Man *explains the passion with which his Bride, the Church, clings to what God has revealed to her about it. It is indeed the very mystery of her existence.*
The doctrine of Christ's divinity *(in opposition to the Jews) and his* humanity *(in opposition to heathen gnosis) are the main pillars of dogma concerning Christ, the development of the truth of the 'hypostatic union' of the divine and human natures in the one divine Person. No purely human individuality or personality in Christ is compatible with this unity (in opposition Nestorius). There is therefore in Christ beside his natural sonship of God no gratuitous adoption as the Son of God (against adoptionism). The two natures remain separate and* distinct *(against monophysitism), distinct and entire. Christ therefore has a real human* intellect *(against*

Apollinaris), a true human soul *(against Arius), his own human* will *and human* actions *(against monotheletism and monergism). But this distinction is not a separation: the human nature also really and truly belongs to the divine Person of the Word of God. This is the basis of Christ's* sinlessness *and* freedom from error *even in his human life, and the lack of any ignorance in him. Thus placed as* mediator *between God and man, he, the second Adam, was able to found a new covenant in his blood, whereby there is glory to God on high, and on earth peace to men of good will.*

This chapter is mainly devoted to doctrinal decrees about the person of Christ. *The doctrine of the* redemption *will be found very largely represented throughout, but the most important texts concerning Christ's Passion and merits will be found in other contexts (cf. in particular No. 223 on original sin; Nos. 711–8, the Council of Trent on justification). In this chapter we offer only a brief summary of the doctrine of redemption in an extract from Pius XI's encyclical* Miserentissimus Redemptor.

The doctrine concerning Christ, the Word made flesh, embraces the following individual truths:
Christ is true God *(135, 234, 247–51, 264, 289, 291, 299–303, 319b, 831, 837, 839) by being born of the* Father *(133, 247, 252, 255, 270, 837, 839) and true* Man *(247–51, 271, 289, 290, 319b, 837, 837c, 839) by being born of Mary (246, 247–51, 252, 255, 259, 270, 283, 837, 837c, 839).*
Thus (against monophysitism) there are two natures *in Christ, the divine and the human (74h, 232, 248–51, 252, 270, 271, 285, 287, 319b) which are distinct (233, 246, 248, 249, 260–2, 271–5, 284, 832, 837, 839). In him also (against monotheletism) there are twofold knowledge, and twofold will and action (251, 276–82, 295, 296).*

Both natures of Christ (against Nestorianism) are united in the one Person *of the Word (231, 234–45, 246, 252, 256–8, 264–6, 270, 282, 286, 319b, 832, 837, 837c, 839b). Therefore Christ's humanity is to be adored (241, 262)* and the characteristics *of the one second divine Person, and his actions and sufferings can be said to belong to* both *natures (237, 245, 253, 263, 268, 270, 839). In Christ then, according to his humanity, there is no sonship by adoption (231, 238, 297, 298, 839).*

On account of its union with the Word, the human nature of Christ is sanctified and sinless (232, 243, 252, 264, 271, 293, 295) and endowed with special knowledge (304–7, 311–3, 319a).

Christ came as Mediator *with the Father for the salvation of man (223, 243, 247, 248, 283, 293, 333, 359, 711, 832, 839). He achieved the redemption by his* Sacrifice of the Cross *(223, 243, 245, 293, 310, 315, 326, 512, 595, 711, 794) by which he made atonement to God (314, 570, 718) and merited all grace for man (333, 718, 747).*

All the faithful are united in the community of his Mystical Body *(316–9, 319a, 331, 334a, 359, 362, 398a–c, 398f, 436, 537a, 567).*

THE COUNCIL OF ROME UNDER
POPE DAMASUS I (382)

Arius (ob. 336) denied that the second Person of God had the same substance as the Father: the Word was freely created in time by the Father. According to Arius the incarnation consists in the Word's assuming not a complete human nature with body and soul, but only a body.

Arius was finally condemned by the first General Council at Nicaea in 325 (Cf. Nos. 829–30).

One of Arius's most zealous opponents was Apollinaris (ca. 310–90) who defended the consubstantiality of the Word with the Father. However, in his explanation of the personality of Christ he allowed himself to be led astray by Arius. The explanation which he put forward in good faith was based on the Platonic division of man into a body, a principle of life, and an intellectual soul. He thought that in Christ the intellectual soul was replaced by the second Person of God. This seemed to him to ensure the unity of Person and above all Christ's absolute freedom from sin.

The Council of Rome dealt with all the errors about the Person of Christ that had up till then arisen: against a double sonship, a natural divine one and a gratuitous human one, against Arius and Apollinaris. The unanimous rejection of Apollinaris's teaching is proof how seriously the mystery of the Incarnation, that is the assumption of a complete human nature by the second Person of the Divinity, was taken in the very earliest days of Christianity.

231
158

6. We anathematize those who say there are two Sons, one from before time and one after the assumption of flesh from the Virgin.

232
159

7. We anathematize those who say that the Word of God was infused into human flesh instead of a rational

and intellectual human soul, since the Son and Word of God did not replace a rational and intellectual soul in his body but he took our soul, i.e. a rational and intellectual soul, and redeemed it.

14. If any one shall say that it was God who suffered the agony of the Cross and not the flesh with a soul which he had put on, 'taking the form of a servant' *(Phil. 2:7)* as Scripture says, he is heretical.[1]

233
166

THE GENERAL COUNCIL OF EPHESUS (431)

Christ is God and man. The extreme representatives of the Antiochian school of theology conceived the distinction of the two natures in Christ as a dual personality. Nestorius came from this school, and from 428 he was Bishop of Constantinople. Here his doctrine met stubborn resistance when the priest Anastasius in a public sermon denied Mary the title of 'Mother of God'. She was not the Mother of God but only the mother of Christ with whom the Person of the Word had joined himself. Nestorius's most ardent opponent was Cyril, Bishop of Alexandria. The final decision fell to the General Council of Ephesus which at its first session solemnly adopted Cyril's second letter (No. 246) as the orthodox formula for the Church's teaching on the incarnation of the Logos. Cyril also laid before the Council his third letter with the twelve anathemas against Nestorius (Nos. 234–45).

These twelve articles cannot be regarded as infallible decisions by the Council, but after Ephesus they were repeatedly accepted as true Catholic doctrine.

Nestorius's teaching is based on the conception that a com-

---

[1]. The expression 'putting on' *(caro cum anima, quam induerat)* is a not entirely unambiguous way of expressing the relationship between Christ's divinity and humanity. The document is of very early date, when theological terminology was still undeveloped and often very clumsy. But that this and other expressions were intended to have the proper meaning is clear from the decisive way erroneous conceptions were rejected.

plete human nature must also necessarily be a human personality. Thus if Christ were wholly man, he must also be a human person, so that human nature in Christ is not united to God to make one person, but is in a relationship of grace to him; the things that are said about the divine and the human in Christ, such as are found in Holy Scripture, apply to two persons; Christ had first to merit this promotion to the relationship of grace with the divine Word.

CYRIL'S TWELVE ANATHEMAS AGAINST NESTORIUS

234
252
1. If anyone do not confess that Emmanuel is truly God and the Blessed Virgin therefore Mother of God because she bore according to the flesh the incarnate Word from God – *anathema sit.*

235
253
2. If any one do not confess that the Word from God the Father was united in the flesh to the Person and that Christ together with his flesh is one, namely the same God and Man at one and the same time – *anathema sit.*

236
254
3. If any one divide the substances once they are united in Christ, joining them only by the external bond of dignity or authority or power, and not rather by a coming together natural to union – *anathema sit.*[1]

237
255
4. If any one apply the words contained in the evangelical and apostolic writings, or what has been said by the saints about Christ, or by him about himself, separately to two Persons or hypostases, applying some to the man especially chosen by the Word of God and others, as being worthy of God, only to the Word of God the Father – *anathema sit.*

1. This rather too great emphasis on the union of the two natures, due to the as yet undeveloped terminology and the determination to reject the teaching of Nestorius, was, among other things, the occasion and starting point for monophysitism.

5. If any one dare to say that Christ was a man bearing God in him and not rather in truth God, as the one, natural Son in whom the Word was made flesh and participated in flesh and blood as we do – *anathema sit*. 238, 256

6. If any one dare to say that the Word from God the Father is God or Lord over Christ and not rather profess that the same Christ is at one and the same time God and man, since the Word became flesh according to the Scriptures – *anathema sit*. 239, 257

7. If any one say that the man Jesus received the power to act from the God the Word and that the glory of the Only-Begotten really belongs to some other than him – *anathema sit*. 240, 258

8. If any one dare to say that the man assumed *(by the Word)* is to be adored and glorified with God the Word and with him to be called God, as of one with another – for so the repeated 'with' gives one to think – and not rather honour Emmanuel with *one* adoration and glorify him with one praise, since the Word became flesh – *anathema sit*. 241, 259

9. If any one say that the one Lord Jesus Christ was glorified by the Holy Spirit as one using a power alien to him given by the Spirit, and that he received from the Spirit power to act against unclean spirits and to fulfil the miracles of the Godhead among men, and do not rather say that it was his own Spirit whereby he worked the signs of Godhead – *anathema sit*. 242, 260

10. Christ, says Divine Scripture, is 'the apostle and high priest of our confession' *(Heb. 3:1)* and 'hath delivered himself for us, an oblation and a sacrifice to God for an odour of sweetness' *(Eph. 5:2)* and to the Father. Wherefore, if anyone say that it was not the Word of God when he was made flesh and became man like us who became our high priest and apostle, but a man separate from him, born of woman, or if anyone 243, 261

say that he offered his sacrifice for himself as well, and not rather solely for us since he had no need of sacrifice who knew no sin – *anathema sit*.

244 11. If any one do not confess that the flesh of the Lord
262 is life-giving and true flesh of the Word of God the Father, but says that it is the flesh of another beside him, joined to him in dignity or merely the possessor of the divine dwelling place, and not rather that it is life-giving (as we have said) because it was made the real flesh of the Word with power to give life to all things – *anathema sit*.

245 12. If any one do not confess that the Word of God
263 suffered in the flesh, and was crucified in the flesh, and in the flesh tasted death, and became the first-born from among the dead, according to which as God he is life and life-giving – *anathema sit*.

CYRIL OF ALEXANDRA'S SECOND LETTER TO NESTORIUS

This letter was read before the Council and solemnly approved

246 ...For we do not say that the nature of the Word
250 became flesh by being changed, nor that it was transformed into a whole man consisting of body and soul, but we do say that the Word united himself in his Person in an inexplicable and incomprehensible way with the flesh animated by a rational soul and thus became man and is called the Son of Man, not solely by his will nor solely by the assumption of a person. And although the natures are different, they truly come together in union to make one Christ and Son for us; not that the difference of natures was removed on account of the union, but because the divinity and

humanity, by their mysterious and ineffable conjunction in one person, constituted for us one Jesus Christ and Son... For it was not in the first place an ordinary man who was born of the Blessed Virgin into whom the Word of God thereafter descended, but he issued united from the very womb and therefore we say that he was born according to the flesh since he made the birth of his flesh into his own birth...

DOGMATIC LETTER (or 'TOME') OF POPE LEO I AGAINST EUTYCHES (449)

The defence against Nestorianism led Cyril of Alexandria's successor Dioscoros *(ob. 454) not only to envisage Christ's unity of divinity and humanity as unity of person but also to recognize only one divine-human (theandric) nature in Christ. Before the union, divinity and humanity were separate, but on union they fused and there remained only one new nature (monophysitism). In Constantinople the monk* Eutyches *adhered to this view. Together, thanks to considerable influence at the Imperial Court, they succeeded in summoning a Council (the so-called Latrocinium of Ephesus, 449), and, by not allowing freedom of voting, in having the new doctrine approved and the main opponents of the heresy deposed from their sees.*
But Leo the Great, *in his famous Tome, addressed to Flavian, Patriarch of Constantinople, had already declared against the new heresy. The Tome contains the clearest expression up to that time of the doctrine of the Incarnation.*
In 451 the Council of Chalcedon met in order to lay down in solemn dogmatic decisions the doctrine of the two natures of Christ united in the second Divine Person.

...This eternal Only-Begotten of the eternal Father was born of the Holy Spirit and the Virgin Mary. This temporal birth took nothing from that divine and eternal   *247*
291

birth, and added nothing to it. Its whole purpose was the redemption of deluded man, to conquer death and to destroy the devil, who had dominion over death. For we could not have overcome the author of sin and death unless he, whom sin could not stain nor death hold fast, had taken our nature and made it his own.

He was conceived by the Holy Spirit in the womb of the Virgin who bore him without loss of virginity as she conceived him without loss of virginity...

292 But this marvellously unique and uniquely marvellous generation must not be understood as if by the new mode of creation some property of the *(human)* race was removed; for the Holy Spirit indeed made the Virgin fruitful, but the true body was taken from the body *(of the Virgin)* – 'Wisdom hath built herself a house' *(Rev. 9:1)* 'And the Word was made flesh, and dwelt among us' *(John 1:14)* that is, in the flesh which he took from man and animated with a rational soul.

248 With the character of both natures unimpaired, there-
293 fore, coming together in one person, humility was assumed by majesty, weakness by strength, mortality by eternity, and in order to wipe out our guilt the inviolable nature was joined to the nature subject to suffering so that, as our salvation demanded, one and the same 'mediator of God and man, the man Christ Jesus' *(1 Tim. 2:5)* could from one element be able to die and from the other not.

249 The true God therefore was born in the complete and
293 perfect nature of man, complete in his *(nature)* and complete in ours...

294 so the Son of God enters this lowly world, descending from his heavenly throne yet not leaving the glory of his Father.

250 *(He comes)* in a new order, born in a new birth. In a
294 new order, because, invisible in his own, he became

visible in ours; the incomprehensible wished to comprehended[1]. Existing before all time, he began in time. The Lord of all things hid his immeasurable majesty to take the likeness of a servant. The impassible God did not disdain to become a man subject to suffering, and the Immortal to subject himself to the laws of death. Born also with a new birth, for inviolate Virginity, knowing no concupiscence, provided his body. His nature the Lord took from his mother, but no guilt. Nor is the nature of the Lord Jesus Christ, born of a virgin, different from ours because his birth was miraculous. For he who is truly God is also truly man, and in this unity there is no lie, for the divine majesty and the human humility penetrate each other. As God is not changed by his mercy, so man is not consumed by this dignity. For each of the two natures does what is proper to it in communion with the other, the Word doing what pertains to the Word, and the flesh doing what pertains to the flesh. One of them shines out with miracles, the other is subjected to insults. And as the Word does not leave the equality of glory with the Father, so also the flesh does not abandon the nature of our race...

251
294

THE GENERAL COUNCIL OF CHALCEDON (451)
(Cf. Note to No. 247)

AGAINST MONOPHYSITISM

Following therefore the holy Fathers we unanimously teach that the Son, our Lord Jesus Christ, is one and the same, the same perfect in divinity, the same perfect

252
301

---

1. *Incomprehensibilis voluit comprehendi.* Bright translates it, 'He who would not be enclosed in space willed to be enclosed', and supports this rendering with a note of parallel passages.

in humanity, true God and true man, consisting of a rational soul and a body, consubstantial with the Father in divinity and consubstantial with us in humanity, 'in all things like as we are, without sin' *(Heb. 4:15)*, born of the Father before all time as to his divinity, born in recent times for us and for our salvation from the Virgin Mary, Mother of God, as to his humanity.

302 We confess one and the same Christ, the Son, the Lord, the Only-Begotten, in two natures unconfused, unchangeable, undivided and inseparable. The difference of natures will never be abolished by their being united, but rather the properties of each remain unimpaired, both coming together in one person and substance, not parted or divided among two persons, but in one and the same only-begotten Son, the divine Word, the Lord Jesus Christ, as previously the prophets and Jesus Christ himself taught us and the Creed of the Fathers handed down to us. *(Sanction)* The above having been considered with all and every care and diligence, this Holy Ecumenical Council has defined that no one may advance any other belief or inscribe, compose, hold or teach it in any other way...

LETTER OF POPE JOHN II TO THE SENATE OF CONSTANTINOPLE (534)

Even after the great decisions made about the person of Jesus Christ, the implications of the mystery of the incarnation remained a closed book to many. The following decision of Pope John II drew the final conclusions.

Conclusions drawn from the Mystery of the Incarnation

253
401 ...Our son, the Emperor Justinian has informed Us, as you have seen from his letter, that disputes have arisen over the following three questions: Whether one can

say of Christ our God that he is 'one of the Trinity', that is, one holy Person of the Three Persons of the Holy Trinity; whether Christ our God who in his divinity cannot suffer did suffer in the flesh; whether Mary, ever Virgin, Mother of our Lord Jesus Christ, should properly and truly be called 'Genitrix of God and Mother of the Divine Word incarnate from her'. We have in these matters confirmed the Catholic belief of the Emperor and we have shown on the basis of the announcements of the Prophets, of the Apostles and the Fathers that it is so. Christ is really one of the Holy Trinity, that is, one holy Person from the three Persons of the Holy Trinity... God did truly suffer in the flesh... the glorious and holy Mary, ever a Virgin, is in a real and true sense Mother of God...

THE SECOND GENERAL COUNCIL OF CONSTANTINOPLE (553)

THE 'THREE CHAPTERS'

In spite of Chalcedon the monophysite schism continued. In order to heal this breach, it was proposed to condemn as Nestorian certain of the main original opponents of monophysitism together with their writings. These were Theodoret of Cyrus, Ibas of Edessa, and Theodore of Mopsuestia, the chief representative of the Antiochian School. Conflict arose about 'the Three Chapters', the name given to the articles condemning these three writers and their work. The prime mover in putting the condemnation through was the Imperial Court in Constantinople which, in fact, called this Fifth General Council. Finally Pope Vigilius gave his assent to the Council's finding.

1. If any one do not confess the *one nature or substance,* **254**
one might and power of the Father, Son and Holy Spirit, *421*

adoring the consubstantial Trinity, *one Godhead* in three beings or persons – *anathema sit*. For there is *one God and Father from whom are all things, and one Lord Jesus Christ through whom are all things, and one Holy Spirit in whom are all things.*

255
422 2. If any one do not confess *two births* of the Word of God, one from eternity from the Father, timeless and incorporeal, the other in recent times of that same *(person)* who came down from heaven and was incarnate from the holy and glorious Mother of God, Mary ever Virgin, and was born of her – *anathema sit*.

256
423 3. If any one say that the divine Word who performed miracles is other than Christ who died, or that the divine Word was with Christ born of woman, or in him, as one in another, and not *one and the same our Lord Jesus Christ* incarnate Word of God, made man, or that the miracles and sufferings which he freely bore in the flesh do not pertain to the same – *anathema sit*.

257
424 4. If any one say that the union of the divine Word with man was only by grace, or in operation only, or by equality of honour, or authority, or relation, or affection or power – by good will in short, as though the man pleased the divine Word (as Theodorus in his madness says); or *(that this union took place)* only homonymously, as the Nestorians who call the divine Word Jesus and Christ, and the man separately Christ and Son and thus clearly speak of two persons but pretend in the nomenclature and honour and dignity and adoration to speak of one Person and one Christ; and if any one do not confess that the union of the divine Word with the flesh animated by a rational and intellectual soul is synthetic or hypostatic, as the holy Fathers taught, and that therefore there is only one hypostasis, namely the Lord Jesus Christ, one of the Holy Trinity – *anathema sit*.

But since the word 'union' *(unitas, ἐνώσις)* is understood in various senses, the adherents of the impiety of Apollinaris and Eutyches maintain a disappearance of the two natures coming together and teach union by fusion, while the adherents of Theodorus and Nestorius maintain the separation but introduce an affective union/ union of relationship[1]. The Holy Church of God, rejecting both these impieties, confesses the union of the divine Word with the flesh as being by composition (synthesis), that is, according to the hypostasis, for in the mystery of Christ union by composition not only preserves from confusion what has come together but also tolerates no separation.

5. If any one understand the term 'one hypostasis' of our Lord Jesus Christ as having the meaning of several hypostases and thus proposes to introduce into the mystery of Christ two hypostases or *two persons* and speaks of the two persons as one person in dignity, honour and adoration, as Theodorus and Nestorius in their madness have written, or falsely accuses the Holy Council of Chalcedon of using the term 'one hypostasis' in this impious way, and does not confess that the Word of God united himself to the flesh in the Person (καθ' ὑπόστασιν) and that therefore there is only one Hypostasis or one Person, and that the Holy Council of Chalcedon confessed the one hypostasis of our Lord Jesus Christ in this sense – *anathema sit*. For the Holy Trinity did not suffer the addition of another Person or hypostasis by the incarnation of one of its number, namely the Divine Word.

6. If any one call the holy and glorious Mary, ever Virgin, Mother of God in an inaccurate or false way, or only relatively, as if a mere man was born from her

---

1. σχετικὴν ἐνώσιν / affectuatem unitatem.

and not the divine Word incarnate, whereby the human birth concerned the divine Word only in so far as he was together with the man who was born; or falsely accuses the Holy Council of Chalcedon of calling the Virgin Mother of God in the impious sense of this view held by Theororus; or call her mother of man, that is, mother of Christ, as if Christ were not God; and do not confess her as really and truly mother of God, since the divine Word was born of the Father before time and in recent times was incarnate and born of her, and that the Holy Council of Chalcedon so confessed her, *anathema sit.*

260
428
7. If any one in saying 'in two natures' do not confess to meaning thereby that he recognizes one Lord Jesus Christ in divinity and in humanity, thus signifying the difference of natures in which the ineffable union was made without fusion, without the divine Word being changed into the nature of flesh nor the flesh being translated into the nature of the Word (for each remained what by nature it was when the union was made hypostatically), but applies this expression to the mystery of Christ in the sense of a separation of parts; or while confessing the number of natures in the same our Lord Jesus Christ, the Word incarnate, do not understand the distinction of natures of which he is composed, which distinction is not abolished by the union (for one is from both and both are in one), but use this number as if the natures were separate and each had its own hypostasis *(person)* – *anathema sit.*

261
429
8. If any one in saying that the union was made out of the two natures of divinity and humanity, or speaking of the one incarnate nature of the Word, do not thereby understand, as the Fathers taught, that a hypostatic union having been made of divine nature and human nature, one Christ came into being, but proposes to introduce by these expressions *one nature or substance* of

the divinity and flesh of Christ – *anathema sit.*

For when we say that the only-begotten Word of God was united to flesh hypostatically we do not say that there was any fusion of the natures one with the other, but rather we mean that the divine Word united himself to the flesh while each *(nature)* remained what it is. Wherefore Christ is one, God and man, consubstantial with the Father in divinity, and consubstantial with us in humanity. For the Church rejects and anathematizes equally those who would cut or divide into parts the mystery of Christ in the divine dispensation and those who would fuse it.   *430*

9. If any one say Christ is adored in two natures whereby two separate adorations are meant, one for the divine Word and one for the man; or in order to do away with the flesh, or to fuse divinity and humanity, falsely speaks of one nature or substance of *(the natures)* which come together, and thus adores Christ, not adoring with *one adoration* the incarnate Word of God together with his flesh, as was handed down to the Church of God from the beginning – *anathema sit.*   262 *431*

10. If any one do not confess our Lord Jesus Christ who was crucified in the flesh to be true God, and the Lord of Glory and *one of the Holy Trinity, anathema sit.*   263 *432*

12. If any one defend the impious *Theodore of Mopsuestia* who says: 264 *434*

(1) that the divine Word is another *(than Christ)*, and Christ, subject to the sufferings of the soul and the desires of the body, is another *(than the Word)*, who gradually raised himself above less perfect men and became better by his progress in works, and by his conversion became spotless, and was baptized as an ordinary man in the name of the Father and of the Son and of the Holy Spirit, and received in baptism the grace of the Holy Spirit and merited sonship, and is adored in the

person of the divine Word, like the picture of an emperor, and was only made immutable in his thoughts and entirely sinless after the resurrection.

(2) And the same impious Theodore said that the union of the divine Word with Christ was such as the apostle speaks of between man and woman: 'they shall be two in one flesh' *(Eph. 5:31)*.

(3) And among other innumerable blasphemies he dared to say that after the resurrection when the Lord breathed on the disciples and said, 'Receive ye the Holy Ghost' *(John 20:22)* he did not give them the Holy Spirit but only breathed on them figuratively.

(4) And further, that the confession made by Thomas when he felt the Lord's hands and side after the resurrection, saying, 'My Lord and my God' *(John. 20:28)* was not said by Thomas of Christ but that Thomas, amazed by the miracle of the resurrection, was glorifying God who had raised Christ.

(5) And what is worse, in his interpretation of the Acts of the Apostles Theodore likened Christ to Plato, Manichaeus, Epicurus and Marcion saying that as each of these on account of the dogma he founded had caused his disciples to be called Platonists, Manichaeans, Epicureans and Marcionites, so also when Christ founded a dogma, his disciples were called Christians after him. If therefore any one defend the said impious Theodore and his impious writings in which he poured out the above and innumerable other blasphemies against our great God and Saviour Jesus Christ, and do not anathematize him together with his impious writings and all those who accept or defend him and say that his interpretation of the Scriptures was orthodox, and those who wrote or write for him or his impious books and thought or think with him, and who have remained or remain in such heresy to the end, *anathema sit.*

13. If any one defend the impious writings of *Theodoret*, which are contrary to the true faith and to the first Holy Council of Ephesus and to blessed Cyril and his twelve articles, or what he wrote for the impious Theodore and Nestorius, or for others who think alike with the said Theodore and Nestorius, defending them and their impiety and therefore calling those Doctors of the Church impious who profess the union of the divine Word with the flesh to be hypostatic, and do not anathematize these writings and those who thought and think likewise, and all who have written against the true faith and against blessed Cyril and his twelve articles and have persisted in such heresy to the end – *anathema sit*. **265** *436*

14. If any one defend the letter said to have been written by *Ibas* to Maris, the Persian, which denies that the divine Word, incarnate of Mary, Mother of God and ever Virgin, became man, and says that a mere man, whom he calls a 'temple', was born of her, so that the divine Word was other than the man; and which accuses blessed Cyril, who preached the true faith of Christians, of being heretical and of having written in the same sense as the impious Apollinaris; which same letter charges the first Holy Council of Ephesus with having condemned Nestorius without question or examination, and calls blessed Cyril's twelve articles impious and contrary to the true faith, and defends Theodore and Nestorius and their impious dogmas and writings. If any one therefore defend the said impious letter and do not anathematize it together with those who say that it is right, or partly right, and those who have written or who write in its favour of the impiety it contains or who presume to defend it or the impiety in it in the name of the holy Fathers or the Holy Council of Chalcedon, and who persist in these things to the end, *anathema sit*. **266** *437*

THE LATERAN COUNCIL UNDER POPE MARTIN I
(649)

Since the first attempt to end the monophysite schism by the condemnation contained in the 'Three Chapters' did not succeed, Sergius, Patriarch of Constantinople 610–638, with the support of the Emperor Heraclius, tried once more to unite the divided Church in order to strengthen the Empire, threatened as it was by the Slavs and Persians. He sought a compromise whereby the duality of natures in Christ would be recognized but only one active principle [1] *and therefore only one will (monotheletism).*

Obviously this doctrine carried to its logical conclusion would lead back to monophysitism. Since all action stems from the nature, the doctrine of one active principle and one will necessarily includes the doctrine of one nature.

Monotheletism was originally condemned by the Italian and African Bishops under Pope Martin I in Rome. Its final solemn condemnation fell to the General Council of Constantinople.

267
501
1. If any one do not truly and rightly confess with the Fathers *the Father, the Son, and the Holy Spirit*, trinity in unity and unity in trinity, that is, one God in three consubstantial Persons, equal in glory, and one and the same Godhead of the three, one nature, one substance, one force, one power, one kingship, one authority, one will, one activity, uncreated, without beginning, incomprehensible, creator and protector of all things – *condemnatus sit.*

268
502
2. If any one do not truly and rightly confess with the Fathers that one of the holy consubstantial and adorable Trinity, the divine Word, came down from heaven, was incarnate of the Holy Spirit and Mary ever Virgin, became man, was crucified in the flesh, of his own free

---

1. = L. *operatio*, Gk. ἐνέργεια

will suffered and was buried, and on the third day rose again, and ascended into heaven, and is seated at the right hand of the Father and will come again in the glory of the Father, with the flesh assumed by him and animated by a rational soul, to judge the living and the dead – *condemnatus sit*.

3. If any one do not truly and rightly confess with the Fathers that the holy, ever virginal and immaculate Mary is *Mother of God*, since in recent days she really and truly conceived, without seed, by the Holy Ghost, the same divine Word who was born before all time and gave birth to him in chastity, her virginity remaining unimpaired after the birth – *condemnatus sit*. 269 503

4. If any one do not truly and rightly confess with the Fathers *two births* of the one same our Lord and God Jesus Christ, one before all time incorporeally and eternally from God the Father, and one corporeally in recent times from the Blessed Virgin Mary Mother of God; and that the one and the same Lord and God Jesus Christ is consubstantial with the Father in divinity and consubstantial with man and his mother in humanity; that he can suffer in the flesh but not in his divinity; that he is circumscribed in the body but not circumscribed in divinity; uncreated and created; terrestrial and celestial; visible and *(only)* perceptible by the intellect; occupying space and not occupying space; so that in the same whole man and God the whole man who fell under sin is reconstituted – *condemnatus sit*. 270 504

5. If any one do not truly and rightly confess with the Fathers *one incarnate nature of the divine Word* whereby the term 'incarnate' means that our substance is perfect and undiminished in Christ God but without sin – *condemnatus sit*. 271 505

6. If any one do not truly and rightly confess with the 272

506   Fathers that one and the same *Lord and God Jesus Christ is of and in two natures substantially united* but distinct and undivided – *condemnatus sit.*

273
507   7. If any one do not truly and rightly confess with the Fathers that *the substantial difference of natures remains distinct and undivided* – *condemnatus sit.*

274
508   8. If any one do not truly and rightly confess with the Fathers that the *substantial union of natures* is in him *undivided and distinct* – *condemnatus sit.*

275
509   9. If any one do not truly and rightly confess with the Fathers that the *natural characteristics* of his divinity and humanity remain *unaffected and undiminished* in him – *condemnatus sit.*

276
510   10. If any one do not truly and rightly confess with the Fathers *two wills*, the divine and the human, harmoniously united, so that he is in both natures the author by will of our salvation – *condemnatus sit.*

277
511   11. If any one do not truly and rightly confess with the Fathers *two active principles*, the divine and the human, harmoniously united, so that he is in both natures the author by activity of our salvation – *condemnatus sit.*

278
512   12. If any one confess with the infamous heretics only one will and one active principle in Christ our God, contrary to the confession of the holy Fathers and the dispensation of our Saviour – *condemnatus sit.*

279
513   13. If any one confess with the infamous heretics, and contrary to the teaching of the Fathers, only one will and one active principle in Christ our God in whom two wills and two sources of activity were maintained and were piously preached by our holy Fathers – *condemnatus sit.*

280
514   14. If any one confess with the infamous heretics one will and one active principle, as they impiously hold, and deny and reject two wills and two active principles, that is, the divine and the human, which are conserved

in union in the same Christ our God and are orthodoxly taught by the Fathers – *condemnatus sit.*

15. If any one with the infamous heretics foolishy take the divine-human (in Greek ϑεανδρικήν) active principle as *one* active principle and do not with the holy Fathers confess it to be twofold, that is, divine and human, or believe that the neologism *(theandric)* denotes one rather than indicating the wonderful and glorious union of both – *condemnatus sit.*

16. If any one with the infamous heretics, by denying the two wills and two active principles, that is, the divine and the human, essentially conserved in union in Christ our God and piously preached by the Fathers, foolishly introduce dissensions and divisions into the mystery of the dispensation, and therefore do not ascribe the sayings of the Gospels and the Apostles concerning the Saviour to one and the same person and essentially one and the same Lord and our God Jesus Christ according to *(the teaching of)* blessed Cyril, so that he is shown to be naturally God and man – *condemnatus sit.*

THE CREED OF THE ELEVENTH COUNCIL OF TOLEDO (675)
(Cf. Note to No. 144)

The Temporal Birth from the Virgin Mary.
...We believe that of these three Persons only the Person of the Son assumed for the liberation of the human race, a true and sinless human nature from the holy and immaculate Virgin Mary of whom he was born in a new order and a new birth: in a new order because, invisible in his divinity, he became visible in the flesh; and he was born in a new birth because the inviolate virginity knew no commerce with man and bore the

matter of his body made fruitful by the Holy Spirit. Which virgin birth can be neither grasped by reason nor shown by example; for if it can be grasped by reason, it is not marvellous, and if it can be shown by example it is not unique. The Holy Spirit, however, is not to be held to be the father of the Son on account of the fact that Mary conceived by being overshadowed by the same Holy Spirit, lest we appear to say there are two fathers of the Son, which it would be wrong to say.

284 In this wonderful conception, in which Wisdom built
534 herself a house, 'the Word was made flesh and dwelt among us' *(John 1:14)*. But the Word was not on that account converted or changed into flesh so that in willing to become man he ceased to be God. The Word was made flesh in such a manner that there is in him not only the Word of God and the flesh of man but also a rational human soul. So the whole must be called God on account of God, and man on account of man.

The Two Natures of Christ

285 And we believe there are two natures in the Son of God,
534 one divine and one human, which so united themselves in the one person of Christ that the divinity can never be separated from the humanity nor the humanity from the divinity. Thus Christ is perfect God and perfect man in the unity of one Person.

286 But when we say there are two natures in the Son, we
534 do not thereby set up two persons, nor does the Trinity become a quaternity. God the Word did not assume the person of a man but the nature, and took the temporal substance of flesh into the eternal Person of the divinity.

287 When, further, we believe the Father and the Son and
535 the Holy Spirit to be of one substance, we do not say that the Virgin Mary generated the unity of this Trinity but only the Son, who alone assumed our nature in the

unity of his Person.

It is also to be believed that the entire Trinity brought about the incarnation of this Son of God for the works of the Trinity are inseparable. But only the Son took 'the form of a servant' *(Phil. 2:7)* in the singularity of the Person, not in the unity of the divine nature, in what is proper to the Son and not in what is common to the Trinity. This form *(of a servant)* was added by him to the unity of Person, that is, so that one Christ is both Son of God and Son of Man: Further, Christ in these two natures consists of three substances, that of the Word which pertains to the essence of God alone, and those of body and soul which belong to the true man.

He has therefore the twofold substance of his divinity and our humanity. *536*

Since he came from the Father without beginning he is only born, not made, nor said to be predestined; since however he was born of the Virgin Mary we must believe that he was born and made and predestined. Both generations in him are thus miraculous, since he was generated before time from the Father without a mother and at the end of time was generated from a mother without a father; who inasmuch as he was God created Mary, and inasmuch as he was made was created by Mary; he is both the father and the son of his mother Mary. *288* *536*

Further, inasmuch as he is God, he is equal to the Father; inasmuch as he is man, he is less than the Father. Further it is to be believed that he is greater and less than himself; for in the form of God he is the Son and greater than himself on account of the humanity which he assumed than which his divinity is greater; but in the form of a servant he is less than himself, that is in his humanity which is less than his divinity. For, as by the flesh which he assumed he is believed to be less not only than the *289* *536*

Father but also than himself, so according to his divinity he is coequal with the Father, and he and the Father are greater than the man who was assumed by the Person of the Son alone.

290 Further, to the question as to whether the Son could be
537 equal to and less than the Holy Spirit in the same way as we believe that in relation to the Father he is now equal, now less, we reply: in the form of God he is equal to the Father and the Holy Spirit; in the form of a servant he is less than the Father and the Holy Spirit; for neither the Father nor the Holy Spirit but only the Person of the Son took flesh, whereby we believe that he is less than these two Persons.

291 Further, this Son, inseparable from the Father and the
537 Holy Ghost, we believe to de a distinct person who took to himself a human nature. Further, the person exists with the man; but with the Father and the Holy Ghost the nature or substance of divinity.

292 It is to be believed, however, that the Son was sent not
538 only by the Father but also by the Holy Spirit, from what he himself said by the Prophet: 'and now the Lord God has sent me, and his Spirit' *(Is. 48:16)*. We must also believe that he was sent by himself inasmuch as not only is the will of the whole Trinity inseparable but its action also. For he who was called the Only-Begotten before all time became the first-begotten in time; only-begotten in the substance of divinity, first-begotten in the nature of the flesh assumed by him.

On redemption

293 And we believe according to the truth of the Gospel that
539 in this assumed form of man he was conceived without sin, born without sin, and died without sin who alone for us 'hath been made sin' *(2 Cor. 5:21)*, that is, a sacrifice for our sins. Yet, his divinity unimpaired, he suffered

his Passion for our failings, was condemned to death, and suffered real death of the flesh on the cross, and on the third day, brought back to life by his own power, he rose from the tomb...

This the statement of the faith of our confession, whereby the dogma of all heretics is destroyed, whereby the hearts of the faithful are cleansed, and whereby one ascends to God for ever and ever. Amen. 294
541

THE THIRD GENERAL COUNCIL OF CONSTANTINOPLE (680–1)
(Cf. Note to No. 267)

Two Wills in Christ

...And we preach, according to the doctrine of the holy Fathers *two natural wills* and two natural active principles inseparably, immovably, undividedly, and unconfusedly in him *(Christ)*. And two natural wills, *not opposing each other*, as heretics assert, *absit*, but his human will following without resistance or reluctance but subject rather to his divine and omnipotent will. For as blessed Athanasius says, the human will had to be moved to submit to the divine will. For, as his flesh is called, and is, the flesh of the Word of God, so his natural will is called, and is, the real will of the Word of God, as he himself says: 'Because I came down from heaven, not to do my own will, but the will of him who sent me' *(John 6:38)*, calling his own will the will of his flesh. For the flesh, too, was his own. For, as his most holy and immaculate flesh, endowed with a soul, was not destroyed by being divinified but remained in its proper status and kind, so also his human will was not destroyed by being divinified, but was preserved as Gregory the theologian says: 'For his will, namely that of the Saviour, is not contrary to God, being wholly divinified'[1]. 295
556

1. Gregory Nazianzen, *Oratio* 30.

296 And we teach *two natural active principles*, **inseparably,**
537 **immovably, unconfusedly and undividedly in the same our Lord Jesus Christ our true God, that is, a divine active principle and a human one, according to the very clear statements of the divine preacher of God, Leo: 'Each form does what is proper to it in communion with the other, that is, the Word doing what is proper to the Word, and the flesh doing what is proper to the flesh'. Nor do we in any way admit one natural active principle of God and the creature, so as neither to raise what is created into the divine nature nor lower what is higher in the divine nature to suit the place of created things. For we ascribe both the miracles and the suffering to one and the same, according to the natures in and of which he consists, as Cyril so admirably says.**

POPE HADRIAN I's LETTER TO THE BISHOPS OF GALICIA AND SPAIN (793)

As Monotheletism was meant to be a sort of settlement with monophysitism, but itself led back to monophysitism, so adoptionism *was intended as a settlement with Nestorianism. In Spain in the eighth century there appeared under the influence of Elipandus of Toledo the doctrine that the divine Word had a natural sonship on account of his eternal birth from the Father, but that Christ the man, born of Mary, only enjoyed an adoptive sonship. This overlooks the fact that sonship applies to a person, not to a nature: Christ is the Son of God because he is the Second Person of the Trinity. Thus ultimately adoptionism was no more than a revival of Nestorianism which posited two persons in Christ. The condemnations of this teaching, which spread from Spain into France, led to a further clarification of the mystery of the Incarnation.*

297 *Christ is not the adopted Son, but the true Son of God.*
(310) ...You have not shrunk from saying with poisoned

tongues that our Redeemer is an adopted Son, as though he were mere man and subject to human weakness. Indeed, it is shameful to say, you have unthinkingly and disrespectfully called him a servant... Are you not ashamed, then, you contentious slanderers, fallen under the wrath of God, to call a servant him who freed you from the service of the devil?... For even if he was called servant in the veiled language of prophecy on account of the outward form of a servant, we yet know... that this was said in the historical sense about John and only in a metaphorical sense about Christ...

CREED OF THE COUNCIL OF FRIAUL (796)

Christ is truly the Son of God
...Nor did that human and temporal birth take anything from the divine and timeless birth, but in the one Person of Jesus Christ there is the true Son of God and the true Son of Man, not a different Son of God and a different Son of Man, but one and the same Son of God and man, in both natures, that is, divine and human, true God and true man, not apparently the Son of God but truly, not adoptive but real, for he was never separated from the Father on account of the man *(human nature)* he assumed... And therefore we confess him in both natures as the real and not adoptive Son of God, because, having taken human nature, one and the same is Son of God and of man.
Naturally Son of the Father in his divinity, and naturally Son of his Mother in his humanity...

298
619

ARTICLES OF MODERNISM CONDEMNED BY POPE PIUS X (1907)
(Cf. Note to No. 64)

[299] 3427   27. The divinity of Jesus Christ is not proved from the Gospels, but is a dogma derived by the Christian conscience from the notion of the Messias.

[300] 3428   28. While exercising his ministry, Jesus did not so speak as to teach that he was the Messias, nor was the purpose of his miracles to prove that he was.

[301] 3429   29. It is permissible to admit that the Christ shown by history is much inferior to the Christ who is the object of faith.

[302] 3430   30. In all Gospel texts the expression 'Son of God' means no more than 'Messias' and in no way signifies that Christ is the true natural Son of God.

[303] 3431   31. The doctrine concerning Christ taught by Paul and John and the Councils of Nicaea, Ephesus and Chalcedon is not that which Jesus taught but *(only)* what the Christian conscience has conceived about Jesus.

[304] 3432   32. The natural sense of the Gospel texts cannot be reconciled with what our theologians teach about the awareness and infallible knowledge of Jesus Christ.

[305] 3433   33. It is obvious to anyone who is not led by preconceived opinions that either Jesus taught in error the proximate advent of the Messias or the greater part of his teaching as contained in the synoptic Gospels lacks authenticity.

[306] 3434   34. A critic cannot claim unlimited knowledge for Christ without supposing what is historically inconceivable and repugnant to the moral sense, that Christ as man had knowledge of God and nevertheless in so many things did not wish to communicate the knowledge to his disciples and to posterity.

[307]   35. Christ was not always aware of his own messianic

dignity. 3435
36. The resurrection of the Saviour is not a true fact [308]
in the order of history but only a fact in the super- 3436
natural order and is neither proved nor provable, but
something that the Christian conscience gradually
developed from other facts.
37. Belief in the resurrection of Christ was not at the [309]
beginning in the actual fact of resurrection but in the 3437
immortal life of Christ with God.
38. The doctrine of the expiatory death of Christ is [310]
not from the Gospels but from Paul. 3438

DECISION OF THE HOLY OFFICE CONCERNING CERTAIN ARTICLES ON CHRIST'S KNOWLEDGE (1918)

The main outlines of dogma concerning Christ are quite clearly set out in the great doctrinal decrees, but it is only then that one sees the outline of the task of penetrating into the mystery of Christ's personality. The fact remains that when he assumed human nature, Christ took with it all the heights and depths of man's psychological life. In all but sin, he was like us. But there can be no doubt that, on account of its hypostatic union with the second Person of the Divinity, Christ's human nature acquired certain privileges such as do not belong to any other man or such as man will only share in the next world. Christian tradition has taught these privileges since the first centuries.

The attempt to penetrate and understand this psychological life was reserved till comparatively recent times. There has been no lack of false attempts to simplify Christ's psychology by pushing these privileges as far as possible into the background. The following articles are directed against such attempts.

(The question is asked) whether the following propositions can safely be taught:

1. It is not certain that there was in the soul of Christ [311]

3645 during his life among men that knowledge which the saints or those enjoying the Beatific Vision have.

[312] 2. Nor can the opinion be called certain which main-
3646 tains that the soul of Christ was ignorant of nothing, but in the Word knew from the beginning all things past, present and future, that is, all things that God knows by intuition.

[313] 3. The opinion of certain innovators about the limited
3647 knowledge of Christ's soul is no less to be received in Catholic schools than the view of the ancients on his universal knowledge.
(Answer:) No.

POPE PIUS XI's ENCYCLICAL *MISERENTISSIMUS REDEMPTOR* ON THE ATONEMENT DUE TO THE SACRED HEART OF JESUS (1928)

Through the incarnation and redemption Christ entered into an intimate community with mankind. In a certain sense redeemed mankind was also drawn into the mystery of the ever-continuing incarnation and the constantly renewed redemption. By reason of the profoundly mysterious bond between the Head and his members, the Christian must carry on in his own life the redemptive expiatory Passion of Christ and complete it. Pius XI's encyclical Miserentissimus Redemptor *expounds this thought in a unique and profound manner.*

314 ...Yet, though the copious redemption of Christ has abundantly 'forgiven us all offences', nevertheless, because of that wonderful dispensation of divine wisdom by which what is lacking of the sufferings of Christ for his body, which is the Church *(Col. 1:24)* is to be filled up in our flesh, we can add, nay even we are bound to add, our own praises and satisfactions to the praises and satisfactions 'which Christ rendered

unto God in the name of sinners.'

But we must always remember that the whole virtue 315
of the expiation depends on the one bloody sacrifice
of Christ, which is renewed without intermission on
our altars in an unbloody manner, 'for the Victim is
one and the same; he who then offered himself on the
cross is now offering through the ministry of priests,
the manner of offering alone being different' *(Trent,
22nd Session; Cf. No. 514)*.

Community of Atonement with Christ

Therefore, with this most august sacrifice of the 316
Eucharist should be joined an oblation of the ministers
and the other faithful so that they also may present
themselves as 'being victims, holy, pleasing to God'
(Rom. 12:1). Nay, even St Cyprian does not hesitate
to declare that 'the Lord's sacrifice is not celebrated
with legitimate sanctification unless our oblation and
sacrifice correspond to his Passion'. Wherefore the
Apostle admonishes us that, 'bearing about in our body
the mortification of Jesus '*(2 Cor. 4:10)* and buried
together with Christ and planted together in the likeness
of his death, we should not only crucify our flesh with
its vices and concupiscences, 'flying the corruption of
that concupiscence which is in the world' *(2 Peter 1:4)*,
but that 'the life also of Jesus should be made manifest
in our bodies' *(2 Cor. 4:10)* and, being made partakers
of his eternal priesthood we should offer 'gifts and
sacrifices for sin' *(Heb. 5:1)*.

Universal Priesthood

Participation in this mystic priesthood and in the office 317
of satisfying and sacrificing is enjoyed not only by
those whom our Pontiff, Jesus Christ, employs as his
ministers to offer up a clean oblation to God's name

in every place, from the rising to the setting of the sun *(Mal. 1:11)*, but the whole Christian people, rightly called by the Prince of the Apostles 'a chosen generation, a kingly priesthood' *(1 Peter 2:9)*, ought to make offering for sin both for itself and for all mankind, in much the same way as every priest and pontiff 'taken from among men, is ordained for men in the things that pertain to God' *(Heb. 5:1)*.

318 The more perfectly our oblation and sacrifice correspond with the Lord's sacrifice, that is to say the more perfectly we immolate our self love and our desires, and crucify our flesh with that mystic crucifixion of which the Apostle speaks, the more abundant fruits of that propitiation and expiation shall we reap for ourselves and for others. For a wonderful living bond of union exists between all the faithful and Christ, a union such as prevails between the head and the other members; moreover, by that mystic Communion of Saints which we profess in the Catholic faith, both individuals and peoples are joined together, not only with one another but also with him 'who is Head, Christ, from whom the whole body being compacted and fitly joined together, by what every joint supplieth according to the operation in the measure of every part, maketh increase of the body, unto the edifying of itself in charity' *(Eph. 4:15f)*. This, indeed, it was that the Mediator between God and men, Jesus Christ, asked of the Father when he was nigh unto death: 'I in them, and thou in me; that they may be made perfect in one' *(John 17:23)*...

319 There is the consideration also that the expiatory passion of Christ is renewed, and in a manner continued and fulfilled, in his mystical body, the Church. For, to use once more the words of St Augustine, 'Christ suffered whatever he was due to suffer; now

nothing is wanting to the measure of his sufferings. Therefore the sufferings were complete, but in the Head; there still remained the sufferings of Christ in his body' *(In Ps. 86)*. This, indeed, our Lord Jesus himself vouchsafed to proclaim when, speaking to Saul, 'still breathing threats and slaughter against the disciples'. *(Acts 9:1)*, he said, 'It is I, Jesus, whom thou persecutest' *(Acts 9:5)*, clearly signifying that when persecutions are stirred up against the Church, the divine Head of the Church is himself attacked and harassed. Quite rightly, then, does Christ, who still suffers in his Mystical Body, desire to have us as the sharers of his expiation, and our intimate union with him of itself demands this, for as we are 'the body of Christ and members of member' *(1 Cor. 12:27)* whatever the Head suffers, all the members must suffer...

PIUS XII's ENCYCLICAL
MYSTICI CORPORIS CHRISTI (1943)
(Cf. Notes to Nos. 334a and 311)

...But the loving knowledge with which the divine Redeemer has pursued us from the first moment of his Incarnation is such as completely to surpass all the searchings of the human mind; for by means of the Beatific Vision, which he enjoyed from the time he was received into the womb of the Mother of God, he has forever and continuously had present to him all the members of his Mystical Body and embraced them with his saving love...

319a
3812

PIUS XII's ENCYCLICAL
SEMPITERNUS REX (1951)
(Cf. Note to 74h)

This short extract condemns two errors arising from the Council of Chalcedon whose 1500th Anniversary it marked. The first was that of the kenoticists, whereby Protestant theology, particularly in the nineteenth century, taught that the Word of God at his Incarnation really gave up some of the characteristics of divinity. The other was that of an extreme assumptus-homo-*theology with the resultant consequences for the psychology of Jesus.*

319b Also completely incompatible with the Creed of Chalcedon is a view, fairly widespread among non-Catholics which gained a foothold and an appearance of authority from a rash and false interpretation of a passage in St Paul's Epistle to the Philippians *(Phil. 2:7)* – the doctrine called 'kenosis' according to which one supposes that Christ 'emptied himself' of the divinity of the Word. This truly blasphemous invention, as well as the opposite error of docetism, is to be condemned, since it reduces the whole mystery of the Incarnation and Redemption to a bloodless and empty shadow. 'God (as Leo the Great impressively teaches) was born in the perfect and unimpaired nature of a true man, wholly in his own nature and wholly in ours' *(Eph. 28; PL. 54, 763; cf. Serm. 23, 2; PL. 54, 201)*.

3905 Although there is nothing to prevent Christ's humanity from being more profoundly studied, even by psychological methods, there are some who in the difficult studies of this kind depart unreasonably far from old ideas in order to introduce new ones and who make use of the authority and definitions of the Council of Chalcedon to support their views. These people put the special state and condition of Christ's human nature so much to the fore as to set it up almost as a '*subiectum sui iurus*', as though it did not subsist in the Person of the Word himself. Now the Council of Chalcedon, in agreement with that of Ephesus, clearly lays down that both natures of our Redeemer come together 'in one person and subsistence' and forbids the positing of two individuals in Christ as if some autonomous '*homo assumptus*' were attached to the Word.

CHAPTER SEVEN

THE MOTHER OF THE REDEEMER

The significance of the Mother of God in the divine plan of salvation and in our order of grace can never be fully brought out in a collection of Church documents. There are comparatively few sections of official pronouncements which deal exclusively with Mary. Generally the doctrine about the Mother of God is so closely bound up with that about Christ and the redemption that, to be complete, we should have to include in this chapter all the great christological documents. In particular, the mystery of the motherhood of God, which is the centre of all Marian doctrine, is also a crucial point in the doctrine about Christ himself[1].
This chapter is intended, then, as a supplement to what has already been said about Christ, a sort of postscript containing the documents about Mary which have not yet appeared in connexion with the teaching on Christ. The principal mysteries concerning the motherhood of God, *the* immaculate conception, sinlessness, and virginity *are gifts made to Mary in view of her vocation to be the Mother of God. Her motherhood of the Word of God is not just an external bringing about of Christ's*

1. Special mention should be made in this connexion of No. 234 in Cyril of Alexandria's Twelve Articles, No. 247 in the Tome of Leo, No. 252 of Chalcedon, No. 255 of Constantinople II, No. 269f of Lateran, and No. 283 of the Toledo Creed.

bodily existence. Mary was mother of the Redeemer in the full sense of being his assistant in the work of redemption. In order to be able to take a worthy part in this work she had to receive her purity and fulness of grace, fruits of the redemption, in advance.

The mystery which completes Mary's cooperation in the work of Christ is her role as Mediatrix of Grace. As her first assent to her choice to be the Mother of God was the first conveyance of all grace, her willingness to be the means of bringing to mankind Christ, the source of all grace, so the help she bore him in his work of redemption, the unbroken loyalty to Christ in his sufferings, are also effective in her supreme position as mediatrix of grace. To Mary's position as the most perfect handmaid corresponds her first place in the distribution of the fruits of the sacrifice.

So the Church's teaching of the universal character of Mary's mediation by her intercession has been ever more and more clearly expressed, especially in the Marian encyclicals of recent popes. All the graces which God accords us on account of Christ's merits come to us directly or indirectly through Mary.

The Church's teaching about Mary is:
She is truly the Mother of God *(234, 252, 253, 259, 269, 288, 328, 330, 828, 832) through the overshadowing by the Holy Spirit (283, 287, 828, 832) without loss of virginity (247, 255, 269, 283, 320, 322, 828, 832, 837c).*
She is distinguished from the rest of mankind by her immaculate conception *i.e. freedom from original sin (226, 323, 324, 325), by her fulness of grace (329, 334) and by complete sinlessness (321, 334a, 760).*
She is Mediatrix of All Grace merited by Christ *(326–34, 334a).*
She was assumed body and soul into Heaven *(334a, b, c).*

LETTER OF POPE SIRICIUS TO ANYSIUS, BISHOP OF THESSALONICA (392)

Bishop Bonosus of Sofia, who died about the beginning of the fifth century, had put forward the doctrine that after the birth of Christ Mary had not remained a virgin but had given birth to other children, 'the brothers of Jesus'. For this he was condemned by the Illyrian Bishops of Thessalonica, but the Bishops referred the matter to Rome for final decision.
In itself Pope Siricius's answer is not definitive, but it is evidence of the unanimous teaching of the Church. The reasoning with which the Pope supports the doctrine seem to be taken from the preaching of St Ambrose who had opposed the heresy.

Mary's Virginity

...Your Holiness is rightly repelled by the idea that any other birth should have taken place from the womb whence Christ was born according to the flesh. Jesus would not have chosen to be born of a virgin if he had had to regard her as being so little continent as to desecrate the place of birth of the Lord's body, that temple of the eternal King, by human intercourse[1]. If anyone believes that, he sides with the Jews in their unbelief, who say that he could not have been born of a virgin...

320
(91)

---

1. This phrase must not, of course, be understood as meaning that the Church regards marital intercourse as 'desecration'. Only that the virginal body which had given birth to the Lord should not then bear other children.

THE GENERAL COUNCIL OF TRENT, SIXTH SESSION (1547)

CANONS ON JUSTIFICATION

In 1476 Pope Sixtus IV had introduced into general use a Mass and Office in honour of the mystery of the Immaculate Conception. At Trent, during the exposition of the sinfulness of all men, the question was once more raised whether Mary was also included in the universal law of original sin and the inability to avoid venial sin. The Council gave no definitive decision on the matter but did lay down that the universality of original sin and inability to avoid all venial sin were not contrary to the Church's doctrine about the exceptional position of Mary.

Mary's Sinlessness

321
1573
23. **If any one shall say that a man once justified... can avoid throughout his life even venial sins, except by a special privilege from God, such as the Church holds concerning the Blessed Virgin** – *anathema sit*.
(Trent on the Immaculate Conception, cf. No. 226).

POPE PAUL IV's CONSTITUTION
CUM QUORUNDAM (1555)

Very soon after the emergence of the Reformers, rationalist theology, which set reason above revelation, made its appearance within Protestantism. Its criticism of traditional dogma was levelled in particular against the Trinity of God (Unitarians, Socinians; Servet, Ochino, Blaudrata, Laelius and Faustus Socinus and others). The following constitution was written during the early days of this movement, but it deals with all the attempts to do away with the fundamental mysteries of revelation by means of rationalist explanations. It can rightly be called the first condemnation of rationalism.

Mary's Virginity
...*(The opinion is condemned that Jesus Christ)* was not 322
conceived according to the flesh by the Holy Spirit in *1880*
the womb of Blessed Mary ever Virgin but, as other
men are, by the seed of Joseph... or that the same
most blessed Virgin Mary is not the true Mother of God
and did not retain her virginity intact before the birth,
in the birth and after the birth in perpetuity...

DU BAY's ERRORS CONDEMNED BY PIUS V
(1567)

The teaching of Du Bay and the Jansenists about Mary is only a part of their rigourist views about the fundamental sinfulness of the human will, to which they admitted of no exception.

Mary's Immaculate Conception
73. Nobody but Christ is free from original sin; hence [323]
the Blessed Virgin died on account of the sin inherited *1973*
from Adam and all her afflictions in this life were, like
those of the rest of the just, punishment for actual or
original sin.

JANSENIST ERRORS CONDEMNED
BY POPE ALEXANDER VIII (1690)

Mary's Immaculate Conception
24. The sacrifice made by the Blessed Virgin Mary in [324]
the temple on the occasion of her Purification, two *2324*
young doves, one as a burnt-offering and one in
atonement for sins, is sufficient evidence that she was in
need of purification and also that her Son (who was
presented) was also stained by the stain of his mother,
according to the word of the Law.

POPE PIUS IX's BULL *INEFFABILIS DEUS* PROCLAIMING THE IMMACULATE CONCEPTION (8 December 1854)

Pope Pius IX's infallible decree raised the doctrine of the Immaculate Conception to an article of faith. This infallible document states that at no moment of her life was Mary under the dominion of sin, and that she was, by anticipation of the redemption by Christ, the one exception to the law of original sin.

325
2803 ... To the glory of the holy and undivided Trinity, to the honour and ornament of the Virgin Mother of God, the exaltation of the Catholic faith and the increase of Christian religion, We, by the authority of our Lord Jesus Christ, of the blessed Apostles Peter and Paul, and by Our own authority declare, pronounce and define that the doctrine which holds that the Most Blessed Virgin Mary from the first moment of her conception was, by the singular grace and privilege of Almighty God, in view of the merits of Christ Jesus the Saviour of the human race, preserved immune from all stain of original sin, is revealed by God and is therefore firmly and constantly to be believed by all the faithful.

2804 Wherefore, if any persons shall dare to think, which God forbid, otherwise than has been defined by Us, let them clearly know that they are condemned by their own judgment, that they have suffered shipwreck to their faith and fallen from the unity of the Church, that they thenceforth subject themselves *ipso facto* to the penalties provided by law if they shall dare to expres their views in speech or writing or in any other way.

POPE LEO XIII's ENCYCLICAL *OCTOBRI MENSE* (1891)

The doctrine of Mary as mediatrix of grace is part of the Church's inheritance from the first centuries of Christianity.

It is no more than the Church's awareness of Mary's special place in God's plan of salvation. Nevertheless it was reserved to more recent times to incorporate this doctrine in the official documents of the Church. We have gathered here only a few of the texts which were decisive in the argument for and explanation of this doctrine in the last few decades.

Mary's Mediatory Role

326 ... The salvation of the human race was achieved in the mystery of the Cross. Christ celebrates his triumph. But on earth the Church is firmly established as the trustee of salvation. At this moment a *new order of Divine Providence* began for the new People. We must consider this divine plan with the greatest respect.

327 The eternal Son of God, when he wished to take the nature of man for the redemption and glorification of 3274 mankind, and wished therefore in a certain sense to enter into a mystical marriage with the whole of the human race, did not do so without first having the *absolutely free consent of his chosen mother* who in a sense personified the whole human race, as it was so truly and aptly expressed by Aquinas: 'In the annunciation the consent of the Virgin was awaited in place of the whole human race' *(S. Th. III, 30, ad 1)*. Whence it is possible to say in a true and exact sense that from that great treasure of grace which the Lord brought – 'grace and truth came by Jesus Christ' *(John 1:17)* – nothing comes to us except, by God's will, through Mary; so that, just as no one can attain to the supreme Father except through the Son, to a certain extent, no one can attain to the Son except through the Mother.

328 Great are the wisdom and mercy of God that shine forth in this plan. For we certainly believe in God's infinite goodness, and we praise it, but we also believe in his infinite justice, and we tremble before it... If

therefore the awareness of our actions cause us to tremble, we need an advocate and a protector, who is powerful before God in his grace, but who is also so full of goodness that no one, even in the greatest despair, will be refused his protection, and that he will inspire new confidence in God's mercy in all who are oppressed and bowed to earth.

Mary is such a one, Mary worthy of all praise; she is powerful, mother of the all-powerful God; but – and this sounds more promising – she looks down on us full of goodness and consideration.

3275 So God gave her to us. He made her the Mother of his only-begotten Son and gave her a mother's heart that knows nothing but love and forgiveness. And so Christ showed her to us: he freely willed to be subject to her and to obey her as a child obeys its mother... We should place ourselves under her protection and loyalty, together with our plans and deeds, our purity and our penance, our sorrows and joys and pleas and wishes. All that is ours we should entrust to her...

POPE LEO XIII's ENCYCLICAL
MAGNAE DEI MATRIS (1892)

Mary, Mediatrix of Grace

329 ...When we ask something of Mary in prayer, we are asking it of the Mother of Mercy. Her attitude to us is such that in every need that oppresses us, and especially when it is a matter concerning our eternal salvation, she immediately and gladly brings us help, even if we do not call upon her for it, and gives us something from the treasury of grace with which she was superabundantly endowed by God from the start of her existence so that she might be a worthy Mother for him. For by this fulness of grace, the most glorious

of the privileges of the Virgin, she stands high above all the orders of angels and men and she alone is next to Christ. 'For there is something great in every saint if he has so much grace that it suffices for the salvation of many. The greatest of all would be to have so much grace that it would suffice for the *salvation of all men on earth*. This is the case in Christ and in the Blessed Virgin' *(Th. A.)*

POPE LEO XIII's ENCYCLICAL *FIDENTEM* (1896)

Mary's Mediatory Role
...No one can think of anyone who has ever or will ever contribute so much to reconciling man to God as she (Mary) has done and does. For she brought the Saviour to man rushing into eternal disaster already then when the news of the peace-bringing mystery was brought to the world by the angel and received by her in her admirable assent in the place of all mankind. She it is from whom Jesus was born, that is, his true Mother, and therefore worthy and acceptable *Mediatrix with the Mediator*... 330 3321

POPE PIUS X's ENCYCLICAL *AD DIEM ILLUM* TO MARK THE FIFTIETH ANNIVERSARY OF THE PROCLAMATION OF THE IMMACULATE CONCEPTION (1904)

Mediatrix of Graces
Is not Mary the *Mother of Christ*? Then she is *our Mother*, too. One thing is unshakeably fixed: Jesus, the incarnate Word, is also the Redeemer of the human race. As God-Man he took the same palpable body as the rest of men. As Restorer of the human race, however, he also took a spiritual, as it were a mystical body, namely the community of those who believe in 331

Christ; 'So, we, being many, are one body in Christ' *(Rom. 12:5)*. Now the Virgin did not give birth to the eternal Son of God only in order that he should become man, taking his human nature from her; no, it was also in order that, *by the nature he took from her he should become the Redeemer of all mortals.* On this account the angel told the shepherds: 'This day is born to you a Saviour, who is Christ the Lord' *(Luke 2:11)*. Christ took flesh in the womb of his most pure Mother and at the same time that spiritual body composed of those who would believe in him. So one can say that Mary bore in her womb the Saviour and at the same time all those whose life was included in the life of the Saviour. All of us, that is, who are bound to Christ, who in the words of the Apostle are 'members of his body, of his flesh, and of his bones' *(Eph. 5:30)*, came from Mary's womb in the manner of a Body joined to its Head. So we may call ourselves in a spiritual and mystical way children of Mary, and she is the Mother of us all. 'Mother according to the spirit, but in fact *mother of the members of Christ, which we are'. (Augustine)*

332 The praise of the most holy Mother of God is not exhausted in that she offered her flesh to the only-begotten Son of God for his birth in a human body so that the victim was made ready for the salvation of the world. Her task went further: to cherish and nourish the Victim and to bring him at the proper time to the altar. Thus came about the *community of life and suffering between Mother and Son* which was never broken... But as the Son's life drew near its end, there stood at the foot of Jesus' cross his mother, not indeed overwhelmed by sorrow 'but rejoicing because her only Son was sacrificed for the salvation of the human race. So intimately had she participated in his Passion that, had it been possible, she would rather have taken upon

herself all the sufferings her Son bore' *(Bonaventure)*. This community of suffering and will between Mary and Christ, promoted her to the high dignity of *restorer of the lost world* and thus the dispenser of all the goods which Jesus won for us by his death and at the price of his blood.   3370

We do not indeed deny that the distribution of these gifts belongs properly and personally to *Christ*. Through his death alone they were won and he by his power is mediator between God and man. Nevertheless, on account of the communion of sorrows and pains between Mother and Son we have spoken of, it has been given to the august Virgin to be 'the most powerful mediatrix and conciliator between the whole world and her only-begotten Son. The *source* is Christ, 'and of his fulness we have all received' *(John 1:16)* 'from whom the whole body, being compacted and fitly joined together... maketh increase of the body, unto the edifying of itself in charity' *(Eph. 4:16)*. Mary indeed... 'is an aqueduct' *(Bernard of Clairvaux)* the neck... of our body through which all spiritual goods are channelled to his mystical body *(Bernardine of Siena)*.   333   3370

It is clear therefore that it is not our intention to ascribe to the Mother of God the power of effecting supernatural grace, which belongs to God alone. But since she stands above all others in sanctity and in union with Christ and was drawn by Christ into the work of man's salvation, she *de congruo*, as the saying is, merits for us what Christ merited *de condigno*, and is *the chief minister in the distribution of graces*. He sits at the right hand of Majesty in heaven, while as Queen she helper of all who are in danger. Where she leads and cares for and protects in her bounty, there is neither fear nor despair.   334   3370

POPE PIUS XII's ENCYCLICAL
MYSTICI CORPORIS CHRISTI (1943)

This encyclical was published on 29 June 1943 and set out in detail the nature of the Church. The passage given here is the epilogue. It is remarkable, for one thing, in the way it summarizes the importance of the Mother of God in the history of salvation, and also because it is the first time a papal doctrinal document speaks of the bodily assumption of the Blessed Virgin into heaven, though this had long been part of the ordinary doctrine of the Church.

334a
(2291)   May these Our fatherly prayers, which are surely also yours, Venerable Brethren, find fulfilment, and all men find a true love for the Church, through the intercession of the Virgin Mother of God. Her most holy soul, more than the souls of all God's creatures together, was filled with the divine Spirit of Jesus Christ. She, 'representing the whole of humanity' gave her consent to 'a spiritual marriage between the Son of God and human nature' *(S. Th. III, 30 ad 1)*. It was she who gave miraculous birth to Christ our Lord, adorned already in her virginal womb with the dignity of Head of the Church, and so brought forth the source of all heavenly life; and it was she who presented him, the new-born Prophet, King and Priest, to those of the Jews and Gentiles who first came to adore him. It was in answer to her motherly prayer 'in Cana of Galilee' that the Only-begotten worked the miracle by which 'his disciples believed in him' *(John 2:11)*. She it was who, immune from all sin, personal or inherited, and ever most closely united with her Son, offered him on Golgotha to the eternal Father together with the holocaust of her maternal rights and motherly love, like a new Eve, for all the children of Adam contaminated through his unhappy fall, and thus she, who was the

mother of our Head according to the flesh, became by a new title of sorrow and glory the spiritual mother of all his members. She too it was who by her most powerful intercession obtained for the new-born Church the prodigious pentecostal outpouring of that Spirit of the divine Redeemer who had already been given on the Cross. She, finally, true Queen of Martyrs, by bearing with courageous and confident heart her immense weight of sorrows, more than all Christians 'filled up those things that are wanting of the sufferings of Christ, for his Body, which is the Church' *(Col. 1:24);* and upon the mystical Body of Christ, born of the broken heart of the Saviour, she bestowed that same motherly care and fervent love with which she fostered and nurtured the suckling infant Jesus in the cradle.

May she, therefore, most holy Mother of all the members of Christ, to whose Immaculate Heart we have trustingly consecrated all men, may she who now, resplendent with glory in body and soul, reigns in heaven with her Son, use her intercession with him so that from that august Head abundance of grace may flow with steady stream into all the members of his mystical Body. May she now, as in times past, keep watch and ward over the Church with her most powerful patronage, and at length obtain from God times more peaceful for her and for the whole family of men.

POPE PIUS XII's APOSTOLIC CONSTITUTION *MUNIFICENTISSIMUS* (1950)

On 1 November 1950 Pope Pius XII solemnly defined Mary's assumption body and soul into the glory of heaven. The Constitution offers a survey of the history of this belief down the centuries which also mentions the way in which the Church's awareness of faith developed this truth from the basic data of revelation about Mary. Here we give the sum-

mary of the theological argument which is the link between the historical survey and the actual definition with which it ends.

334b 3900 All these arguments and considerations of the Fathers and theologians rest on Sacred Scripture for their ultimate foundation. They present to us the beloved Mother of God as most intimately united with her divine Son and as ever sharing his lot. Hence it seems practically impossible to contemplate her who conceived Christ, brought him forth, and nourished him with her milk, held him in her arms and embraced him, as separated in body from him, though not in soul, after her life on earth was over. Since our Redeemer is the Son of Mary and observed the divine law most perfectly, he certainly could not but honour his beloved Mother with an honour second only to that given to his eternal Father. And seeing that by preserving her from the corruption of the tomb he could give her such great honour, we must believe that he actually did so.

3901 Above all it is to be remembered that, ever since the second century, the Fathers thought of the Virgin Mary as the New Eve, who, although subject to the New Adam, was still most closely united with him in the struggle against the infernal enemy. The struggle, as foretold in the Proto-gospel *(Gen. 3:15)*, was to lead to a complete victory over sin and death, two things that were always joined together in the writings of the Apostle of the Gentiles *(cf. Rom. 5 and 6; 1 Cor. 15:21–6; 54–7)*. Hence as the glorious resurrection of Christ was an essential part and the final sign of this victory, in like manner the struggle which the Blessed Virgin endured in common with her Son was to end in the 'glorification' of her virginal body. For, as the same Apostle says, 'when this mortal hath put on immortality, then shall come to pass the saying that is written: 'Death is swallowed up in victory' *(1 Cor. 15:54).*

Thus from all eternity and by 'one and the same decree' *(Bull* **Ineffabilis Deus)** of predestination the august Mother of God is united in a mysterious way with Jesus Christ; immaculate in her conception, a spotless virgin in her divine motherhood, the noble companion of the divine Redeemer, who won a complete triumph over sin and its consequences, she finally obtained as the crowning glory of her privileges preservation from the corruption of the tomb and, like her Son before her, she conquered death and was raised body and soul to the glory of heaven, where as Queen she shines refulgent at the right hand of her Son, the immortal King of Ages *(1 Tim. 1:17).* **3902**

Therefore, since the universal Church, which the Spirit of Truth actively and infallibly directs in perfecting the knowledge of revealed truths, has manifested in various ways down through the centuries her belief, and since the bishops of the entire world almost unanimously petition that the truth of the bodily Assumption of the Blessed Virgin Mary into heaven be defined as a dogma of divine and Catholic faith – which truth is founded on Sacred Scripture, is deeply embedded in the minds of the faithful, has received the approval of liturgical worship from the earliest times, is perfectly in keeping with the rest of revealed truth, and has been lucidly developed and explained by the studies of learned and wise theologians – We deem that the moment pre-ordained in the plan of divine Providence has now arrived for Us to proclaim solemnly this extraordinary privilege of the Virgin Mary...

Wherefore, having directed humble and repeated prayers to God, and having invoked the light of the Spirit of Truth, to the glory of Almighty God, who has bestowed **334c**
3903

his special bounty on the Virgin Mary, for the honour of his Son the immortal King of ages and Victor over sin and death, for the greater glory of his august Mother, and for the joy and exaltation of the whole Church, by the authority of our Lord Jesus Christ, of the blessed Apostles Peter and Paul, and by Our own, We proclaim and define it to be a dogma revealed by God that the immaculate Mother of God, Mary ever Virgin, when the course of her earthly life was finished, was taken up body and soul into the glory of heaven.

3904 Wherefore, if anyone, which God forbid, should wilfully dare to deny or call in doubt what We have defined, let him know that he has certainly abandoned divine and Catholic faith.

CHAPTER EIGHT

THE CHURCH

Christ's work has to go on. Though it is part of the nature of the mystery of the Incarnation that Christ in his appearance as man took upon himself the time and space limitations of an earthly life, he had nevertheless, on account of the universal character of his mission and the absolute necessity that all men should find salvation in him, to provide for the possibility for all men to encounter him. This possibility he created in the Church.
The Church thus embodies two realities.
The first is the divine reality. *However much the Church in its outward appearances is fallible and subject to development, however intimately she may be bound up in an earthly kingdom, as for instance in the Middle Ages, however much her visage may for centuries bear the features of one particular culture – we only really know the Church as a European Church – she has nevertheless been given by Christ marks of her own that do not belong to any purely human community. She is the one, holy, catholic and Apostolic Church which is essentially the same as what was formerly represented by the community of the Apostles, and which will never be complete until all peoples and cultures have found their home in her. 'And thy gates shall be open continually: they shall not be shut day nor night, that the*

strength of the Gentiles may be brought to thee, and their kings may be brought' (Is. 60:11).

The Church's second reality is that she is a human society, *whose framework and construction can be set out in clear rules. In all questions of government and doctrine there is one supreme authority; even the salvific action of the Church is bound up with outward and visible signs in the sacraments, sacraments which are administered by an ordering and regulating authority. Christ's Church must be like this if the Incarnation is not to remain just a passing historical fact but the way of salvation which God has built in the world. Christ's mission and work, his teaching office, his office of shepherd and of priest live on in the hierarchy and priesthood as official states.*

Both realities, divine and human, are found in the Church from the earliest centuries of Christianity. Everything that has been said about the Church in later ages, particularly in recent decades, is only the unfolding and the finding of terms to express what the Church was living from the start.

Thus the earliest documents *about the Church are not really, as it were, self-portraits, but* expressions of her living presence. *They deal partly with the juridical-organizational side of things, concern for true doctrine, and watching over loyalty and community in the Church. Respect for the hierarchy is often much to the fore, together with, at its head, the successors of Peter, the popes of Rome. Most of these utterances refer back, often in so many words, often with the demand for absolute acceptance unthinkable in a purely human community, to the Church's divine institution.*

More detailed statements about the Church *come only comparatively late. An example is the Vatican Council's Decree (1870–Nos. 370ff).*

A summary of doctrine concerning the Church includes:
The Church was founded by Christ *(67, 360, 391, 398g, 398c)* as the sole community of the faithful wished by him *(339–41, 354, 360, 363, 368g)*. She is the mystical body of Christ *(316–9, 319a, 331, 334a, 359, 362, 398a–c, 398f, 537a)*. She is visible *(345–8, 360–2, 398a)*, in her own way a 'perfect society' *(398d)*, and eternal *(366, 398c, 392)*. She has been given special marks by Christ *(354, 355, 356, 828, 831, 834, 841)* and her own wonderful existence is proof of her divine origin *(356)*.

The Church was founded in order to continue Christ's work of salvation as teacher, pastor and priest *(359, 362, 370)*. Revelation is therefore entrusted to her *(38, 61, 64, 67, 126e, 352, 355, 357, 358, 367, 389, 390, 398h, 398i, 858)*. In the course of her ordinary and extraordinary magisterium *(398h, 398i)* the Church explains and proclaims to the faithful *(126e, 352, 353, 357, 367, 368)*. She has also the task of authoritative interpretation of Scripture *(72, 79, 81, 86, 88, 89, 92, 93, 104, 107, 126e, 398h, 398i, 850)*. In the explanation of revelation the universal Church is infallible *(367, 368, 388, 398)*. This infallibility also attaches to the pope by himself if in virtue of his authority he makes a definitive decree in matters of faith and morals *(383–8, 388a, 398)*.

The community of the Church is articulated *(369, 398c, 630, 638, 641)*. Supreme juridical power over the whole Church was given to Peter by Christ *(338, 341, 349, 354, 372–4, 394)* and is passed on to his successors in the See of Rome *(67, 335–7, 338, 341, 342, 343, 344, 348, 349, 354, 375–82, 388a, 395, 396–7, 848, 857, 858)*. Bishops have ordinary jurisdiction over the dioceses entrusted to them *(380, 388a, 398e, 631, 639, 640)*.

The Church is the community of those who have become members of Christ in baptism *(359, 363, 398a, 398b, 398g, 436, 447)*. She is also entrusted with the admini-

stration of the sacraments (426, 851).

Membership of the Church is necessary for salvation *(340, 350, 351, 364, 365, 398a, 398b, 398g). Conditions for membership are: baptism, confession of the true faith, submission to the Church's authority (398a). Blameless ignorance of the Church does not, however, exclude from salvation (351, 365) if the wish and desire to belong exists (398g). This wish can also exist implicitly (398g) but must be associated with supernatural faith and charity (398g).*

Since we are dealing here only with dogmatic matters, we have omitted all documents dealing with developments of the Church's life willed by Christ but not actually put into operation by him, such as, for example, the organizational development or relations between Church and State.

EARLY DOCUMENTS ON THE PRIMACY OF THE ROMAN PONTIFF

The most important ancient and mediaeval testimonies to the primacy of the Bishop of Rome were embodied in the decree of the First Vatican Council (cf. Nos. 375 and 384). Thus we only give an indication of what they consist of.

1. The declaration made by the Papal Legates to the Council of Ephesus (431) about the primacy of the Bishop of Rome. This was unanimously adopted by the Council.   335 (112)

2. The 'Formula of Pope Hormisdas' whose signature by some two hundred and fifty Oriental bishops put an end to the Acacian schism (484–519). This was later adopted by the Eighth General Council (Constantinople IV) in 869.   336 363–4

3. The confession of faith which the Emperor Michael Paleologue as representative of the Eastern Church signed through his ambassadors, before the General Council of Lyons in 1274. The text is given in Nos. 838–48; 848 deals with the primacy of Rome.   337 861

POPE LEO IX's LETTER TO MICHAEL CERULARIUS (1053)

After the Photian schism (cf. Note to No. 202) normal relations were restored between Rome and Constantinople at the beginning of the tenth century, and they remained more or less so until Michael Cerularius became Patriarch in 1043. He tried to arouse a conflict with the Pope as an excuse to break away. He found an excuse in the ritual differences between East and West, particularly in the Western use of unleavened bread for the Eucharist. It got to the point where there was anti-Western rioting in Constantinople.

The letter drafted by the German Cardinal Humbert von Silva and signed by Pope Leo IX, by-passes all questions of ritual, hardly indicating them, and goes straight to the crux of the matter – the primacy of the Roman pope. This is what makes this document so important, written as it was at a decisive moment, just one year before the Papal Legates had to pronounce sentence of excommunication in Hagia Sophia in Constantinople.

The Primacy of the Roman Pontiff

338
(351) Chap. VII... The holy Church is built upon the rock that is Christ, and upon Peter, or Cephas, son of John, previously called Simon, on the rock against which the gates of hell – that is the attacks of heretics which lead foolish men to destruction – shall never prevail. Thus promised Truth himself, by whom what was always true, still is true: 'And the gates of hell shall not prevail against it' *(Mt. 16:18)*, And the Son begged the fulfilment of this promise from the Father, when he assured Peter in the words beginning 'Simon, Simon, behold Satan...' *(Luke 22:31)*. Is it possible to be so blind as to consider this prayer, by One for whom to will is to be able, to be ineffectual? Have not the opinions of all heretics been rejected, refuted and thrown down by the See of the Prince of the Apostles, that is, by the Roman Church through Peter himself and his successors? Are not the hearts of the brethren strengthened in the faith of Peter that has never yet wavered and never will?

THE FOURTH LATERAN GENERAL COUNCIL (1215)

Chap. I – On the Catholic Faith
Denial that the Church was the one community necessary for salvation founded by Christ lay at the heart of the Albigensian heresy. Its condemnation by the Lateran Council thus provides an important document on Church unity. *(Cf. Note to No. 170).*

...There is only one universal Church of the faithful, **339**
outside which none will be saved. In it Jesus Christ is *802*
both priest and sacrifice, whose body and blood are
truly contained in the Sacrament of the Altar under the
species of bread and wine, the bread having by the
power of God been transubstantiated into the body
and the wine into the blood, whereby we receive of his
what he received of ours so that the mystery of unity
may be perfected...

POPE BONIFACE VIII's BULL
UNAM SANCTAM (1302)

*This bull was issued during the conflict between Pope Boniface
and Philip the Fair of France. To start with, the Pope sets out
the foundations of doctrine concerning the Church: her uniqueness, her necessity for salvation and the reason for these
characteristics – Christ the head of the Church. The consequences of this are principally the Church's fulness of
power, first in spiritual matters and then in worldly matters.
While the political content of the bull is only of historical
value, the final sentence (No. 342) imposes a dogmatic
obligation.*

*The Church is Unique, Necessary for Salvation, and
Endowed with the Fulness of Power*

...**That there is only one holy, catholic and apostolic** 340
Church we are compelled by faith to believe and hold, *870*
and we firmly believe in her and simply confess her,
outside whom there is neither salvation nor remission
of sins... She represents one mystical body, the head of
which body is Christ, but the head of Christ is God.
In her there is 'one Lord, one faith, one baptism'
(Eph. 4:5)...
This one and unique Church, therefore, has not two 341
heads, like a monster, but one body and one head, viz. *872*

Christ and his vicar Peter's successor, for the Lord said to Peter personally 'Feed my sheep' *(John 21:17)* 'My' *(sheep)* he said in general, not individually, or these or those; whereby it is understood that he confided all his sheep to him.

If therefore Greeks or others say that they were not confided to Peter and his successors they must necessarily confess that they are not among Christ's sheep, for the Lord said in John *('s Gospel)*, 'there shall be one fold and one shepherd' *(John 10:16)*.

342
875 Furthermore we declare, state and define that it is absolutely necessary for the salvation of all men that they submit to the Roman pontiff.

THE GENERAL COUNCIL OF CONSTANCE
(1414–1418)

Of crucial importance in the following centuries, and in particular at the Reformation, was Wycliffe's conception of the Church. Wycliffe (1320–84) was the forerunner of the Reformation in England. He denied that the Church was founded by God as an outward and visible community with official powers of teaching and government, recognizing only a Church of the 'Predestined'. Only those who in God's eternal decree were predestined for the glory to come were members of the Church, not those whom God knew would be lost, the 'Foreknown'. Of no man, even baptized and believing could it be known whether he belonged to the Church or not, not even of Princes of the Church without particular revelation. The Church thus became a purely interior community. There was no mediation of faith or salvation by any community founded by God, but only individuals had the right and the duty to seek out the truth from the sole source, the Scriptures. Here already we find anticipated the Reformers' acceptance of the Bible as the sole source of faith to the exclusion of tradition. Wycliffe's ideas were adopted by John Hus (1370–1415) and became wide spread in Bohemia.

WYCLIFFE'S ERRORS CONDEMNED

8. If the Pope is a Foreknown and evil, and consequently a member of the devil he has no power over the faithful given him by anybody, unless indeed by the emperor. [343] *1158*

37. The Church of Rome is the synagogue of Satan, and the pope is not the next and immediate vicar of Christ and the Apostles. [344] *1187*

HUS'S ERRORS CONDEMNED

3. The Foreknown are not part of the Church, for no part of the Church finally falls away, because the charity of predestination which binds it together does not fall away. [345] *1203*

5. The Foreknown, even if at some time in a state of grace according to present justice, is never a part of the holy Church. But the predestined man remains always a member of the Church; even if at some time he falls from present grace, he does not fall from the grace of predestination. [346] *1205*

6. Assuming the Church to be the community of the predestined, whether in a state of grace according to present justice or not, in this sense the Church is an article of faith. [347] *1206*

10. Without revelation no one can rationally assert of himself or of another that he is the head of a particular Church, nor is the Roman Pontiff head of the Roman Church. [348] *1210*

THE GENERAL COUNCIL OF FLORENCE
(1438–45)

The Council of Florence, whose main object was reunification of the schismatic East with the Mother Church, naturally had to place some emphasis on the unity of the Church and the primacy of Rome.

DECREE FOR THE GREEKS (1439)

349 *The Primacy of the Roman Pontiff*

1307 ...We decree that the Holy Apostolic See and the Roman Pontiff have primacy in the whole world, and that this Roman Pontiff is the successor of blessed Peter, Prince of the Apostle, and true vicar of Christ, head of the whole Church and father and teacher of all Christians; that to him in blessed Peter was given by our Lord Jesus Christ the full power of feeding, ruling and governing the universal Church as it is contained in the acts of the ecumenical Councils and in the sacred canons.

POPE PIUS IX's ALLOCUTION *SINGULARI QUADAM*
(1854)

Denial of supernatural revelation entails denying the Church as the sole God-given community necessary for salvation. Rationalism and indifferentism (according equal value to all forms of religion) are closely connected. Again and again they were condemned alongside one another in Church documents of the nineteenth century. The present document is of importance because it makes such a clear distinction between the objective necessity of the Church for salvation willed by God and the subjective guilt or innocence of people outside the Church.

...It is to be held as a matter of faith that no one can be saved outside the Apostolic Roman Church. It is the only ark of salvation and anyone who does not enter it must sink in the flood. But it is equally to be held as certain that those who live in ignorance of the true religion, if such ignorance be invincible, will not be held guilty in the eyes of the Lord.

351
2865°

POPE PIUS IX's LETTER TO THE ARCHBISHOP OF
MUNICH-FREISING (1862)
(*Cf.* Note to No. 22)

The Church as Guardian of Revealed Truth
...The Church, by virtue of her divine institution has the duty of most conscientiously maintaining the treasure of divine faith unimpaired and complete and of watching with the utmost zeal over the salvation of souls. She must therefore with painstaking care remove and eradicate anything that is contrary to faith or in any way harmful to the salvation of souls. Thus by virtue of the power accorded her by her divine author, the Church has not only the right but also the duty of not tolerating but of proscribing and condemning all

352

2861

errors if the integrity of the faith and the salvation of souls require it.

POPE PIUS IX's LETTER TO THE SAME (1863)

353 *The Church's Ordinary Magisterium*
2879 ...Let Us admit that they *(certain German theologians)* have confessed to the truth which is of obligation in the Catholic faith. We wish also to be convinced, however, that they do not restrict this obligation, which is binding upon all professors and writers, to those matters alone which are proposed by the infallible judgment of the Church as dogmas of faith to be believed by all. And We are persuaded that they did not wish to declare that that complete adherence to revealed truths, which they acknowledge as being altogether necessary for real scientific progress and the fight against error, could be attained by merely giving credence and obedience to those dogmas expressly defined by the Church. For if it were a matter only of the submission to be made by an act of divine faith this would not be limited to those things which have been expressly defined by decrees of General Councils or of the See of the Roman Pontiffs, but would be extended also to those things which are taught by the ordinary magisterium of the universal Church throughout the world and are therefore held by the general universal consensus of Catholic theologians to be matters of faith.

LETTER OF THE HOLY OFFICE TO THE BISHOPS OF ENGLAND (1864)

In London in 1857 there was founded the 'Association for the Promotion of the Reunion of Christendom' based on the notion that the three great Christian communions, the Roman, Greek and Anglican Churches, were of equal status. The adherence of a number of Catholics to this association was the occasion for the Church to lay down the basis of any possible agreement, namely the unity and unicity of the Church. Christ's foundation lives on only in the Roman Catholic Church, which also bears the marks given her by Christ.

...The true Church of Jesus Christ is by divine authority constituted and distinguished with four marks which we assert as matters of faith in the Creed. Each of these marks is so closely linked to the others that it cannot be separated from them. Hence the Church which truly is and is called Catholic must exhibit at one and the same time the prerogatives of unity, sanctity and apostolic succession. So the Catholic Church is one in conspicuous and perfect unity in the whole world and among all nations, that unity indeed whose beginning, root and origin is the supreme authority and *potior principalitas (Irenaeus)* of blessed Peter, Prince of the Apostles, and of his successors in the Roman cathedra. Nor is there any other Catholic Church but that built upon the one Peter 'compacted and fitly joined together' in one body *(Eph. 4:16)*, growing in the unity of faith and charity. 354 2888

THE FIRST VATICAN GENERAL COUNCIL, THIRD SESSION (1870)

DECREE ON THE CATHOLIC FAITH

In conjunction with the doctrine on revelation (cf. Nos. 31ff) the Vatican Council also had to speak about the Church as guardian and at the same time permanent and visible proof of the divine character of revelation.

Chapter III. Faith

The Church as Protection and Proof of Revelation

355   ...So that we may be able to satisfy the obligation of
3012 embracing the true faith and of consistently persevering in it, God has instituted the Church through his only begotten Son, and has bestowed on it manifest marks of that institution, so that it may be recognized by all men as the guardian and teacher of the revealed Word; for to the Catholic Church alone belong all those many and admirable tokens which have been divinely established for the evident credibility of the Christian faith.

356 Nay more, the Church by itself, with its marvellous
3013 extension, its eminent holiness, and its inexhaustible fruitfulness in every good thing, with its Catholic unity and its invincible stability, is a great and perpetual motive of credibility and an irrefutable witness of its own divine mission. And thus, like a standard set up unto the nations *(Is. 11:12)*, it both invites to itself those who do not yet believe, and assures its children that the faith which they profess rests on the most firm foundation...
(Cf. No. 40)

Chapter IV. Faith and Reason

The Church as Guardian of the truth

357   ...For the doctrine of faith which God has revealed has
3020 not been proposed, like a philosophical invention, to be perfected by human intelligence, but has been delivered as a divine deposit to the Spouse of Christ, to be faithfully kept and infallibly declared. Hence also, that meaning of the sacred dogmas is perpetually to be retained which our Holy Mother the Church has once declared; nor is that meaning ever to be departed from, under the pretence or pretext of deeper comprehension of them...

THE FIRST DRAFT OF THE CONSTITUTION ON THE CHURCH OF CHRIST

The Vatican Council wanted to do other things besides lay down in a solemn and infallible pronouncement the primacy and infallibility of the Pope of Rome. This doctrine was rather a section of the overall picture of the Church which the Council was to work out and proclaim. Since the Council was, however, adjourned before time it got no further than decreeing that one section.

The schema prepared by the Council theologians is, of course, no infallible teaching of the Church; it is not even an official document of ecclesiastical doctrine but only the draft for such a document. Nevertheless, it is of great importance since it embodies the points which were regarded as being ripe for definition. In addition, this schema became to a great extent the basis for dealing with doctrine concerning the Church.

358 Pius, Bishop, Servant of the Servants of God, with the approval of the Sacred Council, for a perpetual remembrance

The Apostolic Office of Supreme Pastor in which the ineffable Providence and mercy of God has placed Us urges Us unceasingly to leave nothing undone so that the way which leads to eternal life and salvation shall be clear to all men, so that those who are in darkness and the shadow of death may attain the light and the knowledge of faith. Since, then, our God and Saviour has placed the truth of the whole of the doctrine of salvation, and the treasures of the means of salvation, in his Church, as in a rich treasury, so *in the first place the true Church herself must be both shown to those in error and urgently commended to the faithful* so that the former may be led into the way of salvation and the later be confirmed and grow in it. Wherefore We hold it to be a duty of Our office to expound the more important articles of true Catholic doctrine concerning the nature of the Church, her characteristics and her powers, and to condemn the contrary errors of the time in the Canons annexed.

Chapter I. The Church is the Mystical Body of Christ

359 The only-begotten Son of God, who enlightens all men coming into this world, who never denies his aid to the poor sons of Adam, in the fulness of time as fore-ordained by the eternal council, appeared in the likeness of man, having assumed the form of our body so that earthly corporeal men, putting on the new man which is created in the image of God in justice and holiness of truth *(Eph. 4:24)* should constitute the mystical body of which he himself is the Head.

In order to effect this unity of the Mystical Body, Christ the Lord instituted the sacred *Lavacrum* of *regeneration and renewal*, whereby the sons of man, so largely divided among themselves, and especially fallen through sin, could be cleansed of all stain of sin, and become members of one another, and joined to the divine Head in faith, hope and charity, that all might be animated by his one Spirit and receive abundant gifts of heavenly grace and charisms.

And this is the sublime form of the Church, which can never be sufficiently proclaimed to the faithful that it may become fixed in their hearts, whose Head is Christ, 'from whom the whole body being compacted and fitly joined together, by what every joint supplieth according to the operation in the measure of every part, maketh increase of the body, unto the edifying of itself in charity' *(Eph. 4:16)*.

Chapter II. The Christian religion can be fully cultivated only in and through the Church founded by Christ

Jesus, the author and perfecter of our faith, himself 360 founded and instituted this Church, which he acquired by his blood and which he has loved from eternity as his one chosen Bride. And he commanded that, brought together from all creation throughout the world by his apostles and their successors, taught and governed by them to the end of time, she should be a holy people 'a people acceptable, a pursuer of good works' *(Tit. 2:14)*. For it is not the meaning of the law of the Gospel that each individual should worship God for himself without bond of community as true worshippers of the Father in spirit and in truth; rather our Saviour wished so to bind his religion to the community founded by him that one should remain entirely bound up and interpenetrated with the other and that outside this community there should be no true Christian religion.

Chapter III. The Church is a true, perfect[1] spiritual and supernatural society

We teach and declare: The Church has all the marks 361 of a true Society. Christ did not leave this society undefined and without a set form. Rather, he himself gave its existence, and his will determined the form of its existence and gave it its constitution. The Church is not part nor member of any other society and is not

---

1. By a 'perfect' society is meant one that disposes in itself of all the means necessary to achieve its goal and which therefore is not dependent on a higher community as, for example, the family is dependent upon the State.

mingled in any way with any other society. It is so perfect in itself that it is distinct from all human societies and stands far above them. It stems from the inexhaustible fount of mercy of God the Father; the incarnate Word laboured to build its foundations; and it was perfected in the Holy Spirit. In the beginning, the Spirit was poured out in the greatest abundance on the apostles, and continues to pour itself out in overflowing measure upon the sons of adoption; thus, enlightened by his light, with one faith in their hearts, they should adhere to God and be bound together among themselves; thus they should bear the earnest of their inheritance in their hearts, tearing out the fleshly concupiscence of the corrupt and sensual world, and strengthened by the one blessed common hope, seek the promised eternal glory of God. Thus they will by good works make sure of their calling and election *(2 Peter 1:10)*. Now since in the Church men increase in these goods and riches by the Holy Spirit and are welded into unity by this bond of the Holy Spirit, so is the Church itself a community in the Spirit and of a wholly supernatural order.

Chapter IV. The Church is a Visible Society

362 No one should believe that the members of the Church are held together only by interior and hidden bonds, so that the Church is an entirely hidden and invisible community. For the eternal wisdom and power of God willed that to the spiritual and invisible bonds wherewith the faithful are bound by the Holy Spirit to the supreme and invisible head of the Church there should correspond external and visible bonds. Whence comes the visible magisterium which publicly lays down what is to be inwardly believed and outwardly confessed.

Whence also the visible ministry which governs and controls the visible mysteries of God that effect the inner salvation of man and the honour due to God. Whence, too, the visible pastorate which orders the unity of the members among themselves and guides and leads the outward and public life of the faithful in the Church. Whence, finally, the whole visible body of the Church to which belong not only the just and the predestined but also sinners who are bound to it by community and confession of faith. Thus the Church of Christ here on earth is by no means hidden or invisible but set before all eyes like a shining city set high on a mountain, which cannot be hidden *(Mt. 5:14)* but which, lit by the Sun of Justice, shines out over the world with the light of its truth.

Chapter V. The Visible Unity of the Church

Such then is the true Church of Christ. We therefore declare: This society, visible to all, is that Church of the divine promises and mercy which Christ wished to bedeck and distinguish with so many prerogatives and privileges. The Church is so completely bounded and determined in her constitution that no society separated from the unity of belief or from communion with this body can in any way be called a part or member of the Church. Further, the Church is not distributed and divided among the various societies that call themselves Christian; she is wholly selfcontained in unity. In the unity visible to all she is an undivided and indivisible body, the mystical body indeed of Christ, of which St Paul says: 'One body and one Spirit; as you are called in one hope of your calling; one Lord, one faith, one baptism: one God and Father of all, who is above all, and through all, and in us all' *(Eph. 4:4–6)*.

Chapter VI. The Church is Necessary for Attaining to Salvation

364 So let all understand how necessary this society, the Church of Christ, is for the attainment of salvation. This necessity corresponds to the greatness of the community and bond between Christ the head and his mystical body. For he nourishes and cherishes no other community as he does his Church, as her and her alone he loved, and for her delivered himself up, to cleanse her by the water of baptism in the word of life, 'that he might present her to himself a glorious Church, not having a spot or wrinkle, or any such thing, but that she should be holy, and without blemish' *(Eph. 5:26f)*. So we teach: The Church is not a free community in which it is indifferent to the salvation of man whether he knows it or not, whether he enters in or leaves it. She is absolutely necessary, and this not solely on account of our Lord's command whereby the Saviour prescribed that all peoples should come into his Church, but also as a means, since, in the order of salvation established by divine Providence, communion with the Holy Spirit and partaking of truth and life cannot be attained except in the Church and through the Church whose head is Christ.

Chapter VII. Outside the Church No One Can be Saved

365 Further, it is an article of faith that outside the Church no one can be saved. Certainly not all those who are in invincible ignorance of Christ and his Church are to be eternally damned solely on account of this ignorance. For it bears no guilt in the eyes of the Lord who wants all men to be saved and to attain to knowledge

of the truth. To all who do their best he gives his grace so that they may attain justification and eternal life. But no one who by his own fault is separated from the unity of belief and community of the Church and thus cuts himself off from this life receives this grace. Who is not in this ark will perish in the flood. So we reject and abhor the doctrine of the equal value of all religions, which is also contrary to human reason. Thus the children of this world would abolish the distinction between true and false and say: The gateway to eternal life stands open to all regardless of what religion they come from. Or: Concerning the truth of a religion there is always only a greater or lesser degree of probability and never any certainty. Equally we condemn the impious opinion of those who close the kingdom of heaven to men with the false pretence that it is unfitting and in any case not necessary to salvation, to leave the religion in which one was born and bred and grew up even if it be false. Indeed, they even upbraid the Church herself who declares that she is the one true religion and who rejects and condemns all religions and sects that are separated from communion with her. They apparently believe that unrighteousness can somehow win a share of righteousness, or darkness a share of light, or that Christ could make a pact with Satan.

Chapter VIII. The Indefectibility of the Church

We further declare: The Church of Christ, whether regarded in its existence or in its constitution is a permanent and indefectible society. No other order of salvation, more complete or more perfect, will follow her in this world. For since the mortal pilgrims of this earth must, until the end of the world, attain to salvation through Christ, his Church is the sole com-

366

munity of salvation which remains unchangeable and unchanged in its constitution. The Church indeed grows – and may she ever increase in faith and charity 'for edifying the body of Christ' *(Eph. 4:12)* – and she indeed develops according to the age and the differences in the environment in which she lives in constant struggle. Nevertheless, she is unchangeable in herself and in the constitution she received from Christ. Never, therefore, can the Church of Christ lose her essential features or her gifts: her magisterium, her ministry and her pastorate. So Christ in his visible body is always and for all men the way, the truth and the light.

Chapter IX. The Infallibility of the Church

367 The Church of Christ would lose her immutability and her dignity, and would cease to be the community of life and necessary means of salvation if she could stray from the saving truth of faith and morals or could in her preaching and teaching deceive herself or others. She is the pillar and foundation of truth, free and untouched by any danger of error or falsehood.
With the approval of the holy and ecumenical Council We teach and declare: The gift of infallibility which has been revealed as an enduring characteristic of the Church of Christ – and it is not to be confused with the gift of inspiration; nor does it mean that the Church is accorded new revelations – is given to the Church so that the word of God in written and oral tradition shall remain authentic throughout the Church, be maintained and protected from change and innovation, as St Paul commanded: 'O Timothy, keep that which is committed to thy trust, avoiding the profane novelties of words, and the oppositions of knowledge falsely so called, which some promising, have erred against the faith' *(1 Tim. 6:20f)*. And again Paul insists: 'Hold

the form of sound words, which thou hast heard of me in faith, and in the love which is in Christ Jesus. Keep the good thing committed to thy trust by the Holy Ghost, who dwelleth in us' (2 Tim. 1:13f).

We therefore teach: The fact of infallibility extends as far as the deposit of faith reaches, and it is made necessary by the duty of guarding this deposit. This privilege of infallibility which the Church of Christ has embraces in the first place the whole revealed word of God, but also all that which, while not itself being revelation, is absolutely necessary to maintain in security what has been revealed, to set it out clearly and definitely as an article of faith and to interpret it, or to defend it against human error and sustain it against the controversies of false science. The object of this infallibility is the unspotted truth of the community of the faithful in matters of faith and morals. It rests on the magisterium which Christ established in his Church for all time when he said to his Apostles: 'Going therefore, teach ye all nations: baptizing them in the name of the Father, and of the Son, and of the Holy Ghost: teaching them to observe all things whatsoever I have commanded you: and behold I am with you all days even to the consummation of the world' *(Mt. 28:19f)*. To his Apostles Christ also promised the Spirit of truth to abide with them forever, to be in them and teach them all things *(John 14:15f, 26)*. 368

Chapter X. The Power of the Church

But the Church of Christ is not a community of equals in which all the faithful have the same rights. It is a society of unequals, not only because among the faithful some are clerics and some are laymen, but particularly because there is in the Church the power from 369

God whereby to some it is given to sanctify, teach and govern and to others not. Two ecclesiastical powers should be distinguished, that of order and that of direction and government. Concerning the latter We teach in particular: It applies not only in the realms of conscience and the sacraments but also in the realm of what is external and public. It is unlimited and complete in legislative, juridical and coercive power. The bearers of this power are the pastors and teachers instituted by Christ. They exercise this power in freedom and independence of any secular power. Thus they direct and govern the Church of God with all fulness of power: by laws which of themselves impose an obligation and are binding in conscience, by judicial decrees, and finally by salutary punishments against those who deserve them, even if they should resist. This direction concerns not only the domains of faith, morals, worship and sanctification but also the external order and governance of the Church. Thus it is an article of faith that the Church of Christ represents a perfect society. And this true and blessed Church of Christ is none other than the one holy, catholic and apostolic Roman Church...

FIRST VATICAN GENERAL COUNCIL, FOURTH SESSION (1870)

FIRST DOGMATIC CONSTITUTION ON THE CHURCH OF CHRIST

In the following constitution, the doctrine of the primacy of the Roman Pontiff is first expounded, followed by the actual definition. Thus only the last sections of the individual chapters are to be taken as infallible decrees.

370
3050 The Eternal Pastor and Bishop of our souls, in order to continue for all time the life-giving work of his

Redemption, determined to build up the Holy Church, wherein, as in the house of the living God, all who believe might be united in the bond of one faith and one charity. Wherefore, before he entered into his glory, he prayed to the Father, not for the apostles only, but for all those who through their preaching should come to believe in him, that all might be one as he the Son and the Father are one *(John 17:20f)*. As then he sent the Apostles whom he had chosen to himself from the world, as he himself had been sent by the Father: so he willed that there should ever be pastors and teachers in his Church to the end of the world. And in order that the episcopate also might be one and undivided, and that by means of a closely united priesthood the multitude of the faithful might be kept secure in the oneness of faith and communion, he set blessed Peter over the rest of the Apostles, and fixed in him the abiding principle of this twofold unity, and its visible foundation, in the strength of which the everlasting temple should arise, and the Church in the firmness of that faith should lift her majestic front to heaven. *3051*

And seeing that the gates of hell with daily increase of hatred are gathering their strength on every side to upheave the foundation laid by God's own hand, and so, if that might be, to overthrow the Church: We, therefore, for the preservation, safe-keeping and increase of the Catholic flock, with the approval of the Sacred Council, do judge it to be necessary to propose to the belief and acceptance of all the faithful, in accordance with the ancient and constant faith of the universal Church, the doctrine touching the institution, perpetuity, and nature of the sacred Apostolic Primacy, in which is found the strength and solidity of the entire Church; and at the same time to proscribe and condemn the contrary errors, so hurtful to the flock of Christ. *371* *3052*

Chapter I. The Institution of the Apostolic Primacy in Blessed Peter

372
3053 We therefore teach and declare that, according to the testimony of the Gospel, the primacy of jurisdiction over the universal Church of God was immediately and directly promised and given to Blessed Peter the Apostle by Christ the Lord. For it was to Simon alone, to whom he had already said, 'Thou shalt be called Cephas' *(John 1:42)*, that the Lord, after the confession made by him, 'Thou art the Christ, the Son of the living God', addressed these solemn words: 'Blessed art thou, Simon Bar-Jona; because flesh and blood have not revealed it to thee, but my Father who is in heaven. And I say to thee that thou art Peter; and upon this rock I will build my Church, and the gates of hell shall not prevail against it. And I will give to thee the keys of the Kingdom of Heaven. And whatsoever thou shalt bind upon earth, it shall be bound also in heaven, and whatsoever thou shalt loose on earth, it shall be loosed also in heaven' *(Mt. 16:16ff)*.

373 And it was upon Simon Peter alone that Jesus after his resurrection bestowed the jurisdiction of Chief Pastor and Ruler over all his fold in the words: 'Feed my lambs; feed my sheep' *(John 21:15ff)*.

3054 At open variance with this clear doctrine of Holy Scripture, as it has ever been understood by the Catholic Church, are the perverse opinions of those who, while they distort the form of government established by Christ the Lord in his Church, deny that Peter in his single person, preferably to all the other apostles, whether taken separately or together, was endowed by Christ with a true and proper primacy of jurisdiction; or of those who assert that the primacy was not bestowed immediately and directly upon Blessed Peter himself, but upon the Church, and through the Church on Peter as her minister.

If any one, therefore, shall say that Blessed Peter the Apostle was not appointed the Prince of all the Apostles and the visible Head of the whole Church Militant; or that he directly and immediately received from the same our Lord Jesus Christ a primacy of honour only, and not of true and proper jurisdiction – *anathema sit.* 374 / 3055

Chapter II. The Perpetuity of the Primacy of Blessed Peter in the Roman Pontiffs

That which the Prince of Shepherds and great Shepherd of the Sheep, Jesus Christ our Lord, established in the person of the Blessed Apostle Peter to secure the perpetual welfare and lasting good of the Church, must, by the same institution, necessarily remain unceasingly in the Church, which, being founded upon a Rock, will stand firm to the end of the world. 'For none can doubt, and it is known to all ages, that the holy and blessed Peter, the Prince and Chief of the Apostles, the pillar of faith and foundation of the Catholic Church, received the keys of the kingdom from our Lord Jesus Christ, the Saviour and Redeemer of mankind, and lives, presides, and judges, to this day and always, in his successors the Bishops of the Holy See of Rome which was founded by him and consecrated by his blood' *(Council of Ephesus)*. 375 / 3056

Whence, whoever succeeds to Peter in this See, does by the institution of Christ himself obtain the primacy of Peter over the whole Church. 'The disposition made by Incarnate Truth before remains, and blessed Peter, abiding in the strength of the Rock that he received, has not given up the direction of the Church undertaken by him' *(Leo the Great)*. 'Wherefore it has at all times been necessary that every Church – that is to say, the faithful 376 / 3057 throughout the world – should agree with the Roman Church on account of its more powerful principality' *(Irenaeus)*; that in that See, from which the rights of communion flow forth to all, being associated as members with the head, they may grow together unto one compacted body.

377
3058 If, then, any one shall say that it is not by the institution of Christ the Lord, or by divine right, that Blessed Peter should have a perpetual line of successors in the primacy over the Universal Church; or that the Roman Pontiff is not the successor of Blessed Peter in this primacy – *anathema sit.*

Chapter III. The Power and Nature of the Primacy of the Roman Pontiff

378
3059 Wherefore, resting on plain testimonies of the Sacred Writings, and adhering to the plain and express decrees both of Our Predecessors, the Roman Pontiffs, and of the General Councils, We renew the definition of the Ecumenical Council of Florence, in virtue of which all the faithful of Christ must believe that the Holy Apostolic See and the Roman Pontiff possess the primacy over the whole world, and that the Roman Pontiff is the successor of Blessed Peter, Prince of the Apostles, and is true Vicar of Christ, and Head of the whole Church, and Father and Teacher of all Christians; and that full power was given to him in Blessed Peter to feed, rule, and govern the Universal Church by Jesus Christ our Lord; as is also contained in the acts of the General Councils and in the Sacred Canons'.

379
3060 Hence we teach and declare that by the appointment of our Lord the Roman Church possesses a *superiority of ordinary power* over all other Churches, and that this power of jurisdiction of the Roman Pontiff, which is truly

episcopal, is immediate; to which all, of whatever rite and dignity, both pastors and faithful, both individually and collectively, are bound by their duty of hierarchical subordination and true obedience, to submit, not only in matters which pertain to faith and morals, but also in those that pertain to the discipline and government of the Church throughout the world, so that the Church of Christ may be one flock under one supreme pastor through the preservation of unity both of communion and of profession of the same faith with the Roman Pontiff. This is the teaching of Catholic truth, from which no one can deviate without loss of faith and of salvation.

But so far is this power of the Supreme Pontiff from being any prejudice to the *ordinary and immediate power of episcopal jurisdiction*, by which bishops, who have been set by the Holy Spirit to succeed and hold the place of the Apostles, feed and govern, each his own flock, as true pastors, that this their episcopal authority is really asserted, strengthened and protected by the supreme and universal pastor; in accordance with the words of St Gregory the Great: 'My honour is the honour of the whole Church. My honour is the firm strength of my brethren. I am truly honoured, when the honour due to each and all is not withheld. 380 3061

Further, from this supreme power possessed by the Roman Pontiff of governing the Universal Church, it follows that he has the *right of free communication* with the pastors of the whole Church, and with their flocks, that these may be taught and ruled by him in the way of salvation. Wherefore we condemn and reject the opinions of those who hold that the communication between this supreme Head and the pastors and their flocks can lawfully be impeded; or who makes this communication subject to the will of the secular power, so as to maintain that whatever is done by the Apostolic See, or by its 3062 authority, for the government of the Church, cannot have force or value unless it be confirmed by the assent of the secular power.

381 And since by the divine right of apostolic primacy, the
3063 Roman Pontiff is placed over the Universal Church, We further teach and declare that he is the *supreme judge of the faithful,* and that in all causes the decision of which belong sto the Church, recourse may be had to his tribunal, and that none may re-open the judgment of the Apostolic See, than whose authority there is no greater, nor any lawfully review its judgment. Wherefore they err from the right path of truth who assert that it is lawful to appeal from the judgments of the Roman Pontifffs to an Ecumenical Council, as to an authority higher than that of the Roman Pontiff.

382 If then any one shall say that the Roman Pontiff has the
3064 office merely of inspection or direction, but not full and supreme power and jurisdiction over the Universal Church, not only in things pertaining to faith and morals, but also in those things that relate to the discipline and government of the Church spread throughout the world; or that he possesses merely the principal part, and not all the fulness of this supreme power; or that this power which he enjoys is not ordinary and immediate, both over each and all the Churches and all the pastors and the faithful – *anathema sit.*

Chapter IV. The Infallible Magisterium of the Roman Pontiff

383 Moreover, that the supreme power of teaching is also
3065 included in the apostolic primacy which the Roman Pontiff as the successor of Peter, Prince of the Apostles, possesses over the whole Church, this Holy See has always held, the perpetual practice of the Church confirms

and Ecumenical Councils have also declared, especially those in which the East met with the West in the union of faith and charity.

For the Fathers of the Fourth Council of Constantinople, following in the footsteps of their predecessors, gave forth this solemn profession: 'The first condition of salvation is to keep the rule of the true faith. And because the sentence of our Lord Jesus Chirst cannot be passed by who said: 'Thou art Peter, and upon this Rock I will build my Church', these things which have been said have been approved by events, because in the Apostolic See the Catholic religion has always been kept undefiled, and its holy doctrine proclaimed. Desiring, therefore, not to be in the least degree separated from the faith and doctrine of that See, we hope that we may deserve to be in the one communion which the Apostolic See preaches, in which is the entire and true solidity of the Christian religion.' And with the approval of the Second Council of Lyons, the Greeks professed that: 'The Holy Roman Church enjoys supreme and full primacy and pre-eminence over the whole Catholic Church, which it truly and humbly recognizes that it has received with the plenitude of power from our Lord himself in the person of Blessed Peter, Prince or Head of the Apostles, whose successor the Roman Pontiff is; and as the Apostolic See is bound before all others to defend the truth of faith, so also if any questions regarding faith shall arise, they must be defined by its judgment' *(Cf. No. 848)*.

Finally, the Council of Florence defined: 'The Roman Pontiff is the true Vicar of Christ, and the Head of the whole Church, and the Father and Teacher of all Christians; and that to him in Blessed Peter was delivered by our Lord Jesus Christ the full power of feeding, ruling, and governing the Universal Church' *(Cf. No. 349)*.

To satisfy this pastoral duty Our Predecessors ever made

3069 unwearied efforts that the salutary doctrine of Christ might be propagated among all the nations of the earth, and with equal care watched that it might be preserved genuine and pure where it had been received. Therefore the bishops of the whole world, now singly, now assembled in Synods, following the long-established custom of Churches and the form of the ancient rule, sent word to this Apostolic See of those dangers especially which sprang up in matters of faith, that the losses of faith might there be most effectually repaired where the faith cannot fail.

And the Roman Pontiffs, according to the exigencies of time and circumstances, sometimes assembling Ecumenical Councils, or asking for the mind of the Church scattered throughout the world, sometimes by particular Synods, sometimes using other helps which Divine Providence supplied, defined as to be held those things
3070 which with the help of God they had recognized as conformable with the Sacred Scriptures and Apostolic Traditions. For the Holy Spirit was not promised to the successors of Peter that by his revelation they might make known new doctrine, but that by his assistance they might inviolably keep and faithfully expound the revelation or deposit of faith delivered through the apostles.

386 And indeed *all the venerable Fathers have embraced*, and the holy orthodox Doctors have venerated and followed *their apostolic doctrine,* knowing most fully that this See of holy Peter remains ever free from all blemish of error according to the divine promise of the Lord our Saviour made to the Prince of his disciples: 'I have prayed for thee that thy faith fail not, and, when thou art converted, do thou confirm thy brethren' *(Luke 22:32).*

387 This gift, then, of truth and never-failing faith was con-
3071 ferred by Heaven upon Peter and his successors in this Chair that they might perform their high office unto the

salvation of all; that the whole flock of Christ, kept by them away from the poisonous food of error, might be nourished with the pasture of heavenly doctrine; that the occasion of schism being removed the whole Church might be kept one, and, resting on its foundation, might stand firm against the gates of hell.

But since in this very age, in which the salutary efficacy of the Apostolic Office is most of all required, not a few are found who take away from its authority, We judge it altogether necessary solemnly to assert the prerogative which the only-begotten Son of God vouchsafed to join with the supreme pastoral office. 3072

Definition of Papal Infallibility

Therefore, faithfully adhering to the tradition received from the beginning of the Christian faith, for the glory of God our Saviour, the exaltation of the Catholic religion, and the salvation of Christian peoples, the Sacred Council approving, We teach and define that it is a dogma divinely revealed: that the Roman Pontiff, when he speaks *ex cathedra*, that is, when in discharge of the office of Pastor and Doctor of all Christians, by virtue of his supreme apostolic authority he defines a doctrine regarding faith or morals to be held by the Universal Church, by the divine assistance promised him in Blessed Peter, is possessed of that infallibility with which the Divine Redeemer willed that his Church should be endowed for defining doctrine regarding faith or morals: and that therefore such definitions of the Roman Pontiff are irreformable of themselves, and not from the consent of the Church. 388 3073 3074

But if any one – which God avert – presume to contradict this Our definition – *anathema sit*. 3075

COLLECTIVE DECLARATION BY THE GERMAN HIERARCHY AND ITS APPROVAL BY PIUS IX (1875)

The following document is important for its bearing on the question of the relationship between papal and episcopal power. After the Vatican Council Bismarck issued a circular dated 14 May 1872 in which he maintained that the Pope's direct and universal primacy of jurisdiction made bishops into mere executive organs of the pope, and that they were thus degraded to the status of mere officials. Against this view, the collective declaration of the German hierarchy was issued (January/February 1875). In an Apostolic Brief of 2 March 1875 Pope Pius IX approved in an unusually solemn form this teaching of the German hierarchy.

The Declaration

388a
3112
With respect to the decrees of the Vatican Council the Circular Despatch *(of Bismarck)* maintains: 'By these decisions the Pope has been placed in a position to take into his own hand the episcopal jurisdiction of every individual diocese and to substitute papal authority for that of the territorial bishops. Episcopal jurisdiction has been absorbed by papal jurisdiction'. 'The Pope no longer exercises as heretofore certain reserved rights, but the whole abundance of episcopal rights lies in his hand.' 'He has in theory replaced every individual bishop,' 'and in practice it depends upon him alone at any moment if he will set himself in their place in relation to the government'. 'The bishops are now nothing but his tools, his officials, without any responsibility of their own', 'as far as the government is concerned, they have become officials of a foreign sovereign', 'a sovereign, indeed, who by virtue of his infallibility is absolute, more so than any absolute monarch in the world.'

All these phrases are without foundation and directly at variance with the wording of the decisions of the Vatican Council and with their proper interpretation thereof repeatedly stated by the Pope, the Hierarchy and the representatives of Catholic science.

According to these decrees, the ecclesiastical power of jurisdiction of the pope is, in fact, a *potestas suprema, ordinaria et immediata* accorded by Jesus Christ the Son of God to the pope in the person of St Peter, the supreme power extending directly over the whole Church including individual dioceses and all the faithful to uphold the unity of the Church's faith, discipline and government, and by no means a mere competence consisting of reserved rights. 3113

This is no new doctrine, however, but a truth of the Catholic faith that has always been acknowledged and a well-known principle of Canon Law, a doctrine which the Vatican Council, in harmony with the declarations of earlier General Councils, renewed and confirmed in opposition to the heresies of the Gallicans, Jansenists and Febronians. According to this doctrine of the Catholic Church the Pope is the Bishop of Rome, not the bishop of any other town or diocese, not the Bishop of Cologne, nor of Breslau, etc. But as Bishop of Rome he is also Pope, i.e. pastor and head of the whole Church, head of all the bishops and all the faithful, and his papal power comes into force not in certain special cases but is always and everywhere valid and binding. In this position which he occupies the Pope has to see that every bishop fulfils the duties of his office, and where a bishop is prevented or other necessity demands, then the Pope has the right and duty, not as bishop of the diocese concerned but as Pope, to make proper dispositions for the administration of the diocese. All the States of Europe have, up to the present time, acknowledged this as belonging to the system of the Catholic Church and in their dealings with the Holy See have always treated its incumbent as the real head of the whole Catholic Church, of bishops as well as the faithful and never as the mere bearer of certain reserved rights.

3114 The decrees of the Vatican Council give no shadow of ground for the assertion that the Pope has by them become an absolute sovereign and, by virtue of his infallibility, 'more absolute than any absolute monarch in the world'. In the first place the domain of the Pope's ecclesiastical authority is essentially different from that in which the sovereignty of a secular monarch is exercised; and the full sovereignty of territorial princes in civil matters is never contested by Catholics. But, apart from that, the description of absolute monarch cannot be applied to the Pope even in relation to ecclesiastical matters, for he is subject to divine law and bound by the rules laid down by Christ for his Church. He cannot change the constitution given the Church by her divine founder in the way that a secular legislator can change a State constitution. In all essential points the constitution of the Church is based on divine ordinance and immune from any arbitrary human action.

3115 The episcopate exists by virtue of the same divine institution upon which the Papacy rests. It, too, has its rights and duties by virtue of the order set up by God himself. It is thus a complete misunderstanding of the Vatican decrees to say that by them 'episcopal jurisdiction has been absorbed by the papal', that 'he has replaced individual bishops', that bishops are 'tools of the Pope, his officials, with no responsibility of their own'. According to the permanent teaching of the Catholic Church, as it was also expressly declared by the Vatican Council, the bishops are not mere tools of the Pope, not just papal officials without any responsibilities of their own, but 'have been set by the Holy Spirit to succeed and hold the place of the Apostles, feed and govern, each his own flock, as true pastors' *(No. 380)*.

As to the assertion that by the Vatican decrees the bishops have become papal officials without any responsibility of their own, we can only deny it with all possible force. It is certainly not the Catholic Church in which the immoral and despotic axiom has found acceptance that the order of a superior frees one unconditionally from one's own responsibility.

Finally, the view that the Pope, 'by virtue of his infallibility, has become a completely absolute sovereign' rests on a totally mistaken conception of the dogma of papal infallibility. As the Vatican Council expressed it in clear and unambiguous words, and as is clear from the nature of the thing itself, it is restricted to being a property of the supreme teaching office of the papacy; this covers exactly the same area as the infallibility of the Church in general and is bound up with the doctrine contained in holy Scripture and in tradition and with the afore-mentioned definitions laid down by the Church's magisterium. As far as the Pope's dealing with secular powers are concerned, here has not been the slightest change. Since, therefore, the opinion that the relationship of Pope to bishops was altered by the Vatican decrees is seen to be entirely groundless, the conclusion drawn from this supposition, that the Pope's relations with governments were changed by the decrees, also loses all basis and foundation.

From Pius IX's Letter of 2 March 1875
...The clarity and firmness of your declaration leave

nothing to be desired and it can only be the occasion for Our most sincere congratulations. But the mischievous attempt by certain newspapers to restore the force of the despatch refuted by you by saying that your refutation is not to be believed because it is a weakening of the Council's decrees and does not correspond to the interpretation of the Holy See, obliges Us to make another more solemn declaration. We therefore reject this cunning and calumnious insinuation and suggestion. Your declaration gives the genuine Catholic doctrine, which is also that of the Holy Council and of this Holy See, defends it with illuminating and irrefutable reasoning, and sets it out so clearly that it is plain to any honest man that there is no innovation in the definitions attacked...

ARTICLES OF MODERNISM CONDEMNED BY POPE PIUS X (1907)

Of the various papal decrees of recent decades, we give here only the modernist articles condemned by Pope Pius X. They deal with the effects of the modernist system (cf. Note to No. 64) on the doctrine of the Church. Leo XIII's great encyclicals, especially Satis cognitum *(1896) are once more a systematic exposition of the Church's teaching, but they contain nothing essentially new or not covered by the Vatican Council schema (Nos. 358ff).*

[389] 3406 6. In the definition of truths, the teaching and the listening Church work together in such a way that there is nothing left to the teaching Church but to ratify the general conceptions of the listening Church.

[390] 3407 7. When the Church proscribes errors she cannot demand of the faithful that internal assent which they give to judgments made by themselves.

[391] 3452 52. It was foreign to the mind of Christ to found a Church to extend like a society over the world and to

endure throughout the long series of centuries. In Christ's mind the kingdom of heaven, and with it the end of the world, were already at hand.

53. The organic constitution of the Church is not unchangeable. Christian society, like human society, is subject to constant evolution. [392] 3453

54. Dogmas, sacraments, and hierarchy, both notionally and really, are nothing but interpretations and developments of the Christian conscience which have increased in external growth and completed the small seed lying hidden in the Gospel. [393] 3454

55. It never occurred to Simon Peter that he was called by Christ to the primacy of the Church. [394] 3455

56. The Roman Church became the head of all Churches not by the ordinance of divine Providence but as a result of mere political conditions. [395] 3456

FROM THE CODE OF CANON LAW (1917)

C. 222 § 1. There can be no Ecumenical Council which has not been called by the Roman Pontiff. 396

§ 2. It belongs to the same Roman Pontiff to preside over the Ecumenical Council in person or by others, to constitute and designate the matters to be treated by it and to establish the order of dealing with them, to transfer, adjourn or dissolve the Council and to confirm its decrees. 397

C. 227 Decrees of a Council have no definitive binding force unless they have been confirmed by the Roman Pontiff and promulgated by his command. 398

C. 1323 § 1. All things which are contained in the word of God whether in writing or in tradition and which are proposed by the Church either in a solemn decree or in her ordinary and universal magisterium for belief as being divinely revealed are to be believed with divine and catholic faith.

§ 2. The pronouncement of such a solemn decree pertains to an Ecumenical Council and to the Roman Pontiff speaking *ex cathedra*.

POPE PIUS XII's ENCYCLICAL
MYSTICI CORPORIS CHRISTI (1943)

We can give here only a few extracts from this most important encyclical (cf. Note to No. 334a), and we have chosen those whose contents were perhaps less clearly and understandably expressed in previous official doctrinal decrees. We have thus omitted equally important passages dealing with already defined truths, such as the primacy of the Pope, which are already clear enough. With this in mind we consider the following to be of special importance: the identification in modern Church usage of the Catholic Church with the Mystical Body of Christ (which is again required by Humani Generis*); the establishment of the requirements for real membership of the Church (as opposed to membership in* voto*); the demonstration that without prejudice to her juridical constitution and the 'offices' necessary to it, the charismatic also belongs to the Church; the unity of the Church of law and the Church of love in the true Church of Christ; the nature and significance of the episcopal office; the Holy Spirit as the 'soul' of the Church, a doctrine which is important in combating a naturalistic conception of the Church with too much emphasis on the sociological and juridical aspects.*

Church and 'Mystical Body'

398a And so to describe this true Church of Christ – which is the Holy, Catholic, Apostolic, Roman Church – there is no name more noble, none more excellent, none more divine, than 'the mystical Body of Jesus Christ', a name which blossoms like a flower from numerous passages of the sacred Scriptures and the writings of the Fathers. That the Church is a body we find asserted again and again in the Sacred Scriptures. 'Christ', says the Apostle, 'is the Head of the Body, the Church' *(Col. 1:18)*. Now if the Church is a body it must be something one and undivided, according to the statement of St Paul: 'Being many, we are one body in Christ' *(Rom. 12:5)*. And not only must it be one and undivided, it must also be something concrete and visible, as Our Predecessor of happy memory, Leo XIII, says in his encyclical *Satis Cognitum:* 'By the very fact of being a body the Church is visible'. It is therefore an aberration from divine truth to represent the Church as something intangible and invisible, as a mere 'pneumatic' entity joining together by an invisible link a number of communities of Christians in spite of their differences in faith...

Membership of the Church
Only those are to be accounted really[1] members of the Church who have been regenerated in the waters of baptism and profess the true faith, and have not cut themselves off from the structure of the Body by their own unhappy act or been severed therefrom, for very grave crimes, by the legitimate authority. 'For in one Spirit,' says the Apostle, 'we were all baptized into one body, whether Jews or Gentiles, whether bond or free' *(1 Cor. 12:13)*. Hence, as in the true community of the faithful there is but one Body, one Spirit, one Lord, and one baptism, so there can be only faith *(Eph. 4:5)* and therefore whoever refuses to hear the Church must,

398b
3802

---

1. This is in distinction from those who belong to the Church *'in voto'*, who with the necessary dispositions (faith and love) can attain salvation because they are 'related to the mystical Body of the redeemer by some unconscious yearning and desire' as this encyclical says later. (Cf. also Nos. 351, 365, 398g).

as the Lord commanded, be considered as the heathen and publican *(Mt. 18:17)*. It follows that those who are divided from one another in faith or government cannot be living in the one Body so described, and by its one divine Spirit.

The Charismatic in the Church

398c
3800 Moreover, just as in nature a body does not consist of an indiscriminate heap of members but must be provided with organs, that is, with members not having the same function yet properly coordinated, so the Church for this special reason merits to be called a body, because it results from a suitable disposition and coherent union of parts, and is provided with members different from one another and harmoniously compacted. And it is thus that the Apostle describes the Church: 'As in one body we have many members, but all the members have not the same office; so we, being many, are one body in Christ; and every one members one of another' *(Rom. 12:4)*.

3801 But it must not be supposed that this coordinated, or organic, structure of the Body of the Church is confined exclusively to the grades of the hierarchy, or – as a contrary opinion holds – that it consists only of 'charismatics', or persons endowed with miraculous powers; though these, be it said, will never be lacking in the Church. It is certainly true that those who possess the sacred power in this Body must be considered primary and principal members, since it is through them that the divine Redeemer himself has willed the functions of Christ as teacher, king and priest to endure through the ages. But when the Fathers of the Church mention the ministries of this Body, its grades, professions, states, orders and offices, they rightly have in mind not only persons in sacred orders, but also all cording to the institution to which they belong; also those who, though living in the world, actively devote themselves to spiritual or corporal works of mercy; and also those who are joined in chaste wedlock. Indeed it is to be observed, especially in present circumstances, that fathers and mothers and godparents, and particularly those among the laity who cooperate with the ecclesiastical hierarchy in spreading the kingdom of the divine Redeemer, hold an honoured though often an obscure place in the Christian society, and that they too are able, with the inspiration and help of God, to attain the highest degree of sanctity, which, as Jesus Christ has promised, will never be wanting in the Church...

But our divine Saviour himself also governs directly the society which he founded: for he reigns in the minds and hearts of men, bending and constraining even rebellious wills to his decree. 'The heart of the king is in the hand of the Lord; whithersoever he will he shall turn it' *(Prov. 21:1)*. And by this interior government he, 'the shepherd and bishop of our souls' *(1 Peter 2:25)*, not only cares for each individual but also watches over the whole Church: enlightening and fortifying her rulers so that they may faithfully and fruitfully discharge their functions; and (especially in circumstances of greater difficulty) raising up in the bosom of Mother Church men and women of outstanding sanctity to give example to other Christians and so promote the increase of his mystical Body. Moreover, Christ looks down from heaven always with singular love upon his immaculate Bride as she labours in this earthly exile, and when he sees her in peril he saves her from the waves of the tempest, either directly himself or through his angels, or through her whom we invoke as Help of Christians, and through other those who have embraced the evangelical counsels and lead either an active life among men or a hidden life in the cloister, or else contrive to combine the two, ac- heavenly protectors; and having calmed the sea, he consoles her with that peace 'which surpasses all understanding'.

The Juridical Church and the Church of Love

398d We therefore deplore and condemn also the calamitous error which invents an imaginary Church, a society nurtured and shaped by charity, with which it disparagingly contrasts another society which it calls juridical. Those who make this totally erroneous distinction fail to understand that it was one and the same purpose – namely that of perpetuating on this earth the salutary work of the Redemption – which caused the divine Redeemer both to give the community of human beings founded by him the constitution of a society perfect in its own order, provided with all its juridical and social elements, and also, with that same end in view, to have it enriched by the Holy Spirit with heavenly gift and powers. It is true that the eternal Father wished it to be the 'kingdom of the Son of his love' *(Col. 1:13)*, but he willed it to be a true kingdom, one, that is, in which all believers would yield the complete homage of their intellect and will, and with humble and obedient hearts be likened to him who for us 'became obedient unto death' *(Phil. 2:8)*. Hence there can be no real opposition or incompatibility between the invisible mission of the Holy Spirit and the juridical office which pastors and teachers have received from Christ. Like body and soul in us, the two realities are complementary and perfect one another, both having their origin in our one and the same Saviour who not only said as he breathed the divine Spirit on the Apostles, 'Receive ye the Holy

Ghost,' *(John 20:22)* but also enjoined aloud, 'As the Father hath sent me, I also send you' *(John 20:21)*, and again, 'He that heareth you heareth me' *(Luke 10:16)*.

The Episcopate

What We have said here of the Universal Church must be said also of the particular communities of Christians, Eastern and Latin, of which the one Catholic Church is composed; for these also are governed by Jesus Christ through the voice and authority of their respective bishops. Therefore the bishops are not only to be regarded as more eminent members of the Universal Church, by reason of the truly unique bond which unites them with the divine Head of the whole Body and so makes them indeed the 'primary parts of the members of the Lord' *(Gregory the Great)*, but each of them is also, so far as his own diocese is concerned, a true Pastor who tends and rules in the name of Christ the flock committed to his care. In discharging this function, however, they are not completely independent but are subject to the proper authority of the Roman Pontiff, although they enjoy ordinary power of jurisdication received directly from the Sovereign Pontiff himself. The people must therefore venerate them as successors of the Apostles by divine institution; and to bishops, graced as they are with the chrism of the Holy Spirit, more than to the greatest of earthly rulers, we must apply the words, 'Touch not my anointed' *(1 Paral. 16:22)*. 398e 3804

The Holy Spirit the Soul of the Mystical Body

The Spirit of Christ is the invisible principle to which we must also attribute the union of all parts of the Body with one another and with their exalted Head, 398f 3808 dwelling as he does whole in the Head, whole in the Body, and whole in each of its members, and assisting these with this presence in divers manners according to their various functions and duties and their higher or lower degree of spiritual perfection. He, with his heavenly breath of life, is the source from which proceeds every single vital and effective salutary action in all the parts of the Body. It is he himself who is present in all the members, and divinely acts in each, through he also acts in the lower members through the ministry of the higher. And, finally, it is he who, while by the inspiration of his grace giving ever new increase to the Church, refuses to dwell by sanctifying grace in members who are completely severed from the Body. This presence and operation of the Spirit of Christ has been vigorously and compendiously described by Our wise Predecessor of immortal memory, Leo XIII, in the following words: 'It is enough to state that, since Christ is the Head of the Church, the Holy Spirit is her soul.'

If, however, this vital source and power, through which the whole community of Christians is upheld by its Founder, is viewed not in itself but in the created effects which proceed from it, then it consists in those heavenly gifts which our Redeemer together with his Spirit bestows upon the Church, and of which he, giver of supernatural light and cause of sanctity, together with his Spirit is the author. Thus the Church, as well as all her holy members, may make her own the eloquent words of the Apostle: 'I live, now not I; but Christ liveth in me'. *(Gal. 2:20)*.

LETTER OF THE HOLY OFFICE TO THE ARCHBISHOP OF BOSTON (1949)

On the 8 August 1949 the Holy Office sent Archbishop Cushing of Boston, Mass. a letter intervening decisively in the 'Boston Heresy Case' (Leonard Feeney). About this time there had been considerable controversy in America over the meaning and application of the axiom Extra Ecclesiam nulla Salus, *in other words of the necessity of Church membership for salvation. (The full Latin text appears in print only in the* American Ecclesiastical Review *77 (1952) pp. 307ff, but Denzinger gives the main body in 3866–73). This letter, of which the most important extracts are given below, is notable not only because it emphasizes once more the ancient doctrine of the necessity of the Church for salvation, as up till then it had been set out not only by theologians but also by the Church's magisterium. It also lays down in a manner up till then unknown in doctrinal utterances the extent to which a* votum Ecclesiae *is absolutely necessary: this* votum *can also be* implicit *in the good intention to act according to God's will, whereby, of course, further explanation will state that such a* votum *only brings justification when it is informed by supernatural faith and supernatural love.*

Among those things that the Church has always preached and will never cease to preach is also that infallible article by which we are taught 'outside the Church there is no salvation'. This dogma is, however, to be understood in the sense in which the Church herself understands it... In the first place the Church teaches that in this we are dealing with a most strict *command* of Jesus Christ... But among the commands of Christ not the lowest place is occupied by that whereby we are ordered to be incorporated by baptism in the mystical Body of Christ, which is the Church, and to adhere to Christ and his vicar through whom he himself governs the Church in a visible manner. No-

398g
3866

3867

body, therefore, will be saved who, knowing the Church to have been divinely instituted by Christ, refuses to submit to her or who refuses obedience to the Roman Pontiff, the vicar of Christ on earth.

3868 But the Saviour did not only give the commandment that all peoples should enter the Church, he also established that the Church is the *means of salvation* without which no one is able to enter the kingdom of heavenly glory.

3869 In his infinite mercy God wished that the effects of this necessary means of salvation, ordained by divine ordinance but not by intrinsic necessity to *(man's)* final end, could also be obtained in certain circumstances when they are applied only *in voto* or by desire. Which we see defined in clear words by the holy Council of Trent concerning both the sacrament of regeneration and that of penance *(Cf. Nos. 713, 732).*

3870 The same must be said, in its way, about the Church as a general aid to salvation. For someone to obtain eternal salvation it is not always demanded that he is in fact *(reapse)* incorporated as a member of the Church, but what is absolutely required is that he should adhere to it by wish and desire. This wish *(votum)* need not always be explicit, as in the case of catechumens, but where a man labours under invincible ignorance God also accepts an *implicit wish*, as it called, for it is contained in that good disposition of the soul whereby a man wishes to conform his will to the will of God.

3871 *(Here there are two passages from* Mystici Corporis Christi *No. 398a quoted and commented).*

3872 With these provident words he *(Pius XII)* reproves those who exclude from eternal salvation those who adhere to the Church by implicit wish alone, and also those who falsely assert that men can equally well be saved in any religion *(Cf. No. 351)*. But it is not to be thought that any sort of wish to enter the Church is sufficient for a man to be saved. It is required that the wish whereby someone is directed to the Church should be informed by *perfect charity (Cf. Nos. 722, 746, 749–51);* nor can an implicit *votum* have effect unless the man has supernatural faith *(Cf. Heb. 11:6; and No. 722).*

POPE PIUS XII's ENCYCLICAL *HUMANI GENERIS* (1950)
(Cf. Note to No. 74a)

The following extract from Humani Generis *is important for a variety of reasons. It brings out once more the ancient teaching (Cf. No. 353) that the theologian as such must give his inner assent to the teaching of the Church's magisterium and allow himself to be guided by it in his studies, not only where a solemn definition or the particular nature of the teaching of the ordinary magisterium requires a real assent of faith to divine and Catholic belief, but also where the Church speaks bindingly in other, not definitive, doctrinal writings. This applies also when what has been an open controversy among theologians up till then is closed but without definition.*

Of equal importance is the other passage quoted here which emphasizes that theology has not come to an end, that Bible theology and positive historical theology do not just demonstrate that the Church's teaching today is a legitimate formulation of Bible doctrine and ancient tradition but both these sciences have to maintain theology as a living science by constantly referring back to the sources, for Scripture is an inexhaustible fountain, far from being exhausted by traditional theology, which alone can prevent all speculation from succumbing to formalistic sterility.

Theology and Magisterium

398h Unfortunately these innovators are easily led on from contempt of scholastic theology into forgetting or even despising the Authority of the Church itself, which has so committed itself to the theology in question. Authority, by their way of it, is a drag on progress, is a bar to the development of science; there are some non-Catholics who think of it as a bridle, which forcibly restrains some few enlightened theologians from revolutionizing the whole system they teach. Is not this Authority a sacred trust, an exact and all-embracing standard of measurement which every theologian must use? Has not our Lord Christ committed to it the task of guarding, preserving, interpreting the whole deposit of faith, not only Sacred Scripture, but the tradition which is no less divine in origin? Have not the faithful a duty of shunning even those errors which approximate, in a more or less degree, to heresy, and therefore of 'obeying even those regulations and decrees by which the Holy See stigmatizes such false opinions, and forbids the propagation of them'? (C.I.C. can. 1324; cf. Conc. Vat. D.B. 1820, Const. *De Fide cath.* cap. 4, *De fide et ratione*, post canones.) Yet the very existence of such a duty sometimes goes unremarked. Let Roman Pontiffs write encyclicals as they will about the nature and constitution of the Church, there are some who are determined to take no notice; they aim at giving currency, instead, to certain vague ideas on the subject, derived (as they claim) from the ancient Fathers, the Greek Fathers particularly. The Popes, they will tell you, have no intention of deciding upon questions which are in dispute among theologians we must go back to primitive sources, and interpret these new decrees, these new regulations, in the light of what was written long ago.

Adroit reasoning, but there is a fallacy in it. It is quite true as a general principle that the Popes give theologians full liberty of speculation over questions which are variously answered by doctors of repute. But history teaches us that many propositions which were at one time freely discussed, have afterwards been settled beyond the possibility of dispute.

Nor is it to be supposed that a position advanced in an encyclical does not, *ipso facto*, claim assent. In writing them, it is true, the Popes do not exercise their teaching authority to the full. But such statements come under the day-to-day teaching of the Church, which is covered by the promise, 'He that heareth you, heareth Me' *(Luke 10:16)*. For the most part the positions advanced, the duties inculcated, by these encyclical letters are already bound up, under some other title, with the general body of Catholic teaching. And when the Roman Pontiffs go out of their way to pronounce on some subject which has hitherto been controverted, it must be clear to everybody that, in the mind and intention of the Pontiffs concerned, this subject can no longer be regarded as a matter of free debate among theologians.

True again, that a theologian must constantly be having recourse to the fountains of divine revelation. It is for him to show how and where the teaching given by the Living Voice of the Church is contained in Scripture and in our sacred tradition, 'be it explicitly, or implicitly, to be found there.' (Pius IX, *Inter gravissimas*, 28 Oct. 1870, *Acta*, vol. I, p. 260). This twofold spring of doctrine divinely made known to us contains, in any case, treasures so varied and so rich that it must ever prove inexhaustible. That is why the study of these hallowed sources gives the sacred sciences a kind of perpetual youth; avoid the labour of probing deeper and deeper yet into the sacred deposit, and your speculations – experience shows it – grow barren. All that is true, but for that very reason theology, even what is called positive theology, must not be put on a level with the merely historical sciences. Side by side with these hallowed sources God has given His Church a Living Voice; thus He would make clear to us, unravel for us, even what was left obscure in the deposit of faith, and only present there implicitly. The task of interpreting the deposit aright was not entrusted by our Divine Redeemer to the individual Christian, not even to the individual theologian; it was the Church's teaching that must be decisive. And when the Church exercises this privilege, as it often has in past ages, whether it be exercised in the way of routine or upon some special occasion, it is plainly wrong to treat its decisions as these people do. They actually use what is obscure to explain what is lucidly clear; as if the opposite procedure did not plainly impose itself on all minds! No wonder that Our predecessor of undying memory, Pius IX, in laying it down that the tracing of the Church's defined doctrines to their source was the noblest office of theology, added certain words of grave but necessary warning; 'in no other sense,' he wrote, 'than that in which they have been defined by the Church.'

THE VENERATION OF SAINTS

The veneration of the saints arises naturally from a lively awareness of the community which binds all those who have been redeemed to Christ their head and to each other. It gives rise to a reciprocal relationship of intercession, merit and satisfaction

It is also an historical fact that the loss of sense of ecclesiality, the dissolution as it were of the Communion of Saints, and the preaching of a purely interior religion have always led to a protest against the Church's veneration of the saints. So it was with Wycliffe, and even more with the Reformers. That is why we have to thank the Council of Trent, which concerned itself with the errors of the Reformers, for the most detailed exposition of Church doctrine on the subject of the Catholic veneration of saints and on relics and pious images. The Council, while on the one hand combatting the errors of the Reformers, did not neglect to speak out against the abuses which had crept in and caused misconception of the real meaning of this form of devotion.

The Church encourages the veneration of Saints (400, 403, 404, 855), and relics (399, 401, 403, 855) and images of saints (399, 402, 403, 855).

Veneration of images was in particular taken under the Church's protection by the Second General Council of Nicaea (787) against the Iconoclasts in the Eastern Roman Empire. This decree is, however, too greatly historically conditioned and is not included here.

THE GENERAL COUNCIL OF CONSTANCE (1414–18)
(Cf. Note to No. 343)

QUESTIONS TO BE PUT TO WYCLIFFITES AND HUSSITES

399
1269
29 Whether he believes and asserts that it is lawful for the faithful of Christ to venerate the relics and images of the Saints.

THE GENERAL COUNCIL OF TRENT, TWENTY-FIFTH SESSION (1563)
(Cf. Note to No. 606)

ON THE INVOCATION, VENERATION, AND RELICS OF SAINTS AND ON SACRED IMAGES

Veneration of Saints

400
1821
The Holy Council commands all bishops and others who hold the office of teaching and have charge of the cure of souls that, in accordance with the usage of the Catholic and Apostolic Church received from the primitive times of the Christian religion, and with the unanimous teaching of the holy Fathers and the decrees of sacred Councils, they above all instruct the faithful diligently in matters relating to *intercession and invocation of the Saints,* the veneration of relics, and the legitimate use of images, teaching them that the saints who reign together with Christ offer up their prayers to God for men, that it is good and beneficial suppliantly to invoke them and to have recourse to their prayers, assistance and support in order to obtain favours from God through his Son, Jesus Christ our Lord, who alone is our redeemer and saviour; and that they think impiously who deny that the saints who enjoy eternal happiness in heaven are to be

invoked, or who assert that they do not pray for men, or that our invocation of them to pray for each of us individually is idolatry, or that it is opposed to the word of God and inconsistent with the honour of the 'one mediator of God and men, Jesus Christ' *(1 Tim. 2:5)*, or that it is foolish to pray vocally or mentally to those who reign in heaven.

Veneration of Relics
Also, that the *holy bodies of the holy martyrs* and of others living with Christ, which were the living members of Christ and the temple of the Holy Spirit, to be awakened by him to eternal life and to be glorified, are to be venerated by the faithful, through which many benefits are bestowed by God on men, so that those who maintain that veneration and honour are not due to the relics of the saints, or that these and other memorials are honoured by the faithful without profit, and that the places dedicated to the memory of the saints for the purpose of obtaining their aid are visited in vain, are to be utterly condemned, as the Church has long since condemned and now again condemns them. 401 1822

Veneration of Images
Moreover, that the images of Christ, of the Virgin Mother of God, and of the other saints are to be placed and retained especially in the churches and that due honour and veneration is to be given them; not, however, that any divinity or virtue is believed to be in them by reason of which they are to be venerated, or that something is to be asked of them, or that trust is to be placed in images, as was done of old by the Gentiles who placed their hope in idols; but because the honour which is shown them is referred to the prototypes which they represent, so that by means of the images which we kiss 402 1823

and before which we uncover our heads and prostrate ourselves, we adore Christ and venerate the saints whose likeness they bear. That is what was defined by the decrees of the Councils, especially the Second Council of Nicaea, against the opponents of images...

(Particular attention should be paid to the use of pictures to instruct in the mysteries of the redemption. They remind the faithful of God's gifts and set salutary examples before their eyes. But any abuses that might lead to false conceptions in matters of faith must be removed.)

FROM THE CODE OF CANON LAW

403 *The Veneration, of Saints, Holy Images and Relics*
C. 1276. It is good and profitable to invoke the aid of the Servants of God who reign together with Christ and to venerate their relics and images. All the faithful should honour with childlike devotion the Blessed Virgin Mary above all others.

404 C. 1277 § 1. Only those Servants of God are to be publicly venerated who by decree of the Church are ranked among the Saints or the Blessed.

CHAPTER NINE

THE SACRAMENTS

I THE SACRAMENTS IN GENERAL

The history of human salvation is the history of the way God came to man. The first step on this way was the bridging of the gulf separating God and man in the person of the one Mediator Jesus Christ and by his work of redemption. By means of his Church Christ makes his grace available to all. Only in this application of redemption to mankind is the redemptive action of Christ completed. The doctrine of the sacraments is the doctrine of the second part of God's way of salvation to us. It deals with the holy signs which Christ instituted as the vehicles of his grace.

The great mystery of the union in Christ of a human nature with the second Person of the Godhead is that the human actions and sufferings of Christ are divine actions and sufferings. The sacraments are a living continuation of this mystery. There are earthly, external signs here which, of themselves, could never acquire any supernatural significance, but the signs of the sacraments have been made by Christ into vehicles of his grace. They effect in men the grace for which Christ made them the sign.

So there are two fundamental ideas which constantly

recur in the Church's teaching, on the sacraments. First there is the Church's concern for these signs instituted by Christ, their number, and their proper preservation and administration; then the grace which Christ has for all time linked with these signs and which is communicated by them.

The second is the effect of the sacraments. They are the signs of Christ's work; the effectiveness of Christ's continuing work in his Church cannot be dependent on man's inadequacy. A sacrament, administered properly in the way established by Christ and with the proper intention, gives the grace it signifies. It is effective not by reason of the power of intercession of priestly prayer nor on account of the worthiness of the recipient, but solely by the power of Christ. The power of Christ lives in the sacraments. The effect of the sacrament is independent of the sinfulness or unworthiness of the minister. The Church has never tolerated any subjectivist qualification of the objective effectiveness of the sacraments ex opere operato. *This would ultimately be to conceive the way of salvation as being man's way to God and not God's way to man.*

The Church accordingly teaches:
There are seven sacraments *(408, 413, 845, 851)*. They were instituted by Christ *(413, 427, 428, 431)* and given to the Church to administer *(425, 426, 851)*. They are necessary for salvation *(416, 431, 437b)*.
The sacraments are the vehicles of grace *which they convey (408, 414, 417, 418, 429, 430, 537b)*. They are validly administered *by the carrying out of the sign with the proper intention (407, 410, 419, 420, 423, 703). Not all are equally qualified to administer all the sacraments (405, 422, 565). The validity of the sacrament is independent of the worthiness of the minister, 405, 406,*

The Sacraments

407, 424, 475, 565, 581).
Three sacraments imprint an indelible character *(411, 421, 432, 581).*
Sacramentals *are instituted by the Church and are effective by virtue of the Church's intercession (433). Institution and alteration of them is reserved to the Holy See (433).*

PROFESSION OF FAITH PRESCRIBED FOR WALDENSIANS – POPE INNOCENT III (1208)

This profession of faith was put to Durandus of Huesca when after his reconversion by St Dominic he came to Rome in 1208 to ask Pope Innocent III for a licence to preach. The profession is aimed at the errors of the time but was not intended to charge Durandus with ever having preached them. In particular the Albigensian and Waldensian heresies are condemned (Cf. Note to No. 170). These heresies professed to be fighting the worldliness and unworthiness of the clergy which they held responsible for the decay of religious life. In the process they confused the person with the office. One of their most crucial errors was the assertion that the validity of a sacrament was dependent on the worthiness of the minister.

405
193 We in no way reject sacraments which are celebrated in her *(the Church)* in cooperation with the inestimable and invisible power of the Holy Spirit even if they are administered by a sinful priest so long as the Church accepts him; nor do we depreciate ecclesiastical offices or blessings celebrated by him but accept them willingly as from one most worthy, for the wickedness of bishop or priest has no harmful effect on the baptism of a child or the consecration of the Eucharist or other ecclesiastical offices carried out for their subjects...

THE GENERAL COUNCIL OF CONSTANCE (1414–18)

Wycliffe's errors (Cf. Note to No. 343) *in sacramental doctrine were inspired by a passionate hatred of the clergy. John Hus (1370–1415) took over Wycliffe's ideas and spread them in Bohemia. After healing the schism, Church reform* and the campaign against these heresies were the most urgent tasks of the Council of Constance.

ERRORS OF WYCLIFFE CONDEMNED

4. If a bishop or a priest is in mortal sin he neither ordains, nor consecrates, nor transubstantiates, nor baptizes. [406] 1154

QUESTIONS TO BE PUT TO WYCLIFFITES AND HUSSITES

22. Whether he believes that a wicked priest, with due matter and form, and the intention of doing what the Church does, really transubstantiates, really absolves, really baptizes and really confers the other sacraments. 407 *1262*

THE GENERAL COUNCIL OF FLORENCE

DECREE FOR THE ARMENIANS (1439)

After the reunion with the Greeks, which remained ineffectual, the Armenians, too, found their way back to the Mother Church at the Council of Florence (22 November 1439). The Armenian delegates bound themselves to the Decretum pro Armeniis *which, after reciting the most important articles of faith from previous Councils and a series of ritual dispositions, contains the important section on the sacraments. It follows very closely St Thomas Aquinas's* On the Articles of Faith and the Sacraments of the Church.

This decree is not an infallible pronouncement, but equally it is not just a description of the administration of the sacraments in the Latin rite, nor is it 'unofficial'. It is indeed a declaration by the Church concerning the essential elements of the sacraments, though it carries no definitive and binding obligation. The question is an important one because here

(No. 625) in agreement with St Thomas the handing over to the ordinand of the chalice with the wine and the paten with the bread are part of the matter of the sacrament of order whereas the laying-on of hands by the bishop is now still, or once more (as it was in the early Church) the sacramental sign. (Cf. 644a).

...For the easier instruction of Armenians... we set out the truth of the sacraments of the Church in the following very brief formula.

1310 There are *seven sacraments* of the New Law, viz. baptism, confirmation, Eucharist, penance, extreme unction, order and matrimony. They are very different from the *sacraments of the Old Law*. For these latter did not confer grace but were only a figure of the grace to be conferred by the Passion of Christ; but our sacraments both *contain grace* and confer it on those who receive them worthily.

1311 The first five of these sacraments are ordained for the *personal spiritual perfection* of every man; the last two for the *government and increase of the whole Church*. For by baptism we are spiritually reborn; by confirmation we grow in grace and are strengthened in faith; reborn and strengthened, we are nourished by the divine food of the Eucharist. If by sin we incur disease of the soul, we are spiritually cured by penance; *(we are cured)* spiritually also, and in the body if it be for the benefit of the soul, by extreme unction; by order the Church is governed and multiplied spiritually, by matrimony it is corporally increased.

1312 All these sacraments are accomplished in three parts, viz. by things as the matter, by words as the form, and by the person of the minister conferring the sacrament with the intention of doing what the Church does. If one of these three should be lacking, the sacrament is not accomplished.

Among these sacraments there are three, baptism, confirmation and order, which impress a character on the soul, that is, and indelible sign which distinguishes them *1313* from the others. Whence they are not repeated in the same person. But the other four sacraments impress no character and admit of repetition...

THE GENERAL COUNCIL OF TRENT, SEVENTH SESSION (1547)

Following upon the doctrine of justification (cf. Nos. 412, 709ff) the Council set forth the teaching on the sacraments. After a brief foreword, the decree starts with thirteen canons dealing with the sacraments in general.
Canon 1, against Luther who could have limited their number to two or three, emphasizes that there are seven; against the Augsburg Confession which attributed confirmation and extreme unction to an apostolic institution, attributes them all to Christ.
Canons 4 and 5 are also directed against Luther who taught that the sacraments are only effective by the faith which they arouse.
Canons 10 and 11 are directed against Luther's teaching that since the sacraments are effective only through the faith of the recipient they are independent of the person or intention of the minister.

Foreword

For the completion of the salutary doctrine on justification which was promulgated with the unanimous consent of the Fathers in the last session it has seemed proper to deal with the most holy sacraments of the Church through which all true justice either begins or, being begun, is increased, or being lost, is restored. Wherefore in order to destroy the errors and extirpate the heresies which in our stormy times are directed against the most holy sacraments, some of which are a revival of heresies *412* *1600* long ago condemned by our Fathers, while others are of recent origin, all of which are exceedingly detrimental to the purity of the Catholic Church and the salvation of souls, the holy, ecumenical and general Council of Trent... adhering to the teaching of the Holy Scriptures, to the Apostolic traditions, and to the unanimous teaching of other Councils and of the Fathers, has thought it proper to establish and enact these present canons; hoping, with the help of the Holy Spirit, to publish later those that are wanting for the completion of the work begun.

Canons on the Sacraments in General

413　1. If any one shall say that the sacraments of the New
1601　Law were not all instituted by our Lord Jesus Christ, or that there are more or fewer than seven, namely, baptism, confirmation, Eucharist, penance, extreme unction, order and matrimony, or that any one of these seven is not truly and intrinsically a sacrament – *anathema sit.*

414　2. If any one shall say that these sacraments of the
1602　New Law do not differ from the sacraments of the Old Law, except that the ceremonies are different and the external rites different – *anathema sit.*

415　3. If any one shall say that these seven sacraments are
1603　so equal to each other that one is not for any reason more excellent than the other – *anathema sit.*

416　4. If any one shall say that the sacraments of the New
1604　Law are not necessary for salvation but are superfluous, and that without them or without the desire of them men obtain from God through faith alone the grace of justification, though all are not necessary for every individual – *anathema sit.*

417　5. If any one shall say that these sacraments have been
1605　instituted solely for the nourishment of faith – *anathema sit.*

6. If any one shall say that the sacraments of the New Law do not contain the grace which they signify, or that they do not confer that grace on those who place no obstacles in its way, as though they are only outward signs of grace or of justice received through faith and are but certain marks of Christian profession whereby among men believers are distinguished from unbelievers – *anathema sit*. 418 *1606*

7. If any one shall say that grace, so far as God's part is concerned, is not imparted through the sacraments always and to all men even if they receive them rightly, but only sometimes and to some persons – *anathema sit*. 419 *1607*

8. If any one shall say that by the sacraments of the New Law grace is not conferred *ex opere operato*, but that faith alone in the divine promise is sufficient to obtain grace – *anathema sit*. 420 *1608*

9. If any one shall say that in three sacraments, namely baptism, confirmation and order, there is not imprinted on the soul a character, that is, a certain spiritual and indelible mark, by reason of which they cannot be repeated – *anathema sit*. 421 *1609*

10. If any one shall say that all Christians have the power to administer the word and all the sacraments – *anathema sit*. 422 *1601*

11. If any one shall say that in ministers when they effect and confer the sacraments there is not required at least the intention of doing what the Church does – *anathema sit*. 423 *1611*

12. If any one shall say that a minister who is in mortal sin, though he observe all the essentials that pertain to the effecting on conferring of a sacrament, neither effects nor confers a sacrament – *anathema sit*. 424 *1612*

13. If any one shall say that the received and approved rites of the Catholic Church accustomed to be used in the administration of the sacraments may be despised or 425 *1613*

omitted by the ministers without sin and at their pleasure, or may be changed by any pastor of the churches to other new ones – *anathema sit.*

TWENTY-FIRST SESSION (1562)
DOCTRINE ON COMMUNION UNDER BOTH KINDS AND COMMUNION OF YOUNG CHILDREN

Chapter II. The Power of the Church Concerning the Dispensation of the Sacrament of the Eucharist

In its twenty-first session the Council dealt with the widely discussed question of the chalice for the laity (cf. Eucharist, No. 503). In the process the argument dealt with the breadth of power given by Christ to the Church to determine the ways and means of administering the sacraments. The results of this discussion are set out in Chapter II.

426
1728 *(The Holy Council)* **furthermore declares that in the dispensation of the sacraments, provided their substance is retained, the Church may, according to circumstances, times and places, determine or change whatever she may judge most expedient for the benefit of those receiving them or for the veneration of the sacraments; and this power has always been hers. The Apostle seems to have clearly intimated this when he said: 'Let a man so account of us as of the ministers of Christ, and the dispensers of the mysteries of God'** *(1 Cor. 4:1);* **and that he himself exercised this power, as in many other things, so in this sacrament, is sufficiently manifest, for after having given some instructions regarding its use, he says: 'The rest I will set in order when I come'** *(1 Cor. 11:34).* **Wherefore, ... Holy Mother Church, cognizant of her authority in the administration of the sacraments...**
(There follows the approval of Communion under one kind)

ARTICLES OF MODERNISM CONDEMNED BY POPE PIUS X (1907)

The Church's doctrine of the institution of the sacraments by Christ and their validity dependent on their administration as such were, for the Modernists, typical of the way religious forms established in the first centuries of Christianity came to stand on their own and be proposed as fixed dogmas by the Church's magisterium. (Cf. also Nos. 470 and 587ff).

39. The opinions on the *origin of the sacraments* with which the Tridentine Fathers were imbued and which undoubtedly influenced them in their dogmatic canons are far removed from those which now rightly obtain among historical investigators of Christianity. [427] 3439

40. The sacraments have their origin in this, that the Apostles and their successors took some idea and intention of Christ and interpreted it under the influence and pressure of circumstances and events. [428] 3440

41. The object of the Sacraments is only to recall to the mind of man the always beneficent presence of the Creator. [429] 3441

POPE PIUS X's ENCYCLICAL *PASCENDI* AGAINST MODERNISM (1907)

The errors of Modernists concerning the sacraments are very grave... Worship, they maintain, arises from a twofold impulse or necessity. One impulse is to make religion tangible, and the other is to make it visible, neither of which can ever be done without some visible form and acts of consecration, which we call sacraments. But for Modernists, sacraments are bare symbols or signs, although not lacking in force. To illustrate this force, they quote the example of words to which a certain virtue is ascribed because they are 430 3489 capable of arousing the imagination and moving the heart. As the words are to ideas, so are the sacraments to the religious sense – and nothing more. They would express it more clearly if they were to say that the sacraments were instituted solely to nourish faith. But this was condemned by the Council of Trent: 'If anyone shall say that these sacraments were instituted solely in order to nourish faith, *anathema sit.*'

FROM THE CODE OF CANON LAW (1917)
THE SACRAMENTS

431 C. 731 § 1. Since all the sacraments of the New Law were instituted by Christ our Lord as the principal means of our sanctification and salvation, the greatest care and respect must be paid to their profitable and proper ministry and reception.

432 C. 732 § 1. The sacraments of baptism, confirmation and order, which impress a special character, cannot be repeated.

SACRAMENTALS

433 C. 1144. Sacramentals are objects or actions which the Church uses in a certain imitation of the sacraments to obtain by their intercession certain effects, mainly spiritual.
C. 1145. Only the Holy See can introduce new sacramentals, make dispositions about those already introduced, or abolish or alter them.

II BAPTISM

Baptism is the sacrament that frees man from original sin and from personal guilt, that makes him a member of Christ and his Church. It is thus the door to a new and supernatural life.
This sacrament has been undisputed in the Church since the beginning of Christian tradition. It has never been rejected by any heresy intending to remain on a Christian basis. Doubts could arise only about the ways and means of administering it and on its effects and way of operation. These things are therefore in essence what Church documents about baptism deal with.

Baptism is a true sacrament *instituted by Christ (408, 413, 436, 440–2, 841, 845, 851). It is* administered *by washing with natural water and at the same time invoking the Most Holy Trinity (437, 441, 443, 456, 837d). Anybody, even an unbeliever or a heretic can validly administer baptism (438, 443, 457). Since it confers grace by the signs' being properly carried out (437) children can and should be baptized even while still infants (224, 434, 435, 451, 452, 455, 459). Baptism is* necessary *for salvation (223, 434, 436, 444, 454, 456, 713).*
Baptism effects *the remission of original sin and actual* sins *(217, 223, 224, 434, 435, 439, 558, 703, 704, 718, 831) and of all* punishment *due to sin (225, 439, 569, 732); it confers sanctifying* grace *(225, 409, 554, 718),* membership in Christ *(359, 398b, 436, 557) and in the* Church *and the obligation to obey the Church's laws (398b, 434, 436, 447, 453, 756, 757) and gives an indelible* character *(411, 421, 432, 434, 450, 458, 629, 644a, 851).*

LETTER OF POPE INNOCENT III TO YMBERTUS, ARCHBISHOP OF ARLES (1201)

The effect of Baptism

434
780
(The baptism of young children is not profitless. As circumcision made men members of the People of Israel, so baptism gives them entry to the kingdom of heaven).
Even though original sin was remitted by the mystery of circumcision and the danger of damnation avoided, it did not lead to the kingdom of heaven,... whose gates the blood of Christ mercifully opened to the faithful. Lest it be that all small children, of whom such a great multitude dies every day should perish, for them, too, the merciful God, who wishes no one to perish, has provided a way to salvation...

Original Sin and Actual Sin – Their Forgiveness
We distinguish two kinds of sin, original and actual; original, which is contracted without consent, and actual, which is committed with consent. Thus, original sin to which man is subject without his consent is remitted by the power of the sacrament; but actual sin which is committed with consent is by no means remitted without consent. Now, even if in baptism original sin is forgiven to a child who cannot give consent, to an adult who is deprived of reason or is asleep, unless he gives his assent to baptism, neither actual nor original sin is forgiven.
One might ask why adults who have lost their reason or are asleep should not at least have their original sin remitted by baptism, like small children. The answer to that is: the Lord who made man whole and entire on the sixth day knows no incomplete work. Therefore he does not forgive sins in part but in entirety.
Further, the punishment for original sin is the loss of

the Beatific Vision, but the punishment of actual sin is the torture of eternal hell.

The Free Nature of Baptism. Its Character
It is contrary to the Christian religion to compel anyone against his will and in spite of his refusal to receive and observe Christianity. Wherefore some, not without reason, distinguish between unwilling and unwilling, between coercion and coercion, because one who by force of terror and punishment is brought to accept the sacrament of baptism to avoid harm to himself, receives, as does one who comes feignedly to baptism, the character of Christianity impressed upon him and must therefore be held to the observance of the Christian faith since in the circumstances he did give his consent even if not unconditionally... But one who never gives his consent but absolutely refuses receives neither the effect nor the character of the sacrament. For express refusal is more than just witholding one's consent. *781*

POPE INNOCENT III's PROFESSION OF FAITH FOR WALDENSIANS (1208)
(Cf. Note to No. 405)

We therefore approve the *baptism of infants*. We profess and believe that if they die after baptism, before they have committed any sins, they are saved. In baptism, we believe all sins are forgiven, original sin and those committed voluntarily... *435*
794

THE GENERAL COUNCIL OF FLORENCE

DECREE FOR THE ARMENIANS (1439)
(Cf. Note to No. 408)

436
1314 The first place of all the sacraments is held by holy baptism, which is the gateway to the spiritual life; by it we are made members of Christ and the body of the Church. And since by the first man death came to all, unless we are reborn of water and the Spirit we cannot, as Truth said, enter into the kingdom of heaven *(John 3:5)*.

437
1314 The *matter* of this sacrament is true natural water; it is irrelevant whether it be hot or cold. The form is: I baptize thee in the name of the Father, and of the Son, and of the Holy Ghost. But we do not deny that true baptism can be administered with the words: 'May the servant of Christ, N, be baptized in the name of the Father, and of the Son, and of the Holy Ghost', or: 'By my hands N is baptized in the name of the Father, and of the Son, and of the Holy Ghost'. For as the principal cause from which baptism derives its virtue is the Holy Trinity, the *instrumental cause* is the minister who performs the externals of the sacrament. If, therefore, the action carried out by the minister is expressed in words, together with the invocation of the Holy Trinity, the sacrament is administered.

438
1315 The *minister* of this sacrament is the priest to whom it belongs by reason of his office to baptize. But in case of necessity not only may a priest or deacon baptize, but also a layman, or a woman, or even a pagan or a heretic, provided he adheres to the Church's form and intends to do what the Church does.

439
1316 The effect of this sacrament is the remission of all original and actual sin together with all punishment due

to that sin. Therefore no satisfaction for past sins is to be enjoined on persons baptized; but if they die before committing any sin they go straight to heaven and the Beatific Vision...

THE GENERAL COUNCIL OF TRENT, SEVENTH SESSION (1547)

CANONS ON THE SACRAMENT OF BAPTISM

Trent did not set out any doctrinal description of the sacrament of baptism but only condemned the errors that had become widespread. Nevertheless, these canons are of decisive importance for the Catholic doctrine of baptism.
Canon 4 contains the final definition of a doctrine which had been firmly held for centuries. From the earliest times the validity of 'heretical baptism' has been proof of the effectiveness of the sacraments in that it does not depend on the faith or worthiness of the minister but on the proper carrying out of Christ's commands.
Canon 6 is directed against Luther who said that the one sin whereby man lost justification was unbelief (cf. Nos. 733, 764).
Canon 14 is directed against Erasmus's 'liberal' conception.

1. If anyone shall say that the baptism of John had the same effect as the baptism of Christ – *anathema sit*. 440 1614
2. If anyone shall say that true and natural water is not necessary for baptism and thus twists into some metaphor the words of our Lord Jesus Christ, 'Unless a man be born again of water and the Holy Ghost' (John 3:5) – *anathema sit*. 441 1615
3. If anyone shall say that in the Roman Church, which is the mother and mistress of all churches, there is not the true doctrine concerning the sacrament of baptism – *anathema sit*. 442 1616
4. If anyone shall say that the baptism which is given by 443

1617	heretics in the name of the Father and of the Son and of the Holy Ghost with the intention of doing what the Church does is not true baptism – *anathema sit*.
444 1618	5. If anyone shall say that baptism is optional, that is, not necessary for salvation – *anathema sit*.
445 1619	6. If anyone shall say that one baptized cannot, even if he wishes, lose grace, however much he may sin, unless he is unwilling to believe – *anathema sit*.
446 1620	7. If anyone shall say that those baptized are by baptism obliged to faith alone but not to the observance of the whole law of Christ – *anathema sit*.
447 1621	8. If anyone shall say that those baptized are free from all the precepts of holy Church, whether written or unwritten, so that they are not bound to observe them unless they should wish to submit to them of their own accord – *anathema sit*.
448 1622	9. If anyone shall say that the remembrance of the baptism received is to be so impressed on men that they may understand that all the vows made after baptism are void in virtue of the promise already made in that baptism, as if by those vows they detracted from the faith which they professed and from the baptism itself, – *anathema sit*.
449 1623	10. If anyone shall say that by the sole remembrance and the faith of the baptism received all sins committed after baptism are either remitted or made venial – *anathema sit*.
450 1624	11. If anyone shall say that baptism, truly and rightly administered, must be repeated in one converted to repentance after having denied the faith of Christ among the infidels – *anathema sit*.
451 1625	12. If anyone shall say that no one is to be baptized except at the age at which Christ was baptized, or on the point of death – *anathema sit*.
452	13. If anyone shall say that children, because they have not

the act of believing, are not after receiving baptism to be numbered among the faithful, and that for this reason they are to be re-baptized when they have reached years of discretion; or that it is better that the baptism of such be omitted than to baptize in the faith of the Church alone those who do not believe by their own act – *anathema sit*.   *1626*

14. If anyone shall say that those who have thus been baptized as children are, when they have grown up, to be asked whether they will ratify what their sponsors promised in their name when they were baptized, and if they answer that they will not, are to be left to their own will; nor are they to be compelled in the meantime to a Christian life by any penalty other than exclusion from reception of the Eucharist and the other sacraments until they repent – *anathema sit*.   453 *1627*

MODERNIST ARTICLES CONDEMNED BY POPE PIUS X (1907)

The articles condemned here by Pius X are a part of the Modernists' attempt to explain the Catholic faith as a development of community life (Cf. Note to No. 64).

42. The Christian community introduced the necessity of baptism, adopting it as a necessary rite and attaching to it the obligations of Christian profession.   [454] *3442*

43. The custom of conferring baptism on infants was a disciplinary development which is one of the reasons why the sacrament resolved into two, baptism and penance.   [455] *3443*

FROM THE CODE OF CANON LAW (1917)

C. 737. § 1. Baptism, the gateway and foundation of the sacraments is for all men necessary, really or by   456 intention, for their salvation. It is validly administered only by washing with true, natural water joined with the prescribed form of words.

457 C. 742 § 1 Without solemn form... baptism can be administered by anyone whomsoever who uses the proper matter and form and has the right intention.

458 C. 745 § 1 Every person in this life who has not yet been baptized is able to be baptized, but no one else.

459 C. 770 § 1 Children should be baptized as early as possible...

III CONFIRMATION

The sacrament of confirmation completes the sacrament of baptism. If baptism is the sacrament of re-birth to a new and supernatural life, confirmation is the sacrament of maturity and coming of age. The real confession of Christ consists in this, 'that the whole man submits himself to Truth, in the judgment of his understanding, in the submission of his will and in the consecration of his whole power of love... To do this, poor-spirited man is only able when he has been confirmed by God's grace' (Bonaventure, Breviloqium *VI, 8).*

This confirmation in the power of the Holy Spirit leading to a firm profession of faith has always been the particular effect *which Catholic tradition has ascribed to the sacrament. It is an effect which complements and completes that of baptism.*

About confirmation the Church teaches:
It is a true sacrament *instituted by Christ (408, 413, 467, 845, 851) and different from baptism (470).*
It is administered *by laying-on of hands and anointing with chrism accompanied by prayer (464, 471, 845). The chrism is blessed by the bishop (460, 464,) and the bishop administers the sacrament (461–3, 465, 469, 472, 845). All baptized persons can and should be confirmed (473). The* effect *of the sacrament of confirmation is to* give strength *in faith and for the confession of faith (409, 466) and to impress an indelible character (411, 421, 432, 629, 851).*

POPE CLEMENT VI's LETTER ON ARMENIAN REUNION (1351)

After a somewhat chequered history, the Armenians were indeed in union with the Mother Church in Rome from 1198 to 1375. Nevertheless the Popes several times wished to assure themselves of their true faith which was variously, and mostly falsely, impugned. So it was that on 29 September 1351 Clement VI sent to the Catholicos Mekhithar (= comforter) a letter containing seventy-four carefully worked out theological questions including some on the sacraments and purgatory.

460 *(I am led to ask you...)*

1068 1. On the blessing of chrism: dost thou believe that chrism can properly and duly be blessed by no priest who is not a bishop?

461 2. Dost thou believe that the sacrament of confirmation
1069 cannot ordinarily be administered ex officio by anyone other than a bishop?

462 3. Dost thou believe that a dispensation to administer
1070 confirmation can be given to priests who are not bishops only by the Roman Pontiff who has the fulness of power?

463 4. Dost thou believe that those who have been anointed
1071 by priests who are not bishops and have not received a commission or concession from the Roman Pontiff in this matter are to be confirmed again by a bishop or bishops?

GENERAL COUNCIL OF FLORENCE

DECREE FOR THE ARMENIANS (1439)
(Cf. Note to No. 408)

...The second sacrament is *confirmation;* of which the *matter* is chrism made of oil, which symbolizes purity of conscience, and balsam whose perfume signifies good repute, blessed by the bishop. The *form* is: 'I sign thee with the sign of the cross and I confirm thee with the chrism of salvation, in the name of the Father, and of the Son, and of the Holy Ghost.' 464 / 1317

The *ordinary minister* is the bishop. Whereas other anointings[1] may be conferred by a simple priest, this may not be conferred except by the bishop. For it is of the Apostles alone, whose place is held by the bishops, that we read that they gave the Holy Spirit by the laying-on of hands, as a reading of the Acts of the Apostles shows: 'Now when the Apostles, who were in Jerusalem, had heard that Samaria had received the word of God, they sent unto them Peter and John. Who, when they were come, prayed for them, that they might receive the Holy Ghost. For he was not as yet come upon any of them; but they were only baptized in the name of Jesus Christ. Then they laid their hands upon them, and they received the Holy Ghost' *(Acts 8:14-17)*. In place of this laying-on of hands the Church has confirmation. But there are also accounts of how for reasonable and urgent cause simple priests, by virtue of permission from the Apostolic See, administered the sacrament of confirmation with chrism prepared by the bishop. 465 / 1318

The *effect* of this sacrament is that in it the Holy Spirit is given for strength, as he was given to the Apostles on 466 / 1319

---

1. Baptism and extreme unction.

the day of Pentecost, so that the Christian may courageously confess the name of Christ. Therefore the confirmand is anointed on the forehead which is the seat of shame so that he shall not blush for the name of Christ and especially his Cross, which is a stumbling block for the Jews and foolishness for the Gentiles *(1 Cor. 1:23)* according to the Apostle; wherefore he is signed with the sign of the Cross...

THE GENERAL COUNCIL OF TRENT, SEVENTH SESSION (1547)

CANONS ON THE SACRAMENT OF CONFIRMATION

The teaching of the Council of Trent on the sacrament of confirmation is limited to the following three canons which teach, mainly in opposition to Luther, Melancthon and Calvin, the real sacramental character of confirmation and its institution by Christ (The Augsburg Confession taught that it was instituted by the Apostles). Melancthon in particular had turned the sacrament into no more than a solemn confession of belief (cf. 467).

Canon 3 lays down who is the ordinary minister of confirmation, the bishop, but is not directed against the Greeks among whom, with the tacit consent of the Church authorities, it is usually administered by priests.

467
1628
1. If anyone shall say that the confirmation of those baptized is an empty ceremony and not a true and proper sacrament; or that of old it was nothing more than a sort of instruction in which those approaching adolescence gave an account of their faith before the Church – *anathema sit.*

468
1629
2. If anyone shall say that those who ascribe any power to the holy chrism of confirmation offer insults to the Holy Spirit – *anathema sit.*

3. If anyone shall say that the ordinary minister of holy confirmation is not the bishop alone but any simple priest – *anathema sit.* 469
1630

ARTICLES OF MODERNISM CONDEMNED BY PIUS X (1907)

From liberal Protestant ideas of the history of dogma, particularly from Harnack, the Modernists adopted the notion that confirmation was originally a part of the rite of baptism and only developed later into a sacrament on its own.

44. There is no proof that the rite of the sacrament of confirmation was used by the Apostles; the formal distinction of two sacraments, namely baptism and confirmation, is unknown in the history of primitive Christianity.   [470]
3444

FROM THE CODE OF CANON LAW (1917)

C.780 The sacrament of confirmation must be administered by laying-on of hands with the anointing of the forehead with chrism and with the words prescribed in pontificals approved by the Church.   471

C. 782 § 1. The ordinary minister of confirmation is the bishop alone.   472

§ 2. An extraordinary minister is the priest to whom this faculty has been granted by the Holy See either as a general or a special right.

C. 786. One not baptized with water cannot be validly confirmed. In addition, for someone to be lawfully and profitably confirmed he must be in a state of grace and, if he has reached the age of reason, be adequately instructed.   473

IV THE EUCHARIST

The doctrine of the holy Eucharist consists of that of the eucharistic sacrifice, *the sacrificial* meal, *and the sacrificial food, or to express it otherwise, it consists of the doctrine of the Mass, of Communion, and of the Real Presence. There is no presence of Christ in the Blessed Sacrament that is not meant first and foremost as food for the faithful people, and there is no sacramental union with Christ in Holy Communion that is not to be thought of as a sacrificial meal: 'For as often as you shall eat this bread, and drink the chalice, you shall show the death of the Lord, until he come'* (1 Cor. 11:26). *The eucharistic meal can only be prepared in the sacrifice of the Mass.*

Thus the mystery of the Eucharist summarizes the whole mystery of our redemption. There are two fundamental relationships *in which Christ stands to us. First, he is our* priestly mediator with God, *and offers him atonement for our sins. But Christ is not a stranger to us, who merely represents us as a propitiator before God. He comes to us in the second relationship by being the mediator of the grace which God gives us on account of his sacrifice. That is the mystery of our union with Christ who is the* source of all grace *for us. 'And of his fulness we have all received, grace for grace'* (John 1:16)

This second community is realized only in the sacrifice of the Cross, *by his giving his life for his Church which he had to ransom for himself. Only in death did Christ seal the deep covenant with the Church whereby she is purified and sanctified and which according to the teaching of St Paul is the image of the most intimate union of human* beings in marriage: 'Husbands, love your wifes, as Christ also loved the Church, and delivered himself up for it; that he might sanctify it, cleansing it by the laver of water in the word of life' (Eph. 5:25f). From the opened side of our crucified Saviour the Church was first born, as Eve was taken from Adam's side. That is the most ancient way of expressing this truth.

This twofold relationship, then, in which Christ stands to us men, as our mediator before God and the bringer of all graces from God, lives on in the mystery of the Eucharist. The Holy Mass is the renewing of the sacrifice which Christ offered for us, of the sacrifice of atonement for our sins; but the sacrifice is also at the same time the preparation of the eucharistic meal, the sacrament of our union with Christ in grace.

We should not be surprised if the doctrine of the real presence of Christ in the Blessed Sacrament occurs more than most doctrines in the documents of the Church. There are few mysteries of the faith where the mystery is so evident and therefore so exposed to the attacks of heresy and unbelief. However, the militant position of the Church should not prevent us from seeing the Real Presence in the context of the whole eucharistic mystery.

The doctrine of the Holy Eucharist is thus made up of:
1. Doctrine about the eucharistic sacrifice.
Holy Mass is a real sacrifice *(512, 513, 521, 530, 853)*, instituted by Christ at the Last Supper *(512, 522)*. It represents Christ's sacrifice of the Cross *(315, 512)*, but in an unbloody manner *(514)*. Priest and victim are both Christ, who offers himself through the priest *(512, 514)*. The laity also offers the sacrifice, but does not have the power to transubstantiate *(644a)*.

The eucharistic sacrifice is offered to God *in praise, thanksgiving, petition and atonement (514, 515, 523),* for the living and the dead *(514, 523, 853)*. Saints may also be commemorated in honour and petition *(515, 525)*. The Church has the responsibility of determining the rites and prayers to be observed *(516–20, 526–9)*. The liturgy as a whole is the public worship by the mystical Body of Christ *(537a)*. In every liturgical activity Christ is present, in a manner that must be properly interpreted *(537b)*.

2. *Doctrine about the eucharistic sacrament, sacrificial meal and sacrificial food:*

The Holy Eucharist is a true sacrament *(408, 413, 845, 851)* instituted by Christ *(484)*. Christ is really present in the Holy Eucharist *(339, 474, 475, 477, 483, 492, 499, 530, 853)* even when not being received *(486, 495)*. It is therefore to be honoured and adored *(488, 497, 498)*. The whole Christ *is present in either kind and in any part of either kind and is received by the communicant (476, 478, 480, 486, 494, 853)*. For the wheat bread and grape wine *(479, 532, 533) are* transubstantiated *by the ordained priest (475, 480) into the flesh and blood of Christ (339, 474, 487, 493, 537c, 846, 853) so that only the appearance of bread and wine remains (493).*

In the Latin rite the laity *receive Communion in only one kind (476, 503–5, 507–9, 534)*. Worthy *reception requires the communicant to be in a state of grace (502, 536, 537). Children below the age of reason are not obliged to receive Holy Communion (506, 510, 536).*

The sacrament effects *union with Christ (481);* it is nourishment for the soul *(409, 481, 485)*, gives increase in grace *(481)* and remits venial sin and punishment *(485, 496).*

OATH OF BERENGARIUS AT THE COUNCIL OF ROME (1079)

Berengarius (ob. 1088) was head of the school of St Martin at Tours. On the basis of philosophical objections he denied the transubstantiation of the bread and wine and the real presence of Christ in the Eucharist. He was thus a forerunner of the symbolical-spiritualistic conception of the Eucharist adopted by the Reformers. After various condemnations he finally had to swear to the following profession before a local Council assembled in Rome.

I, Berengarius, believe with my heart and confess with my mouth that the bread and wine which are placed upon the altar are by the mystery of the sacred prayer and the words of our Redeemer substantially changed into the true and real and life-giving flesh and blood of Jesus Christ our Lord, and that after the consecration there is the true body of Christ which was born of the Virgin and which hung on the cross as a sacrifice for the salvation of the world and which sits at the right hand of the Father, and the true blood of Christ which flowed from his side, not just by the sign and virtue of the sacrament but in its real nature and true substance... 474 700

PROFESSION OF FAITH PRESCRIBED FOR THE WALDENSIANS – POPE INNOCENT III (1208)
(Cf. Note to No. 405)

...The sacrifice, that is, the bread and wine, is after the consecration the true body and true blood of our Lord Jesus Christ. This we believe firmly and without doubt, with pure hearts, and confess without reservation in faithful words. In it, we believe, a good priest effects no more and a bad priest no less, for it is effected not by the merit of the consecrator but by the word of the 475 794

Creator and the power of the Holy Spirit. Whence we firmly believe and confess that no man however honest, religious, holy and prudent can or may consecrate the Eucharist or effect the sacrifice of the altar unless he be a priest regularly ordained by a visible and tangible bishop[1].

Three things, we believe, are necessary for this office: a definite person, that is a priest constituted, as we have said, for that office by a bishop; those solemn words which were placed in the canon by the holy Fathers; and the proper intention of the celebrant. We therefore firmly believe and confess that anyone who believes and professes that he can effect the sacrifice of the Eucharist without previous ordination by a bishop, as we have said, is heretical... and to be separated from the whole holy Roman Church...

THE GENERAL COUNCIL OF CONSTANCE
(1414–18)

DECREE CONCERNING COMMUNION
UNDER ONE KIND

The demand for Communion under both kinds was first raised by the disciples of John Hus. The basis for the demand was the supposed command of Christ and the usage of the early Church. The final word was spoken by the Council of Trent (Cf. Nos. 503, 507f).

476
1198

...Granted that in the primitive Church the Sacrament was received by the faithful under both kinds, but later it was received by celebrants under both kinds but by the laity only under the species of bread, since it is most firmly to be believed and in no wise to be doubted

---

1. The Innovators claimed a grace of ordination directly conveyed to them by the Holy Spirit.

that the whole body and blood of Christ are truly contained both in the species of bread and in the species of wine...

QUESTIONS TO BE PUT TO WYCLIFFITES AND HUSSITES

Wycliffe's false doctrine concerning the Eucharist comprised: bread and wine remain; that the appearances should remain without the substances is contrary to Holy Scripture and tradition; Christ is present in the Eucharist symbolically and by effect only, not as he is in heaven; adoration of the Eucharist is therefore idolatry; the consecration of bread and wine in the Mass is no sacrifice; the Mass has value only when it is celebrated by a pious priest.

16. Whether he believes that after the consecration by the priest there is in the sacrament of the altar under the veil of bread and wine not material bread and material wine but wholly Christ who suffered on the Cross and sits at the right hand of the Father.   477 *1256*

17. Whether he believes and asserts that after the consecration by the priest under the sole species of bread alone, without the wine there is the true flesh of Christ and the blood and soul and divinity and the whole Christ, and the same complete body is present in each of the species separately.   478 *1257*

THE GENERAL COUNCIL OF FLORENCE

DECREE FOR THE ARMENIANS (1439)
(Cf. Note to No. 408)

...The third sacrament is the Eucharist. Its *matter* is wheat bread and grape wine into which before consecration a small amount of water is mixed. The water is mixed because... it can be assumed that the Lord   479 *1320*

himself instituted the sacrament with wine mixed with water. Then it suitably represents our Lord's Passion... *(It also represents the union of the faithful with Christ).* The *form* of this sacrament are the words of the Saviour
480 with which he effected this sacrament, for the priest effects this sacrament speaking in the person of Christ. By virtue of these same words the substance of bread is changed into the body of Christ and the substance of wine into his blood, but in such a way that the whole Christ is contained in the species of bread and the whole Christ in the species of wine. Also in any part of the consecrated host or the consecrated wine, when separated, the whole Christ is there.

481 The *effect* of this sacrament, which operates in the soul
1322 of the worthy recipient, is the union of man with Christ. And since by grace man is incorporated in Christ and united with his members, the consequence is that in those who receive it worthily grace is increased by this sacrament. And all the effects that bodily food and drink have on bodily life, of sustenance, increase, renewal and enjoyment, this sacrament has for the spiritual life. In which, as Pope Urban (IV) says, we celebrate the grateful memory of our Saviour, are held back from evil, confirmed in good, and receive increase in virtue and grace...

THE GENERAL COUNCIL OF TRENT, THIRTEENTH SESSION (1551)

DECREE ON THE MOST HOLY SACRAMENT OF THE EUCHARIST

The setting forth of the true doctrine of the Eucharist was one of the most urgent tasks of the Council (cf. No. 482). The most important questions were dealt with in the thirteenth, twenty-first and twenty-third sessions. First there was the question of the Real Presence, denied by the Innovators, particularly Zwingli and Calvin. The Church's teaching is set out in eight chapters, which are followed by eleven canons condemning heresy.

Chapter I deals with the Real Presence – fact, possibility and proof. It is aimed particularly at Calvin and Zwingli. See Canon 1.

Chapter IV deals with the real change. Luther did not in fact deny the real presence of Christ but he taught that the bread and wine also remained at the same time. In contrast to this the Council taught the true change of substance, leaving only the outward appearances of bread and wine. It also authorized as the proper term the word 'transubstantiation' which had first been used in the Fourth Lateran Council (cf. No. 339).

Foreword

The holy, ecumenical and general Council of Trent... though convened, not without the special guidance and direction of the Holy Spirit, for the purpose of setting forth the true and ancient doctrine concerning faith and the sacraments, and of applying a remedy to all the heresies and the other most grievous troubles by which the Church of God is now miserably disturbed and rent into many and various parts, yet, even from the outset, has especially desired that it might pull up by the roots the cockles of execrable errors and schisms which the enemy has in these our troubled times disseminated regarding the doctrine, use and worship of the Sacred Eucharist, which our Saviour left in his Church as a symbol of that unity and charity with which he wished all Christians to be mutually bound and united.

Wherefore, this Holy Council, stating that sound and genuine doctrine of the venerable and divine sacrament of the Eucharist, which the Catholic Church, instructed by our Lord Jesus Christ himself and by his Apostles, and taught by the Holy Spirit who always brings to her mind all truth, has held and will preserve even to the end

482
1635

of the world, forbids all the faithful of Christ to presume henceforth to believe, teach or preach with regard to the most Holy Eucharist otherwise than is explained and defined in this present decree.

Chapter I. The Real Presence of our Lord Jesus Christ in the Most Holy Sacrament of the Eucharist

483
1636 First of all, the Holy Council teaches and openly and plainly professes that after the consecration of bread and wine our Lord Jesus Christ, true God and true man, is truly, really and substantially contained in the august sacrament of the Holy Eucharist under the appearance of those sensible things. For there is no conflict in this that our Saviour sits always at the right hand of the Father in heaven according to the natural mode of existing, and yet is in many other places sacramentally present to us in his own substance by a manner of existence which, though we can scarcely express it in words, yet with our understanding illuminated by faith,
484
1637 we can conceive and ought most firmly to believe is possible to God. For thus all of our forefathers, as many as were in the true Church of Christ and who treated of this most holy sacrament, have most openly professed that our Redeemer instituted this wonderful sacrament at the Last Supper when, after blessing bread and wine, he testified in clear and definite words that he gives them his own body and his own blood. Since these words, recorded by the holy Evangelists and afterwards repeated by St Paul, embody that proper and clearest meaning in which they were understood by the Fathers, it is a most contemptible action on the part of some contentious and wicked men to twist them into fictitious and imaginary figures of speech by which the truth of the flesh and blood of Christ is denied, contrary to the

universal sense of the Church, which, as the 'pillar and ground of truth' *(1 Tim. 3:15)*, recognizing with a mind ever grateful and unforgetting this most excellent favour of Christ, has detested as satanical these untruths devised by impious men.

Chapter II. The Reason for the Institution of This Most Holy Sacrament

When about to depart from this world to the Father, therefore, our Saviour instituted this sacrament in which he poured forth, as it were, the riches of his divine love towards men, 'making a remembrance of his wonderful works' *(Ps. 110:4)*, and commanded us in the participation of it to reverence his memory and to show forth his death until he comes to judge the world. But he wished that this sacrament should be received as the spiritual food of souls, whereby they may be nourished and strengthened, living by the life of him who said: 'He that eateth me, the same also shall live by me' *(John 6:57)*, and as an antidote whereby we may be freed from daily faults and be preserved from mortal sins. He wished it furthermore to be a pledge of our future glory and everlasting happiness and thus be a symbol of that one body of which he is the Head and to which he wished us to be united as members by the closest bond of faith, hope and charity, that we might all speak the same thing and there might be no schisms amongst us. 485
1638

Chapter III. The Excellence of the Most Holy Eucharist Above the Other Sacraments

The most Holy Eucharist has indeed this in common with the other sacraments that it is a symbol of a sacred thing and a visible form of an invisible grace; but there is found in it this excellent and peculiar characteristic 486
1639

that, whereas the other sacraments first have the power of sanctifying when one uses them, in the Eucharist there is the Author himself of sanctity before it is used. For the Apostles had not yet received the Eucharist from the hands of the Lord when he himself told them that what he was giving them was his own body. This has always been the belief of the Church of God, that immediately after the consecration the true body and the true blood of our Lord, together with his soul and divinity, exist under the form of bread and the blood under the form of wine, by the power of the words; but the same body also under the form of wine and the same blood under the form of bread and the soul under both, by virtue of that natural connexion and concomitance whereby the parts of Christ the Lord, 'who hath now risen from the dead, to die no more' *(Rom. 6:9)* are mutually united; also the divinity on account of its admirable hypostatic union with his body and soul. Wherefore it is very true that as much is contained under either form as under both. For Christ is whole and entire under the form of bread and under any part of that form; likewise the whole Christ is present under the form of wine and under all its parts.

Chapter IV. Transubstantiation

But since Christ our Redeemer declared that which he offered under the form of bread to be truly his own body, it has therefore always been a firm belief in the Church of God, and this Holy Council now declares it anew, that by the consecration of the bread and wine a change is brought about of the whole substance of the bread into the substance of the body of Christ our Lord, and of the whole substance of the wine into the substance of his blood. This change the holy Catholic Church properly and appropriately calls transubstantiation.

Chapter V. The Worship and Veneration to be Shown to this Most Holy Sacrament

There is, therefore, no room for doubt that all the faithful of Christ may, in accordance with a custom always received in the Catholic Church, give to this most holy sacrament in veneration the worship of *latria*, which is due to the true God. Neither is it to be less adored for the reason that it was instituted by Christ the Lord in order to be received. For We believe that in it the same God is present of whom the eternal Father, when introducing him to the world, says: 'And let all the angels of God adore him' *(Heb. 1:6)*; whom the Magi, falling down, adored *(Mt. 2:11)*; who, finally, as the Scriptures testify, was adored by the Apostles in Galilee *(Mt. 28: 17)*...

488
1643

Chapter VI. The Reservation of the Sacrament of the Holy Eucharist and Taking It to the Sick

489
1645

Chapter VII. The Preparation to be Employed that One May Worthily Receive the Sacred Eucharist

490
1646-7

Chapter VIII. The Use of this Admirable Sacrament

491
1648-50

CANONS ON THE MOST HOLY SACRAMENT OF THE EUCHARIST

Canon 1 contains the Catholic doctrine of the true and complete presence of Christ. Zwingli ('only as in a sign') and Calvin ('only as in a force') are expressly condemned.
The importance of Canon 3 lies in its practical consequences: anyone who believes in this cannot demand communion under both kinds as a matter of necessity.
With regard to Canon 4, Melancthon taught that Christ was present only in usu. *Luther was undecided on this.*

492
1651
1. If anyone shall deny that in the sacrament of the most Holy Eucharist are contained truly, really and substantially the body and blood together with the soul and divinity of our Lord Jesus Christ, and consequently the whole Christ, but shall say that he is in it only as in a sign, or figure or force – *anathema sit*.

493
1652
2. If anyone shall say that in the sacred and holy sacrament of the Eucharist the substance of the bread and wine remains conjointly with the body and blood of our Lord Jesus Christ, and deny that wonderful and singular change of the whole substance of the bread into the body and the whole substance of the wine into the blood, the appearances only of bread and wine remaining, which change the Catholic Church most aptly calls transubstantiation – *anathema sit*.

494
1653
3. If anyone shall deny that in the venerable sacrament of the Eucharist the whole Christ is contained under each form and under every part of each form when separated – *anathema sit*.

495
1654
4. If anyone shall say that after the consecration is completed the body and blood of our Lord Jesus Christ are not in the admirable sacrament of the Eucharist, but are there only *in usu*, while being taken, but not before or after, and that in the hosts or consecrated particles which are reserved or which remain after Communion, the true body of the Lord does not remain – *anathema sit*.

496
1655
5. If anyone shall say that the principal fruit of the most Holy Eucharist is the remission of sins, or that other effects do not result from it – *anathema sit*.

497
1656
6. If anyone shall say that in the holy sacrament of the Eucharist Christ, the only begotten Son of God, is not to be adored with the worship of *latria*, also outwardly manifested, and is consequently neither to be venerated with a special festive solemnity nor to be solemnly borne about in procession according to the laudable and uni-

versal rite and custom of Holy Church, or is not to be set publicly before the people to be adored and that the adorers thereof are idolaters – *anathema sit*.

7. If anyone shall say that it is not lawful that the Holy Eucharist be reserved in a sacred place, but immediately after consecration must necessarily be distributed among those present, or that it is not lawful that it be carried with honour to the sick – *anathema sit*.   498 / *1657*

8. If anyone shall say that Christ received in the Eucharist is received spiritually only and not also sacramentally and really – *anathema sit*.   499 / *1658*

9. If anyone shall deny that each and all of Christ's faithful of both sexes, when they have reached the years of discretion, are bound to communicate every year at least at Easter in accordance with the precept of Holy Mother Church – *anathema sit*.   500 / *1659*

10. If anyone shall say that it is not lawful for the celebrant priest to communicate himself – *anathema sit*.   501 / *1660*

11. If anyone shall say that faith alone is a sufficient preparation for receiving the sacrament of the most Holy Eucharist – *anathema sit*. And lest so great a sacrament be received unworthily and hence unto death and condemnation, this Holy Council ordains and declares that sacramental confession, when a confessor can be had, must necessarily be made beforehand by those whose conscience is burdened with mortal sin, however contrite they may consider themselves. Moreover, if anyone shall presume to teach, preach or obstinately assert, or in public disputation defend the contrary, he shall be *ipso facto* excommunicated.   502 / *1661*

THE GENERAL COUNCIL OF TRENT, TWENTY-FIRST SESSION (1562)

THE DOCTRINE OF COMMUNION UNDER BOTH KINDS AND THE COMMUNION OF LITTLE CHILDREN

After being interrupted since 1552, the deliberations of the Council were renewed under Pope Pius IV in 1562. After four sessions dealing with organizational matters, the twenty-first session turned to the question of the chalice for the laity. The points considered were: Whether divine law requires the faithful to communicate under both kinds (Chap. I); If there is no such law, has the Church power to determine the ways and means of dispensing the sacrament? (Chap. II) (cf. No. 426); Is reception of the sacrament under one kind as complete as under both (Chap. III).
The question whether reception under one kind is associated with the same measure of grace was deliberately not answered because the Council never adhered to any particular school. The last question (Chap. IV) dealt with the matter of small children and their not being obliged to communicate.

503
1726–7
Chapter I. Laymen, and Clerics when not offering the Sacrifice, are not bound by Divine Law to Communion under both Species

(The reception of the one species of bread is sufficient for salvation. Advocates of the chalice for the laity cannot properly appeal to John 6:54 etc. since in other contexts Christ himself spoke of the bread alone – e.g. John 6:58).

504
1728
Chapter II. The Power of the Church concerning the Dispensation of the Sacrament of the Eucharist

(The essentials of the sacraments were instituted by Christ, but their dispensation is entrusted to the Church. St Paul taught this and made dispositions in this sense.

The Church thus has the right to prescribe Holy Communion in one kind) (See also No. 426).

Chapter III. Christ, Whole and Entire, and a True Sacrament are Received Under Either Species

505
1729

(Those who receive under one species only are not deprived of any grace necessary to salvation).

Chapter IV. Little Children are not Bound to Sacramental Communion

506
1730

(They are incorporated in Christ by baptism and cannot at their age lose grace. Nevertheless earlier ages when small children did occasionally receive Communion are not to be condemned. But Communion is not necessary for salvation for children below the age of reason.)

CANONS ON COMMUNION UNDER BOTH SPECIES AND THAT OF LITTLE CHILDREN

1. If anyone shall say that each and all of the faithful of Christ are by a precept of God or by the necessity for salvation bound to receive both species of the most holy sacrament of the Eucharist – *anathema sit*. 507 / 1731

2. If anyone shall say that the holy Catholic Church was not moved by just causes and reasons that laymen and clerics when not consecrating should communicate under the form of bread only, or has erred in this – *anathema sit*. 508 / 1732

3. If anyone shall deny that Christ, the found and author of all graces, is received whole and entire under the one species of bread, because, as some falsely assert, he is not received in accordance with the institution of Christ under both species – *anathema sit*. 509 / 1733

4. If anyone shall say that communion of the Eucharist is necessary for little children before they have attained years of discretion – *anathema sit*. 510 / 1734

THE GENERAL COUNCIL OF TRENT, TWENTY-SECOND SESSION (1562)

DOCTRINE CONCERNING THE SACRIFICE OF THE MASS

In the doctrine concerning the holy sacrifice of the Mass, too, a broad exposition as well as brief canons were made necessary by the innovators' many distortions of the Catholic conception of it. The Council proceeded to this question when it next met in September 1562.

Chapter I The salvation of mankind is effected by the sacrifice of the Cross. Holy Mass is not a sacrifice independent of that of the Cross but a re-presentation of it. At the Last Supper Christ made an offering and commanded the Apostles to do likewise. The exposition of the connexion between the sacrifice of the Mass and that of the Cross invalidates the essential Protestant objections to the Mass.

Chapter II The sacrifice of the Mass is a true propitiatory sacrifice whose fruits are shared by all the faithful.

Chapter III A clarification about Masses offered in honour of saints was necessary to meet Protestant objections.

Chapters IV–VIII deal with the development of the rites surrounding the celebration of Mass.

Foreword

511
1738 **So that the ancient, complete and in every way perfect faith and teaching regarding the great mystery of the Eucharist in the Catholic Church may be retained, and with the removal of errors and heresies may be preserved in its purity, the holy, ecumenical and general Council of Trent... instructed by the light of the Holy Spirit, teaches, declares and orders to be preached to the faithful the following concerning it, since it is the true and only sacrifice.**

Chapter I. The Institution of the Most Holy Sacrifice of the Mass

Since under the former Testament, according to the testimony of the Apostle Paul, there was no perfection because of the weakness of the Levitical priesthood, there was need, God the Father of Mercies so ordaining, that 'another priest should arise according to the order of Melchisedech' *(Heb. 7:11)*, our Lord Jesus Christ, who might perfect and lead to perfection as many as were to be sanctified. He, therefore, our God and Lord, though he was by his death about to offer himself once upon the altar of the cross to God the Father that he might there accomplish an eternal redemption, nevertheless, so that his priesthood might not come to an end with his death, at the last supper, on the night he was betrayed, so that he might leave to his beloved spouse the Church a visible sacrifice, such as the nature of man requires, whereby that bloody sacrifice once to be accomplished on the cross might be represented, the memory thereof remain even to the end of the world, and its salutary effects applied to the remission of those sins which we daily commit, declaring himself constituted 'a priest forever according to the order of Melchisedech' *(Ps. 109:4)*, offered up to God the Father his own body and blood under the form of bread and wine, and under the forms of those same things gave to the Apostles, whom he then made priests of the New Testament, that they might partake, commanding them and their successors in the priesthood by these words to do likewise: 'Do this in commemoration of me' *(Luke 22:19; 1 Cor. 11:24f)* as the Catholic Church has always understood and taught. For, having celebrated the ancient Passover which the multitude of the children of Israel sacrificed in memory of their departure from Egypt, he instituted a new

512
1739

1741

Passover, namely himself, to be immolated under visible signs by the Church through the priests in memory of his own passage from this world to the Father, when by the shedding of his blood he redeemed and 'delivered us from the power of darkness and translated us into his kingdom' *(Col. 1:13)*.

513
1742
And this is indeed that clean oblation which cannot be defiled by any unworthiness or malice on the part of those who offer it; which the Lord foretold by Malachias was to be great among the Gentiles, and which the Apostle Paul has clearly indicated when he says that they who are defiled by partaking of the table of devils cannot be partakers of the table of the Lord *(1 Cor. 10:21)*, understanding by table in each case the altar. It is, finally, that *(sacrifice)* which was prefigured by various types of sacrifices during the period of nature and of the Law, which, namely, comprises all the good things signified by them, as being the consummation and perfection of them all.

Chapter II. The Visible Sacrifice is Propitiatory both for the Living and for the Dead

514
1743
And inasmuch as in this divine sacrifice which is celebrated in the Mass there is contained and immolated in an unbloody manner the same Christ who once offered himself in a bloody manner on the altar of the cross, the Holy Council teaches that this is truly propitiatory and has this effect that if, contrite and penitent, with sincere heart and upright faith, with fear and reverence, we draw nigh to God, 'we obtain mercy and find grace in seasonable aid' *(Heb. 4:16)*. For, appeased by this sacrifice, the Lord grants the grace and gift of penitence, and pardons even the gravest crimes and sins. For the victim is one and the same, the same now offering by the

ministry of priests who then offered himself on the cross, the manner of offering alone being different. The fruits of that bloody sacrifice, it is well understood, are received most abundantly through this unbloody one, so far is the latter from derogating in any way from the former. Wherefore, according to the tradition of the Apostles, it is rightly offered not only for the sins, punishments, satisfactions and other necessities of the faithful who are living, but also for those departed in Christ but not yet fully purified.

Chapter III. Masses in Honour of the Saints

And though the Church has been accustomed to celebrate at times certain Masses in honour and memory of the saints, she does not teach that sacrifice is offered to them, but to God alone who crowned them; when the priest does not say, 'To thee, Peter of Paul, I offer sacrifice', but, giving thanks to God for their victories, he implores their favour that they may vouchsafe to intercede for us in heaven whose memory we celebrate on earth.

515
1744

Chapter IV. The Canon of the Mass

And since it is becoming that holy things be administered in a holy manner, and of all things this sacrifice is the most holy, the Catholic Church, in order that it might be worthily and reverently offered and received, instituted many centuries ago the holy canon which is so free from error that it contains nothing that does not in the highest degree savour of a certain holiness and piety and raise up to God the minds of those who offer. For it consists partly of the very words of the Lord, partly of the tradition of the Apostles, and also of pious regulations of holy pontiffs.

516
1745

Chapter V. The Solemn Ceremonies of the Mass

517
1746 And since the nature of man is such that without external means he cannot easily be raised to meditation on divine things, Holy Mother Church has instituted certain rites, namely that some things in the Mass be pronounced in a low tone and others in a louder tone. She has likewise, in accordance with apostolic discipline and tradition, made use of ceremonies such as mystical blessings, lights, incense, vestments and many other things of this kind whereby both the majesty of so great a sacrifice might be emphasized and the minds of the faithful be excited by those visible signs of religion and piety to the contemplation of those most sublime things which are hidden in this sacrifice.

Chapter VI. The Mass in which the Priest alone Communicates

518
1747 The Holy Council wishes indeed that at each Mass the faithful who are present should communicate, not only in spiritual desire but also by the sacramental partaking of the Eucharist, that thereby they may derive from this most holy sacrifice a more abundant fruit; if, however, that is not always done, it does not on that account condemn as private and illicit those Masses in which the priest alone communicates sacramentally, but rather approves and commends them, since these Masses also ought to be considered as truly common, partly because at them the people communicate spiritually and partly also because they are celebrated by a public minister of the Church, not for himself alone but for all the faithful who belong to the body of Christ.

Chapter VII. The Mixture of Water with Wine in the Offering of the Chalice

The Holy Council then calls to mind that the Church has instructed priests to mix water with the wine that is to be offered in the chalice, because it is believed that Christ the Lord did so, and also because from his side there came blood and water; the memory of this mystery is renewed by this mixture, and since in the Apocalypse of St John the peoples are called waters, the union of the faithful people with Christ their head is represented.

519

1748

Chapter VIII. The Mass not Generally to be Celebrated in the Vernacular – Its Mysteries to be Explained to the People

Although the Mass contains much instruction for the faithful, it has nevertheless not been deemed advisable by the Fathers that it should be celebrated everywhere in the vernacular tongue. Wherefore the ancient rite of each Church, approved by the holy Roman Church, the mother and mistress of all churches, being everywhere retained, that the sheep of Christ may not suffer hunger or 'the little ones ask for bread and there is none to break it unto them' *(Lam. 4:4)* the Holy Council commands pastors and all who have the cure of souls that, either themselves or through others, they explain frequently during the celebration of the Mass some of the things read during the Mass, and that among other things they explain some mystery of this most holy sacrifice, especially on Sundays and feast-days.

520

1749

CANONS ON THE SACRIFICE OF THE MASS

Canon 1 contains the principle dogma about the Mass: it is the true sacrifice of Christ. The sacrifice does not consist only in its being given to us in Holy Communion. No exact definition was given of wherein the essence of the sacrifice of the Mass lies, for this is matter of theological opinion. The canon is aimed at the Protestants who recognized only Christ's sacrifice on the cross and therefore denied the sacrificial character of the Mass. For them there was only the Supper and no sacrifice.

Canon 2 relates priests of the new dispensation with the sacrifice of the new Covenant.

Canon 3 states that the sacrifice of the Mass is also a propitiatory sacrifice as that of Calvary was.

Canon 4 invalidates Protestant objections to the Mass by showing the inner connexion between the sacrifice of the cross and that of the Mass.

521　1. If anyone shall say that in the Mass a true and real
1751　sacrifice is not offered to God, or that what is offered is nothing but that Christ is given us to eat – *anathema sit.*

522　2. If anyone shall say that by the words, 'Do this for
1752　a commemoration of me,' Christ did not institute the Apostles priests, or did not ordain that they and other priests should offer his own body and blood – *anathema sit.*

523　3. If anyone shall say that the sacrifice of the Mass is
1753　only one of praise and thanksgiving; or that it is a mere commemoration of the sacrifice consummated on the cross but not a propitiatory one; or that it profits only him who receives Communion, and ought not to be offered for the living and the dead, for sins, punishments, satisfactions, and other necessities – *anathema sit.*

524　4. If anyone shall say that by the sacrifice of the Mass
1754　a blasphemy is cast upon the most holy sacrifice of Christ consummated on the cross, or that the former derogates from the latter – *anathema sit.*

525　5. If anyone shall say that it is an imposture to celebrate
1755　Masses in honour of the saints and in order to obtain

their intercession with God, as the Church intends – *anathema sit.*

6. If anyone shall say that the Canon of the Mass contains errors and therefore should be abrogated – *anathema sit.*   526 / 1756

7. If anyone shall say that the ceremonies, vestments and outward signs which the Catholic Church uses in the celebration of Masses are incentives to impiety rather than stimulants to piety – *anathema sit.*   527 / 1757

8. If anyone shall say that Masses in which the priest alone communicates sacramentally are illicit and are therefore to be abrogated – *anathema sit.*   528 / 1758

9. If anyone shall say that the rite of the Roman Church whereby a part of the canon and the words of consecration are pronounced in a low tone is to be condemned; or that the Mass ought to be celebrated in the vernacular tongue only; or that water ought not to be mixed with the wine that is to be offered in the chalice because it is contrary to the institution of Christ – *anathema sit.*   529 / 1759

FROM THE CODE OF CANON LAW (1917)

C. 801. In the most holy Eucharist under the species of bread and wine, Christ the Lord is himself contained, offered and consumed.   530

C. 802. Priests alone have the power of offering Mass.   531

C. 814. The most holy sacrifice of the Mass is to be offered of bread and wine with which a very small part of water is to be mixed.   532

C. 815. § 1. The bread must be pure wheat and recently made so that there is no danger of corruption.   533
§ 2. The wine must be pure, from the vine, and free of corruption.

C. 852. The most holy Eucharist is to be distributed under the species of bread alone.   534

535 C. 853. Any baptized person who is not legally forbidden can and must be admitted to Holy Communion.

536 C. 854. § 1. The Eucharist is not to be administered to children who on account of not having attained the age of reason have no knowledge or understanding of this sacrament.

§ 2. In danger of death, it is enough that they know how to distinguish the Body of Christ from normal food and reverently adore it that the most holy Eucharist can and should be ministered to children.

§ 3. Outside danger of death, a fuller knowledge of Christian doctrine and a more detailed preparation are rightly demanded, namely they should have the understanding suitable to their capacity of those mysteries of the faith which are necessary as means to salvation and should approach the most holy Eucharist with a devotion suitable to their age.

537 C. 856. No one whose conscience is burdened by mortal sin, however sorry he may consider himself to be, may approach Holy Communion without previous sacramental confession; but if necessity compels and no confessor is available, he must arouse perfect contrition.

POPE PIUS XII's ENCYCLICAL
MEDIATOR DEI (1947)

On 20 November 1947 this encyclical was issued, summing up the results of half a century of the 'liturgical movement' and taking a positive attitude to all the questions which had arisen from this more active participation by the faithful in the Church's worship. It gives us in connexion with the sacrament of order an exposition of the universal priesthood of Christians (Cf. No. 644a). In the following extracts we have the position with regard to two other points: the real nature of the liturgy as a whole and the presence of Christ in the liturgy, the latter a question that had been much debated in Germany.

Although the second extract does not answer all the questions raised by theology on the mode of Christ's presence in the Church's liturgy, in the sacraments and the offering of the sacrifice of the Mass, this declaration of the magisterium must be taken into account if one seeks to penetrate these unresolved questions any further.

The Nature of the Liturgy
The sacred Liturgy, then, is the public worship which our Redeemer, the Head of the Church, offers to the heavenly Father and which the community of Christ's faithful pays to its Founder, and through him to the Eternal Father; briefly, it is the whole public worship paid by the Mystical Body of Jesus Christ, Head and members... 537a
3841

The Presence of Christ in the Liturgy
Therefore in the whole conduct of the liturgy the Church has her divine Founder present with her. Christ is present in the august sacrifice of the altar, in the person of his minister and especially under the Eucharistic species; he is present in the sacraments by his power which he infuses into them as instruments of sanctification; he is present, finally, in the prayer and praise that are offered to God, in accordance with his promise, 'When two or three are gathered together in my name, I am there in the midst of them' *(Mt. 18:20)...* 537b
3840

...Therefore the liturgical year, animated throughout by the devotion of the Church, is no cold and lifeless representation of past events, no mere historical record. It is Christ himself, living on in his Church, and still pursuing that path of boundless mercy which, 'going about and doing good' *(Acts 10:38)* he began to tread during his life on earth. This he did so that the souls of men might come into contact with his mysteries and, so to speak, live by them. And these mys- 3855 teries are still now constantly present and active, not in the vague and nebulous way which certain recent writers describe, but as Catholic doctrine teaches us. The Doctors of the Church tell us that the mysteries of Christ's life are at the same time most excellent models of virtue for us to imitate and also sources of divine grace for us by reason of the merits and intercession of the Redeemer. They live on in their effects on us, since each of them, according to its nature, and in its own way, is the cause of our salvation...

PIUS XII's ENCYCLICAL *HUMANI GENERIS* (1950)
(cf. Nos. 74; 126d; 205; 398a)

Modern research into the innermost structure of matter is bound to raise the question of how the doctrine of transubstantiation fits into the modern picture of nuclear physics. The following extract from Humani Generis *rejects one solution of this question which takes refuge from the difficulties by 'spiritualizing' the dogma out of existence.*

537c
3891
...You will find men arguing that the doctrine of Transubstantiation ought to be revised, depending as it does on a conception of substance which is now out of date. The real presence of Christ in the Holy Eucharist is thus reduced to a kind of symbolic communication, the consecrated species being no more than an effectual sign of Christ's spiritual presence, and of His close union with His faithful members in the Mystical Body.

V PENANCE

If the Church is to fulfil in its entirety her task of saving mankind she needs the power to forgive sins. It is a power essentially different from her mission to preach the Gospel and baptize. In baptism, indeed, all sins and the punishment due to them are remitted. Baptism is the first justification. But the first justification is also the first entry into the realm of the supernatural which works entirely by God's grace and which asks of the person baptized no more than that he turn away from sin and turn in faith to Christ.

Penance is something different. A baptized person who sins again, sins against God to whom, since his baptism in the name of the Most Holy Trinity, he belongs. He also betrays the Church of which he is now a member. Thus the new atonement assumes the character of a legal trial, *with accusation, sentence and satisfaction.*

The practice *of penance has varied considerably down the centuries. In very early days satisfaction, usually in the form of public penance, was very much to the fore. Re-acceptance into the Church community normally took place only after completion of the penance imposed. More and more, however, penance has withdrawn from the public domain and today only the private administration of the sacrament is still in use.*

The development of the system of confession shows that misunderstanding easily arises about the nature of penance. *In the face of all attacks – by Wycliffe, the Reformers, liberal dogmatic historians and modernists – the Church has always maintained the judicial character of the sacrament of penance and drawn the necessary conclusions.*

Church documents teach us the following about penance: The Church has the power to forgive all sins *(554, 556, 574, 587, 588, 731, 766, 828, 841). This forgiveness of sins is a true* sacrament *instituted by Christ (408, 413, 542, 554, 556, 572, 731, 845, 851), different from baptism (557, 558, 573, 732), particularly on account of its judicial form (557). Sins are forgiven only by the sacrament of penance (449, 538, 539, 564, 577, 732, 766). Sins are forgiven by* absolution *(542, 559) which can only be given by an* authorized priest *(539, 540, 542, 565, 581, 589). It is a real judicial pardon (566, 580, 589). The Church has the power to reserve certain cases (541, 551, 567, 582).*

On the part of the sinner *contrition, confession and satisfaction are required (542, 543, 552, 560, 575, 732).* Contrition *is aversion to the sins committed (542, 562, 732). Perfect contrition remits sin even before confession if it is joined with the intention to confess (563) Imperfect contrition (attrition) is sufficient if there is confession ((563), and is a good and salutary thing (544, 545, 563, 576, 745).*

Confession must cover all mortal sins committed since baptism and not previously confessed (538, 539, 542, 546, 547, 564, 577–80, 593, 732). Venial sins (546, 564, 578, 594) and sins already confessed can validly be confessed (594). And satisfaction *(540, 542, 568–71, 583–6, 732). The* effect *of the sacrament is reconciliation with God, that is, the remission of sins and the eternal punishment (409, 542, 548, 561, 731) but not all the temporal punishment (568, 583, 732, 767).*

THE GENERAL COUNCIL OF CONSTANCE
(1414–18)

WYCLIFFE'S ERRORS CONDEMNED

In his teaching about penance, as in other matters, Wycliffe, was the forerunner of the Reformation. According to him the essence of penance was not absolution by the priest by virtue of his priestly power – there was no difference here between the powers of a layman, a priest, a bishop or a pope – but lay solely in contrition. Confession was not even necessary.

7. If a man shall have been duly sorry, external confession is superfluous and useless to him.   [538] *1157*

QUESTIONS PUT TO WYCLIFFITES AND HUSSITES

20. Whether he believes that it is necessary for a Christian for his salvation in addition to heartfelt sorrow to confess, if a suitable priest is available, to a priest alone and not to one or more laymen however good and devout they may be.   539 *1260*

21. Whether he believes that a priest, in cases permitted to him, can absolve the penitent who has confessed and been sorry for his sins, and impose a penance upon him.   540 *1261*

25. Whether he believes that the jurisdictional authority of the Pope, of archbishops and bishops in remitting and retaining *(sins)* is greater than the authority of a simple priest, even if he has the cure of souls.   541 *1265*

THE GENERAL COUNCIL OF FLORENCE

DECREE FOR THE ARMENIANS (1439)
(Cf. note to No. 408)

The fourth sacrament is penance, of which *as it were the matter* consists of the actions of the penitent which are in *three parts.* The first of these is *contrition* of heart, which consists of sorrow for sin committed and the in-   542 *1323* tention not to sin in the future. The second is oral *confession*, whereby the sinner confesses to the priest all the sins he remembers in their entirety. The third is *satisfaction* for sins according to the judgment of the priest, which is mainly achieved by prayer, fasting and almsdeeds. The *form* of this sacrament is the words of absolution spoken by the priest when he says: I absolve thee etc.... The *minister* of this sacrament is the priest who has the authority either ordinary or by commission from his superior, to absolve. The *effect* of this sacrament is absolution from sins.

ERRORS OF MARTIN LUTHER CONDEMNED BY POPE LEO X (1520)
(Cf. Note to No. 553)

[543] 1455   5. The doctrine that there are three parts of penance: contrition, confession and satisfaction is not founded on Holy Scripture nor on the ancient holy Christian Doctors.

[544] 1456   6. Contrition arising from discussion, consideration and detestation of sins, whereby one thinks over one's years in the bitterness of one's heart, pondering on the grievousness, number and ugliness of one's sins, on the loss of eternal happiness and the gain of eternal damnation – such a contrition makes one a hypocrite and a greater sinner than before.

[545[1457   7. Very true, and better than any doctrine so far on the subject of contrition, is the saying: 'The supreme penance is not to do it in future; the best penance is a new life.'

[546] 1458   8. On no account presume to confess venial sins, nor even all mortal sins, for it is impossible that you know all your mortal sins. For that reason only public mortal sins were confessed in the early Church.

9. If we wish to confess everything clearly we behave as if we wished to leave nothing to the mercy of God to forgive. [547] *1459*

10. Sins are not remitted to anyone unless he believes they have been remitted by the priest who remits them; rather, the sin remains unless he believes it remitted; for the remission of the sin and the giving of grace are not sufficient, it is also necessary to believe it has been remitted. [548] *1460*

11. Do not believe you have been forgiven on account of your contrition, but on account of Christ's saying, 'Whatsoever thou shalt loose...' *(Mt. 16:19)*. Hence I say: Have confidence if you have absolution of a priest, and believe firmly that you are absolved, and absolved you will truly be, whatever the state of your contrition. [549] *1461*

12. If, *per impossibile*, the penitent were not sorry, or the priest absolved not seriously but in jest, but if he believe himself absolved, then he is in very truth absolved. [550] *1462*

13. In the sacrament of penance and the remission of guilt the Pope or a bishop does no more than the lowest priest; rather, where there is no priest, any Christian can do as much, even a woman or a child. [551] *1463*

14. No one need be answerable to the priest whether he is sorry, nor should the priest ask it of anyone. [552] *1464*

THE GENERAL COUNCIL OF TRENT, FOURTEENTH SESSION (1551)

DOCTRINE ON THE SACRAMENT OF PENANCE

Penance, the second means of justification, was already mentioned in Chapter XIV of the Sixth Session in connexion with the doctrine of justification (cf. Nos. 731–2). In the following decree the doctrine of penance is expanded in view of the many errors current.

Chapter I – Penance is a true sacrament.
Chapter II – The differences between penance and baptism. The Reformers had taught that every forgiveness of sins was a renewal of the grace of baptism by faith.
Chapter III – The essential elements of the sacrament. In particular Luther's idea, that the penitent's contribution consists solely in the pangs of conscience and in faith, is rejected.
Chapter IV – Contrition, its necessity and effect. Of particular importance is the distinction between perfect contrition, which of itself effects forgiveness when it is coupled with the intention of receiving the sacrament of penance, and imperfect contrition (attrition) which is sufficient for valid reception of the sacrament. Luther had heavily attacked attrition as hypocrisy.
Chapter V – Confession, the obligation in divine law and in the nature of the sacrament (against Luther).
Chapter VI – Absolution. Only a priest can absolve. Validity of absolution is not dependent on the priest's moral state (against Wycliffe). It is a real absolution, not just a statement of fact, for it is not belief in forgiveness that effects the justification, as Luther assumed, but the absolution itself.
Chapters VII–IX. One may note in these last three chapters how much the 'Church of law,' which has to intervene in the matter of the sacrament to maintain and restore order, and the 'Church of love,' whose primary concern is the salvation of souls, are one and the same.

Foreword

553
1667

Although the holy... Council of Trent... has, by reason of a certain necessity induced by the affinity of the subjects, given much consideration to the sacrament of penance in its decree on justification, yet so great is the number of errors concerning this sacrament in our days that it will be of no little general benefit to give to it a more exact and complete definition in which, all errors having been under the guidance of the Holy Spirit

pointed out and refuted, Catholic truth may be made clear and resplendent; which *(truth)* this Holy Council now sets before all Christians to be observed for all time.

Chapter I. Necessity and Institution of the Sacrament

If in all those regenerated there were such gratitude to God that they were constant in safeguarding the justice received in baptism by his bounty and grace, there would have been no need for another sacrament besides that of baptism to be instituted for the remission of sins. But since God, 'rich in mercy' *(Eph. 2:4)*, 'knoweth our frame' *(Ps. 102:14)*, he has given a remedy of life even to those who may after baptism have delivered themselves up to the servitude of sin and the power of the devil, namely the sacrament of penance, whereby the benefit of Christ's death is applied to those who have fallen after baptism. 554 / 1668

Penance was indeed necessary at all times for all men who had stained themselves by mortal sin, even for those who desired to be cleansed by the sacrament of baptism, in order to obtain grace and justice; so that, their wickedness being penanced and amended, they might with a hatred of sin and a sincere sorrow of heart detest so great an offence against God. Wherefore the Prophet says: 'Be converted and do penance for all your iniquities, and iniquity shall not be your ruin' *(Ezech. 18:30)*. The Lord also said: 'Except you do penance, you shall all likewise perish' *(Luke 13:5)*. And Peter, Prince of the Apostles, recommending penance to sinners about to receive baptism, said: 'Do penance and be baptized every one of you' *(Acts 2:38)*. 555 / 1669

Moreover, neither before the coming of Christ was penance a sacrament nor, since his coming, is it such to anyone before baptism. 1670

556 But the Lord then especially instituted the sacrament of
1670 penance when, after being risen from the dead, he breathed upon his disciples and said: 'Receive ye the Holy Ghost, whose sins you shall forgive, they are forgiven them, and whose sins you shall retain, they are retained' *(John 20:22f)*. The consensus of all the Fathers has always acknowledged that by this action so sublime and words so clear the power of forgiving and retaining sins was given to their Apostles and their lawful successors for reconciling the faithful who have fallen after baptism, and the Catholic Church with good reason repudiated and condemned as heretics the Novatians who of old stubbornly denied that power of forgiving. Therefore this Holy Council, approving and accepting that perfectly true meaning of the above words of the Lord, condemns the fictitious interpretations of those who, contrary to the institution of this sacrament, wrongly distort those words to refer to the power of preaching the word of God and of making known the Gospel of Christ.

Chapter II. The Differences Between the Sacraments of Penance and Baptism

557 Besides, it is clear that this sacrament is in many respects
1671 different from baptism. For apart from the fact that it differs very widely in matter and form, which constitute the essence of a sacrament, it is beyond question that the minister of baptism need not be a judge, since the Church exercises judgment on no one who has not entered it through the gate of baptism. 'For what have I to do,' asks St Paul, 'to judge them that are without?' *(1 Cor. 5:12)*. It is otherwise with those who are of the household of the faith whom Christ the Lord has once made members of his own body by the washing of baptism. *(1 Cor. 12:12f.)*

For these, if they should afterwards have defiled themselves by some crime, he wished not to have cleansed by the repetition of baptism, since that is in no manner lawful in the Catholic Church, but to be placed as culprits before this tribunal that by the sentence of the priests they may be absolved not only once but as often as, repentant of the sins committed, they shall have recourse thereto.

Moreover, the fruit of baptism is one thing, that of penance another. For by baptism we 'put on Christ' *(Gal. 3:27)* and are made in him an entirely new creature, receiving a full and complete remission of all sins; to which newness and integrity, however, we are by no means able to arrive by the sacrament of penance without many tears and labours on our part, divine justice demanding this, so that penance has rightly been called by the holy Fathers a laborious kind of baptism. This sacrament is necessary for salvation for those who have fallen after baptism, as baptism is for those who have not been regenerated. 558 *1672*

Chapter III. The Parts and Fruits of this Sacrament

The Holy Council teaches furthermore that the form of the sacrament of penance, in which its efficacy chiefly consists, are those words of the minister: 'I absolve thee...' etc, to which are indeed laudably added certain prayers according to the custom of Holy Church, which, however, do not by any means belong to the essence of the form nor are they necessary for the administration of the sacrament. 559 *1673*

But the acts of the penitent himself, namely contrition, confession, and satisfaction, constitute the matter of this sacrament, which actions, inasmuch as they are by God's institution required in the penitent for the integrity of the sacrament and for the full and complete remission of 560 *1673* sins, are for this reason called the parts of penance.

561 But that which is signified and produced by this sacra-
1674 ment is, so far as its force and efficacy are concerned, reconciliation with God, which sometimes in persons who are pious and who receive this sacrament with devotion is wont to be followed by peace and serenity of conscience with an exceedingly great consolation of
1675 spirit. The Holy Council, while declaring these things regarding the parts and effect of this sacrament, at the same time condemns those who maintain that faith and the terrors that agitate conscience are parts of penance.

Chapter IV. Contrition

562 Contrition, which has the first place among the aforesaid
1676 acts of the penitent, is a sorrow of mind and a detestation of sin committed, together with the purpose of not sinning in the future. This feeling of contrition was at all times necessary for obtaining the forgiveness of sins and thus indeed it prepares one who has fallen since baptism for the remission of sins if it is united with confidence in the divine mercy and the desire to do the other things that are required to receive this sacrament in the proper manner. The Holy Council declares therefore that this contrition implies not only an abstention from sin and the resolution and beginning of a new life, but also a hatred of the old, according to the statement: 'Cast away from you all your transgressions by which you have transgressed, and make to yourselves a new heart and a new spirit' *(Ezech. 18:31)*. And certainly he who has pondered these lamentations of the saints: 'To thee only have I sinned, and have done evil before thee' *(Ps. 50:6)*; 'I have laboured in my groanings, every night I will wash my bed' *(Ps. 6:7)*; 'I will recount thee all my years in the bitterness of my soul' *(Is. 38:15)*, and others of this

kind, will easily understand that they issued from an overwhelming hatred of their past life and from a profound detestation of sins.

The Council teaches furthermore that though it sometimes happens that this contrition is perfect through charity and reconciles man to God before this sacrament is actually received, this reconciliation, nevertheless, is not to be ascribed to the contrition itself without a desire of the sacrament, which desire is included in it. As to imperfect contrition, which is called attrition, since it commonly arises either from the consideration of the heinousness of sin or from the fear of hell and of punishment, the Council declares that if it renounces the desire to sin and hopes for pardon, it not only does not make one a hypocrite and a greater sinner, but is even a gift of God and an impulse of the Holy Spirit, not indeed as already dwelling in the penitent but only moving him, with which assistance the penitent prepares a way for himself unto justice. And though without the sacrament of penance it cannot of itself lead the sinner to justification, it does, however, dispose him to obtain the grace of God in the sacrament of penance. For, struck salutarily by this fear, the Ninivites, moved by the terrifying preaching of Jonas, did penance and obtained mercy from the Lord. Falsely, therefore, do some accuse Catholic writers as if they maintain hat the sacrament of penance confers grace without any pious exertion on the part of those receiving it, something that the Church of God has never taught or ever accepted. Falsely also do they assert that contrition is extorted or forced, and not free and voluntary.

563
1677

1678

Chapter V. Confession

From the institution of the sacrament of penance as already explained the universal Church has always

564
1679

understood that the complete confession of sins was also instituted by the Lord and is by divine law necessary for all who have fallen after baptism, because when about to ascend from earth to heaven, our Lord Jesus Christ left behind him priests, as rulers and judges, to whom all the mortal sins into which the faithful of Christ may have fallen should be brought in order that they may, in virtue of the power of the keys, pronounce the sentence of remission or retention of sins. For it is evident that without a knowledge of the matter priests could not have exercised this judgment, nor could they have observed justice in imposing penalties had the faithful declared their sins in general only and not specifically

1680 and one by one. From which it is clear that *all mortal sins* of which they have knowledge after a diligent self-examination must be enumerated by the penitents in confession even though they are most secret and have been committed only against the last two precepts of the Decalogue, which sins sometimes injure the soul more grievously and are more dangerous than those which are committed openly. Venial sins, on the other hand, by which we are not excluded from the grace of God and into which we fall more frequently, though they may rightly and profitably and without any presumption be declared in confession, as the practice of pious people evinces, may nevertheless be omitted without guilt and can be expiated by many other remedies...

Chapter VI. The Minister of the Sacrament, and Absolution

565
1684 With regard to the minister of this sacrament, the Holy Council declares false and absolutely foreign to the truth of the Gospel all doctrines which perniciously extend the ministry of the keys to all other men as well as

bishops and priests in the belief that those words of the Lord: 'Whatsoever you shall bind upon earth, shall be bound also in heaven, and whatsoever you shall loose upon earth, shall be loosed also in heaven' *(Mt. 18:18)* and 'Whose sins you shall forgive, they are forgiven them, and whose sins you shall retain, they are retained' *(John 20:23)* were, contrary to the institution of the sacrament, addressed indifferently and indiscriminately to all the faithful of Christ in such manner that everyone has the power of forgiving sins, public ones by way of rebuke, if the one rebuked complies, and secret ones by way of voluntary confession to anyone.

It teaches, furthermore, that even priests who are in mortal sin exercise, through the power of the Holy Spirit conferred in ordination, the office of forgiving sins as ministers of Christ, and that the opinion of those who maintain that bad priests do not possess this power is erroneous.

But although the absolution by the priest is the dispensation of another's bounty, yet it is not a bare ministry only either of proclaiming the Gospel or of declaring that sins are forgiven, but it is after the manner of a judicial act by which sentence is pronounced by him as by a judge. The penitent, therefore, ought not so to flatter himself on his own faith as to think that even though he have no contrition and there be wanting on the part of the priest the intention to act in earnest and to absolve effectively, he is nevertheless absolved really and in the sight of God by reason of faith alone. For faith without penance effects no remission of sins, and he would be most negligent of his salvation who, knowing that a priest absolved him jokingly, would not diligently seek another who would act in earnest.

566
1685

Chapter VII. Reservation of Cases

567
1686-8
(Since the sacrament of penance is a juridical function it requires jurisdiction. Thus, for the edification of the people, certain particularly grave sins may be reserved to the Pope or to bishops for absolution. But so that no one shall perish on account of such reservation, all priests may absolve anyone on the point of death from all sins and censures regardless of reservation).

Chapter VIII. The Necessity and Fruits of Satisfaction

568
1689
Finally, as regards satisfaction which, just as it is that part of penance which has at all times been recommended to the Christian people by our Fathers, is also the part which in our age is chiefly assailed under a high-sounding pretext of piety by those who 'have an appearance of piety, but have denied the power thereof' *(2 Tim. 3:5)*, the Holy Council declares that it is absolutely false and contrary to the word of God that the guilt is never remitted by the Lord without the entire punishment's also being remitted. For clear and outstanding examples are found in holy Scripture by which, as well as by divine tradition, this error is refuted in the plainest manner.

569
1690
Indeed, the nature of *divine justice* seems to demand that those who through ignorance have sinned before baptism be received into grace in one manner, and in another manner those who, after having been liberated from the servitude of sin and the devil, and after having received the gift of the Holy Spirit, have not feared knowingly to violate the temple of God and to grieve the Holy Spirit. And it is in keeping with *divine clemency* that sins be not thus pardoned without satisfaction, lest seizing the occasion and considering sins as trivial and offering insult and affront to the Holy Spirit, we should fall into

graver ones, 'treasuring up to ourselves wrath against the day of wrath' *(Rom. 2:5)*. For without doubt these satisfactions greatly restrain from sin, check penitents as it were with a bit and make them more cautious and vigilant in the future; they also remove remnants of sin and by acts of the opposite virtues destroy habits acquired by evil living. Neither was there ever in the Church of God any way held more certain to ward off impending chastisement by the Lord than that men perform with true sorrow of mind these works of penance. Add to this that while making satisfaction we suffer for our sins, we are made conformable to Christ Jesus who satisfied for our sins, from whom is all our sufficiency, having thence also a most certain pledge that 'if we suffer with him, we shall also be glorified with him' *(Rom. 8:17)*. Neither is this satisfaction which we discharge for our sins so much our own as not to be through Christ Jesus; for we, who can do nothing of ourselves as of ourselves, can do all things with the cooperation of him who strengthens us *(Phil. 4:13)*. Thus man has not wherein to glory, but all our glorying is in Christ, in whom we live, in whom we merit, in whom we make satisfaction, 'bringing forth fruits worthy of penance' *(Mt. 3:8)* which have their efficacy from him, by him are offered to the Father, and through him are accepted by the Father.

570

1691

(Therefore priests are obliged to impose penances suitable to the sins, as protection and aid for the future and as punishment for the past.)

1692

Chapter IX. Works of Satisfaction

(We can make satisfaction by penance, undertaken voluntarily or given us by the priest, and also by bearing patiently the sufferings which God sends us.)

571

1693

CANONS ON THE SACRAMENT OF PENANCE

572
1701
1. If anyone shall say that in the Catholic Church penance is not truly and properly a sacrament instituted by Christ the Lord for reconciling the faithful to God as often as they fall into sin after baptism – *anathema sit*.

573
1702
2. If anyone, confounding the sacraments, shall say that baptism is itself the sacrament of penance, as though these two sacraments were not distinct, and that penance is therefore not rightly called a second plank after shipwreck – *anathema sit*.

574
1703
3. If anyone shall say that those Words of the Lord Saviour, 'Receive ye the Holy Ghost, whose sins you shall forgive, they are forgiven, and whose sins you shall retain, they are retained' *(John 20:22f)*, are not to be understood as applying to the power of forgiving and retaining sins in the sacrament of penance, as the Catholic Church has always understood them from the beginning, but distorts them, contrary to the institution of this sacrament, as applying to the authority of preaching the gospel – *anathema sit*.

575
1704
4. If anyone shall deny that for the full and perfect remission of sins three acts are required of the penitent, constituting as it were the matter of the sacrament of penance, namely, contrition, confession, and satisfaction, which are called the three parts of penance; or shall say that there are only two parts of penance, namely the terrors of a smitten conscience convinced of sin and the faith received from the gospel or from absolution by which one believes that one's sins are forgiven through Christ – *anathema sit*.

576
1705
5. If anyone shall say that the contrition which is evoked by examination, recollection and hatred of sins, whereby a person recounts his years in the bitterness of

his soul, by reflecting on the grievousness, the multitude and baseness of his sins, the loss of eternal happiness and the incurring of eternal damnation, with a purpose of amendment, is not a true and beneficial sorrow, does not prepare for grace, but makes a man a hypocrite and a greater sinner; or finally that this sorrow is forced and not free and voluntary – *anathema sit*.

6. If anyone shall deny that sacramental confession was instituted by divine law or is necessary to salvation; or shall say that the manner of confessing secretly to a priest alone, which the Catholic Church has always observed from the beginning and still observes, is at variance with the institution and command of Christ and is a human contrivance – *anathema sit*.   577 *1706*

7. If anyone shall say that in the sacrament of penance it is not required by divine law for the remission of sins to confess each and all mortal sins which are recalled after a due and diligent examination, also secret ones and those that are a violation of the last two commandments of the Decalogue, as also circumstances that change the nature of a sin, but that this confession is useful only to instruct and console the penitent and in olden times was observed only in order to impose a canonical satisfaction; or shall say that they who strive to confess all sins want to leave nothing to the divine mercy to pardon; or finally that it is not permitted to confess venial sins – *anathema sit*.   578 *1707*

8. If anyone shall say that the confession of all sins as it is observed in the Church is impossible and is a human tradition to be abolished by pious people; or that each and all of the faithful of Christ of either sex are not bound thereto once a year in accordance with the constitution of the great Lateran Council, and for this reason the faithful of Christ are to be persuaded not to confess during Lent – *anathema sit*.   579 *1708*

580   9. If anyone shall say that the sacramental absolution
1709   of the priest is not a judicial act but a mere service of pronouncing and declaring to him who confesses that the sins are forgiven, provided only he believes himself to be absolved, even though the priest absolve not in earnest but in jest; or shall say that the confession of the penitent is not necessary in order that the priest may be able to absolve him – *anathema sit*.

581   10. If anyone shall say that priests who are in mortal
1710   sin have not the power of binding and loosing, or that not only priests are the ministers of absolution but that to each and all of the faithful of Christ was it said: 'Whatsoever you shall bind upon earth, shall be bound also in heaven; and whatsoever you shall loose upon earth, shall be loosed in heaven' *(Mt. 18:18)* and 'Whose sins you shall forgive, they are forgiven them, and whose sins you shall retain they are retained' *(John 20:23)*; by virtue of which words everyone can absolve from sins, from public sins by reproof only, provided the one reproved accepts correction, and from secret sins by voluntary confession – *anathema sit*.

582   11. If anyone shall say that bishops have not the right to
1711   reserve cases to themselves except such as pertain to external administration, and that therefore the reservation of cases does not hinder a priest from absolving from reserved cases – *anathema sit*.

583   12. If anyone shall say that God always pardons the
1712   whole penalty together with the guilt and that the satisfaction of penitents is nothing else than the faith by which they perceive that Christ has satisfied for them – *anathema sit*.

584   13. If anyone shall say that the satisfaction for sins, as to
1713   their temporal punishment, is in no way made to God through the merits of Christ by the punishments inflicted by him and patiently borne, or by those imposed

by the priest, or even those voluntarily undertaken, as by fasts, prayers, almsgiving or other works of piety, and that therefore the best penance is merely a new life – *anathema sit*.

14. If anyone shall say that the satisfactions by which penitents atone for their sins through Christ are not a worship of God but traditions of men which obscure the doctrine of grace and the true worship of God and the beneficence itself of the death of Christ – *anathema sit*.   585 *1714*

15. If anyone shall say that the keys have been given to the Church only to loose and not also to bind, and that therefore priests, when imposing penalties on those who confess, act contrary to the purpose of the keys and to the institution of Christ, and that it is a fiction that there remains often a temporal punishment to be discharged after the eternal punishment has by virtue of the keys been removed – *anathema sit*.   586 *1715*

ARTICLES OF MODERNISM CONDEMNED BY POPE PIUS X (1907)
(Cf. Note to No. 454)

46. In the primitive Church the concept of a Christian sinner reconciled by the authority of the Church did not exist, but the Church only very slowly became accustomed to this idea. Rather, even after penance was acknowledged as an institution of the Church it was not called by the name of sacrament for it would have been taken for a shameful sort of sacrament.   [587] *3446*

47. The words of the Lord: 'Receive ye the Holy Ghost. Whose sins you shall forgive, they are forgiven them; and whose sins you shall retain they are retained' *(John 20:22f)* do not refer to the sacrament of penance as the Fathers of Trent were pleased to say.   [588] *3447*

FROM THE CODE OF CANON LAW (1917)

589 C. 870. In the sacrament of penance by the judicial absolution administered by the lawful minister to a properly disposed *(member of the)* faithful, sins committed since baptism are remitted.

590 C. 871. The minister of this sacrament is the priest alone.

591 C. 872. As well as the power of order, the power of jurisdiction, either ordinary or delegated, in relation to the penitent, is required in the minister for the valid absolution of sins.

592 C. 883 § 1. Let the priest remember in hearing confessions that he is at once judge and doctor, that he has been constituted by God to serve divine justice and divine mercy, to consider the divine honour and the salvation of souls.

593 C. 901. Anyone who since baptism has committed mortal sins which have not already been remitted by the keys of the Church must confess all those of which after diligent examination he is conscious and must explain in confession any circumstances which change the nature of the sin.

594 C. 902. Sins committed since baptism, either mortal sins already remitted by the power of the keys or venial sins are sufficient but not obligatory matter for the sacrament of penance.

VI INDULGENCES

The power to forgive sins necessarily includes the power to remit the eternal punishment due to them. But there remains temporal punishment. But besides the power to forgive sins and their eternal punishment Christ also gave his Church the power to remit temporal punishment for sins.

In the remission of temporal punishment, that is, in indulgences, *it is not a matter of regaining the state of grace, or of the essential goods of the supernatural order which we receive in the sacraments and through the objective effects of the sacraments* ex opere operato *(i.e. independently of one's own or the Church's merits but solely by the power of Christ working in the sacramental signs), but of a lessening of the punishments still due for sin. This remission comes about on the basis of the* value as satisfaction of the works and sufferings of Christ *and of all who can accomplish such works in the grace of Christ, i.e. of* all persons in a state of grace. *The application of this satisfying value, however, is not attached to any sacramental sign in itself but to certain actions which can be prescribed by the Church. Thus, the twofold basis of the doctrine of indulgences is: first, the* satisfying and supernaturally meritorious value of all works done in a state of grace, *and second, the* community of saints, *of all, that is, who have been redeemed by Christ and live and work in his grace, in communion with Christ and with one another.*

Since the gaining of indulgences is related to certain actions, great abuses and scandals have been possible. The in part very abusive practice in the matter of in-

dulgences at the end of the Middle Ages served the Reformers as a symbol of a mechanistic organization of supernatural life, of the wordly character and avarice of the Church who touted holy things in the market-place. Against them, the Church declared her power to grant indulgences, and their value for the faithful, but at the same time she put all her force into the campaign against abuses.

The Church, then, teaches she has received from Christ, on the basis of the treasury of his merits, the power to grant to the faithful on certain conditions indulgences *i.e. the remission of temporal punishment due to sin (596, 598–602, 606, 856). Indulgences may be applied to the dead (605, 608). Abuses are to be avoided (607). The use of indulgences is salutary for the people of Christ (603–5, 856).*

POPE CLEMENT VI's JUBILEE BULL
UNIGENITUS DEI FILIUS (1343)

Pope Boniface VIII had proclaimed the year 1300 to be a Jubilee year, which was to be celebrated every hundred years, with a plenary indulgence for all who made the pilgrimage to Rome and fulfilled certain conditions there. In 1343 Clement VI proclaimed that every fiftieth year should be a Jubilee year, starting with 1350. He took the occasion to set out the basic truths about indulgences. The doctrinal matter of this Bull embraces three points: Christ's merits are superabundant; he has entrusted the treasury of his merits to the Church; to this treasury of Christ's merits are added the merits of the saints.

595
1025 The only-begotten Son of God... 'who of God is made unto us wisdom, and justice, and satisfaction, and redemption' *(1 Cor. 1:30)* 'neither by the blood of goats,

or of calves, but by his own blood, entered into the holy of holies... obtained eternal redemption *(Heb. 9:12)*, redeemed us 'not with corruptible things as gold or silver... but with (his own) precious blood, as of a lamb unspotted and undefiled' *(1 Peter 1:18f)*. On the altar of the Cross, he the innocent Victim, shed not just one drop of his blood – which on account of the union with the Word would have sufficed for the redemption of the entire human race – but poured it out in abundance so that 'from the sole of the foot to the top of the head there was no soundness' *(Is. 1:6)* found in him. Now if this so merciful shedding of blood were not to be useless, pointless and superfluous, *how great a treasure it won for the Church militant*. The good Father wanted to make his son rich, so that thus there should be 'an infinite treasure to men, which they that use, become the friends of God' *(Wis. 7:14)*.

Which treasure... he put at the disposal of blessed Peter, the Keybearer, and his successors, his own vicars on earth, to be salutarily distributed among the faithful, for pious and reasonable causes, for the remission, sometimes total, sometimes partial, of the temporal punishment due to sins, to be mercifully applied generally or specially, as it seems good before God, to those who truly repent and confess. 596 / 1026

To this mass of treasure, we know, are added the *merits of the blessed Mother of God and of all the elect* from the first to the last. There is no need to fear that it may be consumed or diminished, not only because of the infinite merits of Christ of which we have spoken but also because the more men attain righteousness by its application the more does their stock of merit increase. 597 / 1027

THE GENERAL COUNCIL OF CONSTANCE
(1414–18)

QUESTIONS TO BE PUT TO WYCLIFFITES AND HUSSITES

Since Wycliffe's system recognized no visible Church (cf. Notes to Nos 343 and 406) he also denied the ecclesiastical power to remit the punishment due to sin.

598
1266   26. Whether he believes that the Pope, for a pious and just cause, can grant to all Christians who are truly sorry and confess indulgences in the remission of sins, especially to those visiting holy places and giving a helping hand.

599
1267   27. And whether he believes that those who visit churches on account of such a concession, and those who assist, can obtain such indulgences.

ERRORS OF MARTIN LUTHER CONDEMNED BY POPE LEO X (1520)
(Cf. Note to No. 606)

[600]   17. The treasures of the Church from which the Pope
1467   gives indulgences are not the merits of Christ and the saints.

[601]   18. Indulgences are a pious fraud on the faithful and
1468   a remission from good works; they are among those things that are lawful, but not those that are expedient.

[602]   19. Indulgences, for those who really gain them, do
1469   not signify the remission of the punishment for actual sins due to the divine justice.

[603]   20. They are led astray who believe that indulgences
1470   are salutary and spiritually fruitful.

[604]   21. Indulgences are necessary only for public crimes

and are properly conceded only to the hardened and impatient. *1474*

22. For six kinds of men indulgences are neither necessary nor useful, viz: the dead and the dying, the infirm, the lawfully hindered, those who have not committed crimes, those who have committed crimes but not public ones, those who lead a better life. [605] *1472*

THE GENERAL COUNCIL OF TRENT, TWENTY-FIFTH SESSION (1563)

The twenty-fifth session of the Council of Trent still had to deal with various questions of importance in the conflict with the Reformers: Purgatory (Cf. No. 824), the honour paid to saints, relics and pictures (Cf. Nos. 400ff) and finally indulgences. Abuses in all these spheres, but particularly in the matter of indulgences, were the occasion of much falling away from the Church. In addition, in the course of the years of bitter struggle the grossest misunderstandings about indulgences had become current.

However the very poor state of Pope Pius IV's health, and other reasons, led to the Council's proceedings, being brought to as rapid a conclusion as possible. Unable to go into great preparatory detail, the Council restricted itself almost entirely to disciplinary decrees. The decree on indulgences issued at this time condemned the denial of the Church's power to grant indulgences and the denial of the utility of indulgences for the faithful.

DECREE CONCERNING INDULGENCES

Since the power of granting indulgences was conferred by Christ on the Church, and even in the earliest times she made use of the power divinely given her, the Holy Council teaches and commands that the use of indulgences, most salutary to the Christian people and approved by the authority of the Holy Councils, is to be 606 *1835* retained in the Church, and it condemns with anathema those who assert that they are useless or deny that there is in the Church the power of granting them.

607
1835 In granting them, however, it desires that, in accordance with the ancient and approved custom of the Church, moderation be observed, lest by too great facility ecclesiastical discipline be weakened... *(Abuses must be got rid of, and all evil traffic in indulgences must be abolished. The people must be instructed and the bishops must restore good order. Questions arising must be solved in conjunction with the Holy See.*

FROM THE CODE OF CANON LAW

608 C. 911. All should prize indulgences or the remission before God of the temporal punishment due to sins whose guilt has been forgiven. The Church authority concedes them from the Church's treasury for the living by means of absolution, and for the dead by means of intercession.

609 C. 925 § 1. To be capable of gaining an indulgence one must be baptized, not excommunicated, in a state of grace at least at the end of the prescribed works, and a subject of the person conceding the indulgence.

§ 2. In order to gain indulgences in fact, the qualified person must have the intention, at least a general intention, of gaining them and must complete the works enjoined in the time and manner prescribed by the concession.

VII EXTREME UNCTION[1]

As confirmation by conferring the Holy Spirit completes the sacrament of baptism, so extreme unction is the complement and completion of penance. Penance restores the justification lost by sin, extreme unction takes away the infirmity left by sin; it 'removes that state which might be an obstacle to the clothing with glory *of the resurrection'; and, as every sacrament makes us men in some respect like Christ, 'so we become by extreme unction* like the risen Christ *because it will be given to the dying as a sign of the glory to come in which everything mortal will be stripped from the elect' (Albertus Magnus). According to the teaching of great theologians, the holy anointing makes the man who stands at the threshold of eternity and loyally cooperates with the grace of the sacrament ready to enter directly upon the Beatific Vision.*

That this sacrament was provided for the sick to strengthen them and prepare them for a happy passage to the hereafter was for centuries an undisputed part of tradition. The ancient prayers accompanying the anointing of the sick are evidence of this. The Church only had to concern herself officially with the doctrinal side of it when particular questions cropped up or errors appeared. For this reason the earliest documents deal more with the question of the minister and the external rites.

1. I am aware of and in sympathy with the move to call this sacrament by a more meaningful name in English, but until some other term is *officially* adopted in English-speaking countries it seems better to retain the text-book translation of *extrema unctio* (Tr.).

It was not until the Reformation denied the sacramentality of extreme unction and its institution by Christ that a more exact exposition was demanded of the Council of Trent.
The Church teaches about extreme unction:
It is a true sacrament *(408, 413, 614, 617, 845, 851) instituted by Christ (613, 614, 617) and proclaimed by St James (614).*
It is administered *by anointing with blessed oil accompanied by prayer (610, 612, 614, 619, 621). Only a priest can validly administer it (611, 612, 616, 620, 622).*
It can be received by any baptized person who has reached the age of reason and is on account of sickness or age in danger of death (616, 623).
Its effect *is the strengthening of the soul (409, 612, 615, 618), often of the body as well (409, 612, 615) and in the necessary conditions remission of sins (615, 618).*

LETTER OF POPE INNOCENT I TO DECENTIUS (416)

Although the question put by Bishop Decentius of Gubbio only concerned the administration of extreme unction by a bishop, the answer provides us with clear evidence concerning the sacrament in general at the beginning of the fifth century. The holy oil was blessed by the bishop, but in those days was used for other pious customs besides the sacramental use. As well as the priest, the bishop was also, of course, the minister. The fact that it is described as a sacrament is not in itself any proof that it was regarded as one in the modern sense, for the word had not at that time a defined meaning, but the fact that those undergoing penance are excluded makes it clear that this was something more than just a pious custom.

610
216
(Your next question) concerns the text from the epistle of the Blessed Apostle James: 'Is any man sick among

you? Let him call the priests, and let them pray over him, anointing him with oil in the name of the Lord; and the prayer of faith will save the afflicted man, and the Lord will raise him up; and if he has sinned, it is remitted him' *(James 5:14)*. This must undoubtedly be accepted and understood as applying to the anointing of the faithful who are sick, who can be anointed with the holy oil of chrism, prepared by the bishop, which can be used not only by priests but also by all Christians for anointing in case of their own necessity or that of their people.

The question of whether the bishop can do what priests undoubtedly may, seems superfluous. For priests come into it because bishops are prevented by other occupations and cannot visit all the sick. But if the bishop is in a position to do so, and thinks it suitable, he can himself without hesitation visit the sick to bless them and anoint them with chrism, for it is he who prepares the chrism. But it may not be used on those undergoing penance for it is of the nature of a sacrament. How should one think that one kind of sacrament should be allowed to those to whom the rest are denied? 611
216

THE GENERAL COUNCIL OF FLORENCE

DECREE FOR THE ARMENIANS (1439)
(Cf. Note to No. 408)

The fifth sacrament is extreme unction, whose *matter* is olive oil blessed by the bishop. This sacrament may not be given except to a sick person whose life is feared for. He is to be anointed in these places: the eyes on account of sight, the ears on account of hearing, the nostrils for the sense of smell, the mouth for taste and speech, the 612
1324

hands for touch, the feet for movement, and the loins as the seat of desire.

The *form* of this sacrament is as follows: 'Through this holy unction and his own most tender mercy, may the Lord pardon thee whatever faults thou hast committed', and the same for the other members.

1325 The *minister* of this sacrament is a priest. The *effect* is the healing of the mind and, as far as it is good for the soul, of the body as well. Of this sacrament blessed James the Apostle says: 'Is anyone sick among you? Let him bring in the priests of the Church that they may pray over him, anointing him with oil in the name of the Lord; and the prayer of faith will save the sick man, and the Lord will raise him up; and if he be in sins, they are forgiven him' *(James 5:14f)*.

THE GENERAL COUNCIL OF TRENT, FOURTEENTH SESSION (1551)

The Council of Trent set out the doctrine concerning extreme unction in immediate conjunction with, and at the same session as, the sacrament of penance. Of all the documents of the Church, this one gives the most complete summary of the Church's teaching on the subject.

The foreword places this sacrament in the context of the other sacraments and in Christian life as a whole.

Chap. I deals with the institution of the sacrament and its announcement by St. James. Since extreme unction is according to theological conceptions the sacrament of 'completion not only of penance but also of the whole Christian life' which could only be administered in the fulness of the Holy Spirit, several mediaeval theologians taught that it was instituted by the Apostles. But all sacraments are instituted by Christ, that is to say that he determined the signs under which he wished to give his grace. It is here expressly taught that this sacrament was instituted by Christ but first pro-

claimed by St James the Apostle. This chapter also gives the essential elements of the sacrament.
Chap. II gives the effects of the sacrament: strengthening the soul, expiation of sins and the remains of sin, and, if expedient, restoration of bodily health.
Chap. III. The minister of the sacrament is an ordained priest, and the recipient one who is dangerously ill.

Foreword

It has seemed good to the Holy Council to add to the preceding document on penance the following concerning the sacrament of extreme unction, which was considered by the Fathers as the completion not only of penance but also of the whole Christian life, which ought to be a continual penance. First, therefore, with regard to its institution, it teaches that our most benevolent Redeemer, who wished to have his servants at all times provided with salutary remedies against all weapons of all enemies, as in the other sacraments he provided the greatest aids by means of which Christians may during life keep themselves free from every graver spiritual evil, so did he fortify the end of life by the sacrament of extreme unction as with the strongest defence. For though our adversary seeks and seizes occasions throughout our whole life to devour our souls in any manner, *(1 Pet. 5:8)* **yet there is no time when he strains more vehemently all the powers of his cunning to ruin us utterly, and if possible to make us lose even faith in the divine mercy, than when he perceives that the end of our life is near.**

613
1694

Chapter I. The Institution of the Sacrament of Extreme Unction

This sacred anointing of the sick was instituted by Christ our Lord as truly and properly a sacrament of the New

614
1695

Law, alluded to indeed by Mark *(6:13)* but recommended and announced to the faithful by James the Apostle and brother of the Lord. 'Is any man sick among you?' he says, 'Let him bring in the priests of the Church and let them pray over him, anointing him with oil in the name of the Lord; and the prayer of faith shall save the sick man, and the Lord shall raise him up; and if he be in sins, they shall be forgiven him' *(James 5:14f)*. In which words, as the Church has learned from apostolic tradition received from hand to hand, he teaches the matter, form, proper administration and effect of this salutary sacrament. For the Church has understood that the matter is the oil blessed by the bishop, because the anointing very aptly represents the grace of the Holy Spirit with which the soul of the sick person is invisibly anointed. The form, furthermore, consists of those words: 'By this unction etc....'

Chapter II. The Effect of this Sacrament

615
1696
Moreover, the significance and effect of this sacrament are explained in the words: 'And the prayer of faith shall save the sick man, and the Lord shall raise him up, and if he is in sins they shall be forgiven him' *(James 5:15)*. For the thing signified is the grace of the Holy Spirit whose anointing takes away the sins if there be any still to be expiated, and also the remains of sin, and raises up and strengthens the soul of the sick person by exciting in him great confidence in the divine mercy, supported by which the sick one bears more lightly the miseries and pains of his illness and resists more easily the temptations of the devil who lies in wait for his heel *(Gen. 3:15)*; and at times when expedient for the welfare of the soul, restores bodily health.

Chapter III. The Minister of this Sacrament and the Time when It Ought to be Administered

(Ministers of this sacrament are the bishop and priests. The sacrament should be given to the dangerously ill). 616 1697-1700

CANONS CONCERNING EXTREME UNCTION

Canon 1, against Luther, Calvin and Melancthon, teaches that extreme unction is a true sacrament instituted by Christ. Canon 2, against Melancthon and Calvin, emphasizes the spiritual effect. Like many modern Protestants, Calvin wanted to see in the anointing of the sick of which James speaks the charism of healing as it existed in the first centuries of Christianity.
Canon 4 designates the minister. Here, as in the case of other sacraments, Protestants tried to find support in Scripture for their rejection of ordained priests as the sole ministers, interpreting 'presbyters' to mean not the official priesthood but the elders of the community.

1. If anyone shall say that extreme unction is not truly and properly a sacrament instituted by Christ our Lord and announced by the blessed Apostle James, but is only a rite received from the Fathers or a human invention – *anathema sit*. 617 1716

2. If anyone shall say that the anointing of the sick neither confers any grace nor remits any sins nor comforts the sick, but that it has already ceased, as if it had been only the grace of healing in olden days, – *anathema sit*. 618 1717

3. If anyone shall say that the rite and usage of extreme unction which the holy Roman Church observes is at variance with the statement of the blessed Apostle James, and is therefore to be changed and may without sin be despised by Christians – *anathema sit*. 619 1718

620
1719
4. If anyone shall say that the priests *(presbyteri)* of the Church whom blessed James exhorts be brought to anoint the sick are not the priests *(sacerdotes)* who have been ordained by a bishop but the elders in each community, and that for this reason the proper minister of extreme unction is not the priest alone – *anathema sit*.

FROM THE CODE OF CANON LAW (1917)

621 C. 937. The sacrament of extreme unction must be conferred by holy anointings using properly blessed olive oil and the words prescribed in ritual books approved by the Church.

622 C. 938 § 1. Every priest, but only a priest, can validly administer this sacrament.

623 C. 940 § 1. Extreme unction cannot be given except to one of the faithful who, having reached the age of reason, is in danger of death from sickness or age.

624 C. 944. Although this sacrament of itself is not necessary for salvation by necessity of means, no one should neglect it...

VIII ORDER

The supreme task which Christ had to fulfil was his priestly work of atonement which he completed as mediator between God and man. *By the union in himself of humanity and divinity Christ is by nature the mediator. As a man from among men, Christ is our mediator with the Father; yet he is also capable of offering a worthy sacrifice to God because, by virtue of the union of his human nature with the Second Person of the Godhead, his human actions have an infinite value. In this fullest sense, the priesthood belongs to Christ alone.*

But if Christ wished to live on and continue his work in the Church, the first thing he had to do was to provide for the continuance of his sacerdotal and mediatory function. *Above all, if Christ wished to renew the sacrifice of the Cross throughout the ages and all over the world as the sacrifice of the New Law in the Holy Mass, he had to allow other men to share in his priesthood. For if there is to be a true sacrifice, there must be a priesthood ordained and authorized by God from whose hands God will accept the sacrifice.*

All attacks on the priesthood of the Catholic Church thus go back to a denial that the Holy Mass is a true sacrifice, entrusted by Christ to his Church, and ultimately to the denial of any visible Church to which Christ entrusted his work as mediator and redeemer. So the attacks of Wycliffe, the Reformers and the 'liberal' historians regarded the setting up of an official priesthood as the result of the evolution of Christian life in the early Christian communities.

The priesthood is ordained in the first place for the

offering of sacrifice and therefore for the solemnization of the Church's formal worship. The arrangements for these celebrations demand also a corresponding ministry and thus graded ministers to the altar. This grading of the ministry goes in part back to direct institution by Christ, but in part was introduced by the Church.

The degrees of order – the four minor and three major orders with the highest of all, that of bishop – signify an order of rank in the mediation of grace. It must be distinguished from the other order of rank which concerns jurisdiction, magisterium and pastorate. The latter are not essentially linked with the powers of mediation of grace, but in the concrete order established by God there are close relationships between the two kinds of power. For example, the fact that the power of forgiving sins exists in the Church does not, in itself, say anything about who has this power. But in the divine order, only a priest can have it.

Besides the conflict about the fact of the sacrament of order, its institution by Christ and its hierarchical structure, it has always been a principal concern of the Church to raise the priesthood to the high moral level suitable to its sublime duties. In the West, a most important step in this direction was the insistence on celibacy. But as we are concerned here solely with doctrinal matters, documents on this are not given.

The Church's doctrine on the sacrament of order is as follows:

Order is a true sacrament *(408, 413, 628, 635, 636, 845, 851) instituted by Christ (413, 635) who ordained the Apostles at the Last Supper (512, 522, 626).*

It is administered *by the laying on of hands and the key phrases of the ordination preface (625, 628, 637, 644b). Only a bishop can validly ordain (625, 631, 639, 643).*

Order is a purely ecclesiastical concern *(632, 639)*.
The effect *of the sacrament of order is to impart the* Holy Spirit *(565, 625, 628, 636) and to impress an indelible* character *(411, 421, 432, 629, 636, 851) which permanently distinguishes those in orders from the laity (629, 630, 636, 641). The laity also has a part in Christ's priesthood, but in another manner (644a).*
The office of bishop *is above the priesthood (which in turn is above the diaconate) and gives special powers of consecration (631, 634, 638, 639, 640). To the* priesthood *belong the celebration of Holy Mass and the power of forgiving sins (512, 522, 565, 581, 590, 633).*
The subdiaconate *belongs with the priesthood and diaconate to the 'major orders' (627, 634, 642). In addition, the four 'minor orders' were instituted by the Church (627, 634).*
Conditions *for the valid reception of order are baptism and being of the male sex (644).*

THE GENERAL COUNCIL OF FLORENCE

DECREE FOR THE ARMENIANS (1439)
(Cf. Note to No. 408)

The sixth sacrament is that of order, whose *matter* **is that which is conferred by its administration; thus the priesthood is conferred by the handing over of the chalice with the wine and the paten with the bread**[1]**; the diaconate by giving the book of the Gospels; the subdiaconate by**

625
1326

---

1. In the doctrine of matter and form the decree *pro Armeniis* follows the teaching of St Thomas Aquinas which is now almost universally rejected by theologians. The matter is the laying-on of hands, and the form the solemn preface which is immediately recited by the bishop. Since in this document we are not dealing with an infallible decree, this divergence of opinion is possible. See also 644a.

giving the empty chalice covered by the empty paten; and similarly for the others by the assignment of the things pertaining to their office. The *form* for a priest is this: 'Receive the power of offering sacrifice in the Church for the living and the dead, in the name of the Father and of the Son and of the Holy Ghost'. And similarly for the forms of the other orders as they are contained in full in the Roman pontifical. The *effect* is the increase of grace so that one may be a suitable minister of Christ.

THE GENERAL COUNCIL OF TRENT, TWENTY-THIRD SESSION (1563)

DOCTRINE ON THE SACRAMENT OF ORDER

According to the ideas of the Reformers there was no real priestly status into which one entered by the sacrament of order. In their ideas, faith is not communicated to us by a visible teaching body, the Church is not governed by an authority instituted by Christ, and grace is not given to man on the basis of outward signs but by confident faith. The Reformers therefore did not recognize any specific status instituted by Christ for the ministry of this grace. Since they did not recognize the sacrifice of the Mass, they did not need a sacrificing priesthood either.

The Council had rejected the basis of the Reformers' doctrine in its decree on justification; here it is a matter of drawing the most important conclusions therefrom. It is also a fact that this session, and that concerned with justification, required the hardest and most thorough preparatory work,

Chapter I. The Institution of the Priesthood of the New Law

626
1764 *Sacrifice and priesthood* are by the ordinance of God so united that both have existed in every law. Since, therefore, in the New Testament the Catholic Church

has received from the institution of Christ the holy, visible sacrifice of the Eucharist, it must also be confessed that there is in that Church a *new, visible and external priesthood* into which the old has been translated. That this was instituted by the same Lord our Saviour, and that to the Apostles and their successors in the priesthood was given the power of consecrating, offering and administering his body and blood, as also of forgiving and retaining sins, is shown by the Sacred Scriptures and has always been taught by the tradition of the Catholic Church.

Chapter II. The Seven Orders

But since the ministry of so holy a priesthood is something divine, in order that it might be exercised in a more worthy manner and with greater veneration, it was consistent that in the most well-ordered arrangement of the Church there should be *several distinct orders of ministers*, who by virtue of their office should minister to the priesthood, so distributed that those already having the clerical tonsure should ascend through the minor to the major orders. For the Sacred Scriptures mention unmistakably not only the priests but also the deacons, and teach in the most definite words what is especially to be observed in their ordination.

627
1765

And from the very beginning of the Church the names of the following orders and the duties proper to each one are known to have been in use, namely those of subdeacon, acolyte, exorcist, lector, and porter, though these were not of equal rank; for the subdiaconate is classed among the major orders by the Fathers and Holy Councils, in which we also read very often of other, inferior orders.

Chapter III. Order is Truly a Sacrament

628 Since from the testimony of Scripture, apostolic tradition
1766 and the unanimous agreement of the Fathers it is clear that grace is conferred by sacred ordination, which is performed by words and outward signs, no one ought to doubt that order is truly and properly one of the seven sacraments of Holy Church. For the Apostle says: 'I admonish thee that thou stir up the grace of God which is in thee by the imposition of my hands. For God has not given us the spirit of fear, but of power and of love and of sobriety' *(2 Tim. 1:6ff)*.

Chapter IV. The Ecclesiastical Hierarchy and Ordination

629 But since in the sacrament of order, as also in baptism
1767 and confirmation, a *character* is imprinted which can neither be effaced nor taken away, the Holy Council justly condemns the opinion of those who say that the priests of the New Testament have only a temporary power, and that those who have once been rightly ordained can again become laymen if they do not exercise the ministry of the word of God.

630 And if anyone should assert that *all Christians* without
1767 distinction are priests of the New Testament, or that they are all *inter se* endowed with an equal spiritual power, he is seen to do nothing else than derange the ecclesiastical hierarchy, which is 'an army set in array' *(Cant. 6:3)*; as if, contrary to the teaching of St Paul, all are apostles, all prophets, all evangelists, all pastors, all doctors *(cf. 1 Cor. 12, 29)*.

631 Wherefore the Holy Council declares that, besides the
1768 other ecclesiastical grades, the *bishops,* who have succeeded the Apostles, principally belong to this hierarchical order and have, as the same Apostle says, been

placed by the Holy Spirit to rule the Church of God *(Acts 20:28)*; that they are superior to priests, administer the sacrament of confirmation, ordain ministers of the Church, and can perform many other functions over which those of an inferior order have no power.

The Council teaches, furthermore, that in the ordination of bishops, priests and the other orders, the consent, call or authority, whether of the people or of any *civil power or magistrate*, is not required in such wise that without it the ordination is invalid; rather does it decree that all those who, called and instituted only by the people or by the civil power or magistrate, ascend to the exercise of these offices, and those who by their rashness assume them, are not ministers of the Church, but are to be regarded as thieves and robbers who have not entered by the door *(John 10:1)*. 632 *1769*

CANONS ON THE SACRAMENT OF ORDER

1. If anyone shall say that there is not in the New Testament a visible and external priesthood, or that there is no power of consecrating and offering the true body and blood of the Lord and of forgiving and retaining sins, but only the office and bare ministry of preaching the Gospel; or that those who do not preach are not priests at all – *anathema sit*. 633 *1771*

2. If anyone shall say that besides the priesthood there are not in the Catholic Church other orders, both major and minor, by which, as by certain steps, advance is made to the priesthood – *anathema sit*. 634 *1772*

3. If anyone shall say that order or sacred ordination is not truly and properly a sacrament instituted by Christ the Lord, or that it is some human contrivance devised by men unskilled in ecclesiastical matters, or that it is only a certain rite for choosing ministers of the word of 635 *1773*

God and of the sacraments – *anathema sit*.

636   4. If anyone shall say that by sacred ordination the Holy
1774   Spirit is not imparted and that therefore the bishops say in vain, 'Receive ye the Holy Spirit', or that a character is not imprinted by it, or that he who has once been a priest can again become a layman – *anathema sit*.

637   5. If anyone shall say that the holy anointing which the
1775   Church uses in ordination is not only not required but is detestable and pernicious, as also are the other ceremonies of order – *anathema sit*.

638   6. If anyone shall say that in the Catholic Church there
1776   is not instituted a hierarchy by divine ordinance, which consists of bishops, priests and ministers – *anathema sit*.

639   7. If anyone shall say that bishops are not superior to
1777   priests, or that they have not the power to confirm and ordain, or that the power they have is common to them and to priests, or that orders conferred by them without the consent or call of the people or of the secular power are invalid, or that those who have been neither rightly ordained nor sent by ecclesiastical and canonical authority, but come from elsewhere, are lawful ministers of the Word and of the sacraments – *anathema sit*.

640   8. If anyone shall say that the bishops who are chosen
1778   by the authority of the Roman Pontiff are not true and legitimate bishops but merely human deception – *anathema sit*.

FROM THE CODE OF CANON LAW (1917)

641   C. 948. According to Christ's institution order distinguishes the clergy from the laity in the Church for the guidance of the faithful and the ministry of divine worship.

642   C. 949. In the canons which follow, by *major* or *holy* orders are understood the priesthood, diaconate and

subdiaconate; and by minor orders, acolyte, exorcist, lector and doorkeeper.

C. 951. The ordinary minister of holy ordination is a consecrated bishop; an extraordinary minister, one who while not having the character of bishop has received by right or by special indult of the Holy See the power to confer certain orders. 643

C. 968. Only a baptized male can validly receive holy ordination... 644

POPE PIUS XII's ENCYCLICAL
MEDIATOR DEI (1947)
(Cf. Note to No. 537a; Nos. 317–9)

The Priesthood of the Faithful

The fact that the faithful take part in the Eucharistic Sacrifice does not mean that they also possess the power of the priesthood. The members of your flocks, Venerable Brethren, must be made to understand this very clearly. 644a / 3849

There are some who, holding a view not far removed from errors that have already been condemned, teach that the New Testament knows of no priesthood other than that which is common to all the baptized; that the command which Jesus Christ gave to his Apostles at the Last Supper, to do what he himself had done, was addressed directly to the whole community of the faithful; and that thence and only later the hierarchical priesthood took its rise. They therefore maintain that the people possess the true priestly power, and that the priest acts only in virtue of a function delegated to him by the community. Consequently they regard the Eucharistic Sacrifice as a true 'concelebration', and think that it is much better for priests to assist and 'concelebrate' with the people than to offer the sacrifice privately when the people are not present. 3850

It is not necessary to show how plainly these captious

errors contradict the truths We asserted above in speaking of the special position that the priest holds in the Mystical Body of Jesus Christ. One thing We think it advisable to repeat: that the priest acts in the name of the people precisely and only because he represents the person of our Lord Jesus Christ, considered as Head of all the members and offering himself for them; that the priest, therefore, approaches the altar as Christ's minister, lower than Christ, but higher than the people; that the people, on the other hand, because it in no way represents the person of the divine Redeemer and is not mediator between itself and God, can in no way possess the priestly right.

All this is certain with the certainty of faith. Yet it must be said that the faithful do also offer the divine victim, though in a different way...

3851 ...The rites and prayers of the Mass show no less clearly that the offering of the Victim is made by the priest together with the people. After the offertory of the bread and wine the sacred minister turns to the people and says: 'Pray, brethren, that my sacrifice and yours may become acceptable in the sight of God the Father Almighty.' Moreover, the prayers by which the divine Victim is offered to God are said for the most part in the plural, and they more than once indicate that the people have a part in this sacrifice as being offerers of it; for example, '...For whom we offer to thee, or who offer to thee... We beseech thee, Lord, graciously to receive this offering of thy servants, indeed of the whole of thy household... We, thy servants, indeed the whole of thy holy people, offer to thy august Majesty, from the gifts that thou hast given us, a pure victim, a holy victim, a spotless victim'.

And there is no wonder that the faithful are accorded this privilege: by reason of their baptism Christians are in the Mystical Body and become by a common title members of Christ the Priest; by the 'character' that is graven upon their souls they are appointed to the worship of God, and therefore, according to their condition, they share in the priesthood of Christ himself...

...To avoid any mistake in this very important matter We must clearly define the exact meaning of the word 'offer'. The unbloody immolation by which, after the words of consecration have been pronounced, Christ is rendered present on the altar in the state of victim, is performed by the priest alone, and by the priest in so far as he acts in the name of Christ, not in so far as he represents the faithful. But precisely because the priest places the divine Victim on the altar he presents it as an oblation to God the Father for the glory of the Blessed Trinity and for the benefit of the whole Church. Now, understood in this restricted sense, the oblation is in their own way shared by the faithful, and for two reasons: first because they offer the sacrifice *through* the priest, and secondly because, in a certain sense, they offer it *with* him. And because they have this part in the Sacrifice, the people's offering also pertains to liturgical worship.

That the faithful offer the sacrifice through the priest is clear from the fact that the minister at the altar acts in the person of Christ considered as Head, and as offering in the name of all the members; and this is why it is true to say that the whole Church makes the offering of the Victim through Christ.

But when the people are said to offer with the priest, this does not mean that all the members of the Church, like the priest himself, perform the visible liturgical rite; this is done only by the minister divinely appointed for the purpose. No, they are said to offer with him inasmuch as they unite their sentiments of praise, entreaty, expiation and thanksgiving with the sentiments or intention of the priest, indeed with those of the High Priest himself, in order that in the very oblation of the Victim, those sentiments may be presented to God the Father also by the priest's external rite. The external rite of sacrifice must of its very nature be a sign of internal worship; and what is signified by the Sacrifice of the New Law is that supreme homage by which Christ, the principal offerer, and with him and through him all his mystical members, pay due honour and veneration to God...

POPE PIUS XII's APOSTOLIC CONSTITUTION
SACRAMENTUM ORDINIS (30 Nov. 1947)
(*Cf.* Note to No. 408; No. 625)

644b
3859 ...By virtue of Our supreme Apostolic Authority We declare with certain knowledge and, as far as it may be necessary, we determine and ordain: the *matter* of the holy orders of diaconate, priesthood and episcopate is the laying-on of hands alone; and the sole *form* are the words determining the application of the matter, whereby the *effects* of the sacrament are unequivocally signified – that is, the power of order and the grace of the Holy Spirit – and which are accepted and used as such by the Church. This leads Us to declare ... and ordain that ... if it has ever been lawfully laid down otherwise ... at least in the future the handing over of the instruments is not necessary for the validity of the holy orders of diaconate, priesthood and episcopate[1].

1. The Constitution then goes on to lay down in detail that in the Latin rite the *first* imposition of hands is the matter for priests and to establish the forms for the three orders; these are certain words in the 'Prefaces' which follow the laying-on of hands, not those which in the case of deacons and bishops accompany the action. Thus, for the future (but only for the future) the old dispute is settled as to whether the handing over of the instruments customary since the Middle Ages was necessary for the rite of ordination.

IX MATRIMONY

Matrimony is the marriage contract between Christians raised by Christ to the dignity of a sacrament. The theological and dogmatic treatment of this sacrament does not look very much to its main features of unity and indissolubility which are basic characteristics of all marriage in natural ethics; they are rather premisses, though of course they attain greater significance and depth and stability in marriage as a sacrament. The fact, then, that these features take up a considerable amount of space in Church documents must not be allowed to hide the theological content of this sacrament which comes to us from revelation and belongs to the supernatural order. As a sacrament matrimony is entirely oriented on man's supernatural goal. *Matrimony and order are the two sacraments which not only serve the individual in reaching this goal but are there for the* benefit of the community. *Matrimony is there for the mutual help of the spouses and the increase of the people of God. Devotion to this twofold end is the way of salvation for married couples, a way sanctified by the sacrament. 'Yet she shall be saved through childbearing; if she continue in faith, and love, and sanctification, with sobriety'* (1 Tim:2:15).
The mutual sacrifice and devotion of husband and wife is a true picture of Christ's sanctifying sacrifice and devotion to his Church. '*Matrimony has its significance in the first place from Christ who took the Church as his bride at the price of his own blood. And also because when he offered his life as the price of her ransom, he stretched out his arms in an embrace of supreme love. And thirdly: as Eve was formed from the side of Adam*

while he slept, so the Church was formed from the side of the dying and dead Christ, as the two chief sacraments poured from his side – the blood of redemption and the water of absolution' (Albertus Magnus).

It is only from this point of view that one can understand the Church's unceasing struggle against any attempt to see marriage as something unholy or something merely profane, of no concern to religion. The campaign began with those countless rigorist or dualist sects in early times and in the Middle Ages; it defended the religious nature of marriage against the Reformers for whom it was just a civil affair; it represented the demands of the Church in the matter of matrimonial legislation in various countries and defended the indissolubility of the marriage contract and the sacrament in the encyclicals of Leo XIII and Pius XI.

Since marriage is also of the greatest civic significance, jurisdiction in matrimonial matters was one of the commonest causes of differences between Church and State. Since this is solely a question of dogmatic viewpoints, the relevant documents are omitted.

For the same reason Church documents dealing mainly with matrimonial morality are omitted.

Church teaching on matrimony, so far as it is represented in the documents in this book, embraces the following truths:

Marriage is willed by God and was raised to a sacrament *by Christ (408, 413, 646, 650, 651, 663, 667, 674, 677, 845, 851). It is therefore good (167, 168, 645, 837d) but may not be put before the state of virginity (659, 660).*

The sacrament of matrimony consists of the marriage contract *(646, 665, 666, 668, 677), so that for Christians the contract and the sacrament are inseparable (665, 675, 677). Therefore marriage comes into the* legal competence of the Church *(653–9, 664–5)*. *The Church may establish impediments (653–5, 847), including diriment impediments which invalidate a marriage (653, 654, 659) and forbidding impediments which make a marriage illegal (653). She may determine the form and rite to be observed (661). Matrimonial causes fall to ecclesiastical courts (662, 679).*

The purpose of marriage is the increase of the people of God (409, 646, 670, 678) and mutual help for the partners in loyalty and love (646, 671, 678). The sacrament gives married people a claim on the graces necessary to their state (649, 663, 674–6).

Only monogamy is valid (648, 652, 671, 678, 847). A new marriage is allowed after the death of one party (645, 847). Marriage is indissoluble (645, 646, 647–9, 655, 672, 673, 678) even in case of adultery (657). An unconsummated marriage can in certain circumstances be dissolved by the Church (656). Once it is consummated, a separation only is possible; the marriage bond cannot be dissolved (658).

PROFESSION OF FAITH PRESCRIBED FOR WALDENSIANS – POPE INNOCENT III (1208)

With Waldensians and Albigensians it was a question of dualistic errors. On the basis of the two 'principles' of good (spirit) and evil (matter), marriage was entirely rejected by 'the Perfect' (cf. also Note to No. 405)

We do not deny... that true marriages may be contracted. We forbid properly contracted marriages to be divorced. We believe and confess that a man can be saved even if he has a wife, and we do not condemn a second or even further marriage.

645
794

THE GENERAL COUNCIL OF FLORENCE

DECREE FOR THE ARMENIANS (1439)
(Cf. Note to No. 408)

646
1327 The seventh is the sacrament of matrimony which is the sign of the union of Christ and his Church according to the Apostle who says: 'This is a great sacrament; but I speak in Christ and in the Church' *(Eph. 5:32)*. The *efficient cause* is the mutual consent regularly expressed in words relating to the present. *A triple good* attaches to matrimony. The first is the begetting of *children* and their education to the worship of God. The second is the faithfulness which each spouse owes to the other. The third is the indissolubility of marriage because it represents the indissoluble union of Christ and the Church. But although it is permitted to have a separation of bed on account of fornication, it is contrary to divine law to contract another marriage since the bond of a legitimately contracted marriage is permanent.

THE GENERAL COUNCIL OF TRENT, TWENTY-FOURTH SESSION (1563)

By denying the seventh sacrament the Reformers had removed marriage from the realm of the supernatural and consequently rejected the Church's juridical functions in matrimonial matters. The assertion of the supernatural character of matrimony as a sacrament and the responsibility of the Church in matrimonial matters were thus the two main concerns of the Council in dealing with the question at their twenty-fourth session. After an introductory passage which recites the main points of revelation concerning the sacrament come the canons directed against the current heresies of the time.
In the second canon the Council deliberately had in mind the

compliancy of the Reformers, Luther in particular, in the case of Philip of Hesse's bigamous marriage. In any case, it is a matter of one of the basic characteristics of Christian marriage.

Canons 3 and 4 support the rights of the Church in matrimonial matters. The sacraments are entrusted to the administration of the Church. If the marriage contract is a sacrament, the Church must necessarily be responsible in matrimonial legislation as well.

Canon 7 deals with the question of whether adultery looses the bond of marriage and makes a new marriage possible. Tradition on this point was not absolutely clear. Above all it was desired not to offend the non-united Greeks who allowed remarriage in such cases. The wording is thus carefully designed so that it only demands acceptance of the Latin standpoint without expressly condemning the other. In Casti Connubii *(1930)* Pius XI declared the teaching of the Latin Church to be universally binding. Referring to this canon, he says: 'If the Church was not, and is not now, in error when she taught and still teaches this doctrine; and if, consequently, it is certain that the marriage bond cannot be dissolved even on the ground of adultery, then clearly all the other grounds of divorce, much less serious, which are commonly advanced, have even less validity, and are to be entirely dismissed' (93).

Canon 9 is so contrived that it does not exclude marriage before ordination which was customary in the Eastern Churches.

Canon 10 brings out the value of the unmarried State which, according to Protestant ideas, was contrary to divine order.

Canon 12 is of great significance and was not set out without the most detailed study. It is not intended to deny that many juridical matters concerning marriage do also fall to State authorities. In particular, Canon Law has interpreted this canon in a manner that leaves State responsibility untouched as far as the civil rights consequent upon a marriage contract are concerned.

DOCTRINE OF THE SACRAMENT OF MATRIMONY

647
1797
The perpetual and indissoluble bond of matrimony was expressed by the *first father of the human race* when, under the influence of the divine Spirit, he said: 'This now is bone of my bones and flesh of my flesh. Wherefore a man shall leave father and mother and shall cleave to his wife, and they shall be two in one flesh' *(Gen. 2:23f).*

648
1798
But that by this bond two only are united and joined together, *Christ the Lord* taught more plainly when referring to those last words as having been spoken by God, he said: 'Therefore now they are not two, but one flesh' *(Mt. 19:6)* and immediately ratified the firmness of the bond so long ago proclaimed by Adam with these words: 'What therefore God has joined together, let no man put asunder' *(Mt. 19:6).*

649
1799
But the *grace* which was to perfect the natural love and confirm that indissoluble union and sanctify the persons married Christ himself, the instituter and perfecter of the venerable sacraments, merited for us by his Passion, which Paul the Apostle intimates when he says: 'Husbands, love your wives, as Christ also loved the Church, and delivered himself up for it' *(Eph. 5:25);* adding immediately: 'This is a great sacrament, but I speak in Christ and in the Church' *(Eph. 5:32).*

650
1800
Since therefore matrimony in the evangelical law surpasses in grace through Christ the ancient marriages, our Holy Fathers, the Councils and the tradition of the universal Church have with good reason always taught that it is to be numbered among the *sacraments of the New Law*; and since with regard to this teaching ungodly men of this age, raving madly, have not only formed false ideas concerning this venerable sacrament but, introducing as is their habit under the pretext of the Gospel

a carnal liberty, have by word and writing asserted, not without great harm to the faithful of Christ, many things that are foreign to the teaching of the Catholic Church and to the usage approved since the time of the Apostles, this holy and general Council... *(propounds the following canons).*

CANONS ON THE SACRAMENT OF MATRIMONY

1. If anyone shall say that matrimony is not truly and properly one of the seven sacraments of the evangelical law, instituted by Christ the Lord, but has been devised by men in the Church and does not confer grace – *anathema sit.*   651 *1801*

2. If anyone shall say that it is lawful for Christians to have several wives at the same time and that this is not forbidden by any divine law – *anathema sit.*   652 *1802*

3. If anyone shall say that only those degrees of consanguinity which are expressed in Leviticus can hinder matrimony from being contracted and dissolve it when contracted, and that the Church cannot dispense in some of them or declare others that hinder and dissolve it – *anathema sit.*   653 *1803*

4. If anyone shall say that the Church cannot establish impediments dissolving marriage *(diriment impediments)* or that she has erred in establishing them – *anathema sit.*   654 *1804*

5. If anyone shall say that the bond of matrimony can be dissolved by heresy, or irksome cohabitation, or by reason of the voluntary absence of one of the parties – *anathema sit.*   655 *1805*

6. If anyone shall say that matrimony contracted but not consummated is not dissolved by the solemn religious profession of one of the parties – *anathema sit.*   656 *1806*

7. If anyone shall say that the Church errs in that she taught and teaches that in accordance with evangelical   657 *1807*

and apostolic doctrine *(Mt. 19:6ff; Mark 10:6ff; 1 Cor. 7:10ff)* the bond of matrimony cannot be dissolved by reason of adultery on the part of one of the parties, and that both, or even the innocent party who gave no reason for adultery, cannot contract another marriage during the lifetime of the other, and that he is guilty of adultery who, having put away the adulteress, shall marry another, and she also who, having put away the adulterer, shall marry another – *anathema sit.*

658
1808
8. If anyone shall say that the Church errs when she declares that for many reasons a separation may take place between husband and wife with regard to bed and cohabitation for a determinate or indeterminate period *anathema sit.*

659
1809
9. If anyone shall say that clerics constituted in sacred orders or regulars who have made solemn professions of chastity can contract marriage, and that the one contracted is valid notwithstanding the ecclesiastical law or vow, and that the contrary is nothing but a condemnation of marriage, and that all who feel that they have not the gift of chastity, even though they have made such a vow, can contract marriage, *anathema sit,* since God does not refuse that gift to those who ask for it rightly, neither does 'he suffer us to be tempted above that which we are able' *(1 Cor. 10:13).*

660
1810
10. If anyone shall say that the married state excels the state of virginity or celibacy, and that it is better and happier to be united in matrimony than to remain in virginity or celibacy – *anathema sit.*

661
1811
11. If anyone shall say that the prohibition of the solemnization of marriages at certain times of the year is a tyrannical superstition derived from the superstition of the heathen, or condemns the blessings and other ceremonies which the Church makes use of therein – *anathema sit.*

12. If anyone shall say that matrimonial causes do not belong to ecclesiastical judges – *anathema sit*. 662
1812

POPE LEO XIII's ENCYCLICAL *ARCANUM DIVINAE SAPIENTIAE* (1880)

Marriage is a Sacrament
Christ the Lord raised matrimony to the dignity of a sacrament and at the same provided that the spouses, sheltered and strengthened by the grace which his merits had won, should attain sanctification in marriage itself; and in it, marvellously modelled on the pattern of his mystical marriage with the Church, he has both perfected the love proper to human nature and by the bond of divine love strengthened the naturally indissoluble partnership of man and woman. 'Husbands', says St Paul, 'love your wives, as Christ also loved the Church, and delivered himself up for it' *(Eph. 5:25)*... 663
3142

The Church's Authority over Marriage
When Christ therefore renewed matrimony and raised it to such a great excellence *(as a sacrament)*, he gave and confided to the Church the *entire legislation* in the matter. And the Church has at all times and in all places exercised this power over the marriages of Christians in such a manner that it has been clear that it is something proper to her, not a concession sought from men but a property accorded her by God through the will of her Founder... 664
3144

The civil marriage contract and the sacrament are not separable
Let no one be misled by the distinction which supporters of the civil power try to make whereby they 665
3145

separate the nuptial contract from the sacrament so that, leaving the sacramental aspects to the Church, the contractual element becomes subject to the power and judgment of the civil power. For there is no basis for such a distinction, or rather such a disruption, for it is clear that in Christian marriage the *contract cannot be dissociated from the sacrament;* thus there can be no true and legitimate contract which is not thereby a sacrament. For Christ the Lord raised matrimony to the dignity of a sacrament, and matrimony is that contract if it is legally made.

The Internal Proof that the Contract itself is the Sacrament

666
3146

In addition, matrimony is a sacrament for this reason that it is a sacred and efficient sign of grace and the *image of the mystical marriage of Christ with his Church.* This form and figure are expressed by the bond of most intimate union by which man and woman bind themselves together, which bond is nothing other than matrimony itself. Hence it is apparent that every proper marriage between Christians is, in and of itself, the sacrament; and nothing is further from the truth than that the sacrament is a sort of added ornament, or an extrinsic property that can be separated from the contract should man think fit.

Thus there is no proof from reason or from history that the civil power has ever legitimately had authority over the marriage of Christians. If in this matter rights have been violated, let no one say that it has been done by the Church.

POPE PIUS XI's ENCYCLICAL
CASTI CONNUBII (1930)

In the introduction Pope Pius refers to Leo XIII's encyclical (No. 663ff)
Taking our starting point from that encyclical, which is concerned almost entirely with vindicating the divine institution of matrimony, its dignity as a sacrament, and its perpetual stability, let us first recall this immutable, inviolable and fundamental truth: 667

Marriage as a Divine Institution
Matrimony was not instituted or re-established by men but by God; not men, but God, the Author of Nature, and Christ our Lord, the restorer of nature, provided marriage with its laws, confirmed it and elevated it; and consequently those laws can in no way be subject to human wills or to any contrary pact made even by the contracting parties themselves... 3700

The Part Played by the Human Will
But although matrimony by nature is of divine institution, yet the human will has a part, and a very noble part, to play in it. Each individual marriage, in so far as it is a conjugal union between a particular man and a particular woman, arises only out of the free consent of the two parties; and this free act by which each yields and receives the specifically marital right is so necessary for the constitution of a true marriage that no human power can supply its place. 668 3701

The Limits of this Freedom
But the only function of this human freedom is to decide that each of the contracting parties in fact wishes to enter the state of matrimony, and to marry 669 3701

this particular person. The freedom of man has no power whatever over the nature of matrimony itself, and therefore when once a person has contracted matrimony he becomes subject to its essential laws and properties...

Offspring

670
3704 The Creator of the human race himself, who in his goodness has willed to use human beings as his ministers in the propagation of life, taught us this truth when in instituting matrimony in the Garden of Eden he bade our first parents, and through them all married persons who should come after them: 'Increase and multiply...' *(Gen. 1:28)*

3705 Christians parents should understand, moreover, that their duty is not only to propagate and maintain the human race on earth; it is not even merely to rear worshippers of the true God. They are called to give children to the Church, to beget fellow-citizens of the saints and members of the household of God, in order that the worshippers of our God and Saviour may increase from day to day...

Fidelity

671
3706 The second of the blessings of marriage... is fidelity, that is, the mutual faithfulness of husband and wife in observing the matrimonial contract. This implies that the right which in virtue of this divinely ratified agreement belongs exclusively to each companion will neither be denied by the one to the other nor be granted to any third party...

Marriage as a Sacrament

672
3710 But the complement and crown of all is the blessing of Christian marriage which... we have called sacra-

ment. It denotes both the indissolubility of the matrimonial bond, and the consecration of this contract by Christ, who elevated it to rank of a sign which is a cause of grace...

The Supernatural Mystery of Marriage
If we seek with reverence to discover the intrinsic reason of this divine ordinance *(indissolubility of marriage)* ...we shall easily find it in the mystical signification of Christian wedlock, seen in its full perfection in consummated marriage between Christians. The Apostle in the Epistle to the Ephesians... tells us that Christian wedlock signifies that most perfect union which subsists between Christ and the Church: 'This is a great sacrament, but I speak in Christ and in the Church' *(Eph. 5:32);* and this is a union which certainly as long as Christ lives and the Church lives by him, can never cease or be dissolved. The same teaching is thus set forth by St Augustine: 'This is what is observed in Christ and in the Church: married persons must never break their married life by any divorce. This sacrament is esteemed so highly in the City of God, that is in the Church, that when women marry or are married for the purpose of proceating offspring it is not lawful to leave a wife, even though she be sterile, to marry another who may bear children. If anyone were to act in this way he would not be condemned by the law of this world... but according to the law of the Gospel such a man is guilty of adultery; and so too is his wife if she marry another man' (Augustine)...

673
3712

The Graces of the Sacrament
But in addition to this permanent indissolubility, the blessing of which we are speaking includes other far

674
3713

greater advantages, which are most aptly designated by the word sacrament. For on the lips of a Christian this is no empty word. When our Lord, who instituted and perfected the sacraments, raised the marriage of his faithful to the dignity of a true and real sacrament of the New Law, he really made it the sign and the source of that special interior grace 'which was to perfect the natural love and confirm that indissoluble union and sanctify the persons married' *(Trent XXIV – No. 649).*

675
3713 And because Christ has made the valid matrimonial consent among the faithful to be a sign of grace, the essence of the sacrament is so closely bound up with Christian wedlock that there can be no true marriage between baptized persons which is not at the same time a sacrament. When the faithful, therefore, give that consent with a sincere heart they open for themselves the treasury of sacramental grace, from which they can draw supernatural strength enabling them to fulfil their obligations and functions faithfully, holily, and perseveringly until death.

676
3714 For this sacrament, if its fruit is not frustrated by any obstacle, not only increases in the soul sanctifying grace, the permanent principle of supernatural life, but also adds special gifts, good impulses, and seeds of grace, amplifying and perfecting the powers of nature and enabling the recipients not only to understand with their minds, but also to relish intimately, grasp firmly, will effectively, and fulfil in deed all that belongs to the state of wedlock and its purpose and duties; it also gives them the right to obtain the help of actual grace whenever they need it for the discharge of their matrimonial tasks.

FROM THE CODE OF CANON LAW (1917)

C. 1012 § 1. Christ the Lord raised the matrimonial contract between baptized persons to the dignity of a sacrament.   677

§ 2. Therefore there can be no valid matrimonial contract between baptized persons that is not in itself a sacrament.

C. 1013 § 1. The primary end of marriage is the procreation and education of offspring; the secondary end, mutual help and the remedy of concupiscence.   678

§ 2. Essential properties of marriage are unity and indissolubility, which in Christian marriage acquire special strength by reason of the sacrament.

C. 1960. Matrimonial causes between baptized persons belong by proper and exclusive right to an ecclesiastical judge.   679

CHAPTER TEN

GRACE

The doctrine of grace embraces revealed truth concerning man's supernatural life. We have already dealt with the first step taken by God for man's elevation, the incarnation of the eternal Word and his work of redemption, and the means whereby Christ communicates his grace to man – the sacraments. All that remains is to see how this elevation of man functions in man himself and what it is that God effects in man – the new life of grace which will be perfected at the end of time in the Beatific Vision.

A condition for the life of grace is that man be freed from sin; this is achieved by justification. *As man by original sin became a sinner before God, this guilt relationship is removed by the application of redemption. It is not just that man is as though justified; he is justified. In this the Church's doctrine on justification is diametrically opposed to that of the Reformers who admitted only an external justification, a sort of attribution of Christ's righteousness to man while inwardly man remained a stranger to righteousness.*

Above and beyond this, with justification man receives grace. It is a free gift from God by virtue of which he becomes a son of God, temple of the Holy Spirit and partaker of the divine nature.

The life of grace is beyond anything which human nature

can lay claim to. And in fact grace is given to an infant in baptism without any action on his part. But an adult must play his part if he is to acquire grace. Thus the doctrine of grace faces the question which can never be entirely answered of how divine grace *and* human freedom *work together. Left to himself, man can never be in a position to take the first step in the supernatural life. Supernatural life is lived on a completely different plane, a plane to which man must be raised before he can do anything on it. But once grace has raised him, man must cooperate.*

Historically *the question of the nature of grace for a long time took second place to that of its action. Here it is a matter of truths which radically affect human life and whose resolution determines the form which Christian life takes. Thus the Church documents we find here deal principally with the conflict with heresies about grace, and owe their existence to combating the erroneous attempts to explain the cooperation between grace and free will. It was only when the Reformers so discounted man's cooperation with grace as to deny human nature's elevation to the supernatural life that the Church's great answer given by Trent (No. 717f) included an exposition on the nature of grace. But even this confined itself to essentials without going into detail or settling any theological conflicts.*

The Church's teaching about grace covers:
1. The doctrine of sanctifying grace. *In justification not only are all sins forgiven (704–7, 712, 717–9, 721, 731, 748) but also* new life is given *(225, 409, 712, 713, 717, 719, 720, 748). The Holy Spirit lives in the soul (563, 718, 720, 807a, 833), by regeneration man shares in the divine life (771) and becomes a living member of the mystical Body of Christ (359, 436, 557, 721). Man be-*

Grace

comes a son of God and heir to heaven (713, 717, 734).
Grace is active and is increased by keeping the commandments and by good works (446, 447, 724, 726, 727, 756–8, 761–3) which gain merit for eternal life (695, 734–6, 763, 768, 769, 774). In justification, the virtues of faith, hope and charity are infused (721, 748).
Grace is gratuitous and supernatural (35, 710, 714, 722, 723, 771, 788, 807a, 807b).
Grace is lost by every mortal sin (445, 731, 733, 764).

2. The doctrine of actual grace
Without supernatural grace there are purely natural good works (744, 775–83, 787–9, 795–9, 801–4). But only grace raises them to be actions of supernatural value (688, 690, 691, 693–5, 698–, 701, 702, 710, 738, 739, 740). Grace gives the first impulse on the way to justification (691, 693, 694, 696–701, 714, 738–40), but it must be actively accepted by man (37, 695, 714, 741). Grace does not remove man's freedom (714, 741, 791, 793, 805–7).
With the help of grace man must prepare himself for justification (695, 714, 715, 741–6) particularly by faith, which is necessary for justification (35, 39, 699, 715, 722) but which does not achieve justification by itself (722, 723, 726, 746, 749–51).
Actual grace is necessary to persevere in avoiding grievous sin (680–2, 689). Final perseverance is a special grace (729, 730, 753, 759).
Everyone receives the grace he needs to keep the commandments (365, 702, 725, 755, 777, 790) but not to avoid all venial sins (683–5, 725, 760).
3. The doctrine of predestination. God's desire for the salvation of all men (365, 794); no one is predestined to evil (702, 743, 754). Nobody can with certainty maintain that he is predestined for eternal life (728, 752, 753).

THE LOCAL COUNCIL OF CARTHAGE (418)

In the midst of the decline and degeneration of the Roman Empire the British monk Pelagius came to Rome at the beginning of the fifth century and gave his strict moral sermons Since Constantine had made Christianity into the State religion a great deal of worldliness had found its way into the Church. Against this decay Pelagius preached the moral seriousness of Christianity. Nature, freedom, law and acquired virtue were the watchwords of his very stoical sermons. His disciple Caelestius organized his thought into a system.

The kernel of the Pelagian heresy is the assumption of complete freedom in man who, without disturbing the balance of good and evil can achieve his own salvation by his own powers. Sin arose only from the personal decision of individuals in favour of evil. Original sin on the basis of the solidarity of the human race found no place in the system of Pelagius and Caelestius (cf. p. 134) The effect of Adam's sin was only that of bad example, copied by his descendants in their personal sins. In his nature, man with his concupiscence and mortality was in the same state as Adam before the fall.

The work of Christ was confined to the forgiveness of personal sins. Man did not necessarily need *actual grace to keep the commandments and attain salvation. The effect of grace consisted solely in illuminating instinct and making* moral actions easier.

The most significant condemnation of Pelagius took place at the Council of Carthage where he had spent some time after Alaric's conquest of Rome. The sentence of the two hundred bishops present was confirmed by Pope Zosimus.

680
225 **3. ...whoever shall say that the grace of God, whereby man is justified through Jesus Christ, our Lord, serves only for the remission of sins already committed but not as a help to their not being committed** – *anathema sit.*

4. And whoever shall say that this same grace of God 681
through Jesus Christ our Lord only helps us not to sin 226
because by it an understanding of the commandments is
opened to us and made clear so that we know what we
should seek and what we should avoid but not that we
should be willing and able to do what we know to be our
duty – *anathema sit*.

For, as the Apostle says: 'Knowledge puffeth up; but
charity edifieth' *(1 Cor. 8:1)*, it is therefore impious to
believe that we have the grace of Christ for what puffs
us up and not for that which edifies, for both are the gift
of God, both knowing what we should do and loving to
do it, so that edified by love we are not puffed up by
knowledge. As it is written of God that 'he teacheth man
knowledge' *(Ps 93:10)*, so also is it written that 'love
is of God' *(1 John 4:7)*.

5. And whoever shall say that the grace of justification is 682
given to us so that we may by virtue of grace more easily 227
carry out what we are required to do, by our free will, as
if even without grace we could, not easily indeed but
possibly, fulfil the divine commandments – *anathema sit*.
For when the Lord spoke of the fruits of the commandments he did not say that without him we could do things
with greater difficulty, but, 'Without me you can do
nothing' *(John 15:5)*.

6. And whoever shall so understand the words of St John 683
the Apostle: 'If we say that we have no sin, we deceive 228
ourselves, and the truth is not in us' *(1 John 1:8)* as to
mean that we must say out of humility that we have sins
and not because it is true – *anathema sit*. For the Apostle
carries on to say: 'But if we confess our sins, he is faithful and just, to forgive us our sins, and to cleanse us from
all iniquity' *(1 John 1:9)*. Whence it is sufficiently obvious that this is said not just out of humility but in truth.
The Apostle could have said: If we say that we have no

sin, we are boasting, and humility is not in us, but since he did say, 'we deceive ourselves and the truth is not in us' it is clear enough that anyone who says he has no sin does not speak truly but falsely.

684
229 7. And whoever shall say that the saints in saying in the Lord's Prayer 'Forgive us our trespasses' *(Mt. 6:12)* do not say it for themselves, because the petitition is unnecessary for them, but for others in his people who are sinners, and therefore none of the saints says, 'Forgive me my trespasses' but 'Forgive us our trespasses' so that the just man is understood to pray for others rather than for himself – *anathema sit*. For the Apostle James was a holy and just man, and he said, 'In many things we all offend' *(James 3:2)*. For why should he insert the word 'all' if not to bring it into accord with the psalm where we read: 'And enter not into judgment with thy servant: for in thy sight no man living shall be justified' *(Ps.: 142:2)*; and in the prayer of the most wise Solomon 'There is no man who sinneth not' *(3 Kgs. 8:46)*; and in the book of holy Job: 'He sealeth the hand of every man, that every man may know his weakness' *(Job. 37:7)*[1]. Whence also the holy and just Daniel, when he used the plural in his prayer, saying, 'We have sinned, we have committed iniquity' *(Dan. 9:5, 15)*, and the other things which he there truly and humbly confesses, lest it be thought, as some think, that he spoke not of his own sins but rather of those of his people, added afterwards, 'While I was... praying, and confessing my sins, and the sins of my people...' *(Dan. 9:20)* to the Lord my God he did not want to say 'our sins' but said the sins of his people and his own sins, for as a prophet he foresaw how they would falsely interpret him in the future.

685
230 8. And whoever wants to understand the words of the

1. This does not correspond to the original text but is translated from the Latin quoted by the Council.

Lord's Prayer where we say, 'Forgive us our trespasses' as being said by the saints out of humility but not truthfully, *anathema sit*. For who can tolerate that one who prays lies not just to men but to the Lord himself, saying with his lips that he wishes to be forgiven and in his heart that he has nothing that needs forgiveness?

THE INDICULUS

In the struggle with the Pelagians, particularly with the clever Julian of Eklanum, Augustine put all his weight into tackling the difficult questions of the relationship between human freedom and divine grace, between the divine will for universal salvation and the divine predestination of the elect. There were severe battles, especially in Southern Gaul. People accepted the authoritative pronouncements of the Church, but would not accept Augustine's teaching, on the basis that all men, being equal before God, God gives all men equal grace; any difference in the bestowal of grace comes solely from differences in the willingness of men themselves; that was also true of the first communication of sanctifying grace. Outstanding opponent of this Semi-Pelagianism, *which unlike Pelagianism professed to admit the necessity of grace for any good work (that is, any work corresponding to the present supernatural order of salvation), though in fact it did not do so because it attributed the original distribution of grace not to God's free generosity but to man's merit, was Prosper of Acquitaine. About the middle for the fifth century his 'Indiculus' made its appearance. It was a summary of the doctrine of grace based on papal pronouncements, pronouncements of the African Councils which had received papal approval, and of the faith as it was expressed in the Church's liturgy, and it presented in classical form the Church's teaching on the action of grace. By the end of the fifth century it was already accepted as the* standard exposition of the Church's doctrine of grace *and thus in due course acquired great significance. It is not a decree; it was not even written by a pope; but on account of its universal acceptance in the Church it must be considered to be a sure expression of the Church's teaching.*

686
238
Because some who glory in the name of Catholic, remaining whether from wickedness or ignorance in the toils of condemned heresies, presume to set themselves against the most loyal supporters *(of the faith)* and, while they do not hesitate to condemn Pelagius and Caelestius, contradict our teachers, as if they had gone beyond the necessary bounds, and profess to obey and accept only what the most Holy See of the Blessed Apostle Peter has by the ministry of its rulers sanctioned and taught against the enemies of divine grace, it

687
has been necessary to investigate with the greatest care what the leaders of the Roman Church have pronounced in judgment on heresies that have arisen in their times, and their conception of divine grace in opposition to the most harmful defenders of 'free will'. To this we have added certain propositions of the African Councils which the apostolic pastors have approved and made their own.

In order therefore that those who are in doubt on any point may be more fully instructed, we are publishing in this short *Indiculus* the constitutions of the holy Fathers, in which anyone who does not wish to be contentious must admit the results of disputations are contained in short and authoritative statements which leave no grounds for contradiction for those who believe with Catholics and confess:

The Judgment of the Popes

688
240
2. No one is good of himself, unless he who alone is good gives him of himself. Which the same Pope *(Innocent III)* testifies in the same letter *(to the Council*

of Carthage) where he says: 'What uprightness is henceforward to be expected from men who think they should attribute to themselves the fact that they are good and not consider him whose grace they daily receive, and trust to themselves to achieve so much without him?'

3. Nobody, not even one renewed by the grace of baptism, is capable of overcoming the wiles of the devil or the lusts of the flesh unless he receives perseverance in good conduct through the daily help of God. Which is confirmed by the teaching of the same Pontiff in the same pages, where he says: 'For though he has redeemed man from his past sins, knowing that he could sin again, he also retained many graces for reparation, to bring him back thereafter, giving him those daily remedies. And if we do not rely with firm confidence upon them, we shall never be able to overcome human errors. For it is necessarily so, that if we conquer with his help, without his help we are conquered.'   689 *241*

5. All efforts and all works and merits of the saints must be referred to the praise and glory of God, for no one can please him otherwise than by what he himself has given...   690 *243*

6. God so works in the hearts of men and in their free will that a holy thought, a pious decision, and every movement of good will come from God, for through him we can do good but without him we can do nothing *(John 15:5)*. For the same teacher Zosimus gave us instruction in this doctrine when speaking to the bishops of the whole world about the help of divine grace, said: 'Is there any time when we do not need his help? We must pray to him as our helper and protector in all our actions, affairs, thoughts and feelings. It is pride when human nature arrogates anything to itself...'   691 *244*

The Judgment of the Councils

692
245
7. We also embrace as proper to the Holy See what is constituted among the decrees of the Council of Carthage, as defined in Cap. 3 *(No. 680 above)*
and in Cap. 4 *(No. 681 above)*
and in Cap. 5 *(No. 682 above)*

The Liturgy

693
246
8. But as well as these inviolable decrees of the Holy Apostolic See in which our most holy Fathers having overthrown the upsurge of dangerous new opinion, have taught us to refer to the grace of Christ the start of good works, the increase in efforts pleasing to God, and persistence in them to the end, let us also consider the sacred mysteries of priestly intercession which in accordance with apostolic tradition are celebrated uniformly throughout the whole world and in the whole of the Catholic Church so that the *law of prayer may establish the law of belief.* For if the leaders of the holy people carry out the mission given to them, they represent the affairs of the human race before the divine bounty, they pray unceasingly in union with the supplication of the whole Church that faith be given to the faithless, that idolators be freed from their godless errors, that the veil be removed from the hearts of the Jews *(2 Cor. 3:15)* and the light of truth be seen, that heretics once more return to a true conception of the Catholic faith, that schismatics receive the spirit of revived love, that those who have fallen receive the remedy of penance, and finally that catechumens who have been led to the sacraments of regeneration find the gates of heavenly mercy open to them. That these prayers are not offered to God pointlessly or in vain is shown by the actual effect, for God deigns to draw many to him from all kinds of error, to deliver them

from the power of darkness and translate them into the kingdom of the Son of his love *(Col. 1:13)* and of vessels of wrath make vessels of mercy *(Rom. 9:22f)*. So strong is the conviction that all this is God's work, that thanksgiving and praise are unceasingly offered to God who does all this for their enlightenment and correction...

Through these rules of the Church and these documents based on divine authority we are strengthened by the help of God so that we recognize God as the author of all good sentiments and works, of all desires and virtues whereby from the beginning of faith we tend towards God, and so that we do not doubt that his grace precedes all human merits, for he works in us both to will and to accomplish any good *(Phil. 2:13)*. 694 / 248

By this help and gift of God free will is not removed but is made free, so that instead of being in darkness it is enlightened; instead of deformed, straight; instead of sick, healthy; instead of imprudent, provident. For so great is God's bounty towards all men that he wishes his gifts to us to be our merits and to give us eternal reward for what he has bestowed upon us. For he works in us so that we want and do what he wants, and he does not suffer to lie idle in us what he has given us to use and not to neglect, so that we too are co-workers with the grace of God. And if we see that something in us is sick from lack of use, let us have immediate recourse to him who heals all our diseases and redeems our life from destruction *(Ps. 102:3f)* and to whom we daily pray 'Lead us not into temptation; but deliver us from evil' *(Mt. 6:13)*... So we hold that what is contrary to the above articles is by no means Catholic. 695 / 248 / 249

THE SECOND COUNCIL OF ORANGE (529)

Conflicts with semi-Pelagianism continued into the next century. In southern France they only came to an end in 529 under Bishop Caesarius of Arles at the small provincial synod of Orange whose findings were approved by Pope Boniface II in 531. In the following canons the relationship between grace and freedom is set out entirely in the spirit, and to a great extent in the words, of St Augustine (Cf. Nos. 218f).

Canons on Grace

696
373
3. If anyone says that the grace of God can be conferred by human invocation and that grace itself does not effect it, as it is invoked by us, he is contradicting the prophet Isaias, or the Apostle who says the same: 'I was found by them that did not seek me: I appeared openly to them that asked not after me' *(Rom. 10:20; Is. 65:1).*

697
374
4. If anyone contends that God waits upon our will to cleanse us from sins and does not confess that our desire to be cleansed comes about in us by the infusion and operation of the Holy Spirit, he opposes the Holy Spirit himself, who, speaking through Solomon, says: 'The will shall be prepared by the Lord' *(Prov. 8:35)*[1] and *(denies)* the salutary teaching of the Apostle: 'For it is God who worketh in you, both to will and to accomplish, according to his good will' *(Phil. 2:13).*

698
375
5. If anyone says that, as the increase, so also the beginning of faith, indeed even the pious readiness to believe, whereby we believe what justifies the impious and attain to the regeneration of holy baptism, is not in us by a gift of grace, that is, by inspiration of the Holy Spirit changing our will from unbelief to belief,

---

1. This is from the Septuagint Greek and does not correspond to the original text.

from impiety to piety, but occurs naturally, shows himself to be an enemy of the apostolic teaching of St Paul who says that we are 'confident of this very thing, that he, who hath begun a good work in you, will perfect it unto the day of Christ Jesus' *(Phil. 1:6)*; and: 'For unto you it is given for Christ, not only to believe in him, but also to suffer for him' *(Phil. 1:29)*; and: 'For by grace you are saved through faith, and that not of yourselves, for it is the gift of God' *(Eph. 2:8)*. For those who say that the faith by which we believe in God is natural, define as faithful also all those who are strangers to the Church.

6. If anyone says that the divine mercy will be accorded to those of us who without God's grace believe, will, desire, endeavour, pray, watch, strive, petition, seek, and demand, and does not confess that the fact that we believe, and will, and are capable of doing all these things as they should be done, occurs in us by the infusion and inspiration of the Holy Spirit, or who subordinates the help of grace to humility and human obedience and does not admit that it is a gift of grace that we are humble or obedient, opposes the Apostle who says: 'What hast thou that thou hast not received?' *(1 Cor. 4:7)*, and: 'By the grace of God, I am what I am' *(1 Cor. 15:10)*...   699 *376*

15. By his sin Adam was changed from the state in which God created him to a worse state. But the believer, by the grace of God is changed from the state brought about by sin to a better state. The first change was the work of the first sinner; the second, as the psalmist says, 'is the change of the right hand of the Most High' *(Ps. 76:11)*.   700 *385*

The Teaching of Tradition on Grace
Thus in accordance with the articles of Holy Scripture   701

396 quoted above, or the definitions of the Fathers, we must with God's held preach and believe: by the sin of the first man human free will was made so weak and infirm that thereafter no man was able either to love God as he ought, nor to believe in God, nor to do good for God's sake, unless the grace of divine mercy were first accorded him. Hence we also believe that the righteous Abel, and Noe, and Abraham, Isaac and Jacob, and all the multitude of saints of old received that glorious faith celebrated by the Apostle *(Heb. 11)* not from the natural good that there had previously been in Adam but by the grace of God. We also know and believe that even after the coming of the Lord this grace is given to all those who seek baptism not by any action of their free will but by the generosity of Christ, according to the much quoted words of the Apostle Paul: 'For to you the grace is given not only to believe in Christ, but also to suffer for him' *(Phil. 1:29)*; and also: 'God who hath begun a good work in you, will perfect it unto the day of Christ Jesus' *(Phil. 1:6)*; and again: 'For by grace you are saved through faith, and that not of yourselves, for it is the gift of God' *(Eph. 2:8)*; and what the Apostle says of himself: 'I obtained mercy so that I should be faithful'[1] – he does not say 'because I was' but 'so that I should be'; and again: 'What hast thou that thou hast not received?' *(1 Cor. 4:7)*; and 'Every best gift, and every perfect gift, is from above, coming down from the Father of lights' *(James 1:17)*; and: 'A man cannot receive anything, unless it be given him from heaven' *(John 3:27)*.

---

1. *Misericordian consecutus sum, ut fidelis essem.*
Two references are given: 1 Cor. 7:25 and 1 Tim. 1:13.
Neither Douay nor Knox of either passage corresponds at all closely to the Latin here quoted, but the sense is clear in both that mercy precedes faith and not vice-versa.

The testimonies of the sacred Scriptures which could be put forward as proof of grace are innumerable, but they have been omitted for the sake of brevity, for indeed if a few are not enough more will serve no purpose.

The Teaching of Tradition about Predestination

This too we also believe according to the Catholic faith, that all baptized persons, once they have received grace by baptism, can and must, with the help and cooperation of Christ, achieve what is necessary for the salvation of the soul if they are willing to work loyally. Not only do we not believe that some by divine power are destined for evil, but if any there be who wish to believe so much evil, we anathematize them with all detestation. But this we salutarily profess and believe that in every good work it is not we who begin and are afterwards helped by God's mercy, but that he first inspires us with belief and love for himself without any previous merits *(of ours)*, so that we may faithfully seek baptism and after baptism by his help do what is pleasing to him. Whence it is very clearly to be believed that that wonderful faith of the thief whom the Lord called to paradise *(Luke 23:43)*, and the Centurion Cornelius to whom an angel of the Lord was sent *(Acts 10:3)*, and of Zacchaeus who was privileged to receive the Lord himself *(Luke 19:6)*, was not from nature but was the gift of the divine generosity.

702
397

PROPOSITIONS OF LUTHER CONDEMNED BY POPE LEO X (1520)
(Cf. Note to No. 709)

1. It is an heretical but widespread opinion that the sacraments of the New Law give justifying grace to those who set no obstacle in the way.

[703]
1451

[704] 2. To deny that sin remains in a child after baptism
1452 is to spurn both Paul and Christ.
[705] 3. Even if there is no actual sin, the *fomes peccati*
1453 hinders a soul leaving the body from entering into heaven.
[706] 31. The just man sins in every good work.
1481
[707] 32. A good work however well done is a venial sin.
1482
[708] 36. After sin, free will is just nominal; and when a man
1486 does his best he sins mortally.

THE GENERAL COUNCIL OF TRENT, SIXTH SESSION (1547)

DECREE ON JUSTIFICATION

Preparatory work on this most important Tridentine decree took a good seven months. Its object was not only to reject the basic heresy of Luther, which lay in his doctrine of justification, but also to give a perspective of the whole doctrine of grace.

Luther's teaching can be briefly summarized as follows: In his original state *man bore God's image. The fall destroyed it.* Original sin *(cf. Note to No. 220; Nos. 220–6) is the hereditary corruption of nature, the* concupiscence *that makes man inwardly bad. Everything done by man, who is and always remains the bearer of this corrupt nature, is sin. The man of faith can in no way cooperate in his own* justification. *Believing confidence is the only way to it, and is at the same time the sign of it. But this justification does not consist in an interior renewal of the man but in the* declaration of justice by virtue of which the merits of Christ are applied to him. *Man's works cannot merit heaven, for human nature, the source of man's actions, is not made inwardly good by justification.*

In its essentials this doctrine of sin and justification was accepted by the other Reformers. To it, however, Calvin added the unconditional divine predestination not only of the good to heaven but also of the wicked to evil and hell quite independently of any human merit or guilt.

The structure of the decree. *The decree is not concerned with the justification of children, who receive the grace of justification by baptism alone without their cooperation, but with that of adults.*

Chaps. I–III deal with God's plan of salvation. Chap. I – Fallen man's impotency; Chap. II – Christ's work of redemption; Chap. III – The communication of the grace of redemption.

Chaps. IV–IX deal with the realization of God's plan, the first justification. Chap. IV – The way of justification shown by God; Chap. V–VI The Preparation of man, the cooperation of nature and grace; Chap. VII – The nature and causes of justification; Chaps. VIII and IX – The relationship between faith and justification, especially in relation to the Protestant conception.

Chaps. X–XIII deal with the state of justfication. Chap. X – The increase of grace through good works; Chap. XI – The necessity and possibility of keeping the commandments; Chaps. XII & XIII – The grace of perseverance.

Chaps. XIV & XV deal with the second justification. Chap. XIV – The sacrament of atonement, and its difference from the first justification of baptism; Chap. XV – The necessity of this sacrament since grace is lost by every mortal sin, not only by loss of faith.

Chap. XVI deals with the merits of good works.

Introduction

Since there is being disseminated at this time, not without the loss of many souls and grievous detriment to the unity of the Church, a certain erroneous doctrine concerning justification, the holy, ecumenical and general Council of Trent... intends... to expound to all the faithful of Christ the true and salutary doctrine of justification

709
1520

which the 'sun of justice' *(Mal. 4:2)*, Jesus Christ, 'the author and furnisher of our faith' *(Heb. 12:2)*, taught, which the Apostles transmitted and the Catholic Church under the inspiration of the Holy Spirit has always retained; strictly forbidding that anyone henceforth presume to believe, preach or teach otherwise than is defined and declared in the present decree.

Chapter I. The Impotency of Nature and the Law to Justify Man

710
1521 The Holy Council declares first that, for a correct and clear understanding of the doctrine of justification, it is necessary that each one recognize and confess that since all men had lost innocence in the transgression of Adam *(Rom. 5:12ff)* having become unclean and, as the Apostle says, 'by nature children of wrath' *(Eph. 2:3)*, as has been set forth in the decree on original sin, they were so far the servants of sin and under the power of the devil and of death, that not only the Gentiles by the force of nature, but even the Jews by the very letter of the Law of Moses, were un able to be liberated or to rise therefrom, though free will, weakened as it was in its powers and downward bent, was by no means extinguished in them.

Chapter II. The Dispensation and Mystery of the Advent of Christ

711
1522 Whence it came to pass that the heavenly Father, 'the father of mercies and the God of all comfort' *(2 Cor. 1:3)*, 'when the blessed fulness of the time was come' *(Eph. 1:10)*, sent to men Jesus Christ, his own Son, who had both before the Law and during the time of the Law been announced and promised to many of the holy fathers, that he might redeem the Jews who were under

the Law, and that the Gentiles who followed not after justice might attain to justice *(Rom. 9:30)*, and that all men might receive the adoption of sons. Him has God proposed as a propitiator through faith in his blood for our sins, and not for our sins only but also for those of the whole world *(1 John 2:2)*.

Chapter III. Who Are Justified through Christ

But though 'he died for all' *(2 Cor. 5:15)*, yet all do not receive the benefit of his death, but only those to whom the merit of his Passion is communicated; because as truly as men would not be born unjust if they were not born through propagation of the seed of Adam, since by that propagation they contract through him, when they are conceived, injustice as their own, so if they were not born again in Christ, they would never be justified, since in that new birth there is bestowed upon them, through the merit of his Passion, the grace by which they are made just. For this benefit the Apostle exhorts us always 'to give thanks to the Father, who hath made us worthy to be partakers of the lot of the saints in light, and hath delivered us from the power of darkness, and hath translated us into the kingdom of the Son of his love, in whom we have redemption and remission of sins' *(Col. 1:12–14)* 712 1523

Chapter IV. A Brief Description of the Justification of the Sinner and its Mode in the State of Grace

In which words is given a brief description of the justification of the sinner, as being a translation from that state in which man is born a child of the first Adam to the state of grace and of the adoption of the sons of God through the second Adam, Jesus Christ, our Saviour. Since the promulgation of the Gospel, however, this translation cannot be effected except through the bathing 713 1524 of regeneration, or the desire for it, as it is written: 'Unless a man be born again of water and the Holy Ghost, he cannot enter into the kingdom of God' *(John. 3:5)*.

Chapter V. The Necessity of Preparation for Justification in Adults, and Whence it Proceeds

714
1525
It is furthermore declared that in adults the beginning of that justification must proceed from the predisposing grace of God through Jesus Christ, that is, from his vocation, whereby, without any merits on their part, they are called; that they who had been cut off from God by sin may be disposed through his quickening and helping grace to convert themselves to their own justification by freely assenting to and cooperating with that grace; so that, while God touches the heart of man through the illumination of the Holy Spirit, man himself neither does absolutely nothing while receiving that inspiration, since he can also reject it, nor yet is he able by his own free will and without the grace of God to move himself to justice in his sight. Hence, when it is said in the sacred Scriptures, 'Turn ye to me, and I will turn to you' *(Zach. 1:3)*, we are reminded of our liberty; and when we reply, 'Convert us, O Lord, to thee, and we shall be converted' *(Lam. 5:21)* we confess that we need the grace of God.

Chapter VI. The Manner of Preparation

715
1526
Now they *(the adults)* are disposed to that justice when, aroused and aided by divine grace, receiving faith by hearing, they are moved freely towards God, believing to be true what has been divinely revealed and promised, especially that the sinner is justified by God 'by his grace, through the redemption that is in Christ Jesus' *(Rom.*

3:24); and when, understanding themselves to be sinners, they, by turning themselves from the fear of divine justice, by which they are salutarily aroused, to consider the mercy of God, are raised to hope, trusting that God will be propitious to them for Christ's sake; and they begin to love him as the fount of all justice, and on that account are moved against sin by a certain hatred and detestation, that is, by that repentance that must be performed before baptism, to begin a new life and to keep the commandments of God.

Of this disposition it is written: 'He that cometh to God must believe that he is, and is a rewarder to them that seek him' *(Heb. 11:6)* ; and, 'Be of good faith, son, thy sins are forgiven thee' *(Mt. 9:2)*; and, 'The fear of the Lord draweth out sin' *(Eccles. 1:27);* and 'Do penance, and be baptized every one of you in the name of Jesus Christ, for the remission of your sins, and you shall receive the gift of the Holy Ghost' *(Acts 2:38)*; and 'Going, therefore, teach ye all nations, baptizing them in the name of the Father, and of the Son, and of Holy Ghost, teaching them to observe all things whatsoever I have commanded you, *(Mt. 28:19f)*; finally, 'Prepare your hearts unto the Lord' *(1 Kings 7:3)*.

716
1527

Chapter VII. In What the Justification of the Sinner Consists, and What are its Causes

This disposition or preparation is followed by justification itself, which is not only a remission of sins but also the sanctification and renewal of the inward man through the voluntary reception of the grace and gifts whereby an unjust man becomes just and from being an enemy becomes a friend, that he may be 'an heir according to hope of life everlasting' *(Tit. 3:7)*.

717
1528

The causes of this justification are: the *final cause* is the

718

1529 glory of God and of Christ and life everlasting; the *efficient cause* is the merciful God who washes and sanctifies gratuitously, signing and anointing 'with the Holy Spirit of promise who is the pledge of our inheritance' *(Eph. 1:13f)*; the *meritorious cause* is his most beloved only-begotten, our Lord Jesus Christ, who, 'when we were enemies', for 'the exceeding charity wherewith he loved us' *(Eph. 2:4)* merited for us justification by his most holy Passion on the wood of the Cross and made satisfaction for us to God the Father; the *instrumental cause* is the sacrament of baptism, which is the sacrament of faith, without which no man

719 was ever justified; finally the single *formal cause* is the justice of God, not that by which he himself is just but that by which he makes us just, that, namely, whereby being endowed with it by him, we are renewed in the spirit of our mind, and not only are we reputed but are truly called and are just, receiving justice within us, each one according to his own measure, which the Holy Spirit distributes to everyone as he wills *(1 Cor. 12:11)*, and according to each one's disposition and cooperation.

720
1530 For though no one can be just except him to whom the merits of the Passion of our Lord Jesus Christ are communicated, yet this takes place in that justification of the sinner when, by the merit of the most holy Passion, 'the charity of God is poured forth by the Holy Ghost in the hearts' *(Rom. 5:5)* of those who are justified, and inheres in them.

721
1530 Whence man, through Jesus Christ in whom he is ingrafted, receives in that justification, together with the remission of sins, all these infused at the same time, namely, faith, hope and charity.

1531 For faith, unless hope and charity be added to it, neither unites a man perfectly with Christ nor makes him a living member of his body. For which reason it is most truly said that 'faith without works is dead' *(James 2:17)* and of no profit, and 'in Christ Jesus neither circumcision availeth anything nor uncircumcision, but faith that worketh by charity' *(Gal. 5:6)*. Conformably to apostolic tradition, catechumens ask this faith of the Church before the sacrament of baptism when they ask for the faith that gives eternal life, which without hope and charity faith cannot give. Whence also they hear immediately the word of Christ: 'If thou wilt enter into life, keep the commandments' *(Mt. 19:17)*. Wherefore, when receiving true and Christian justice, they are commanded, immediately on being born again, to preserve it pure and spotless as the first robe *(Luke 15:22)* given them through Christ in place of that which Adam by his disobedience lost for himself and for us, so that they may bear it before the tribunal of our Lord Jesus Christ and may have life eternal.

Chapter VIII. How the Gratuitous Justification of the Sinner by Faith is to be Understood

But when the Apostle says that man is justified 'by faith' and 'freely' *(Rom. 3:22, 24)*, these words are to be understood in the sense in which the uninterrupted unanimity of the Catholic Church has held and expressed them, namely that we are therefore said to be justified by faith because faith is the beginning of human salvation, the foundation and root of all justification, 'without which it is impossible to please God' *(Heb. 11:6)* and to come to the fellowship of his sons; and we are therefore said to be justified gratuitously because none of those things that precede justification, whether faith or works, merits the grace of justification. For 'if by grace, it is not now by works', 'otherwise' as the Apostle says, 'grace is no more grace' *(Rom. 11:6)*.

722
1532

Chapter IX. Against the Vain Confidence of Heretics

723
1533 But though it is necessary to believe that sins neither are nor ever have been remitted except gratuitously by divine mercy for Christ's sake, yet it must not be said that sins are or have been forgiven to anyone who boasts of his confidence and certainty of the remission of his sins, resting on that alone, though among heretics and schismatics this vain and ungodly confidence may be, and in our troubled times indeed is, found and preached with
1534 untiring fury against the Catholic Church. Moreover, it must not be maintained that those who are truly justified must necessarily, without any doubt whatsoever, convince themselves that they are justified and that no one is absolved from sin and justified except him who believes with certainty that he is absolved and justified, and that absolution and justification are effected by this faith alone, as if he who does not believe this doubts the promises of God and the efficacy of the death and resurrection of Christ. For as no pious person ought to doubt the mercy of God and the merit of Christ and the virtue and efficacy of the sacraments, so each one, when he considers himself and his own weakness and indisposition, may have fear and apprehension concerning his own grace, since no one can know with the certainty of faith, which cannot be subject to error, that he has obtained the grace of God.

Chapter X. The Increase of the Justification Received

724
1535 Having, therefore, been thus justified and made the friends and 'domestics of God' *(John. 15:15 / Eph. 2:19)*, advancing from virtue to virtue *(Ps. 83:8)*, they are renewed, as the Apostle says, day by day *(2 Cor. 4:16)*, that is, 'mortifying the members' *(Col. 3:5)* of their flesh and pre-

senting them as instruments of justice unto sanctification *(Rom. 6:13, 19)*, they, through the observance of the commandments of God and the Church, faith cooperating with good works, increase in that justice received through the grace of Christ *(James 2:22)* and are further justified, as it is written: 'He that is justified, let him be justified still' *(Apoc. 22:11)*; and, 'Be not afraid to be justified even to death' *(Ecclus. 18:22)*; and again, 'Do you see that by works a man is justified; and not by faith only?' *(James 2:24)*. This increase of justice holy Church asks for when she prays: 'Give unto us, O Lord, an increase of faith, hope and charity' *(13th S. after Pent.)*.

Chapter XI. The Observance of the Commandments and the Necessity and Possibility Thereof

But no one, however much justified, should consider himself exempt from the observance of the commandments; no one should use that rash statement, once forbidden by the Fathers under anathema, that the observance of the commandments of God is impossible for one that is justified. For God does not command impossibilities, but by commanding admonishes thee to do what thou canst and to pray for what thou canst not, and aids thee that thou mayst be able. 'His commandments are not heavy' *(1 John 5:3)*, and 'his yoke is sweet and burden light' *(Mt. 11:30)*. For they who are the sons of God love Christ, but they who love him keep his commandments, as he himself testifies *(John 14:23)*; which, indeed, with the divine help, they can do. For though during this mortal life men, however holy and just, fall at times into at least light and daily sins, which are also called venial, they do not on that account cease to be just, for that petition of the just, 'forgive us our trespasses', is both humble and true; for which reason the just ought to

725
1536

1537

feel themselves more obliged to walk in the way of justice, for 'being now freed from sin and made servants of God' *(Rom. 6:22)*, they are able, 'living soberly, justly, and godly' *(Tit. 2:12)* to proceed onward through Jesus Christ by whom they have access to this grace *(Rom. 5:2)*. For God does not forsake those who have once been justified by his grace unless he be first forsaken by them.

726
1538 Wherefore no one ought to flatter himself with faith alone, thinking that by faith alone he is made an heir and will obtain the inheritance, even though he do not 'suffer with Christ, that he may be also glorified with him' *(Rom. 8:17)*. For even Christ himself, as the Apostle says, 'whereas he was the Son of God, he learned obedience by the things which he suffered, and being consummated, he became to all who obey him the cause of eternal salvation' *(Heb. 5:8f)*. For which reason the same Apostle warns those justified saying, 'Know you not that they who run in the race, all run indeed, but one receiveth the prize? So run that you may obtain. I therefore so run, not as at an uncertainty; I so fight, not as one beating the air, but I chastise my body and bring it into subjection; lest perhaps when I have preached to others, I should myself become a castaway' *(1 Cor. 9:24, 26f)*. So also the Prince of the Apostles, Peter: 'Labour the more, that by good works you may make sure your calling and election. For doing these things, you shall not sin at any time' *(2 Peter 1:10)*.

727
1539 From which it is clear that they are opposed to the orthodox teaching of religion who maintain that the just man sins, venially at least, in every good work; or what is more intolerable, that he merits eternal punishment; and they also who assert that the just sin in all works if, in order to arouse their sloth and to encourage themselves to run the race, as well as the principal objective that

God may be glorified, they have the eternal reward also in view, since it is written: 'I have inclined my heart to do thy justifications on account of the reward' *(Ps. 118:112)* and the Apostle says of Moses that 'he looked unto the reward' *(Heb. 11:26)*.

Chapter XII. Rash Presumption of Predestination is to be Avoided

No one, moreover, so long as he lives this mortal life, ought in regard to the sacred mystery of predestination so far presume as to state with absolute certainty that he is among the number of the predested, as if it were true that the one justified cannot sin any more, or if he does sin, that he ought to promise himself an assured repentance. For, except by special revelation, it cannot be known whom God has chosen to himself.

728
1540

Chapter XIII. The Gift of Perseverance

Similarly with regard to the gift of perseverance, of which it is written: 'He that shall preserve to the end, he shall be saved' *(Mt. 10:22)*, which cannot be obtained from anyone except from him who is able to make him stand who stands *(Rom. 14:4)*, that he may stand perseveringly, and to raise him who falls, let no one promise himself herein something as certain with an absolute certainty, though all ought to place and repose the firmest hope in God's help. For God, unless men themselves fail in his grace, as 'he has begun a good work, so will he perfect it, working to will and to accomplish' *(Phil. 2:13)*.

729
1541

Nevertheless, let those who think themselves to stand take heed lest they fall *(1 Cor. 10:12)* and 'with fear and trembling work out their salvation' *(Phil. 2:12)*, in

730
1541

labours, in watchings, in almsdeeds, in prayer, in fastings and chastity *(Cf. 2 Cor. 6, 3f)*. For knowing that they are born again unto the hope of glory, and not as yet unto glory, they ought to fear for the combat that yet remains with the flesh, with the world and with the devil, in which they cannot be victorious unless they be with the grace of God obedient to the Apostle who says: 'We are debtors, not to the flesh, to live according to the flesh; for if you live according to the flesh, you shall die, but if by the spirit you mortify the deeds of the flesh, you shall live' *(Rom. 8:12f)*.

Chapter XIV. The Fallen and their Restoration

731
1542 Those who through sin have forfeited the received grace of justification can again be justified when, moved by God, they exert themselves to obtain through the sacrament of penance the recovery, by the merits of Christ, of the grace lost. For this manner of justification is restoration for those fallen, which the holy Fathers have aptly called a second plank after the shipwreck of grace lost. For on behalf of those who fall into sin after baptism Christ Jesus instituted the sacrament of penance when he said, 'Receive ye the Holy Ghost, whose sins you shall forgive, they are forgiven them, and whose sins you shall retain, they are retained' *(John 20:22f)*.

732
1543 Hence it must be taught that the repentance of a Christian after his fall is very different from that at his baptism, and that it includes not only a determination to avoid sins and a hatred of them, or a 'contrite and humble heart' *(Ps. 50:19)*, but also the sacramental confession of those sins, at least in desire, to be made in its season, and sacerdotal absolution, as well as satisfaction by fasts, alms, prayers and other devout exercises of the spiritual life, not indeed for the eternal punish-

ment, which is, together with the guilt, remitted either by the sacrament or by the desire of the sacrament, but for the temporal punishment which, as the sacred writings teach, is not always wholly remitted as is done in baptism, to those who, ungrateful to the grace of God which they have received, have grieved the Holy Spirit *(Eph. 4:30)* and have not feared to 'violate the temple of God' *(1 Cor. 3:17)*. Of which repentance it is written: 'Be mindful whence thou art fallen; do penance, and do the first works' *(Apoc. 2:5)*; and again: 'The sorrow that is according to God worketh penance, steadfast unto salvation' *(2 Cor. 7:10)*; and again, 'Do penance, and bring forth fruits worthy of penance' *(Mt. 3:8, Luke 3:8)*.

Chapter XV. By Every Mortal Sin Grace is Lost, but not Faith

Against the subtle wits of some also, who 'by pleasing speeches and good words seduce the hearts of the innocent' *(Rom. 16:18)*, it must be maintained that the grace of justification once received is lost not only by infidelity *(unbelief)* whereby also faith itself is lost, but also by every other mortal sin, though in this case faith is not lost; thus defending the teaching of the divine law which excludes from the kingdom of God not only unbelievers but also the faithful *(who are)* fornicators, adulterers, effeminate, liers with men, thieves, covetous, drunkards, railers, extortioners *(1 Cor. 6:9f)*, and all others who commit deadly sins, from which with the help of divine grace they can refrain, and on account of which they are cut off from the grace of Christ.

Chapter XVI. The Fruits of Justification: That is, the Merit of Good Works, and the Nature of that Merit

733
1544

734
1545 Therefore, to men justified in this manner, whether they have preserved uninterruptedly the grace received or recovered it when lost, are to be pointed out the words of the Apostle: 'Abound in every good work, knowing that your labour is not in vain in the Lord' *(1 Cor. 15:58)*. 'For God is not unjust, that he should forget your work, and the love which you have shown in his name' *(Heb. 6:10)*; and, 'Do not lose your confidence, which hath a great reward' *(Heb. 10:35)*. Hence, to those who work well unto the end *(Mt. 10:22)* and trust in God, eternal life is to be offered, both as a grace mercifully promised to the sons of God through Jesus Christ, and as a reward promised by God himself to be faithfully given to their good works and merits. For this is the crown of justice which after his fight and course the Apostle declared was laid up for him, to be rendered to him by the just judge, and not only to him but also to all that love his coming *(2 Tim. 4:7f)*.

735
1546 For since Christ Jesus himself, as the head into the members and the vine into the branches *(John. 15:5)*, continually infuses strength into those justified, which strength always precedes, accompanies and follows their good works, and without which they could not in any manner be pleasing and meritorious before God, we must believe that nothing further is wanting to those justified to prevent them from being considered to have, by those very works which have been done in God, fully satisfied the divine law according to the state of this life and to have truly merited eternal life, to be obtained in its *(due)* time, provided they depart *(this life)* in grace, since Christ our Saviour says: 'If anyone shall drink of the water that I will give him, he shall not thirst forever; but it shall become to him a fountain of water springing up unto life everlasting' *(John 4:13f)*. Thus, neither is our own justice established as our own from ourselves nor

is the justice of God ignored or repudiated, for that justice which is called ours, because we are justified by its inherence in us, that same is *(the justice)* of God, because it is infused into us by God through the merit of Christ. Nor must this be omitted, that although in the sacred writings so much is attributed to good works that even 'he that shall give a drink of cold water to one of his least ones', Christ promised, 'shall not lose his reward' *(Mt. 10:42)*; and the Apostle testifies that 'that which is at present momentary, and light of our tribulation, worketh for us above measure exceedingly an eternal weight of glory' *(2 Cor. 4:17)*; nevertheless, far be it that a Christian should either trust or glory in himself and not in the Lord *(1 Cor. 1:31)*, whose bounty towards all men is so great that he wishes the things that are his gifts to be their merits. And since 'in many things we all offend' *(James 3:2)*, each one ought to have before his eyes not only the mercy and goodness but also the severity and judgment *(of God)*; neither ought anyone to judge himself, even though he be not conscious to himself of anything; because the whole life of man is to be examined and judged by the judgment not of man but of God, 'who will bring to light the hidden things of darkness, and will make manifest the counsels of the hearts, and then shall every man have praise from God' *(1 Cor. 4:5)* who, as it is written, 'will render to every man according to his works' *(Rom. 2:6)*.

736
1548

1549

After this Catholic doctrine on justification, which whoever does not faithfully and firmly accept cannot be justified, it seemed good to the Holy Council to add these canons so that all may know not only what they must hold and follow but also what to avoid and shun.

737
1550

CANONS CONCERNING JUSTIFICATION

738
1551
1. If anyone shall say that man can be justified before God by his own works, whether done by his own natural powers or through the teaching of the Law, without divine grace through Jesus Christ – *anathema sit*.

739
1552
2. If anyone shall say that divine grace through Jesus Christ is given for this only, that man will be more easily able to live justly and to merit eternal life, as if by free will he were able to do both, though with hardship and difficulty – *anathema sit*.

740
1553
3. If anyone shall say that without the predisposing inspiration of the Holy Spirit and without his help man can believe, hope, love, or be repentant as he ought, so that the grace of justification be bestowed on him – *anathema sit*.

741
1554
4. If anyone shall say that man's free will moved and aroused by God, by assenting to God's call and action, in no way cooperates towards disposing and preparing itself to obtain the grace of justification, that it cannot refuse its assent if it wishes, but that, as something inanimate, it does nothing whatever and is merely passive – *anathema sit*.

742
1555
5. If anyone shall say that after Adam's sin man's free will was lost and destroyed, or that it is a thing only in name, indeed a name without a reality, a fiction introduced into the Church by Satan – *anathema sit*.

743
1556
6. If anyone shall say that it is not in man's power to make his ways evil, but that the works that are evil as well as those that are good God produces, not only permissively but *proprie et per se*, so that the treason of Judas is no less his own proper work than the vocation of St Paul – *anathema sit*.

744
1557
7. If anyone shall say that all works done before justification, in whatever manner they be done, are truly sins

or merit the hatred of God; that the more earnestly one strives to dispose oneself for grace, the more grievously he sins – *anathema sit*.

8. If anyone shall say that the fear of hell, whereby by grieving for sins we flee to the mercy of God or abstain from sinning, is a sin, or makes sinners worse – *anathema sit*. 745
1558

9. If anyone shall say that the sinner is justified by faith alone, meaning that nothing else is required to cooperate in order to obtain the grace of justification, and that it is not in any way necessary that he be prepared and disposed by the action of his own will – *anathema sit*. 746
1559

10. If anyone shall say that men are justified without the justice of Christ whereby he merited for us, or by that justice are formally just – *anathema sit*. 747
1560

11. If anyone shall say that men are justified either by the sole imputation of the justice of Christ or by the sole remission of sins, to the exclusion of the grace and the charity that is poured forth in their hearts by the Holy Spirit and remains in them, or also that the grace by which we are justified is only the good will of God – *anathema sit*. 748
1561

12. If anyone shall say that justifying faith is nothing else but confidence in divine mercy, which remits sins for Christ's sake, or that it is this confidence alone that justifies us – *anathema sit*. 749
1562

13. If anyone shall say that in order to obtain the remission of sins it is necessary for every man to believe with certainty and without any hesitation on account of his own weakness and indisposition that his sins are forgiven him – *anathema sit*. 750
1563

14. If anyone shall say that man is absolved from his sins and justified because he firmly believes that he is absolved and justified, or that no one is truly justified except him who believes himself justified, and that by this 751
1564

faith alone absolution and justification are effected – *anathema sit*.

752
1565
15. If anyone shall say that a man who is born again and justified is bound *ex fide* to believe that he is certainly in the number of the predestined – *anathema sit*.

753
1566
16. If anyone shall say that he will for certain, with an absolute and infallible certainty, have that great gift of perseverance even to the end, unless he shall have learned this by a special revelation – *anathema sit*.

754
1567
17. If anyone shall say that the grace of justification is shared by those only who are predestined to life, but that all others who are called are called indeed but receive not grace, as if they are by divine power predestined to evil – *anathema sit*.

755
1568
18. If anyone shall say that the commandments of God are, even for one who is justified and constituted in grace, impossible to observe – *anathema sit*.

756
1569
19. If anyone shall say that nothing besides faith is commanded in the Gospel, that other things are indifferent, neither commanded nor forbidden but free; or that the ten commandments in no way pertain to Christians – *anathema sit*.

757
1570
20. If anyone shall say that a man who is justified and however perfect is not bound to observe the commandments of God and the Church, but only to believe, as if the Gospel were a bare and absolute promise of eternal life without the condition of obeying the commandments – *anathema sit*.

758
1571
21. If anyone shall say that Christ Jesus was given by God to men as a redeemer in whom to trust and not also a legislator to obey – *anathema sit*.

759
1572
22. If anyone shall say that one who is justified either can preserve in the justice received without the special help of God, or cannot do so with it – *anathema sit*.

760
23. If anyone shall say that a man once justified can sin

no more, nor lose grace, and that therefore he that falls *1573* and sins was never truly justified; or, on the contrary, that he can during his whole life avoid all sins, even venial ones, except by a special privilege from God, as the Church holds in regards to the Blessed Virgin – *anathema sit.*

24. If anyone shall say that the justice received is not preserved and also increased before God through good works, but that those works are merely the fruits and signs of justification obtained, but not the cause of its increase – *anathema sit.* **761** *1574*

25. If anyone shall say that in every good work the just man sins at least venially, or, what is more intolerable, mortally, and hence merits eternal punishment, but that he is only not damned on this account because God does not impute these works unto damnation – *anathema sit.* **762** *1575*

26. If anyone shall say that the just ought not for the good works done in God to expect and hope for an eternal reward from God through his mercy and the merit of Jesus Christ, if they persevere to the end in doing well and keeping the divine commandments – *anathema sit.* **763** *1576*

27. If anyone shall say there is no mortal sin except unbelief, or that grace once received is not lost through any sin however grievous and enormous other than the sin of unbelief – *anathema sit.* **764** *1577*

28. If anyone shall say that with the loss of grace through sin faith is also lost, or that the faith that remains is not a true faith, even if it is not a living one, or that he who has faith without charity is not a Christian – *anathema sit.* **765** *1578*

29. If anyone shall say that he who has fallen after baptism cannot by the grace of God rise again, or that he can indeed recover again the lost justice by faith alone without the sacrament of penance, contrary to what the holy Roman and Universal Church, instituted by Christ the Lord and his Apostles, has hitherto professed, ob- **766** *1579*

served and taught – *anathema sit*.

767 30. If anyone shall say that after reception of the grace of
1580 justification the guilt is so remitted and the debt of eternal punishment so blotted out for every repentant sinner that no debt of temporal punishment remains to be discharged either in this world or in purgatory before the gates of heaven can be opened – *anathema sit*.

768 31. If anyone shall say that one justified sins when he
1581 performs good works with a view to an eternal reward – *anathema sit*.

769 32. If anyone shall say the good works of one justified
1582 are in such a manner the gifts of God that they are not also the good merits of him justified; or that one who is justified does not truly merit by the good works that he does by the grace of God and the merit of Jesus Christ, whose living member he is, an increase of grace, eternal life, and in case he dies in grace, the attainment of eternal life itself and also an increase of glory – *anathema sit*.

770 33. If anyone shall say that the Catholic doctrine of
1583 justification as set forth by the Holy Council in this present decree derogates in some respect from the glory of God or the merits of our Lord Jesus Christ, and does not rather illustrate the truth of our faith and no less the glory of God and of Christ Jesus – *anathema sit*.

PROPOSITIONS OF MICHAEL DU BAY CONDEMNED BY POPE PIUS V (1567)

Even after the Reformation the relationship between nature and grace remained one of the principal concerns of the Church's teaching on grace. In 1567 it was necessary to condemn 79 propositions by the Lyons professor Michael du Bay which were heavily contaminated by Protestant influence. They were taken from various of his works and set out quite unsystematically. In order to get a proper perspective, the more important of them are set out here in accordance with the main lines of his system. The best way of relating them is in terms of the three states of human nature: original state, fallen state, and justification.

Du Bay's doctrine on man's original state *is as follows:* Grace, immortality, and freedom from concupiscence were owed *to man and were incorporated in him at creation. They were not additional free gifts from God. In this state man had the direct possibility to earn eternal life by living according to God's commandments, and to do so on his own* merits *without grace. This leads directly to his teaching on merit as it concerns justified man.*

On the fall *Du Bay taught: Since Adam's sin, man is corrupted by an inherent evil attitude of will. Original sin is in him. Whence it follows: first, that* concupiscence *as a wrong attitude of will is a constant transgression of the law 'Thou shalt not covet'. Only, this sin is not counted against redeemed man. And second his concept of freedom which is closely linked with the foregoing. The freedom which is necessary if there is to be sin, does not consist of the freedom to choose between good and evil but in freedom from external constraint. Everything, therefore, which arises from human nature as an active principle is free. But since human nature is corrupted by its inherent evil attitude of will, every human action deriving from it is 'free' and therefore sinful.*

On redemption *du Bay taught: Man has to thank Christ for his new state of justification. It is grace. (But what it works in him is his merit alone). Grace consists in the capability of fulfilling God's commandments. Grace is not dependent upon any sacrament, but is purely the work of God. The sacrament of penance, satisfaction and punishment have only the function of cancelling outstanding punishment. Justification is accompanied by pure love which is the opposite of concupiscence and is alone capable of being the principle of moral action.*

Man's Original State

21. The sublimation and exaltation of human nature to participation in the divine nature was due to the [771] *1921*

integrity of the first state and is therefore to be called natural and not supernatural.

[772] 55. God could not have created man from the begin-
1955 ning as he is now born.

[773] 78. The immortality of the first man was not a gift of
1978 grace but a natural condition.

Merit

[774] 13. Good works done by the sons of adoption do not
1913 acquire merit because they are done through the spirit of adoption dwelling in the hearts of the sons of God but only because they conform to the law and because by them obedience is paid to the law.

Sin

[775] 20. No sin is of its nature venial, but every sin deserve
1920 eternal punishment.

[776] 50. Evil desires to which the reason does not consent
1950 and which men suffer against their will are prohibited by the commandment 'Thou shalt not covet' *(Ex. 20:17)*

[777] 54. The principle that God has not commanded man
1954 to do the impossible is falsely attributed to Augustine since it is of Pelagius.

[778] 67. Man sins and merits damnation even in that which
1967 he does of necessity.

[779] 68. Purely negative unbelief[1] in those things which
1968 Christ did not preach is a sin.

[780] 74. For those who have been reborn and relapsed into
1974 mortal sin and in whom it now reigns, concupiscence, like other evil habits, is a sin.

---

1. *Infidelitas pure negativa*, i.e. unbelief due without personal guilt to ignorance of revelation.

The Impotency of Fallen Nature, and Free Will

25. All works of the unbelieving are sins, and the virtues of the philosophers are vices. [781] *1925*

27. Free will, without the help of God's grace, is of no use except for sinning. [782] *1927*

28. It is a Pelagian error to say that free will can serve to avoid any sin. [783] *1928*

The Concept of Freedom[1]

39. What is done voluntarily, even if it is done of necessity, is done freely. [784] *1939*

41. Under the term freedom in the Scriptures there is not to be found freedom from necessity but only freedom from sin. [785] *1941*

66. Only force is inconsistent with human freedom. [786] *1966*

Charity and Fulfilling the Law

16. There is no true obedience to the law without charity. [787] *1916*

34. That distinction of a twofold love, viz: the natural love by which God is loved as the author of nature, and the gratuitous by which God is loved as the one who makes us blessed, is a vain distinction, and deceptive, and thought out from sacred Scriptures and many past witnesses in order to deceive. [788] *1934*

38. In a rational creature all love is either a vicious cupidity, whereby one loves the world, which is forbidden by John, or that praiseworthy charity 'poured forth in our hearts by the Holy Ghost' *(Rom. 5:5)* whereby God is loved. [789] *1938*

---

1. The more detailed definition of freedom as man's selfdetermination without interior or exterior compulsion will always remain an essential starting point for determining the relationship between grace and free will.

ERRORS OF CORNELIUS JANSEN CONDEMNED BY POPE INNOCENT X (1653)

The condemnation by Innocent X of five of Jansen's propositions was of the greatest importance. The following points are dealt with: 1 – The possibility of keeping God's commandments; 2 & 4 – The possibility of resisting grace; 3 – the concept of freedom; 5 – Predestination.

[790] 2001 1. Some of the commandments of God are impossible for just men who wish and try to fulfil them with their existing powers; and the grace which would make them possible is also lacking.

[791] 2002 2. In the state of fallen nature there is never any resistance to interior grace.

[792] 2003 3. In the state of fallen nature freedom from necessity is not required in man for merit or demerit but only freedom from compulsion.

[793] 2004 4. The semi-Pelagians admitted the necessity for antecedent interior grace for individual actions and for the beginning of faith; in this they were heretical in that they made the grace such that human will could resist it or comply with it.

[794] 2005 5. It is semi-Pelagian to say that Christ died or shed his blood for all men.

PROPOSITIONS OF PASQUIER QUESNEL CONDEMNED BY POPE CLEMENT XI (1713)

Jansenist propositions were condemned on several further occasions, for example by Alexander VIII in 1690 (cf. No. 324). In general, the propositions condemned were just new ways of expressing the old errors. Quesnel (1634–1719) however, had a new conception of the 'grace of Christ' which was the principle of renewal in man. Without this grace man was wholly corrupt, but the grace itself was irresistible. It en-

dowed man with pure charity, the only moral motive for action. In the decree Unigenitus, *the last and most thorough rebuttal of Jansenism, Clement XI condemned 101 propositions by Quesnel.*

Propositions Denying all Moral Good in the Natural Order Without Grace

1. What remains to the soul which has lost God and his grace but sin and the consequences of sin, proud poverty and slothful indigence, that is, a general inability to work or pray or do any good thing? [795] *2401*

38. Without the grace of the Redeemer the sinner is not free except for evil. [796] *2438*

39. The will which is not prompted by grace has no light except to error, no ardour except to cast itself down, no strength except to harm itself. It is capable of all evil and incapable of any good. [797] *2439*

40. Without grace we can love nothing, except to our own damnation. [798] *2440*

41. All knowledge of God, even natural, even among heathen philosophers, cannot come but from God; and without grace it produces nothing but presumption, vanity and opposition to God himself instead of sentiments of adoration, gratitude and love. [799] *2441*

59. The prayer of sinners is a new sin and what God grants them is a new judgment on them. [800] *2459*

Propositions denying the Existence of a Natural Moral Love as Well as Pure Love of God and Concupiscence

44. There are but two loves whence all our willing and doing arise: the love of God which does all things for God's sake and which God rewards; and the love with which we love ourselves and the world, which does not refer to God what should be referred to God, and is therefore evil. [801] *2449*

[802] 45. If the love of God no longer reigns in the heart of
2445 sinners, then of necessity fleshly cupidity reigns and corrupts all its actions.

[803] 46. Either cupidity or charity makes the use of the
2446 senses evil or good.

[804] 47. Obedience to the law flows from a fount, and this
2447 fount is charity. When the love of God is its interior principle and the glory of God its end, then what is seen outwardly is pure; otherwise it is nothing but hypocrisy or false righteousness.

Propositions Concerning the Compulsive Force of Divine Grace

[805] 10. Grace is the operation of the hand of almighty God
2410 which nothing can hinder or delay.

[806] 11. Grace is nothing but the almighty will of God, or-
2411 dering and carrying out its orders.

[807] 23. God himself conveyed to us the concept of the
2423 almighty operation of his will, indicating it by that operation which produces creatures out of nothing and gives life back to the dead.

PIUS XII's ENCYCLICAL
MYSTICI CORPORIS CHRISTI (1943)

This encyclical devoted to the nature of the Catholic Church as the Mystical Body of Christ also contains a notable passage concerning the doctrine of grace. Whereas Trent was concerned with rebutting an actualist and forensic doctrine of justification and thus paid attention primarily to the sanctifying grace of justification in so far as it embraced a created, supernatural inherent 'habit' in man, here attention is expressly paid to 'uncreated grace', the self-communication of the triune God. Principles are formulated for a theologically balanced expression of this 'indwelling' to protect it against pantheistic interpretation as well as against its being regarded as a mere consequence of the inherence of created grace.

Created and Uncreated Grace

807a We are by no means unaware that when men seek to understand and explain this mysterious doctrine – concerning our union with the divine Redeemer, and particularly the indwelling of the Holy Spirit in the soul – their feeble vision is obstructed by many veils which enshroud the truth in a sort of mist. But We know also that from a right-minded and earnest investigation of this subject, and from the clash of conflicting opinions and a rivalry of views, so long as the enquiry is inspired by the love of truth and conducted in due obedience to the Church, precious light emerges and promotes a real advance even in these sacred subjects. We have therefore no word of blame for those who follows various paths and methods in their efforts to reach, and as far as possible illustrate, this profound mystery of our marvellous union with Christ. But, 3814 under pain of departing from pure doctrine and from the true teaching of the Church, they must all hold this as quite certain: that any explanation of this mystical union is to be rejected if it makes the faithful in any way pass beyond the order of created things and so trespass upon the divine sphere, that even one single attribute of the eternal God could be predicated of them in the proper sense. Moreover, this certain truth must be firmly borne in mind, that in these matters all things are to be held common to the Blessed Trinity, so far as the same relate to God as the supreme efficient cause. It must also be remembered that we are dealing with a 3815 hidden mystery which during our exile on earth can never be completely unveiled, never altogether understood, nor adequately expressed in human language.

The Divine Persons are said to 'indwell' inasmuch as, being present in a mysterious way to living intellectual creatures, they are attained by these through knowledge and love, but in a manner which transcends all nature and is quite intimate and unique. If we would reach some little understanding of this we shall do well to use the method recommended by the *(First)* Vatican Council in such matters, the method by which light is successfully sought for some partial perception of God's hidden truths in a comparison of mysteries with one another and with the last end to which they are directed. Thus, when Our wise Predecessor of happy memory, Leo XIII, was treating of this union of ours with Christ and the indwelling of the divine Paraclete within us, he appropriately turned his gaze to that beatific vision wherein one day in heaven this mystical union will find its perfect consummation. 'This marvellous union', he wrote, 'known by the special name of indwelling, differs only by reason of our condition or state from that union in which God embraces and beatifies the citizens of heaven.' In that vision it will be granted to the eyes of the mind, its powers augmented by supernatural light, to contemplate the Father, the Son, and the Holy Ghost, for all eternity to witness close at hand the processions of the Divine Persons, and to enjoy a beatitude very similar to that with which the most holy and undivided Trinity is blessed.

POPE PIUS XII'S ENCYCLICAL
HUMANI GENERIS (1950)
(Cf. Nos. 74, 126e)

In the endeavour, right in itself, to create in the actual order of salvation in which we are as close a tie and mutual interpenetration of nature and grace as possible, theories were developed here and there, particularly in France, in the years preceding Humani generis, *which appeared to interpret the actual orientation of nature to grace in the present order of salvation in such a way that it was logically impossible for God to create a spiritual person without calling him to a direct vision of God and therefore to grace. It is against such theories that* Humani generis *is written.*

The Supernatural Nature of the Order of Salvation and Grace [807b] 3891

...others destroy the gratuitous character of the supernatural order by suggesting that it would be impossible for God to create rational beings without ordaining them for the Beatific Vision and calling them to it...

CHAPTER ELEVEN

THE LAST THINGS

Cornerstone of the Church's doctrinal edifice is eschatology, the doctrine of the end of things. Man came from God, and to God he will return. The doctrine of the last things is what gives the deepest supernatural meaning to the history of the world, which is ultimately the history of salvation to the glory of God.

At the last judgment Christ will finally reveal himself as the head of the Church, as the redeemer and the victor over death and hell, and will lay his kingdom at his Father's feet.

Naturally the position of Christ and his Church in eschatology has not always been proclaimed with the same emphasis at all times and in every individual decree. Almost always the Church's decrees are aimed at heresies which arise and these mostly concern the last things as they affect individuals. In this way the Church's magisterium lays no claim to systematize the inner structure.

In its dealing with heresy concerning the last things the Church has stressed three main fundamental truths:

1 – *The nature of the* direct vision of God *in the next world which is essentially different from the indirect knowledge of God in this world.*

2 – *The* dignity of the human body *and with it the whole*

of material creation as opposed to that form of dualism in which matter stems from the principle of evil and is thus incapable of redemption or supernatural life. Throughout the Early and Middle Ages the Church had to engage in this struggle for the dignity and value of the human body and at the same time to fight for the basic facts of a true anthropology.
3 – *The* discharge in the next world of the punishment due to sin – *purgatory. This doctrine had to be defended in particular against the East and the Reformers.*

Concerning the completion of man and the kingdom of God, the Church teaches: –
Souls which depart this life without sin or punishment due to sin, go to eternal happiness (813, 816, 818–21, 828, 834, 837, 841, 843). The happiness of heaven consists in the direct vision of God *(807a, 819, 823, 827, 843). For this vision, an end which is not owed to man (807b), man needs the Light of Glory (34, 207, 213, 817).*
The soul which has temporal punishment still due goes to purgatory *(767, 814, 823, 843, 854). The faithful can help the holy souls by prayer and good works (514, 523, 605, 608, 814, 824, 825, 843, 854).*
Souls which depart this life in grievous sin go to hell *(813, 815, 822, 837). Hell is* eternal *(808, 813, 815, 837). For souls burdened with original sin alone it consists of the loss of the Beatific Vision (434, 812, 843), but for those in actual sin there are also the torments of hell (434, 812, 843).*
At the end of time souls are re-united with their risen bodies *(809, 810, 813, 828, 834, 837, 841, 844) following Christ's example (809). Christ will then pronounce the last judgment (809, 813, 822, 828, 829, 831, 832, 834, 837, 839, 844) and hand over his kingdom to the* Father *(811).*

PROVINCIAL SYNOD OF CONSTANTINOPLE (543)
CANONS AGAINST THE ORIGENISTS
(Cf. Note to No. 163)

Canon 9 is mainly directed at the followers of Origen who denied the eternity of the punishment of hell.

9. If anyone says or believes that the punishment of demons or wicked men is but temporary and that after a certain time it will end and there will be restitution or reintegration (ἀποκατάστασις) of demons or wicked spirits, *anathema sit*.

808
411

PROFESSION OF FAITH OF THE ELEVENTH
COUNCIL OF TOLEDO (675)
(Cf. Note to No. 144)

The first two part of this great profession of faith are at Nos. 144–54 and 283–93. Here we have the third and last main part. The closing formula appears at No. 294.

We confess that, after the example of our Head, there will be a true *resurrection of the body* of all the dead. We do not believe that we shall rise again in some aerial body or any other body (as some foolishly maintain) but in that in which we live, move and have our being. When he had given the example of this this sacred resurrection, *our Lord and Saviour* by his ascension resumed his paternal throne which in his divinity he had never left. There, seated at the right hand of the Father, he is awaited to the end of time as judge of all the living and dead. Thence he will come with the holy angels and men to give judgment and to render to each his due reward according as in the body he did good or evil.

809
540

810 We believe that the holy Catholic Church which he
540 purchased at the price of his blood will reign eternally with him. Living in his bosom, we believe and confess one baptism for the remission of all sins. In which faith we truly believe in the resurrection of the dead and await the joys of the world to come.

811 This only must we pray for and petition, that when the
540 judgment has been made and completed and the Son delivers up the kingdom to God the Father, he will make us partakers in his kingdom so that through the Faith. by which we cleave to him we may reign with him for ever.

POPE INNOCENT III's LETTER TO YMBERTUS, BISHOP OF ARLES (1201)

812 The punishment of original sin is the deprivation of the
780 sight of God, but the punishment of actual sin is the torment of eternal hell.

THE FOURTH LATERAN GENERAL COUNCIL (1215)
(Cf. Notes to Nos. 155, 170, 171)

Chapter I – On the Catholic Faith

813 Jesus Christ... will come at the end of time to judge the
801 living and the dead, to render to each according to his works, to the rejected and to the elect; who will all arise with their own bodies which they now have so that they may receive, according as their works were good or bad, either perpetual punishment with the devil or eternal glory with Christ.

POPE INNOCENT IV's LETTER TO THE BISHOP OF TUSCULUM (1254)

Differences of doctrine concerning the last things were also among the obstacles to reunion between the Greeks and Rome. The Greeks still prayed for the dead but they were not prepared to accept any place between heaven and hell, nor any suffering of atonement in the next world where there was only final reward for good or evil. On the Latin side, on the contrary, purgatory was repeatedly stressed, especially in the (particular) decree for the Church in Cyprus contained in a letter from Pope Innocent IV to the Bishop of Tusculum, the Papal Legate to the Greeks, and in the great profession of faith of the Emperor Michael Paleologue which, with one important addition, was incorporated by the Council of Florence in the Decree for the Greeks (No. 843). In 1575 it was again prescribed for the Greeks by Gregory XIII.

Truth says in the Gospel, he that shall blaspheme against the Holy Spirit, it will not be forgiven him in this world nor in the world to come *(Mt. 12:32)* whereby we are given to understand that some sins will be forgiven in the present world and some in the world to come; and the Apostle says: 'The fire shall try every man's work, of what sort it is'; and: 'If any man's work burn, he shall suffer loss; but he himself shall be saved, yet so as by fire' *(1 Cor. 3:13, 15)*. And the Greeks themselves are said to believe truly and without doubt and to affirm that the souls of those who have undertaken penance but not completed it, or who die without mortal sin but with venial and minor sins, are *cleansed after death* and can be helped by the intercession of the Church. Because, however, they say that the place of purgation has not been shown them with certainty and by name by their teachers, We now wish that that place which according to the tradition and

814
838

authority of the holy Fathers is called Purgatory should by them also be called by this name. For in that temporary fire sins, not indeed mortal or capital sins not previously remitted by penance, but lesser sins which still weigh upon us although forgiven in this life, are purged.

815　But whoever dies in mortal sin without penance will
839　without any doubt suffer for ever in the fires of eternal hell.

816　But the souls of children after baptism and of adults
839　who die in charity, who are not bound by sin or by satisfaction due for sin, fly directly to their eternal home.

THE GENERAL COUNCIL OF VIENNE (1311-12)

CONDEMNED PROPOSITIONS OF THE BEGUARDS AND BEGUINES CONCERNING THE STATE OF PERFECTION

'Beguards and Beguines' or 'Brothers and Sisters of the Free Spirit' are general terms covering a series of pseudo-mystical sects which made their appearance from the middle of the thirteenth century on the Rhine, in the Netherlands and in northern France. They rejected fundamental Christian doctrine (creation, redemption, eternal recompense), the external structure of the Church, and the moral law. Their pantheistic mystique denied the gratuitous and supernatural nature of the Beatific Vision. Since this is precisely what is taught by the doctrine of the Light of Glory (Lumen gloriae), *the following condemnation by the Council is of particular significance.*

[817]　**5. Any spiritual nature is in itself naturally happy and**
895　**the soul has no need of the light of glory to raise it to see God and enjoy him in happiness.**

POPE BENEDICT XII's CONSTITUTION *BENEDICTUS DEUS* ON THE BEATIFIC VISION AND THE LAST THINGS (1336)

The Avignon Pope John XXII had maintained in sermons in 1331 that the soul of the elect would enjoy the Beatific Vision only after the last judgment and the resurrection of the body. Before then they enjoyed only an imperfect happiness. In the following year he preached the same sort of thing about the punishment of the damned. These were not solemn papal pronouncements but only private expressions of opinion.

There was immediate reaction among the Dominicans, in France in particular, and among the Franciscans, particularly among those adherents of Ludwig the Bavarian unfriendly to the Pope. The Pope gave up his private opinion in favour of the traditional teaching of the Church and wanted to set the latter down in a solemn decree but it was not until after a more detailed study of the question that his successor Benedict XII was able to issue the solemn definition in the constitution Benedictus Deus.

In this perpetually valid Constitution by apostolic authority We define: 818 / 1000

In accordance with God's universal ordinance, since the ascension of our Lord and Saviour Jesus Christ into heaven, the souls of all saints who departed from this world before the passion of our Lord Jesus Christ and those of the holy Apostles, Martyrs, Confessors, Virgins and other faithful departed who died after receiving the baptism of Christ in whom there was nothing to purge when they died, or in whom there will be nothing to purge when they die in future, or in whom anything to be purged has or shall have been purged after death, and the souls of children regenerated or to be regenerated by the same baptism of Christ if they die before the use of free will, were, are, and will be immediately after death, or 819 / 1000 after the aforesaid purgation in the case of those who need it, and before resuming their bodies and before the general judgment in heaven, gathered together with Christ and the holy angels in the kingdom of heaven and the heavenly paradise.

And after the passion and death of the Lord Jesus Christ they have seen, and see, the divine essence intuitively and face to face so that as far as the object seen is concerned no creature acts as a medium of vision, but the divine essence shows itself to them plainly, clearly and openly.

820
1000 In this vision they are filled with the enjoyment of the divine essence, and by this vision and enjoyment the souls of those who have already died are truly happy and have life and eternal rest. Also the souls of those who will die in future will see and enjoy the same divine essence before the general judgment.

821
1001 Such vision and enjoyment of the divine essence remove from them the acts of faith and hope inasmuch as faith and hope are real theological virtues.

And once such intuitive and face-to-face vision and enjoyment shall have begun or shall begin in them, this vision and enjoyment continues without intermission or lessening and will continue until the last judgment and thereafter into eternity.

822
1002 We further define that in accordance with God's universal ordinance the souls of those who die in actual mortal sin descend immediately after death to hell where they are tormented by eternal punishment; and that nonetheless at the day of judgment all men will appear with their bodies to give an account of their own deeds 'before the judgment seat of Christ, that every one may receive the proper things of the body, according as he hath done, whether it be good or evil' *(2 Cor. 5:10).*

POPE CLEMENT VI's LETTER ON ARMENIAN REUNION (1351)
(Cf. Note to No. 460)

On Purgatory 823

We ask: if thou hast believed and believest there is a 1066
purgatory to which the souls of those who die in grace
but have not yet by penance made complete satisfaction
for their sins descend.

And if thou hast believed and believest that they are 1067
burned for a time by fire and that as soon as they are
purged, even before the day of judgment, they attain to
true eternal happiness which consists of seeing God
face to face and in love.

THE GENERAL COUNCIL OF TRENT, TWENTY-FIFTH SESSION (1563)
(Cf. Note to No. 460)

DECREE ON PURGATORY

Since the Catholic Church, instructed by the Holy Spirit, 824
has, following the sacred writings and the ancient tra- *1820*
dition of the Fathers, taught in sacred Councils and very
recently in this ecumenical Council that *there is a pur-*
gatory, **and that the souls detained therein are aided by**
the suffrages of the faithful and chiefly by the acceptable
sacrifice of the altar,

the Holy Council commands the bishops that they strive 825
diligently to the end that the sound doctrine of purgatory, *1820*
transmitted by the Fathers and sacred Councils, be be-
lieved and maintained by the faithful of Christ and be
everywhere taught and preached. The more difficult and
subtle questions, however, and those that do not make for
edification and from which for the most part there is no

increase in piety, are to be excluded from popular instructions to uneducated people. Likewise, things that are uncertain, or that have the appearance of falsehood, they shall not permit to be made known publicly and discussed. But those things that tend to a certain kind of curiosity or superstition, or that savour of filthy lucre, they shall prohibit as scandals and stumbling blocks to the faithful...

ROSMINI'S PROPOSITIONS CONDEMNED BY LEO XIII (1887)
(Cf. Note to No. 18)

The importance of this condemnation lies in the more precise definition of the object of the Beatific Vision, which is not God as he reveals himself in his handiwork but the wealth of the inner life of Godhead itself.

[826] 3239 39. The traces of wisdom and goodness which shine in creatures are necessary for the triumphant, for they *(the traces)*, gathered together in the eternal Exemplar, are that part of him which is accessible to them and they provide the matter of the praises that the blessed sing to God for eternity.

[827] 3240 40. Since God cannot communicate himself entirely to finite beings, even by the light of glory, he could not reveal and communicate his essence to the triumphant except in a way suitable to finite understanding; that is to say, God reveals himself to them, in so far as he has any relationship with them, as their creator, provider, redeemer and sanctifier.

CHAPTER TWELVE

CREEDS AND PROFESSIONS OF FAITH

THE APOSTLES' CREED

The present form of the Apostles' Creed was accepted throughout the western Church in the ninth century, largely due to the influence of Charlemagne under whom it was incorporated into imperial law. Probably, however, the form dates back to the fifth century.
But even before that there were many forms of the Creed which differed little from the present one and go back to the second century of the Christian era. There is no historical basis for the old tradition that the Creed was put together by the apostles soon after the Ascension.

I believe in God, the Father almighty, creator of heaven and earth. And in Jesus Christ, his only Son, our Lord, who was conceived by the Holy Ghost, born of the Virgin Mary, suffered under Pontius Pilate, was crucified, dead and buried. He descended into hell. The third day he rose again from the dead. He ascended into heaven, sitteth at the right hand of God the Father. From whence he shall come to judge the living and the dead. I believe in the Holy Ghost, the holy Catholic Church, the communion of saints, the forgiveness of sins, and life everlasting. 828 30

THE PROFESSION OF FAITH OF THE COUNCIL OF NICAEA (325)

The Council of Nicaea condemned the heresy of Arius that the second Person of the Godhead was not equal to the Father but created by him in time. The true belief in the unity of nature between Father and Son was set out by the Council in a profession of faith to which the condemnation of the Arian heresy was added.

829
125 We believe in one God, the Father almighty, maker of all things visible and invisible. And in one Lord Jesus Christ, the Son of God, only-begotten, born of the Father, that is, of the substance of the Father, God of God, light of light, true God of true God, born, not made, of one substance with the Father, through whom were made all things in heaven and earth. Who for us men and our salvation came down, was incarnate and made man and suffered, and rose again the third day, and ascended into the heavens, and will come to judge the living and the dead. And in the Holy Ghost.

830
126 But those who say 'There was a time when he was not,' and 'Before he was born, he was not,' and 'that he was made out of nothing' or out of some other substance or essence, or that the Son of God is changeable or mutable, those the Catholic Church anathematizes.

THE NICAEO-CONSTANTINOPOLITAN PROFESSION OF FAITH known as the NICENE CREED (381)

This profession of faith was the answer to the heresy denying the divinity of the Holy Spirit. Either taken over as an already fixed formula by the Council of Constantinople in 381 or prepared by it as a standard formula of belief, this creed emphasizes the divinity of the Holy Spirit, calling him 'Lord' and praising him as the 'giver of life' – that is, the source of the life of grace in man. It is still today the form of creed common to the Western and schismatic Eastern Churches and has been introduced into the Western Mass.

I believe in one God, the Father almighty, maker of heaven and earth, and of all things visible and invisible. And in one Lord Jesus Christ, the only-begotten Son of God. Born of the Father before all ages. God from God, Light from Light, true God from true God. Begotten not made, consubstantial with the Father: through whom all things were made. Who for us men and for our salvation came down from heaven. And was incarnate by the Holy Ghost of the Virgin Mary: and was made man. He was crucified also for us under Pontius Pilate, suffered and was buried. He rose again the third day according to the Scriptures; and ascended into heaven: and is seated at the right hand of the Father. And he will come again with glory to judge the living and the dead. And of his kingdom there will be no end.

And *(I believe)* **in the Holy Ghost, the Lord and giver of life; who proceeds from the Father (and the Son)**[1]**. Who together with the Father and the Son is adored and glorified: who spoke through the prophets.**

And *(I believe)* **in the one holy, Catholic and apostolic Church. I acknowledge one baptism for the remission of sins. And I look for the resurrection of the dead. And the life of the world to come. Amen.**

831
150

---

1. *Filioque* (and from the Son) was first introduced into the Creed in Spain. In Carolingian times it came into common use throughout France but it was only officially introduced into the Creed of the Roman Church by Benedict VIII at the request of the Emperor St Henry II.

THE CREED OF EPIPHANIUS (ca. 374)

This profession of faith is an explanatory elaboration of the Nicene Profession and is important on account of the outstanding position of its author Epiphanius (ob. 403) who, as Bishop of Cyprus, was in a very close relationship with all the Mediterranean Churches.

832   We believe in one God, the Father almighty, creator of
44   all things visible and invisible. And in one Lord Jesus Christ, the Son of God, only born begotten by God the Father, that is, from the substance of the Father, God of God, light of light, true God of true God, begotten not made, consubstantial with the Father, through whom all things were made which are in the heavens and in earth, visible and invisible. Who for us men and for our salvation came down, and was incarnate, that is, was perfectly begotten by the Holy Spirit of Mary ever a virgin; was made man, that is, assumed the perfect man, soul and body and mind and all that is man, excepting sin, not by seed of man, nor as if merely inhabiting a man, but transferred that flesh to himself and joined it to him in one holy unity, not in the way in which he inspired the prophets and spoke and acted in them, but he became fully man; for 'the Word was made flesh' *(John 1:14)*; nor did any change take place, nor was his divinity changed into the nature of man, but he joined it in unity with his holy perfection and divinity. For the Lord Jesus Christ is one and not two; the same Lord, the same God, the same King. Who suffered in the flesh, and rose again, and ascended into heaven with the same body; and sits at the right hand of the Father in glory; and will come with the same body in glory to judge the living and the dead; and of his kingdom there will be no end.

833   We believe also in the Holy Spirit, who spoke in the Law

and preached through the prophets, and descended to Jordan, and spoke through the Apostles and lives in the faithful. Thus then we believe in him, that he is the Holy Spirit, the Spirit of God, the perfect Spirit, the Paraclete, uncreated, proceeding from the Father and receiving from the Son, in whom we believe.

We believe also in the one catholic and apostolic Church, and in one baptism of penance, and in the resurrection of the dead, and a just judgment of souls and bodies, and in the kingdom of heaven and life everlasting.

Those, however, who say that there was a time when the Son or the Holy Spirit did not exist, or that they were made from nothing, or from another hypostasis or substance, and those who say that the Son of God or the Holy Spirit are subject to change or mutation, all those the catholic and apostolic Church, your mother and ours, condemns with anathema. And we condemn also those who do not confess the resurrection of the dead, as well as all heresies which are not in accord with this holy faith.

Since you now, dearly beloved, and your children do so believe, and since your wish is to obey the commandments arising therefrom, We hope that you pray for us that We may always partake of this community of faith in loyal fulfilment of the commandments. Pray for us, both you and anyone who holds this faith and keeps the Lord's commandments in Christ Jesus our Lord, through whom and with whom be glory to the Father and the Holy Spirit for all eternity. Amen.

THE 'ATHANASIAN' CREED

The Quicumque vult *or so-called Athanasian Creed did not originate with St Athanasius but was written, originally in Latin, some time between the end of the fourth century and the end of the sixth century. St Ambrose may have been the author. It comprises what is one of the clearest formulations of the mystery of the Blessed Trinity and the Incarnation.*

836 Whoever wishes to be saved must first of all hold the
75 Catholic faith, for anyone who does not maintain this whole and inviolate will surely be lost eternally.

And the Catholic faith is this, that we worship one God in Trinity, and Trinity in Unity, neither confounding the Persons nor dividing the substance. For there is one person of the Father, another of the Son, and another of the Holy Spirit. But the godhead of the Father, of the Son and of the Holy Spirit is all one, the glory equal, the majesty co-eternal. As the Father is, so is the Son, and so is the Holy Spirit. Uncreated the Father, the Son uncreated, and the Holy Spirit uncreated. The Father immeasurable, the Son immeasurable, and the Holy Spirit immeasurable. The Father eternal, the Son eternal, and the Holy Spirit eternal. And yet there are not three eternals but one eternal. Just as there are not three uncreated nor three immeasurables, but one uncreated and one immeasurable. Likewise the Father is almighty, the Son is almighty, and the Holy Spirit is almighty; yet not three almighties, but one almighty. Thus God the Father, God the Son, and God the Holy Spirit; yet not three Gods but one God. Thus the Father is Lord, the Son is Lord, and the Holy Spirit is Lord; yet there are not three Lords, but one Lord. For as we are compelled by Christian truth to acknowledge that each Person by himself is God and Lord, we are forbidden by the true Catholic religion to say that there are three Gods or Lords. The Father is made by none, nor created nor begotten. The Son is from the Father alone, not made nor created but begotten. The Holy Spirit is from the Father and the Son, not made nor created nor begotten, but proceeding. So there is one Father, not three Fathers; one Son, not three Sons; and one Holy Spirit, not three Holy Spirits. And in this Trinity none is before or after another, none is greater or less, but all three Persons are co-eternal with one another and co-equal. So that in all things, as has already been said above, both Unity in Trinity and Trinity in Unity are to be adored. Therefore whoever will be saved must believe this of the Trinity.

For eternal salvation it is further necessary that we faithfully believe in the incarnation of our Lord Jesus Christ. The right faith is therefore this: that we believe and confess that our Lord Jesus Christ the Son of God is both God and man; God of the substance of the Father, begotten before time, and man of the substance of his mother born in time; perfect God and perfect man, consisting of a rational soul and human body; equal to the Father in his divinity, less than the Father in his humanity; who, although both God and man is not two but one Christ; one, however, not by the conversion of the Godhead into flesh but by the assumption of manhood into God. Wholly one, not by fusion of substance but by unity of person. For as the rational soul and the body are one man, so God and man are one Christ. Who suffered for our salvation, descended into hell, rose again from the dead on the third day, ascended into heaven, sits at the right hand of the Father, whence he will come to judge the living and the dead. When he comes, all men will rise again with their bodies and give an account of their own deeds, and those who have done good will enter into eternal life, and those who have done evil into eternal fire. This is the Catholic faith. And if anyone shall not faithfully and firmly believe it, he cannot be saved.

THE PROFESSION OF FAITH OF THE ELEVENTH COUNCIL OF TOLEDO (675)

837a
525–41
The first part, on the Trinity (Denz. 525–32) is at Nos. 144–54; the second part, on Christ (Denz. 533–9) is at Nos. 283–93; the third part, on the fate of man after death (Denz. 540) is at Nos. 809–11; and the closing formula (Denz. 541) is at No. 294.

THE PROFESSION OF FAITH OF THE FOURTH GENERAL LATERAN COUNCIL (1215)
(Cf. Notes to Nos. 155, 171, 339)

837b
800
We firmly believe and simply confess that there is only one true God, eternal, immeasurable and unchangeable, incomprehensible, almighty and ineffable, Father, Son and Holy Spirit: three persons indeed but one essence, substance or wholly simple nature: the Father from no one, the Son from the Father alone, and the Holy Spirit equally from both: and without beginning, always, and without end; the Father generating, the Son being born, the Holy Spirit proceeding; consubstantial, co-equal, co-omnipotent and co-eternal; one origin of all things: the Creator of all things visible and invisible, spiritual and corporal. Who by his almighty power created both orders of creation out of nothing from the beginning of time, the spiritual and corporeal, that is the angelic and the earthly, and then the human order which being constituted of spirit and body is as it were common to both. For the devil and other wicked spirits were indeed created by God good by nature, but they became evil of themselves. Man indeed sinned at the suggestion of the devil. This holy Trinity, undivided in its common essence but distinct in the properties of the Persons, first communicated its doctrine of salvation to the human race to Moses and

then to the holy prophets and to others of his servants according to the most perfect plan for the times.
And finally the only-begotten Son of God Jesus Christ, incarnate by the whole Trinity working in common, conceived of Mary ever a Virgin by the cooperation of the Holy Spirit, made true man, composed of a rational soul and a human body, one person in two natures, showed the way of life more clearly. That very same *(person)* although immortal and impassible in his divinity became passible and mortal in his humanity; he suffered on the wood of the cross for the salvation of mankind and died, descended into hell, rose from the dead, and ascended into heaven: but he descended in the soul and rose in the body; but ascended equally in both. He will come at the end of time to judge the living and the dead, to render to each according to his works, to the rejected as well as to the elect; who will also rise with their own bodies which they now have so that they may receive according to their works, whether they were good or evil, the latter perpetual punishment with the devil, the former eternal glory with Christ. 837c 801

There is indeed one universal Church of the faithful, outside which no one at all is saved. In it the same Jesus Christ is at once priest and victim, whose body and blood are truly contained in the Sacrament of the altar under the species of bread and wine, the bread being transubstantiated into the body by the divine power, and the wine into the blood, so that we receive of his what he received of ours to complete the mystery of unity. And no one can effect this sacrifice but a priest duly ordained by the *(power of the)* keys of the Church which the same Jesus Christ gave to the Apostles and their successors. The sacrament of baptism (which is effected in water with the invocation of the undivided Trinity, viz. the Father, Son and Holy Spirit) is efficient for the salvation of both 802 children and adults when duly administered by anyone according to the Church's form. If anyone after receiving baptism shall have fallen into sin, he can always be restored by true penance. Not only virgins and *continentes* but also married persons, if they are pleasing to God by true faith and good works, are worthy to attain eternal happiness.

THE PROFESSION OF FAITH OF MICHAEL PALEOLOGUE[1] (1274)

In 1261 the Emperor Michael Paleologue had overthrown the Latin Empire, set up by the Crusaders in Constantinople in 1204, and had reconstituted the Eastern Roman Empire. Once more he sought reunion of the schismatic East with Rome. At the fourth session of the Council of Lyons in 1274 the legates of the Emperor of the East bound themselves to the formula of belief proposed by Pope Clement IV to the Emperor in 1267 and usually called after the Emperor, Michael Paleologue.

The first part comprises, with minor variations, the formula which before the Eastern schism had been sent by Pope Leo IX to Peter of Antioch, but most of which goes back to some time in the fifth century (Statuta ecclesiae antiqua). *The second part covers those doctrines which were of significance in the split between East and West.*

The importance of this document lies precisely in this clear presentation of the doctrinal differences between East and West.

838
851

We believe in the holy *Trinity,* **Father, Son and Holy Spirit, one almighty God, and in the Trinity the whole Godhead, of the same essence and substance, equally eternal and equally almighty, having one will, power and majesty, maker of all creatures, by whom and in whom and through whom are all things which are in heaven and**

1. This profession was repeated by the Council of Florence with an addition which is given here between //and// (p.434)

earth, visible and invisible, corporeal and spiritual. And we also believe that each single Person in the Trinity is true God, complete and perfect.

We believe in the *Son of God* himself, the Word of God, eternally born of the Father, consubstantial, co-omnipotent and in all things equal with the Father in divinity, born in time of the Holy Spirit and Mary ever a Virgin, with a rational soul, having two births, one eternal birth from the Father, the other temporal from his mother; true God and true man, real and perfect in both natures; not adoptive, not just apparent, but the one and only Son of God; in and from two natures, that is, divine and human natures, in the unity of one person; in divinity impassible and immortal, but having in his humanity truly suffered with bodily suffering for us and for our salvation; that he died and was buried, and descended into hell, and the third day rose again from the dead in a true resurrection of the body; that on the fortieth day after his resurrection he ascended into heaven with the body in which he rose again and with his soul; that he is seated at the right hand of God the Father, whence he will come to judge the living and the dead, and render to each according to his works, whether they have been good or evil. 839 852

We believe also in the *Holy Spirit*, fully, perfectly and truly God, proceeding from the Father and the Son, co-equal and consubstantial and co-omnipotent and co-eternal in all things with the Father and the Son. We believe that this holy Trinity is not three Gods, but one God, almighty, eternal, invisible and immutable. 840 853

We believe that the holy, catholic and apostolic *(Church)* is the *one true Church*, in which there is one true baptism and true remission of all sins. And we believe in the true resurrection of this body which we now bear, and in life eternal. 841 854

842	We believe also that the almighty God and Lord is the
854	one author of the New and Old Testaments, of the Law
855	and the Prophets and the Apostles. This is the true Catholic faith and the most holy Roman Church holds and preaches it.
843	Yet on account of various errors, some introduced by
855	ignorance and some by malice, she says and preaches: that those who fall into sin after baptism are not to be re-baptized but attain forgiveness of their sins by true
856	penance. But if they die truly repenting in charity before making satisfaction by worthy fruits for what they have done or omitted to do, their souls are *purged after death* ... by the punishments of purgation and purification. The intercession of the living faithful is effective in lessening this punishment, by the sacrifice of the Mass, prayer, alms-giving and other pious works which the faithful are wont to do for one another according to the
857	constitution of the Church. But the souls of those who after holy baptism have acquired no stain of sin at all, and those who having incurred the stain of sin are cleansed either while still in the body or after death as described above, are received immediately into heaven// and clearly see God himself, Three in One, as he is, yet
858	some more perfectly than others according to their different merits//. But the souls of those who die in mortal sin or just in original sin go down immediately to hell, to be punished, however, by different punishments.
844	This same most holy Roman Church firmly believes and
859	firmly proclaims that nevertheless on the day of judgment all men will appear before the *judgment seat of Christ* with their bodies to give an account of their own deeds.
845	The same holy Roman Church holds and teaches that
860	there are *seven sacraments* of the Church: the one baptism mentioned above; then the sacrament of confirmation which bishops confer by laying on their hands

and anointing the regenerated; then penance, Eucharist, the sacrament of order, matrimony, and extreme unction which is administered to the sick according to the teaching of St James.

The same Roman Church prepares the sacrament of the *Eucharist* from unleavened bread, holding and teaching that in this sacrament the bread is truly transubstantiated to the body of our Lord Jesus Christ and the wine to his blood.   846 *860*

Of *matrimony* indeed she teaches that a man may not have more than one wife at one time, nor a woman more than one husband. But if a legitimate marriage is dissolved by the death of one other of the spouses, second and third successive marriages are allowed provided there is no other ground for a canonical impediment.   847 *860*

Also the same holy *Roman Church* has supreme and full *primacy* and dominion over the universal catholic Church, which she recognizes in truth and humility she received with full powers from the Lord himself in Blessed Peter, prince or head of the Apostles, whose successor the Roman Pontiff is. And as she above others is obliged to defend the truth of faith, thus if any questions are raised about faith they must be decided by her judgment. And anyone who is in difficulties in matters pertaining to the ecclesiastical forum can appeal to her; and in all causes within the purview of ecclesiastical enquiry recourse may be had to her judgment; and to it all Churches are subject and their prelates give obedience and reverence. And this fulness of power consists in this, that she allows participation in her cares by the other Churches, many of which, particularly the patriarchal Churches, she has honoured with various privileges while maintaining her own prerogatives both in general Councils and in other matters.   848 *861*

THE TRIDENTINE PROFESSION OF FAITH
(1564)

The Council of Trent demanded of all Church dignitaries a profession of faith and declaration of obedience to the Roman Pontiff. The formula was set out by Pope Pius IV, largely under pressure from St Peter Canisius, in the Bull Iniunctum Nobis *and is known as the Tridentine Creed although it was not the work of the Council. It also appears as the Profession of Catholic Faith prefacing the Code of Canon Law.*

849
1862 I. N, with steadfast faith believe and confess each and all the things contained in the symbol of faith which the Holy Roman Church uses, namely, 'I believe in one God...' *(Here follows the text of the Nicaeo-Constantinople Creed, No. 831)*

850
1863 I most firmly acknowledge and embrace the Apostolical and ecclesiastical traditions and other observances and constitutions of the same Church. I acknowledge the sacred Scripture according to that sense which Holy Mother Church has held and holds, to whom it belongs to decide upon the true sense and interpretation of the holy Scriptures, nor will I ever receive and interpret the Scriptures except according to the unanimous consent of the Fathers.

851
1864 I profess also that there are truly and properly *seven sacraments* instituted by Jesus Christ our Lord and necessary for the salvation of the human race, though not all are necessary for each, namely baptism, confirmation, Eucharist, penance, extreme unction, order and matrimony, and that they confer grace, and that of them baptism, confirmation and order may not be repeated without sacrilege. I also receive and accept all the received and approved rites of the Catholic Church in the solemn administration of the above sacraments.

852 I embrace and receive all things and every single thing

that were defined and declared by the sacred Council of   1865
Trent concerning *original sin* and *justification*.
I also profess that in the Mass a true, real and propi-   853
tiatory sacrifice is offered to God, for the living and the   *1866*
dead, and that in the most holy sacrament of the Eucharist there are truly, really and substantially the body
and blood together with the soul and divinity of our Lord
Jesus Christ, and there takes place the conversion of the
whole of the substance of bread into the body and the
whole of the substance of wine into the blood, which
conversion the Catholic Church calls transubstantiation.
And I further confess that the whole integral Christ and
the true sacrament are consumed even under one species
alone.
I hold unswervingly that there is a *purgatory* and that   854
the souls detained there are helped by the intercession of   *1867*
the faithful;
likewise that the *Saints* reigning with Christ are to be   855
venerated and invoked, and that they offer God prayers   *1867*
on our behalf, and that their relics are to be venerated.
I firmly assert that images of Christ and of the ever-
virgin Mother of God, as well as of other Saints, are to
be possessed and retained and that due honour and
veneration should be accorded them.
I also affirm that the power of *indulgences* was left in the   856
Church by Christ and that their use is very salutary for   *1867*
Christian people.
I acknowledge the holy, catholic and apostolic *Roman*   857
Church as mother and mistress of all Churches; and I
promise and swear true obedience to the Roman Pontiff,
successor to Blessed Peter, Prince of the Apostles, and
Vicar of Jesus Christ.
Also I receive without doubt and profess all that has   858
been handed down, defined and declared by the sacred
canons and ecumenical Councils, and especially by the

sacred Council of Trent // and the ecumenical Vatican Council //, // in particular what concerns the primacy and infallible magisterium of the Roman Pontiff //.¹

859
1869 And at the same time I condemn, reject and anathematize all things contrary thereto and whatever heresies have been condemned, rejected and anathematized by the Church.

1870 This true Catholic belief without which no one can be saved, which I here freely profess and truly hold, I, N, promise, vow and swear by the help of God to hold and confess entire and undefiled most constantly to the last breath of life, and I shall endeavour, as far as in me lies, that it be held, taught and preached by my subordinates and by those whose care is entrusted to me in my office, so help me God and these holy Gospels of God.

The two phrases between // and // were added by the Congregation of the Council and since then must be incorporated when this profession of faith is made.

CHRONOLOGICAL LIST OF DOCUMENTS QUOTED

(Figures in parentheses are dates; other figures refer to the items where the documents are quoted.)

Apostles' Creed – 828
Pope Dionysius' Letter to Bishop Dionysius of Alexandria (ca 260) – 127–8
Profession of Faith of the First General Council of Nicaea (325) – 829–30
Epiphanius' Profession of Faith (ca 374) – 832–5
Roman Council under Pope Damasus I (379) – 129–43; 231–3
Nicaeo-Constantinopolitan Profession of Faith (The Nicene Creed) (381) – 831
'Athanasian' Creed *(Quicumque vult)* (end of 4th to end of 6th Century) – 836–7
Letter of Pope Siricius to Anysius, Bishop of Thessalonica (392) – 320
Letter of Pope Innocent I to Decentius (416) – 610–1
Provincial Council of Carthage (418) – 206; 680–5
General Council of Ephesus (431)
  Twelve Articles of Cyril of Alexandria against Nestorius – 234–45
  Letter of same against Nestorius – 246
'Tome of Leo' – Letter of Pope Leo I to Flavian, Bishop of Constantinople, against Eutyches (449) – 247–51
General Council of Chalcedon (451) – 252
Indiculus of Papal Decisions Relating to Grace (mid-5th Cent). – 217; 686–95
II Council of Orange (529) – 218–9; 696–702

Letter of Pope John II to the Senate of Constantinople (534) – 253
Provincial Council of Constantinople: Canons against the Origenists (543) – 163; 199; 808
II General Council of Constantinople (553) – 76; 254–66
Council of Braga, against the Priscillians (561) – 164–9; 200–1
Lateran Council under Pope Martin I (649) – 77; 267–82
Profession of Faith of XI Council of Toledo (675) – 144–54; 283–94; 809–11; 837a
III General Council of Constantinople (680–1) – 295–6
II General Council of Nicaea (789) – 78
Letter of Pope Hadrian I to the Bishops of Gaul and Spain (793) – 297
Profession of Faith of the Council of Friaul (796) – 298
IV General Council of Constantinople (869–70) – 202
Letter of Pope Leo IX to Michael Caerularius (1053) – 338
Berengarius' Profession of Faith before the Council of Rome (1079) – 474
Letter of Pope Innocent III to Ymbertus, Bishop of Arles (1201) – 434; 812
Pope Innocent III's Profession of Faith against the Waldensians (1208) – 170; 405; 435; 475; 645
IV Lateran General Council (1215)
  Profession of Faith – 155; 171; 339; 813; 837b–d
  Condemnation of Abbot Joachim – 156
Letter of Pope Innocent IV to the Bishop of Tusculum (1254) – 814–6
Profession of Faith of Michael Paleologue (1274) – 838–48
Pope Boniface VIII's Bull *Unam Sanctam* (1302) – 340–2
General Council of Vienne (1311–2)
  Condemned Propositions of Beguards and Beguines – 817
  Against the Errors of Olivi – 203
Articles of Eckhart condemned by Pope John XXII (1329) – 172–6
Pope Benedict XII's Constitution *Benedictus Deus* (1336) – 818–22

Chronological List of Documents Quoted

Armenian Errors condemned by Pope Benedict XII (1341)– 204

Pope Clement VI's Jubilee Bull *Unigenitus Dei Filius* (1343) – 595–7

Pope Clement VI's Letter on Armenian Reunion (1351) – 460–3; 823

General Council of Constance (1414–8)
    Wycliffe's Errors Condemned – 343–4; 406; 538
    Regulation on Communion Under One Kind – 476
    Hus's Errors Condemned – 345–8
    Questions Posed to Wycliffites and Hussites – 399; 407; 477–8; 539–41; 598–9

General Council of Florence (1438–45)
    Decree for the Greeks – 349
    Decree for the Armenians – 408–11; 436–9; 464–6; 479–81; 542; 612; 625; 646
    Decree for the Jacobites – 79; 157–62; 177; 350

V Lateran General Council (1512–7) – 205

Articles of Martin Luther condemned by Pope Leo X (1520) – 543–52; 600–5; 703–8

General Council of Trent (1545–63)
    4th Session (1546) – 80–6
    5th Session (1546) – 220–6
    6th Session (1547) – 321; 709–70
    7th Session (1547) – 412–25; 440–53; 467–9
    13th Session (1551) – 482–502
    14th Session (1551) – 553–86; 613–20
    21st Session (1562) – 426; 503–10
    22nd Session (1562) – 511–29
    23rd Session (1563) – 626–40
    24th Session (1563) – 647–62
    25th Session (1563) – 400–2; 606–7; 824–5

Tridentine Creed (1564) – 849–59

Pope Paul IV's Constitution *Cum quorundam* (1555) – 322

Errors of Michael du Bay condemned by Pope Pius V (1567) – 207–210–227–30; 323; 771–89

Errors of Cornelius Jansen condemned by Pope Innocent X (1653) – 790–4

Jansenist Propositions condemned by Pope Alexander VIII (1690) – 324
Propositions of Pasquier Quesnel condemned by Pope Clement XI (1713) – 795–807
Articles Subscribed by Bautain (1840) – 1–6
Pope Pius IX's Encyclical *Qui pluribus* (1846) – 7–10
Pope Pius IX's Bull *Ineffabilis Deus* (1854) – 325
Pope Pius IX's Allocution *Singulari quadam* (1854) – 11–14; 351
Articles Subscribed by Bonnetty (1855) – 15–17
Provincial Council of Cologne (1860) – 178–88; 211–6
Ontologist Errors condemned by Pope Pius IX (1861) – 18–21
Letters of Pope Pius IX to the Archbishop of Munich-Freising
(1862) – 22–5; 352
(1863) – 353
Letter of the Holy Office to the English Bishops (1864) – 354
Pope Pius IX's 'Syllabus of Errors' (1864) – 26–30; 189
I Vatican General Council (1869–70)
   3rd Session (1870) – 31–61; 87–91; 190–7; 355–7
   First Draft Constitution on the Church of Christ – 358–69
   4th Session (1870) – 370–88
   Declaration by the German Bishops and its Approval by Pope Pius IX (1875) – 388a
Pope Leo XIII's Encyclical *Arcanum divinae Sapientiae* (1880) 663–6
Propositions of Rosmini condemned by Pope Leo XIII (1887) – 62–3; 826–7
Pope Leo XIII's Encyclicals:
   Octobri Mense (1891) – 326–8
   Magnae Dei Matris (1892) – 329
   Providentissimus Deus (1893) – 91–103
   Fidentem (1896) – 330
Pope Pius X's Encyclical *Ad diem illum* (1904) – 331–4
Modernist Propositions condemned by Pope Pius X in the Decree *Lamentabili* (1907) – 104–20; 299–310; 389–95; 427–9; 454–5; 470; 587–8

Chronological List of Documents Quoted   443

Pope Pius X's Encyclical *Pascendi* (1907) – 430
Decision of the Bible Commission on the Historical Nature of the First Chapters of Genesis (1909) – 198
Form of Oath against Modernism Prescribed by Pope Pius X (1910) – 64–74
Canons from the Code of Canon Law (1917) – 396–8; 403–4; 431–3; 456–9; 471–3; 530–7; 589–94; 608–9; 621–4; 641–4; 677–9
Decision of the Holy Office on Certain Propositions concerning Christ's Knowledge (1918) – 311–3
Pope Benedict XV's Encyclical *Spiritus Paraclitus* (1920) – 121–6
Pope Pius XI's Encyclicals:
Miserentissimus Redemptor (1928) – 314–9
Casti connubii (1930) – 667–76
Pope Pius XII's Encyclicals:
Mystici Corporis Christi (1943) – 319a; 334a; 398a; 398c–f 807a
Divino afflante Spiritu (1943) – 126a–c
Mediator Dei (1947) – 537a; 537b; 644a
Pope Pius XII's Constitution *Sacramentum Ordinis* (1947) – 644b
Letter of Bible Commission to Cardinal Suhard on the Authorship and Historicity of the Pentateuch (1948) – 126d
Letter of the Holy Office to Archbishop Cushing of Boston (Mass.) on Membership of the Church Being Necessary for Salvation (1949) – 398g
Pope Pius XII's Encyclical *Humani generis* (1950) – 74a–f; 126e–f; 205a; 205b; 398h; 398i; 537c; 807b
Pope Pius XII's Constitution *Munificentissimus Deus* (1950) – 334b; 334c
Pope Pius XII's Encyclical *Sempiternus Rex* (1951) – 74h; 319b

INDEX

Except for those preceded by 'p' (= page), references are to paragraph numbers; those in *italic* refer to the introductory matter to the paragraph cited. The reference to complex subjects is usually only to the introductory matter where detailed references are given.

Absolution p. 306
Adam 198, 206, 207, 211
– original sin transmitted by, p. 132
– original state of, p. 105
Ad diem illum, 331–4
Adoptionism, *297*; 238, 297, 298, 839
Adoration of Christ, 241, 262
– of the Eucharist, 488, 497, 498
Albigensians, *155*; 170, *203*, 339, 405, 645
– Innocent III's profession of faith for, 170, 405, 435, 475, 645
Alexander VIII, condemnation of Jansenism, 324
Anastasius, preacher against title 'Mother of God', 234
Angels, p. 105; 398c
Anointing, Confirmation, 464, 471, 845
– of the sick, cf, Extreme Unction
Antioch, School of, *234*, *254*
Anysius, letter to, 320
Apokatastasis, 808

Apollinaris, *231*; 257, 266; p. 144
Apostles' Creed, 828
Arcanum divinae sapientiae, 663–6
Arianism, p. 86
– consubstantiality of the Son, *231*, *839*
Armenians, articles condemned, 204
– Clement VI's Letter, 460–3, 823
– Council of Florence, *408* & cf. Sacraments
'Assumptus homo' Theology, 319b
Athanasian Creed, 836–7
Atonement, Christ, 315, 316, 570, 718
– the Mass, 514, 523
Attrition, 544, 545, 549, 563, 576, 745
Baptism, pp. 265 ff
– in the name of the Trinity, 143
Bay, M. du, Articles condemned, 207–10, 227–30, 323, *771*, 771–89

Beatific Vision, p. 419; 819, 826, 827, 843
Beguards and Beguines, 817
Benedict XII, on Beatific Vision, 818–22
– and the Armenians, 204
Benedict XV, *Spiritus Paraclitus*, 121–6
Benedictus Deus, 818–22
Berengarius, 474
Bible, authorship, p. 53 f
– canon, 82–3
– exegesis, p. 53 f
– inerrancy, p. 53 f
– inspiration, p. 53 f
Biblical Commission, Pontifical, on first chapters of Genesis, 198
Biblical Theology, 398i
Birth of Christ, from the Father p. 85 f
– from Mary, p. 181 f
Bishops, general, p. 339 f
– powers of, 380, 388a, 398e, 631
Bismarck, 388a
Body and soul, 203, 205
– dignity of, *164*; 168, 169
– resurrection of, p. 414
Body... cf. also Mystical Body
Bonald, *1*
Boniface II, *696*
Boniface VIII, *Unam Sanctam*, 340–2
Bonnetty, *1*;
– articles subscribed by, 15–17
Bonosus, *320*
Boston Heresy, 398g
Braga, Council of 164–169, 200–201
Caelestius, p. 134; *680*
Caerularius, *338*
Caesarius of Arles, *696*
Calvin, *467*, *482*, *492*, *617*
Canon of Holy Scripture, 81–3, 87
– Luther's, *80*
– Oriental, *79*
– of the Mass, 516, 526
Canon Law on Baptism, 456–9
– Church and Primacy, 396–8
– Confirmation, 471–3
– Eucharist, 530–7
– Extreme Unction, 621–4
– Indulgences, 608–9
– Matrimony, 677–9
– Order, 641–4
– Penance, 589–94
– Sacraments, 431–3
– Veneration of Saints, 403–4
Carthage, Council of, 206, 680–5
– significance of, p. 13
Casti connubii, 667–76
Chalcedon, Council of, *247*; 252
– *Sempiternus Rex*, 74h, 319b
Chalice for the laity, 476, 503–5, 507–9, 534
Character, sacramental, cf. Baptism, Confirmation, Order
Charismatics, 398c
Charlemagne, *828*
Children of God p. 369
– baptism of, *220*; p. 265
– & Holy Communion, 506, 510, 536
Chrism, p. 273
Christ, cf Jesus Christ
Church, general, p. 197
– necessary for salvation, p. 200
– founded by Christ, 67, 360, 391, 398c, 398g
– juridical power, 369, 381
– permanence, 366, 392
– visibility, 345–8, 360–2
– Vatican I Schema, 358–69
– and culture, 47
– and revelation, p. 19; 64, 67
– and science, 45
– and the State, 388a
Circuminsession, 153, 161
Clement VI, Jubilee Bull, 595–7

Index

- on Armenian reunion, 460–3, 823
Clement XI, on Quesnel, 795–807
Clergy, p. 339 f.
Cologne, Provincial Council of 178–88, 211–6
Commandments, possibility of keeping, p. 369
Community of the faithful, p. 199; cf also Mystical Body
Concupiscence, before the Fall, 198, 214
- after the Fall, p. 132
Confession, p. 305; cf. also Penance
Confirmation, p. 273
- priest as extraordinary minister, 463, 465, 472
Constance, General Council of 343–8, 399, 406–7, 476–8, 538–41, 598–9
Constantinople, General Councils of,
- I, *129*; 831
- II, 76, 77, 254–66, 384
- IV, 202
- Provincial Council, 163, 199, 808
Consubstantiality, p. 85 f
Contrition, 542, 562, 563, 732
Corpus Christi, Feast of, 488, 497
Creation p. 103
- account of, 96, 198
Cum quorundam, 322
Cushing, Abp., Letter from Holy Office, 398g
Cyril of Alexandria, *234*; 266, 282
- Twelve Articles against Nestorius, 234–45
- significance of, p. 14
- Letter against Nestorius, 246
Damasus I, Council of Rome under, 129–43, 231–3
Damnation, eternal, p. 414

Death, pp. 105, 132
Decentius, Letter from Innocent I to, 610–1
Deism, 50
Devil, created as good angel, 165, 171
Diaconate, 638
Dialectical Materialism, 74g
Dionysius, Bishop, Letter from Pope Dionysius, 127–8
Dionysius, Pope, Letter to Bishop Dionysius, 127–8
Dioscurus, *247*
Dissolution of uncomsummated marriage, 656
Divinity of Christ, p. 143
Divino afflante Spiritu, 126a-c
Dogma, pp. 19, 199
- and Scripture, 107, 119–20
- Development of, 28, 48, 51, 68, 74, 74c, 74h, 398h, 398i, 807a
Dogmatic significance of Documents, p. 12
Doubt, 41, 58
Dualism, p. 103; *164*; 165, 170, 177
Durandus of Osca, *405*
Eckhart, Articles condemned, 172–6
Elipandus, *297*
Ephesus, Council of, 74h, 234–46, 319b, 335
Epiphanius, Creed of, 832–5
Erasmus, on Baptism *440*; 453
- on Scripture, *80*
Eschatology, p. 413
Eternal Life, p. 414
Eternity of God, 155, 157, 190, 838
- of the divine Persons, 127, 132
Eucharist, p. 278
- worthy reception of, 502, 536, 537
Eunomius, 131
Eutyches, 257; cf also Tome of Leo

Eve, made from Adam, 198
- and Mary, 334b
Exegesis, Scriptural, p. 55
Existence of God, p. 26
- proof of, p. 333
Existentialism, 74d, 74g
Extreme Unction, p. 331
Faith, p. 20
- and justification, p. 367
- and knowledge, p. 20
- and reason, p. 20
Feeney, Leonard, 398g
Fideism, *1, 7, 31, 131*; 1–6, 49, 53, 66
Fidentem, 330
Florence, Council of, cf Armenians, Greeks, Jacobites
Primacy, 384
Form, of the body, Soul as, 203, 205
- of sacraments 410
Freedom, and grace 714, 741, 791, 793, 805–7
- in scriptural exegesis, 104–7, 111, 119, 120
- of the Church, 380
- of God, p. 103
- of human will, p. 104; despite the Fall, p. 132
- of science, p. 20
Friaul, Council of, 298
Frohschammer, 22–5
Genesis, Historicity of, 198
Ghost, Holy, cf Spirit
Gioberti, *18*
Gnosticism, *79, 164,* 809
God, Knowledge of, innate 18–21, 62–3 natural, p. 19
- Children of, p. 369
Good Works, p. 369
Grace, p. 367
- and freedom, cf Freedom
- increase of, p. 111
- loss of, 445, 731, 733, 764
- mediation of, 326–34
- necessary for faith, 37, 57
- for perseverance in faith, 38
- sanctifying, p. 368
- before the Fall, 198, 211–3

- supernatural nature of, pp. 105, 368
Greek Church, *338, 349*
- Council of Florence, Decree for, 349
- and Matrimony, *647*
- and Purgatory, *814*
Gregory XIII, *814*
Guenther, *178*
Hadrian I, Letter, 297
Happiness, eternal, p. 419
- of man as the end of creation 180, 186, 187
Heaven, p. 414
Hell, p. 414
Heraclius, *267*
Hermes, *7, 178*; 57, 58
Hierarchy, p. 199
Historical nature of theology, 74c, 74h
- science and revelation, p. 20
Science and Scripture, p. 55
Holy Office, Letter to English Bishops, 354
- Abp. Cushing, 398g
- on Christ's knowledge 311–3
Holy Scripture, p. 54 cf. also Bible
- and Modernism, 104–20
- and Rationalism, *104*
Holy Souls, p. 414
- Indulgences for, 608
- Masses for, p. 280
Holy Spirit, p. 85
- as the soul of the Church, 398f
Hormisdas, 336
Humani generis, 74a-f, 126e-f, 205a, 205b, 398h, 398i, 537c, 807b
Humbert von Silva Candida, *338*
Hus, *343, 406*; 345–8, 476
Hypostasis, cf Person
Hypostatic Union, p. 143
Ibas of Edessa, *254*; 266
Idealism, 74d, 74g
Images, Veneration of, 399, 402–3, 855

Immaculate Conception, p. 182; *321*; 226, 323–5
Immanentism, 74d, 74g
Immortality of the Soul, 205
Impediments to Marriage, p. 353
Indiculus, 217, 686, 695
Indifferentism, cf Church, necessary for salvation
Indissolubility of Marriage, 645–9, 655, 657, 672, 673, 678
Individuality of the human soul, 205
Indulgences, applicable to Holy Souls, 608
– Church's power to grant, 596, 598–602, 606 utility of, 603–5, 856
Ineffabilis Deus, 325
Inerrancy of Bible, p. 55
Infallible Decrees, p. 12
Infallibility, p. 199
Iniunctum nobis, 849–59
Innocent I, Letter to Decentius 610–1
Innocent III, *155, 170*
– Letter to Ymbertus, 434, 812
– Profession of Faith for Waldensians, 170, 405, 435, 475, 645
Innocent IV, Letter, 814–6
Innocent X, Jansenist errors, 790–4
Inspiration of the Bible, p. 55.
Intention in the administering of sacraments, p. 254
Intercession, for the dead, p. 414
– of our Lady, 326–34
– of the Church in sacramentals, 433
– of the Saints, 400, 403, 404, 855
Jacobites, Decree for (Council of Florence), 79, 157–62, 177, 350

Jansen, Errors condemned, 790–4
Jansenist articles condemned, 324
Jesus Christ, Beatific Vision of, 311f.
– Divine-human actions, 251, 276–82, 295, 296
– Divinity of, p. 144
– Founder of the Church, 67, 360, 391, 393
– Humanity, p. 144 f.
– Incarnation, p. 144 f.
– Inerrability, 304–7, 311–3
– Merits, 333, 718, 747
– Passibility, p. 145
– The Word, 237, 245, 253, 262, 268, 271, 839
Joachim de Fiore, 156
John II, Letter, 253
John XXII, condemns Eckhart 172–6
– on heaven, *818*
Julian of Eclanum, *686*
Judgment, p. 414
Justification, p. 368
– and baptism, p. 265
– and faith, p. 368 f. & cf. Faith
Kenosis, 319b
Knowledge, Christ's, p. 145
– religious, p. 19
Laity, Chalice for, cf Chalice Priesthood of, 644a
Lamennais, *1*
Lamentabili, cf Modernism
Last Supper, Institution of Eucharist and Mass, 512
– Institution of Order, 522, 626
Last Things, p. 413
Lateran, IV General Council, *190*; 155–6, 171, 339, 813, 837b–d
– V General Council, 205
Latrocinium, *247*
Leo I, The Tome of Leo, 247–51, 319b

Leo III, 298
Leo IX, *338*; 838
Leo X, cf Luther
Leo XIII, and Rosmini, 62–3, 826–7
– Encyclicals: *Ad diem illum*, 331–4
– *Arcanum divinae sapientiae*, 663–6
– *Divinum illud*, 398f
– *Fidentem*, 330
– *Magnae Dei Matris*, 329
– *Octobri mense* 326–8
– *Providentissimus Deus*, 92–103
Light of Glory, 817
Liturgy, 537a
– Presence of Christ in, 537b
Lumen Gloriae, 817
Luther and Baptism, *440*
– confirmation, *467*
– Eucharist, *482*
– Extreme unction, *617*
– grace, 703–8; *709*
– indulgences, 600–5
– loss of grace, 440
– Mass, *511*, *521*
– Matrimony, *647*
– Order, *626*
– original sin, *220*
– penance, 543–52
– sacraments, *412*
– Scripture & tradition *80*
Lyons, General Council of, Profession of faith of M. Paleologue, 838–48
Macedonianism, p. 86
Magisterium of the Church, p. 199
– ordinary, 353
Magnae Dei Matris, 329
Manicheism, *164*, *170*, *177*, *220*, *809*; *167*, *179*
Marcion, 127
Martin, Pope, Council in Lateran, 77, 267–82
Mary, p. 181
– Immaculate Conception, *321*; 226, 323–5
– Mediatrix of all grace, 326–34
– Sinlessness, 321, 760
Mass, p. 279
– Canon of, 516, 526
Materialism, *31*, *190*
Matrimonial Causes, *647*; 662, 679
Matrimony p. 351
– impediments, p. 353
– uncomsummated, dissoluble 656
Matter of sacraments, 410
Mediator Dei, 537a, 537b, 644a
Melanchthon, *467*, *492*
Membership of Christ, p. 199
– of the Church, 436, 447, 453
Mennas, *163*
Miracles, p. 20
– accounts of, 113, 116
Miserentissimus Redemptor, 314–9
Modernism, *64*
– Oath against, 64–74
– *Pascendi*, 430
– and Baptism, 454–5
– and Christ, 299–310
– and the Church, 389–95
– and confirmation, 470
– and penance, 587–8
– and the sacraments, 427–9
– and tradition and Scripture, 104–20
cf also Dogma, development of
Monarchy, divine, 127
Monogamy, p. 353
Monogeny, 205b
Monophysitism, p. 143
Monotheletism, *267*, *297*; 251, 276, 282, 295–6
Mortal sin, grace to avoid, 702, 725, 755, 777, 790
– loss of grace, p. 369
– punishment of, p. 414
Munificentissimus Deus, 334b, 334c

Index

Mysteries, p. 20
Mystical Body of Christ, 316–9, 319a, 331, 334a, 359, 362, 398a–c, 398f, 436, 537a, 557
Mystici Corporis Christi, 319a, 334a, 398a, 398c-f, 807a
Mythology, 126d, 126f
Natural cognition of God, p. 19; 16, 31, 49, 65
Natural science and Scripture, p. 55
Nature, single in God, p. 85
– dual in Christ, p. 145
Necessity of grace, p. 369
Nestorianism, *234, 254, 297*; 257, 258
– Cyril's twelve articles against, 234–45
– Cyril's letter against, 246
New Testament, origin, 79, 81, 170, 177
– canon, 83
– minor orders, 627, 634
Nicaea, I General Council, *129, 231*
– Creed, 829–30
– II General Council, *78*; p. 249
'Nicene' Creed, 831
Nouvelle Théologie, *74a*
Oath against Modernism, 64-74
Octobri mense, 326–8
Old Testament, canon, 82
– origin, 79, 81, 170, 177
Olivi, 203
Omnipotence of God, 128, 134, 137, 149, 155, 157, 190, 838
Omniscience of God, 134, 137, 190, 192
Ontologist errors condemned, 18–21, 62–3, 826–7
Orange, Council of, 218–9, 696–702
– significance of, p. 13
Origenists, on creation, 163
– on hell, 808
– on transmigration, 199
Origin of man, 126d, 205a

Original sin, p. 131; *204*
– effect on human understanding, 6, 13, 14 remission, p. 133
Paleologue, Profession of faith of Michael, 838–48
Pantheism, p. 86; *18, 31, 190*; 178
Papacy, infallibility, p. 199
– primacy, p. 199
Parables, 112
Pascendi, *64*; 430
Paul IV, *503*
– *Cum quorundam*, 322
Pelagius, *206, 217, 220, 680*; 218
Penance, Sacrament of, p. 305
Perichoresis, 153, 161
Perseverance, p. 369
Person, One in Christ, p. 144
– Three in God, p. 85
Peter Lombard, *155*; 156
Philosophy, p. 18
Photius, *202*
Pius IV, *606, 849*
Pius V, cf du Bay
Pius IX, letters, 23–5, 352–3
– ontologist errors, 18–21
– Syllabus of Errors, 26–30, 189
– *Ineffabilis Deus*, 325
– *Qui pluribus*, 7–10
– *Singulari quadam*, 11–14, 351
Pius X, *64, 121, 198*
– *Pascendi*, 430
– cf also Modernism
Pius XI, *Casti connubii*, 667–76
– *Miserentissimus Redemptor*, 314–9
Pius XII, Apostolic Constitution on Order, 644b
– *Divino afflante Spiritu*, 126a-c
– *Humani generis*, 74a–f, 126e-f, 205a, 205b, 398h, 398i, 537c, 807b
– *Mediator Dei*, 537a, 537b, 644a

- *Munificentissimus Deus*, 334b, 334c
- *Mystici Corporis Christi*, 319a, 334a, 398a, 398c–f, 807a
- *Sempiternus Rex*, 74h, 319b
Pomponazzi, *205*
Prayers of the Mass, 516, 520, 526–9
Predestination, p. 369
Presence of Christ in the Eucharist, p. 280
- in the Church's worship, 537b
Priesthood, of Christ, 243, 314
- official, p. 339
- universal, 317–9, 644a
Primacy, cf Papacy
Priscillian, *164*
- Council of Braga, 164–9, 200–1
Procession of Blessed Sacrament, 488, 497
- of Holy Spirit, p. 87
Prosper of Acquitaine, *686*
Providence, p. 105
Providentissimus Deus, 92–103
Provincial Councils, p. 13
Psychology of Christ, 319b
Purgatory, p. 414
Quesnel, condemned propositions, 795–807
Quicumque vult, 836–7
Qui pluribus, 7–10
Rationalism, 7, *22*, *31*, *49*, *64*, *104*, *322*; 7–8, 22–30, 59–61
Redemption, p. 145
Relativism, 74e
Relics, 399, 401, 403, 855
Reserved cases, p. 306
Resurrection of the body, p. 414
Revelation, p. 17
- Sources of, p. 55
Rome, Council of, under Damasus, 129–43, 231–3
- under Martin, 77, 267–82
Rosmini, Propositions condemned, 62–3, 826–7
Sabellius, 127, 130
Sacramentals, 433
Sacraments, p. 253
- necessary for salvation, 416, 431
Saints, Masses in honour, of 515, 525
- Veneration of, 400, 403, 404, 855
Salvation, God's plan, 702, 743, 754, 794
- Supernatural order of, p.p. 105, 369
Satisfaction, by Christ, 315, 316, 570, 718
- in sacrament of penance, p. 306
Semipelagianism, *686*
Sempiternus Rex, 74h, 319b
Sergius of Constantinople, *267*
Sin, cf Mortal, Original, Venial
Singulari quadam, 11ff
Sinlessness of Christ, 232, 24,3, 253, 264, 271, 293, 295
- of Mary, 321, 760
Siricus, Pope, Letter of, *320*
Sixtus IV, *321*; 226
Socinians, *322*
Soul, human, p. 105
Spirit, Holy, p. 85 f
Spiritus Paraclitus, 121–6
Subdiaconate, 627, 634, 642
Supernatural gifts in Paradise, p. 132
- knowledge, p. 19
- works, p. 369
Syllabus of Errors, cf Pius IX
Temporal punishment of sin, p.p. 279f, 295, 322
Textual criticism of Scripture, 95, 98
Theodore of Mopsuestia, *254*; 257–9, 264
Theodoret of Cyrus, *254*; 265
Theological Virtues, 721
Theology, biblical, 126e
- bases of, 11, 29

Index

- historical nature of, 74c, 74h
- and magisterium, 352, 353, 398h, 398i
Thomas Aquinas, on sacraments, *408*
'Three Chapters, The', *254*; 254–66
Toledo, Council of, Profession of faith, 144–54, 283–94, 809–11
Tome of Leo, 247–51
Tradition, p. 55
- Protestant view, *80*
Traditionalism, *1*, *31*; 1–6, 49, 55–6
Traducianism, *204*
Transubstantiation, 339, 474, 487, 493, 537c, 846, 853
Transcendence of God, p. 86
Trent, Council of, cf List of Documents
Tridentine Creed, 849–59
Trinity, p. 86 f.
Unam sanctam, 340–2
Unitarians, *322*
Unity of mankind, 198, 205b
Unleavened bread, *338*
Vatican I, General Council, cf List of Documents
Veneration of Saints, relics and images, p. 249
Venial Sin, in confession, 546, 564, 578, 594
- committed by all, 683–5, 760
Vienne, Council of, 203, 205, 817
Vigilius, Pope, *163*, *254*
Virginity, 659, 660
- of Mary, 247, 255, 269, 283, 320, 322, 328, 832
Vulgate, *80*; 85, 87
- as standard version, 126a
Waldensians, *170*, *171*, *203*, *405*, *645*
- Innocent III, profession of faith for, 170, 405, 435, 475, 645
Will, free, cf Freedom
- twofold in Christ, 251, 276–82, 295, 296
Wine in Eucharist, 479, 532, 533
Wycliffe, *343*, *406*, *477*, *538*, *553*, *598*; 343–4, 406, 538
- questions put to his disciples, 399, 407, 477–8, 539–41, 598–9; p. 328
Ymbertus, Bishop of Arles, 434, 812
Zosimus, Pope, *206*, *217*
Zwingli, *482*, *492*

CONCORDANCE DENZINGER/ NEUNER-ROOS

1. Denzinger to Neuner-Roos

The attached table is in three columns. Col. Dl gives the Denzinger numbers for editions earlier than XXXIII (1965), and column D 2 gives those of the XXXIII Edition. In order that in both columns all references may be found in their correct numerical order, in spite of certain rearrangements in Denzinger, some entries occur twice, e.g.

82	176–7	143		54	125–6	829–30
86	150	831	and	86	150	831
91	–	320		59	153	129

The third column (N-R) gives the Neuner-Roos number

2. Neuner-Roos to Denzinger.

Each paragraph has its Denzinger number in *italic* under its own number. Should there be no such number, the text does not occur in Denzinger. References are to the XXXIII Edition except in cases where the earlier editions have a text since omitted; in that case the references are in parentheses.

References to the XXXIII Edition can be translated to earlier editions by use of the attached table.

Notes

(a) Not all texts appear in each work and some are more extensively quoted in one than in another.
(b) The paragraphing is sometimes different in the different works; e.g. the entry

| 285 | 536–8 | 288–92 |

indicates that what was one paragraph in the earlier Denzingers has in the latest edition been divided into three, and that these correspond to five in Neuner-Roos.

(c) Neuner-Roos references in parantheses (335) mean that a summary of the relevant text is given in that paragraph.

D 1	D 2	N–R	D 1	D 2	N–R
6	30	828	203	403	199
13	44	832–4	210	410	163
14	45	835	211	411	808
39–40	75–6	836–7	212	–	76
48	112	127	213–5	421–3	254–5
51	115	128	216	424–5	257
54	125–6	829–30	217–9	426–8	258–60
86	150	831	220	429–30	261
59–61	153–5	129–31	221–2	431–2	262–3
64–5	158–9	231–2	224–5	434–5	264
68–71	162–5	132–5	226–7	436–7	265–6
72	166	233	235	455	164
74–80	168–74	136–42	236	456	200
82	176–7	143	237–8	457–8	165–6
86	150	831	239	459	201
91	–	320	241–3	461–3	167–9
99	216	610–1	254–69	501–16	267–82
101	222	206	270	517	77
103–8	225–30	680–5	275	525	144–5
129	238	686–7	276–7	526–7	146–7
130	239	217	278	528	148–9
131–2	240–1	688–9	279	529	149
134–5	243–4	690–1	280	530	150–1
136–8	245	692, 680–2	281	531–2	152–3
139	246	693	282	533	283
141	248	694–5	283	534	284–6
111a	250–1	246	284	535	287
112	3056c	(335)	285	536–8	288–92
113–24	252–63	234–45	286	539	293
129–41 –			287	540–1	294, 809–11
see above			291–2	556–7	295–6
143	293	248–9	308	609	78
144	294	249–51	310	–	297
148	301–3	252	314a	619	298
171	363–4	336	338	657–8	202
174	370–1	218	351	–	338
175	372	219	355	700	474
176–9	273–6	696–9	410–1	780–1	812, 434
188	385	700	421	790	170
199–200	396–7	701–2	424	793–4	405, 435,
201–2	401	253			475, 465

D 1	D 2	N–R	D 1	D 2	N–R
428	800	155, 171, 837b	698	1320–2	479–81
			699	1323	542
429	801	813, 837c	700	1324–5	612
430	802	339, 837d	701	1326	625
432	804–6	156	702	1327	646
456	838	814	703	1330	157–60
457	839	815–6	704	1331	161–2
461–3	851–3	838–40	706–7	1333–6	177
464	854–9	841–4	706	1334	79
465	860	845–7	714	1351	350
466	861	848, (337)	738	1440	205
468	870–2	340–1	741–3	1451–3	703–5
469	873–5	342	745–54	1455–64	543–52
475	895	817	757–62	1467–72	600–5
481	902	203	771–2	1481–2	706–7
501–3	951–3	172–4	776	1486	708
526–7	976–7	175–6	783	1501	80–1
530	1000–1	818–21	784	1502–5	82–4
531	1002	822	785–6	1506–7	85–6
533	1007	204	787–91	1510–4	220–4
550–2	1025–7	595–7	792	1515–6	225–6
570s	1066–7	823	792a	1520	709
571–4	1068–71	460–3	793–7	1521–5	710–4
584	1154	406	798	1526–7	715–6
587	1157	538	799	1528–9	717–9
588	1158	343	800	1530–1	720–1
617	1187	344	801	1532	722
626	1199	476	802	1533–4	723
629	1203	345	803	1535	724
631–2	1205–6	346–7	804	1536–9	725–7
636	1210	348	805	1540	728
666–7	1256–7	477–8	806	1541	729–30
670–1	1260–1	539–40	807	1542–3	731–2
672	1262	407	808	1544	733
675	1265	541	809	1545–7	734–5
676–7	1266–7	598–9	810	1548–50	736–7
679	1269	399	811–33	1551–73	738–60
694	1307	349	833	1573	321
695	1310–3	408–11	834–43	1574–83	761–70
696	1314–6	436–9	843a	1600	412
697	1317–9	464–6	844–56	1601–13	413–25

D 1	D 2	N–R	D 1	D 2	N–R
857–70	1614–27	440–53	984–6	1821–3	400–2
871–3	1628–30	467–9	987–8	1824–5	(402)
873a	1635	482	989	1835	606
874	1636–7	483–4	993	1880	322
875	1638	485	994–5	1862–3	849–50
876	1639–41	486	996	1864–5	851–2
877	1642	487	997	1866	853
878	1643–4	488	998	1867	854–6
879	1645	(489)	999	1868	857
880	1646–7	(490)	1000	1869–70	858–9
881	1648	(491)	993	1880	322
883–93	1651–61	492–502	1013	1913	774
893a	1667	553	1016	1916	787
894	1668–70	554–6	1020	1920	775
895	1671–2	557–8	1021	1921	207, 771
896	1673–5	559–61	1025	1925	781
897	1676	562	1026	1926	208
898	1677–8	563	1027–8	1927–8	782–3
899	1679–80	564	1034	1934	788
902	1684–5	565–6	1038	1938	789
903	1686–8	(567)	1039	1939	784
904	1689–91	568–70	1041	1941	785
905–6	1692–3	(570–1)	1046–9	1946–9	227–30
907–9	1694–6	613–5	1050	1950	776
910	1697–1700	(616)	1054	1954	777
911–25	1701–15	572–86	1055	1955	209, 772
926–9	1716–9	617–20	1066	1966	786
930	1726–7	(503)	1067–8	1967–8	778–9
931	1728	426	1073	1973	323
931–3	1728–30	(504–6)	1074	1974	780
934–7	1731–4	507–10	1078	1978	210, 773
937a	1738	511	1092–6	2001–5	790–4
938	1739–41	512	1314	2324	324
939–46	1742–9	513–20	1351	2401	795
948–56	1751–9	521–9	1360–1	2410–1	805–6
957–9	1764–6	626–8	1373	2423	807
960	1767–70	629–32	1388–9	2438–9	796–7
961–8	1771–8	633–40	1390–1	2440–1	798–9
969	1797–9	647–9	1394–7	2444–7	801–4
970–82	1800–12	650–62	1409	2459	800
983	1820	824–5	1622–7	2751–6	1–6

D 1	D 2	N–R	D 1	D 2	N–R
1635	2776	7	112	3056c	(335)
1636	2777	8–9	1825–7	3058–60	377–9
1637	2778	9	1828–9	3061–2	380
1638	2779	9–10	1830–2	3063–5	381–3
1639	2780	10	1833–5	3064–8	384
1641	2803–4	325	1836	3069–70	385–6
1642	–	11–12	1837–8	3071–2	387
1643–4	–	13–14	1839	3073–4 }	388
1647	2865°	351	1840	3075 }	
1649–51	2811–3	15–17	1853	3142	663
1659–62	2841–4	18–21	1854	3145–6	665–6
1668–9	2850–1	22–3	1891	3201	62
1670–1	2853–4	24–5	1895	3205	63
1675–6	2860–1	352	1929–30	3239–40	826–7
1683	2879	353	1940a	3274	327, 330
1686	2888	354	1943	3283	93
1701–2	2901–2	189	1944–5	3284–5	94
1703–5	2903–5	26–8	1946	3286	95
1708–9	2908–9	29–30	1947	3287–8	96
1782–4	3001–3	190–2	1949–51	3290–2	97–91
1785	3004	31–2	1952	3293	100–1
1786	3005	33–4	1953	3294	102
1787	3006	87–8	1978a	3370	332, 334
1788	3007	89	2001–4	3401–4	104–7
1789–92	3008–11	35–8	2006–7	3406–7	389–90
1792	3011	90	2009–19	3409–19	108–18
1793	3012	39, 355	2023–4	3423–4	119–20
1794	{ 3013 / 3014	356 / 356, 40–1	2027–38 / 2039–41	3427–38 / 3439–41	299–310 / 427–9
1795–8	3015–8	42–5	2042–3	3442–3	454–5
1799	3019	46–7	2044	3444	470
1800	3020	48, 357	2046–7	3446–7	587–8
1801–5	3021–5	193–7	2052–6	3452–6	391–5
1806–8	3026–8	49–51	2089	3489	430
1809	3029	(52), 91	2123	3514	198
1810–5	3031–6	53–8	2145	3537–42	64–9
1816–8	3041–3	59–61	2146	3543–7	70–3
1821	3050–2	370–1	2147	3548–50	74
1822	3053–4	372–3	2183–5	3645–7	311–3
1823	3055	374	2186	3652	122–4
1824	3056–7	375–6	2187	3653	125–6

D 1	D 2	N–R	D 1	D 2	N–R
2225	3700–1	667–9	2300	3849–52	644a
2226	3702	670	–	3859	644b
2229	3705		–	3866	398g
2231	3706	671	2305	3876	74a
2234	3710	672	2309–12	3881–4	74c–f
2236	3712	673	2313	3884–5	398h
2237	3713–4	674–6	2314	3886	398i
2286	3802	398a	2315	3887	126e
2287	3804	398e	2317	3890	74b
2288	3807–8	398f	2318	3891	537c, 807b
2289	3812	319a	2323	3894	74g
2290	3814–5	807a	2327–8	3896–7	205a–b
2291	–	334a	2329	3898	126f
2292	3825	126a	2331	3900–2	334b
2293	3826–8	126b	2332	–	
2294	3829–30	126c	2333	3903–4	334c
2297	3840, 3855	537b	2334	3905	319b
2298	3841	537a			